International Conference on Big Data Analytics, Data Mining and Computational Intelligence 2018, International Conference on Theory and Practice in Modern Computing 2018 and International Conference on Connected Smart Cities 2018

Held at the Multi-Conference on Computer Science and Information Systems (MCCSIS 2018)

Madrid, Spain
17 – 20 July 2018

Editors:

Ajith P. Abraham
Jorg Roth
Guo Chao Peng

ISBN: 978-1-5108-7012-3

Printed from e-media with permission by:

Curran Associates, Inc.
57 Morehouse Lane
Red Hook, NY 12571

Some format issues inherent in the e-media version may also appear in this print version.

Printed by Curran Associates, Inc. (2018)

International Association for Development of the Information Society (IADIS)
Rua Sao Sebastiao Da Pedreira
No. 100, 30, 1050-209
Lisbon, Portugal

Phone: 351 21 3151373
Fax: 351 21 3151244

secretariat@iadis.org

Additional copies of this publication are available from:

Curran Associates, Inc.
57 Morehouse Lane
Red Hook, NY 12571 USA
Phone: 845-758-0400
Fax: 845-758-2633
Email: curran@proceedings.com
Web: www.proceedings.com

INTERNATIONAL CONFERENCES ON

BIG DATA ANALYTICS, DATA MINING AND COMPUTATIONAL INTELLIGENCE 2018

THEORY AND PRACTICE IN MODERN COMPUTING 2018

and

CONNECTED SMART CITIES 2018

part of the

MULTI CONFERENCE ON COMPUTER SCIENCE AND INFORMATION SYSTEMS 2018

PROCEEDINGS OF THE INTERNATIONAL CONFERENCES

BIG DATA ANALYTICS, DATA MINING AND COMPUTATIONAL INTELLIGENCE 2018

THEORY AND PRACTICE IN MODERN COMPUTING 2018

and

CONNECTED SMART CITIES 2018

Madrid, Spain
JULY 17 - 20, 2018

Organised by
IADIS
International Association for Development of the Information Society

Volume Editors:
Ajith P. Abraham, Jörg Roth and Guo Chao Peng

Computer Science and Information Systems Series Editors:
Piet Kommers and Pedro Isaías

Associate Editor: Luís Rodrigues

TABLE OF CONTENTS

THEORY AND PRACTICE IN MODERN COMPUTING

CONNECTED SMART CITIES

SHORT PAPERS

BIG DATA ANALYTICS, DATA MINING AND COMPUTATIONAL INTELLIGENCE

THEORY AND PRACTICE IN MODERN COMPUTING

CONNECTED SMART CITIES

REFLECTION PAPERS

BIG DATA ANALYTICS, DATA MINING AND COMPUTATIONAL INTELLIGENCE

POSTERS

BIG DATA ANALYTICS, DATA MINING AND COMPUTATIONAL INTELLIGENCE

FOREWORD

These proceedings contain the papers of the 3rd International Conference on Big Data Analytics, Data Mining and Computational Intelligence 2018, the 7th International Conference on Theory and Practice in Modern Computing 2018 and of the 4th International Conference on Connected Smart Cities, which were organised by the International Association for Development of the Information Society, from 17 - 20 July, 2018. These conferences are part of the Multi Conference on Computer Science and Information Systems 2018, 17 - 20 July, which had a total of 617 submissions.

The aim of the Big Data Analytics, Data Mining and Computational Intelligence (BigDaCI) 2018 is to serve as a forum to present current and future work as well as to exchange research ideas in this field.

BigDaCI'18 invites authors to submit their original and unpublished work that demonstrate current research using big data analytics, computational intelligence and other intelligent computing techniques and their applications in science, technology, business and commerce.

Submissions were accepted under the following areas and topics:

- Big Data Algorithms and Architectures
- Computational Intelligent Frameworks for Big Data Processing
- Data Mining Topics and Applications
- Big Data Applications
- Multi-Agent Systems: Models, Architectures and Applications

The International Conference on Theory and Practice in Modern Computing (TPMC 2018) provides a forum for research and developments in the field of computing foundations and technology. Modern computing comes not only with efficient concepts and their application, but also it often addresses networking and mobility topics. Hence, the view in TPMC ranges from fundamentals like new or improved algorithms to very recent and modern applications like ubiquitous scenarios or even everyday computing.

Submissions were accepted under the following four main topics

- Design Foundations
- Mobility Communication and Services
- Realization Aspects
-Networking and Grid Approaches

The Connected Smart Cities (CSC 2018) aims to provide a cutting-edge and premier annual forum on smart cities. It aims to bring in leading scholars from multiple disciplines (including information systems, computer science, telecommunication engineering, urban studies, and business and economics) to share their ideas, knowledge and latest research findings related to the main issues concerning the whole ecosystem (e.g. M2M infrastructure, cloud platforms, big data analytics, mobile applications, citizen needs, user engagement, and new business/economic models) of future smart cities.

The CSC conference also aims at discussing the social, behavioral, technical, economic, and environmental impacts of the introduction of smart city applications and services.

Submissions were accepted under the following seven main topics:

- Wireless Connectivity in Smart Cities
- New Business Concerns in Smart Cities
- Data and Software Applications in Smart Cities
- User-Centric Smart Cities
- Security, Privacy and Identity Issues in Smart Cities
- Greenness and Sustainability of Smart Cities
- Smart City as an Integrated Ecosystem

These conferences received 132 submissions from more than 24 countries. Each submission has been anonymously reviewed by an average of five independent reviewers, to ensure that accepted submissions were of a high standard. Consequently, only 22 full papers were approved which means an acceptance rate of 17%. A few more papers were accepted as short papers, reflection papers and posters. An extended version of the best papers will be published in the IADIS International Journal on Computer Science and Information Systems (ISSN: 1646-3692) and also in other selected journals, including journals from Inderscience.

Besides the presentation of full, short and reflection papers and posters, the conferences also included one keynote presentation from an internationally distinguished researcher. We would therefore like to express our gratitude to Professor Pedro Larrañaga, Department of Artificial Intelligence, Technical University of Madrid, Spain for accepting our invitation to be the keynote speaker.

This volume has taken shape as a result of the contributions from a number of individuals. We are grateful to all authors who have submitted their papers to enrich the conference proceedings. We wish to thank all members of the organizing committee, delegates, invitees and guests whose contribution and involvement are crucial for the success of the conference.

Last but not the least, we hope that everybody had a good time in Madrid, and we invite all participants for the next edition of these conferences, that will be held in Porto, Portugal.

Ajith P. Abraham, Machine Intelligence Research Labs (MIR Labs), USA
Big Data Analytics, Data Mining and Computational Intelligence 2018 Program Chair

Jörg Roth, University of Applied Sciences Nuremberg, Germany
Theory and Practice in Modern Computing 2018 Program Chair

Guo Chao (Alex) Peng, School of Information Management, Sun Yat-sen University, Guangzhou, China
Connected Smart Cities 2018 Program Chair

Piet Kommers, University of Twente, The Netherlands
Pedro Isaías, The University of Queensland, Australia
MCCSIS 2018 General Conference Co-Chairs

Madrid, Spain
July 2018

PROGRAM COMMITTEE

BIG DATA ANALYTICS, DATA MINING AND COMPUTATIONAL INTELLIGENCE

PROGRAM CHAIR

Ajith P. Abraham, Machine Intelligence Research Labs (MIR Labs), USA

THEORY AND PRACTICE IN MODERN COMPUTING

PROGRAM CHAIR

Jörg Roth, University of Applied Sciences Nuremberg, Germany

CONNECTED SMART CITIES

PROGRAM CHAIR

Guo Chao (Alex) Peng, School of Information Management, Sun Yat-sen University, Guangzhou, China

MCCSIS GENERAL CONFERENCE CO-CHAIRS

Piet Kommers, University of Twente, The Netherlands
Pedro Isaías, The University of Queensland, Australia

BIG DATA ANALYTICS, DATA MINING AND COMPUTATIONAL INTELLIGENCE

COMMITTEE MEMBERS

Abdel-badeeh Salem, Ain Shams University, Egypt
Abderrafiaa Koukam, Université de Technologie de Belfort-Montbeliard, France
Alessandro Giuliani, University of Cagliari, Italy
Alexander Gelbukh, Instituto Politécnico Nacional, Mexico
Alla Anohina-Naumeca, Riga Technical University, Latvia
Amalia Foka, University of Ioannina, Greece
Ambra Molesini, Università di Bologna, Italy
Andrei Olaru, University Politehnica of Bucharest, Romania
Anirban Kundu, West Bengal University of Technology, India
Archil Maysuradze, Lomonosov Moscow State University, Russia
Audrone Lupeikiene, VU Institute of Data Science and Digital Technology, Lithuania
Boris Kovalerchuk, Central Washington University, USA
Carson K. Leung, University of Manitoba, Canada
Christos Kalloniatis, University of the Aegean, Greece
Christos Makris, University of Patras, Greece
Daniela Briola, Università Degli Studi di Milano Bicocca, Italy
Daniela Zaharie, UVT, Romania

THEORY AND PRACTICE IN MODERN COMPUTING

COMMITTEE MEMBERS

CONNECTED SMART CITIES

COMMITTEE MEMBERS

KEYNOTE LECTURE

BAYESIAN NETWORKS BASED MULTI-DIMENSIONAL CLASSIFICATION"

Professor Pedro Larrañaga,
Department of Artificial Intelligence, Technical University of Madrid, Spain

ABSTRACT

In this talk, the problem of multi-dimensional classification (a generalization of multi-label classification) will be approached with Bayesian networks. Multi-dimensional Bayesian network classifiers will be introduced and, under this paradigm, we will see that the classification problem can be formulated as the finding of the most probable explanation. As this is an NP-complete problem, in order to alleviate its computational burden, a special type of multi-dimensional Bayesian network classifiers called class-bridge decomposable will be introduced. Methods for learning this type of models from data, both based on score+search and on estimating the Markov blanket of each class variable, will be presented. Some variants of the general framework that consider the use of chain classifiers, or super-classes or even tratable (from the point of view of inference) models will be explained. How this kind of models can be updated in data stream settings will be also discussed. Finally, the application of the methodology real word problems in neuroscience, industry 4.0 and sports will be presented.

Full Papers

IS MARKET EFFICIENCY ENHANCED IN SUB-SECOND TRADING MARKET?

Mieko Tanaka-Yamawaki[1], Yumihiko S. Ikura[1] and Masanori Yamanaka[2]
[1]*Meiji University, 1-21-4 Nakano, Nakano-ku, Toyko, 164-8525 Japan*
[2]*Dept. Physics, School of Science and Engineering, Nihon University, 14-8-1, Kanda-Surugadai, Chiyoda-ku Tokyo 101-8308, Japan*

ABSTRACT

In order to clarify the long-standing question on the statistical nature of price fluctuation, we explore ultrafast time series of the newly developed stock trading system called "arrowhead trading system" in Tokyo Stock Exchange Market. The first question is whether the statistical distribution is Gaussian or non-Gaussian. If Gaussian, price fluctuation obeys the pure random walk and there is practically no room to discuss how to win the market. If it is non-Gaussian, the second question is whether it is a certain kind of stable distribution or not. If it is one of the stable distributions, the third question is to determine the index characterizing the stable distribution. However, even more interesting question is whether such a question makes sense only in a limited time range or not. Following the scaling method developed by Mantegna and Stanley for one-minute data of American stocks, we analyze the 5 second Japanese stocks and 0.1second Japanese stocks and compare them. It is shown that the empirical distributions obtained in our study obey the scaling law of the Lévy stable distribution of index α ranging from 1.4 to 2.0.

KEYWORDS

Stock Time Series; Arrowhead Market, Statistical Distribution, Scaling Phenomena, Market Efficiency

1. INTRODUCTION

Since the work of Luis Bachelier (Bachelier, 1900), the nature of price fluctuation is known to be the random walk (Brownian motion) and the theory of financial technology is established on this base to evaluate, e.g., derivative prices such as Black-Sholes-Merton (BSM) formula (Black, & Scholes, 1973; Merton, 1969; 1973, 1976). However, the BSM formula has several kinds of difficulty, and often fails to describe the real world. For example, the parameter σ (volatility) is assumed to be a certain constant in the above formula because there is no reliable way to compute its value theoretically. A commonly used substitute for the volatility is the 'historical volatility', or the realized volatility', that is the average values of the standard deviation over the historical price data over a fixed length, such as 2 weeks. Another substitute is the 'implied volatility' to obtain σ by inversely solving the BSM formula from for the actual price time series of the option prices. However, the obtained values σ are not a constant but varies as a function of K (the target price of each option) of the same option for different terms T. This is known as the 'smile curve' because the σ-K plot shapes concave and resembles the 'smile' mark. Considering the importance of the derivation of the BSM formula in financial engineering, it is essential to solve the problem of σ.

More serious problem of the BSM formula lies in the basic assumptions of Gaussian nature of price fluctuation, which is incompatible with the observed 'fat-tail', or 'narrow-neck' nature of the actual statistics of the price fluctuation. In order to remedy this situation, a scale-invariant distribution called Lévy stable distribution is proposed and the index α=1.4 was discussed widely (Mandelbrot, 1963; Mantegna, & Stanley, 1995). Although the infinite variance in Lévy stable distribution is not mathematically compatible to framework of option pricing theory, actual price fluctuations behave more like Lévy stable distribution than Gaussian. Thus it is a highly challenging problem to clarify the statistical nature of price fluctuation in various range of time resolutions.

Our thrust is to investigate the new world of arrowhead stock market, not only to determine the shape of the statistical distribution but also to examine various results obtained so far, such as cross correlation between different stocks using random matrix theory-oriented principal component analyses and related techniques

(Tanaka-Yamawaki, Kido, & Itoi, 2011; Yang, Mikamori, & Tanaka-Yamawaki, 2013), for the stock market of normal speed to the results on this newly developed arrowhead market. We also try to investigate whether or not the current "arrowhead" market is approaching the efficient market (Nagata, & Inui, 2014).

In this paper, we report the statistical distributions of price fluctuation obtained from the sub-second range to a few minutes, in order to show their scale invariant property. The rest of the paper is structured as flows. In Section 2, we summarize the formulation of price dynamics. In Section 3, we show the result of our former analysis using five-second sampled prices of 100 companies of Tokyo market in 2013, in which the average stock prices per 5 second are well described by Lévy stable distribution of index α=1.4, based on the fact that the distribution follows the scale invariance for a wide range of time scale Δt=1 to 12 (Tanaka-Yamawaki, 2017). In Section 4, we analyze newly obtained full arrowhead stock price data of the years 2015-2016 to show that the scale invariance seems to hold in the range of 0.8 second to one hour, although the estimated range of index α is rather broad ($1.4<\alpha<2.1$). Finally, Section 5 is devoted to the conclusion.

2. FORMULATION OF PRICE DYNAMICS

We are interested in the statistical distribution of the price increment, which is often called as log-return

$$Z(t) = logX(t + \Delta t) - log\,X(t) \tag{1}$$

of the asset price $X(t)$ at time t and the same price $X(t+\Delta t)$ at $t+\Delta t$, to clarify whether the statistical distribution of the price returns is not purely Gaussian but has fat-tails and narrow necks. Several decades ago, it was pointed out by Mandelbrot then followed by Mantegna and Stanley that the probability distribution of asset returns follow Lévy stable distribution, defined as

$$f_{\alpha,\beta}(Z) = \frac{1}{2\pi}\int_{-\infty}^{\infty} e^{ikZ-\beta|k|^{\alpha}}\,dk \tag{2}$$

which is the Fourier transform of the kernel $F(k)$ given by

$$F_{\alpha,\beta}(k) = e^{-\beta|k|^{\alpha}} \tag{3}$$

The first parameter $\boldsymbol{\alpha}$ characterizes the distribution and is called Lévy index, taking the range of $\mathbf{1} \leq \boldsymbol{\alpha} \leq \mathbf{2}$, and the second parameter $\boldsymbol{\beta}$ is proportional to the time interval Δt, as follows.

$$\boldsymbol{\beta} = \boldsymbol{\gamma\Delta t} \tag{4}$$

Equation (4) can be understood as follows. The stable distribution holds the same index $\boldsymbol{\alpha}$ under convolution of two stochastic variables following the same stable distributions: *i.e.,* $z=x+y$ follows Lévy stable distribution of index α if both x and y follow Lévy stable distribution of the same index $\boldsymbol{\alpha}$**.** This means that the distribution of asset returns at 5 seconds ($\Delta t=1$) follows the same distribution as the same asset returns at 10 seconds **(**$\Delta t=2$**).**

$$f_{\Delta t=2}(z) = \int_0^z f_{\Delta t=1}(x) f_{\Delta t=1}(z-x)dx \tag{5}$$

In the Fourier space, a convolution is reduced to a product of the Fourier kernels.

$$F_{\Delta t=2}(k) = (F_{\Delta t=1}(k))^2 \tag{6}$$

which can be generated to the case of n steps to have

$$F_{\Delta t=n}(k) = (F_{\Delta t=1}(k))^n \tag{7}$$

A series of n steps yields β to be multiplied by n, without changing the Lévy index α. However, this model of price movements naturally assumes a limitation on the maximum number of steps, n.

Note that (2) can be integrated for two special cases, α=1 and α=2, first of which is the Lorentz distribution,

$$P_{\alpha=1,\beta}(Z) = \frac{\beta}{\pi}\frac{1}{\beta^2+Z^2} \tag{8}$$

and the second is the normal (Gaussian) distribution.

$$P_{\alpha=2,\beta}(Z) = \frac{1}{2\sqrt{\pi\beta}} exp\left(-\frac{Z^2}{4\beta}\right) \quad (9)$$

For general values of α, the distribution is computed by numerically integrating Eq. (2).

The scale invariant property of Lévy stable distribution is derived from Eq. (2),

$$P_{\alpha,\beta}\left(Z/(\Delta t)^{1/\alpha}\right) = (\Delta t)^{1/\alpha}\ P_{\alpha,\beta\Delta t}(Z) \quad (10)$$

Setting Z=0 in Eq. (10), Lévy index $\boldsymbol{\alpha}$ is estimated by comparing the height of the distribution $P_{\Delta t}(0)$ for various values of Δt.

$$log\ (P_{\alpha,\beta\Delta t}(0)) = -\frac{1}{\alpha} log\ (\Delta t) + log(P_{\alpha,\beta}(0)) \quad (11)$$

The above scenario was applied on American stock index S&P500, per 1 minute for 1984-1985, and per 15 seconds for 1986-1989, which was well-fitted to Lévy stable distribution around the center of the distribution, and the scale invariant property was proved in the range of Δt =1-1000 min. (Mantegna, & Stanley, 1995).

The scale invariant property of Lévy stable distribution is derived from Eq. (2),

$$P_{\alpha,\ \beta}(Z_s) = (\Delta t)^{1/\alpha}\ P_{\alpha,\ \beta\Delta t}(Z) \quad (12)$$

$$Z_s = Z/(\Delta t)^{1/\alpha} \quad (13)$$

3. PRELIMINARY RESULT BY 5 SECOND SAMPLED DATA

Although the arrowhead trading system was introduced in Tokyo Security Exchange (TSE) on January 4, 2010, it was hard for us to access to the full numerical data due to its huge size. Tokyo Market Impact View (TMIV, www.tse.marketimpactview.com/) offered us an opportunity to download sampled prices of 100 selected stocks per 5 seconds for a limited time from April to December, 2013 (Data-A).

We investigated the statistical property of the price increment of TMIV, and obtained the empirical probability distribution of the average of the 100 stock prices for various time intervals Δt=1, corresponding to the interval of 5 seconds, 3, 6, 12, 24, corresponding to the interval of 2 minutes, as shown in Figure 1. If the statistical distribution if the price increments $Z(t)$ is indeed the scale-invariant distribution, those histograms of five different values of Δt should overlap each other after the scaling transformations of Eq. (12) and Eq. (13).

As shown in Figure 2, histograms of various values of the scale parameter Δt in Figure 1 overlap on a single distribution by rescaling acording to Eq.(12) if the paraneter α is chosen to the value α=1.4.

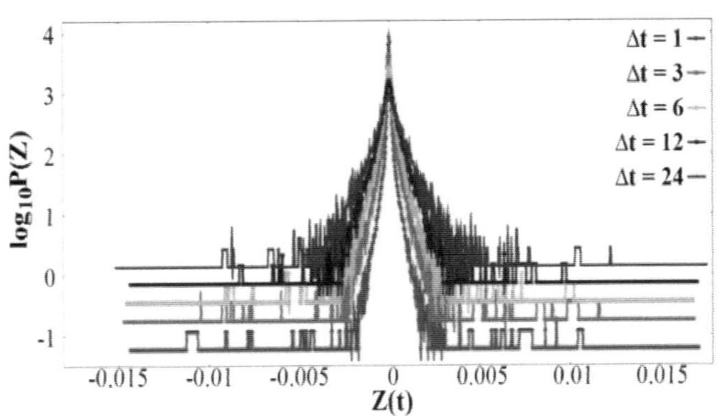

Figure 1. The histograms of statsitical distribution of Z for Δt=1 (5 sec), 3 (15 sec), 6 (30 sec), 12 (1 min), and 24 (2 min)

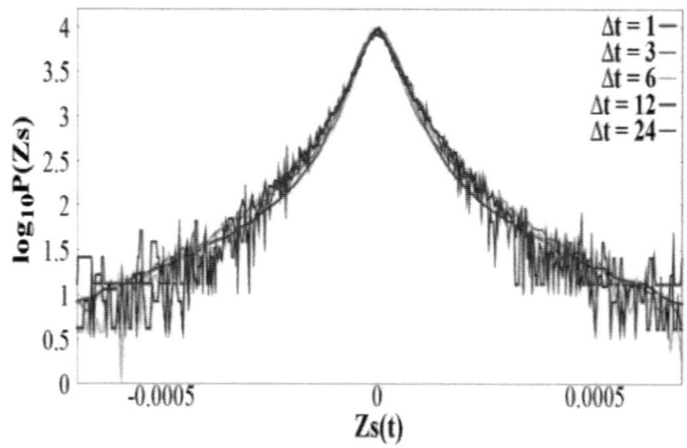

Figure 2. The histograms in Fig.1 are well scaled by Zs vs. $\log_{10}P(Zs)$ for Δt=1(equivalent to 5s), 3(15s), 6(30s), 12(1 min), and 24(2 min) for the case of $\alpha = 1.4$

The scale invariance of the statistical distribution of price increments can be checked using two other methods. One way is to use Eq. (11) for checking the straightness of the log-log plot of P(0) vs. Δt and also to obtain the Lévy index α from the slope ($-1/\alpha$) of the plot. By means of the least square fit, the best fit line turns out

By using this data set, we investigated the statistical distribution of the price increment

$$\log P(0) = -0.709 \log(\Delta t)+2.56 \tag{14}$$

as shown in Figure 3. The Lévy index α obtained from this result is α=1/0.709=1.41, which is consistent to the result from Figure 2.

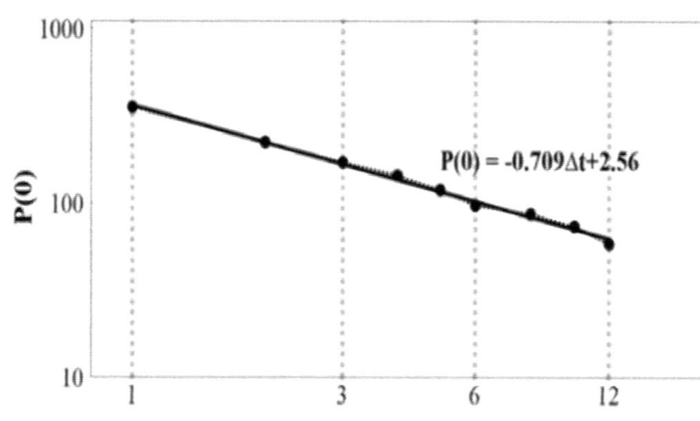

Figure 3. The least square fit derives α =1.41, consistent to the result from Figure 2

So far, we have seen that our analyses on Data-A (5 seconds resolution of TSE arrowhead market) gave us a consistent result. However, a question remains. The price increments looked like purely random in early 20th century. However, it was shown that the price changes are governed by the scale invariance under high resolution analyses. Also, it became clear that the probability distribution of the price changes is featured by the fat-tails and a narrow neck. We have to clarify to what level of resolution this phenomenon goes on. We need to determine whether or not the scale invariant property is valid under the arrowhead market in which the assets are traded under ultra-high resolution shorter than a millisecond.

Before getting into the arrowhead market, we attempted to check our results to another independent data of 1 minute resolution, downloaded from Google Finance site (finance.google.com/finance) for the duration of June 16, 2015 to November 4, 2015. We call this data Data-B. However, the time resolution (frequency) of this Data set is not as small as the previous Data-A and the scaling method is not suitable to analyze this data. We need a different method for Data-B. Since we cannot compare the distributions of different time resolutions, we adopt another method to search for the best value of α to minimize Kulbuck-Leibler divergence (K-L divergence) between two probability distributions *p(x)* and *q(x)* defined by

$$D(p||q) = \sum_{x \in X} p(x) log \frac{p(x)}{q(x)} \quad (15)$$

We compute *D(p||q)* in Eq. (15) by setting *p(x)* and *q(x)*, as the probability distribution of the 1- minute price increments (return) and the corresponding Lévy stable distribution for various values of α and β. The best fitted result for those parameters is consistent with the case of Data-A.

4. FULL ARROWHEAD PRICE DATA

Recently, full arrowhead price data became available via the web page of JPX (www.jpx.co.jp/). Compared to the Data-A, the data sizes are incredibly large. They are compared in Table 1. Note that the Data-A consists of 100 selected stocks, each stock of which has 640,80 data points (720 points per hour times 5 hours times 179 days.). The most active stock in Nov. 2016 has over 36 million data points in one month. The times of trades are utterly irregular in the case of arrowhead data, while Data-A has exactly 3600 points each day. Moreover, price time series of all the traded stocks are recorded in the same data file named by its year and month, such as 201611 for November, 2016, for example, in the ascending order of the stock codes. Also, the number of traded companies vary each month. For example, 3806 companies are listed in 201611, 3820 companies in 201612, and so on.

We began our analysis from the most active stock, code number 8306, and obtained empirical probability distribution by using two different ways of data processing.

Table 1. The data sizes of active companies in full arrowhead data are compared to Data-A

Stock code	Data-A	Full Arrowhead Data	
	(Apr.1-Dec.25, 2013)	Nov., 2016	Dec., 2016
# companies	100	3806	3820
7203	640,80	13,430,448	10,297,008
8306	640,80	36,330,455	31,418,450

4.1 Data Sampled by 100 Millisecond Intervals

We first pick up the stock prices every 100 millisecond interval to make a time series of the stock prices of fixed time interval from October, 2015 to December 2016. Since the original data do not necessarily have a price at every 100 milliseconds, the nearest price before that point is filled for that position. Thus a long queue of the same price is created if no trade occurs for a long time.

An example of the created fixed-time interval data is illustrated in Figure 2. This example shows a case where the price was 572.9 at the 13-hour-42-minute-54-second, and so on.

Fixed time interval of 0.1 second	
13 42 54.0	572.9
13 42 54.1	572.9
13 42 54.2	573.0
13 42 54.3	573.0

Figure 5. The original arrowhead data is formed into time series of a fixed time interval of 100 milliseconds

Based on this data file, we draw the empirical probability distributions for various values of *Δt*. We focus on the graphs for *Δt*= 8, 16, 32, 64, 128, 256, 512, 1024, 2048, 4096, and 8192 (×100ms). Those eleven graphs are simultaneously shown in Figure 6.

The graph for Δt= 8 has the smallest width on the horizontal axis Z and the tallest height on the vertical axis $\log_2 P(Z)$, and the graph for Δt= 16 is slightly smaller width in Z and shorter height in the vertical axis. Those histograms of regularly increasing time scales seem to obey some regularity. If they obey a scale-invariant distribution such as Lévy stable distribution, we should be able to identify the scaling factor $c = (\boldsymbol{\Delta t})^{1/\alpha}$. For example, the graphs for Δt= 8 should overlap the graph for Δt= 16 by multiply Z by the factor $c=\mathbf{2}^{1/\alpha}$ and divide the vertical axis by the same factor c. Applying the same rule on all the eleven histograms, they should be able to overlap on a single distribution if the factor c is properly chosen. This is done by choosing c=1.5 as shown in Figure 7. All the eleven histograms corresponding to Δt= 8-8192 (×100ms) can be scaled to a single curve by choosing c=1.5 and the corresponding index is around α=1.7.

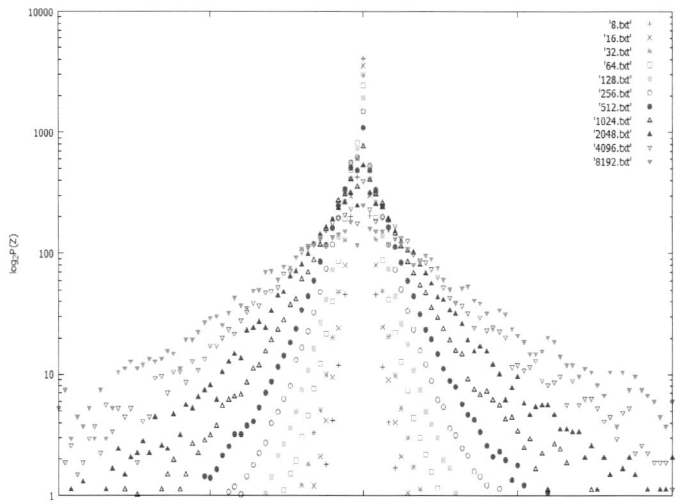

Figure 6. The histograms of 100ms returns are compared for various levels of coarse graining, 8.txt, 32.txt,.., 8192.txt, corresponding to the time scales, Δt =8-8192 (unit 100ms)

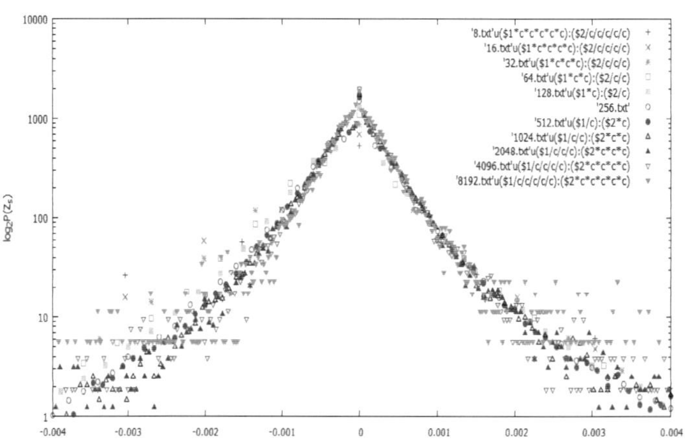

Figure 7. The eleven histograms in Figure 6 of different time resolutions, Δt =8, 16, 32,.., 8192 (unit 100ms) can be rescaled to overlap on a single curve by choosing $c = (\Delta t)^{1/\alpha}$. This figure shows the case of c=1.5 which derives the index α =1.7

Table 2. The scale factor and the values of Lévy index

$c = (\mathbf{2})^{-1/\alpha}$	1.4	1.5	1.6
α	2.06	1.71	1,47

Unfortunately, the resolution of this estimate is not high and the accuracy of the factor c varies in the range of $1.4 < c < 1.6$ according to the estimation of P(0). This uncertainty of c implies the uncertainty of the index α, in the range of $1.4 < \alpha < 2$, or $\alpha = 1.7 \pm 0.3$ as shown in Table 2. The uncertainty of P(0) comes from the excess zeros created in the process of making the price data per 100 milliseconds.

Thus we conclude our result as follows. The result of scaling analysis using 100 millisecond price fluctuation indicates that the statistical distribution of price return defined in Eq. (1) obeys the scaling law of the Lévy stable distribution of index α, which has the center value $\alpha = 1.7$ and the range $1.4 < \alpha \leq 2$ including the error bars. Considering that the range of this analysis covers 0.8 second to a few minutes, this result can be understood as follows. Our previous result on Data-A was $\alpha = 1.4$ for slightly larger time intervals: 5 second to a few minutes, and our current result indicates a larger value of $\alpha = 1.7$. This may be a signal of approaching the efficient market as we proceed towards the higher time resolution.

4.2 All Prices Used Disregarding Time Stamps

In order to remove excess zeros, we adopted another way of setting the arrowhead data. Instead of forming the price data by a fixed time interval, all the price data by disregarding the time stamps are used, as illustrated in Figure 8. In doing so, we can use the entire set of arrowhead price data, in exchange of sacrificing the information of actual time stamps. By drawing histograms for various levels of coarse graining parameter dt=8,…,2048, we recognize a similar scaling property observed in the first method of analysis shown in Figure 6. The nine histograms in Figure 8 are tested for the possibility of scaling. It turns out that the scaling is achieved at the value of the parameter $\alpha = 2$. Although this value stays within the range of error bar of the result in the first way of data processing, $\alpha = 2$ implies Gaussian distribution, which conflicts the fat-tail distribution widely accepted nowadays.

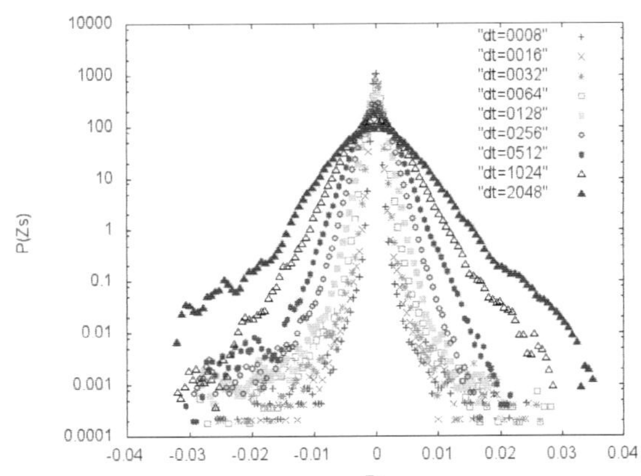

Figure 8. The histograms of stock code 8306 for various levels of coarse graining, dt=8-2048 processed in the second way

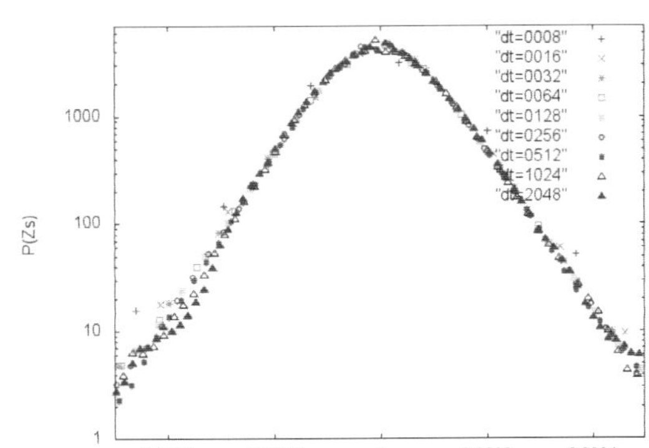

Figure 9. The nine curves in Figure 8 are rescaled to overlap on a single curve by $\alpha = 2$

5. CONCLUSION

We focused in this work to discover possible new elements to characterize the price changes under ultrafast market transactions of sub-millisecond intervals in the arrowhead market, operated in Tokyo market from 2010. In particular, we investigated the shape of the statistical distribution of the price increments. Especially, we obtained the probability distribution of the asset returns and examined the central part of the distribution utilizing its scale-invariant property.

In our previous work using 5 second resolution data (Tanaka-Yamawaki, 2017), however, the distribution turned out to be the same as the result of one-minute resolution data (Mantegna, &Stanley, 1995). In this paper we show, using the new data of 100 millisecond resolution, that the same kind of scale-invariant statistical distribution holds for the sub-second motion of price changes, although the index to characterize the scale invariance comes out to be $\alpha = 1.7 \pm 0.3$.

Although its lower limit $\alpha = 1.4$ is consistent to our previous result, the upper limit $\alpha = 2.0$ means the Gauss distribution. This fact might suggest us that the stable distribution of index $\alpha = 1.4$ holds only in the time interval ranging from a few hundred millisecond to a few minutes. Does this mean an efficient market has already been realized the sub-second price fluctuation in the latest stage “Arrowhead Stock Exchange Market”?

REFERENCES

Bachelier, L. J. B. (1900). Theory of Speculation.

Black, F., & Scholes, M. (1973). The Pricing of Options and Corporate Liabilities. *Journal of Political Economy*, 81, 637-654.

Mandelbrot, B. B. (1963). The variation of Certain Speculative Prices. *J. Buisiness*, 36, 394-419.

Mantegna, R. N., & Stanley, H.E.(1995). Scaling behaviour in the dynamics of an economic index. *Nature*, 376, 46-49.

Merton, R. (1969). Lifetime Portfolio Selection under Uncertainty: the Continuous-Time Case. *The Review of Economics and Statistics*, 51, 247–257.

Merton, R. C. (1973). Theory of Rational Option Pricing. *The Bell Journal of Economics and Management Science*, 4, 141–183.

Merton, R. C. (1976). Option Pricing When Underlying Stock Returns Are Discontinuous. *Journal of Financial Economics*, 3, 125-144.

Nagata, S., & Inui, K. (2014). Does high-speed trading enhances market efficiency? Empirical Analysis on "Arrowhead" of Tokyo Stock Exchange. *Journal of Trading*, 3, 75-81.

Tanaka-Yamawaki, M. (2017). Statistical Distribution of the Arrowhead Price Fluctuation. *Procedia Computer Science*, 112, 1439–1447.

Tanaka-Yamawaki, M., Kido, T., & Itoi, R. (2011). Trend-extraction of Stock Prices in the American Market by Means of RMT-PCA. *Intelligent Decision Technologies (SIST10,Springer)*, 637-646.

Yang, X., Mikamori, Y., & Tanaka-Yamawaki, M. (2013). Predicting the security levels of stock investment by using the RMT-test. *Procedia Computer Science*, 22, 1172-1181.

2CNN - MODULAR IMAGE RECOGNIZER WITH CONVOLUTIONAL NEURAL NETWORKS

Kamil Szyc and Henryk Maciejewski
Wrocław University of Science and Technology, Poland

ABSTRACT

Deep convolution neural networks (CNN) have demonstrated remarkable performance on visual recognition tasks. This performance is feasible due to availability of massive datasets used for training of the networks, and requires long training time even on fast GPUs. One of the challenges related to application of CNN for image recognition is training a new class/category into the model. This usually requires that training data for the already learned classes is available to be used for re-training the model with the training examples for the new class. In this work we propose a modular architecture of image recognition based on n CNNs trained to recognize n individual image categories rather than train one CNN with n-way Soft Max as the last layer. We empirically show that this approach offers comparable performance with state-of-the-art CNNs, while allowing for much easier expansion in terms of classes learned by the model as compared with standard models based on a single CNN with an n-way Soft Max.

KEYWORDS

CNN, Modular, Re-Training Model

1. INTRODUCTION

Since a remarkable success of a deep convolution neural networks (CNN) reported in 2012 ImageNet (Russakovsky el al., 2015) Large Scale Visual Recognition Challenge (Krizhevsky, Sutskever, & Hinton, 2012), interest of machine learning community in deep learning has risen sharply. The CNN reported in (Krizhevsky el al, 2012) referred to as AlexNet, realized ca. 15% error in the task of recognition of 1000 categories of images, the performance far beyond the capabilities of any other competing image recognition algorithm. Since then significant improvements have been proposed in CNNs architectures or in convolution or pooling layers (Goodfellow, Bengio, Courville, & Bengio, 2016; Graham, 2014; Howard, 2013; He, Zhang, Ren, & Sun, 2015). This all results in performance of state-of-the-art CNNs for image recognition reported to surpass human-level performance on some benchmarking datasets (e.g. CNN reported in (He et al., 2015) realized below 5% error on ImageNet, with human-level error on this set reported above 5%; or performance of a CNN on MNIST hand-written digit recognition below 0.3%, also deemed better that human level (Goodfellow el al., 2016)).

Despite so excellent performance, there are still challenges related to understanding how networks build representations of objects they recognize (Szegedy el al., 2013). This motivated some research in CNNs to visualize and understand the process of representation building, see e.g. (Zeiler, & Fergus, 2014). However, one of most important challenges related to training / maintenance of CNNs for large scale (many category) image recognition consists of difficulties in adding new categories (classes of images) to be recognized by the CNN. Usually standard CNN models with the n-way Soft Max layer are trained to recognize only one or n categories. Learning a new class requires re-training the whole network – using training data for the all existing classes (including training examples for the new class). This is usually challenging, because assumes availability of the (usually big) training data for the old classes, and is computationally intensive. Continuous learning approaches have been recently proposed (Li & Hoiem, 2017; Hoi, Sahoo, Lu, & Zhao, 2018) as a way to tackle this problem.

In this work we propose another approach to improve flexibility of CNN-based image recognition in terms of adding new classes to the models. Rather than building a single CNN with the wide Soft Max layer trained to recognize one of n classes, we propose a modular architecture with n CNNs trained to recognize individual classes combined as a voting system, performing as an n-class image classifier. We denote these building-block CNNs trained to recognize individual classes as 2CNN. Adding the capability to recognize a new class requires that a new CNNs is trained specifically to recognize this class, without the need to re-train other classes, hence without the need that training data for the previously learned classes is available.

We show feasibility of this approach using the CIFAR-10 a popular image recognition benchmarking data set. We implement our modular CNNs model to recognize the 10 image categories and compare performance of this with the state-of-art models trained of CIFAR-10. Our method realizes similar performance as a single CNN with 10-way Soft Max, however adding a new class to our model is much easier than re-training a standard CNN with 10-way Soft Max. The cost of our method is related to longer training process of our 10 2CNN models, however this process can be parallelized.

2. CONCEPT OF MODULAR IMAGE RECOGNIZER

Traditional Convolutional Neural Networks(CNN) have specific structure. In general - first layer is an input image represented as a tensor - three (red, green and blue colors channels) matrices (width and height). Next, each CNN contains convolution and pooling layers which are responsible for feature extraction. There are fully connected layers on the very end with final Soft Max output layer. Each final neuron represents a single label that the network can recognize. There are some additional ways to improve the networks to obtain better results (mostly better accuracy) - for example inception module (Szegedy el al., 2016), Residual module (He, Zhang, Ren, & Sun, 2016) or Fractional MaxPooling(Graham, 2014).

We have chosen a very popular images dataset (CIFAR-10) for a better presentation of our idea and to have a possibility of comparing the results. Following the official website: The CIFAR-10 dataset consists of 60000 32x32 color images in 10 classes (airplane, automobile, bird, cat, deer, dog, frog, horse, ship and truck), with 6000 images per class. There are 50000 training images and 10000 test images. Fractional Max-Pooling is a state-of-the-art algorithm, which can classify objects from that database with 96.53% accuracy.

The main idea behind our concept is to build as many Convolutional Neural Networks as labels, which are to be recognized. Each CNN in our project is constructed in a way that allows for only one simple label recognition. Then we can compare outputs form each CNN and choose one real label to get result similar to traditional CNN.

Following CIFAR-10 database as an example we can build ten (number of labels in that database) special CNNs and the first one can recognize only airplanes, the next one only automobiles, the next only birds and so on. Each of that CNNs has only two output neurons, which we named "true" and "false" output labels. "True" label means that the image is recognized as an object class for specific CNN. "False" label is an opposite to that. Because of our last operation in each CNN we use Soft Max function that have two numbers as output. Both values are from 0 to 1 and are summed up to 1(Soft Max function). So we can easily compare outputs from different 2CNN to get the final result. You can see a schematic diagram below - figure 1.

To properly classify object, we execute all ten CNN and compare results. There are several different scenarios of this comparison:

1. All "true" labels are equal to 0
2. None of "true" labels are equal to 1 and a maximum value exists
3. None of "true" labels are equal to 1 and there is no maximum value
4. Only one of "true" label is equal to 1
5. More than one of "true" label is equal to 1
6. All "true" labels are equal to 1

Ideal situation is when we have one of "true" label which is greater than the others (scenario 2 and 4). Then we just pick a label, which is assigned to that CNN. This situation is most often. Another problem we had was to choose a proper first class. Scenarios 1,3 and 6 do not occur in real cases. Scenario 5 occurs relatively often, but there is no good solution for what to do in such case, so we most often choose the random result.

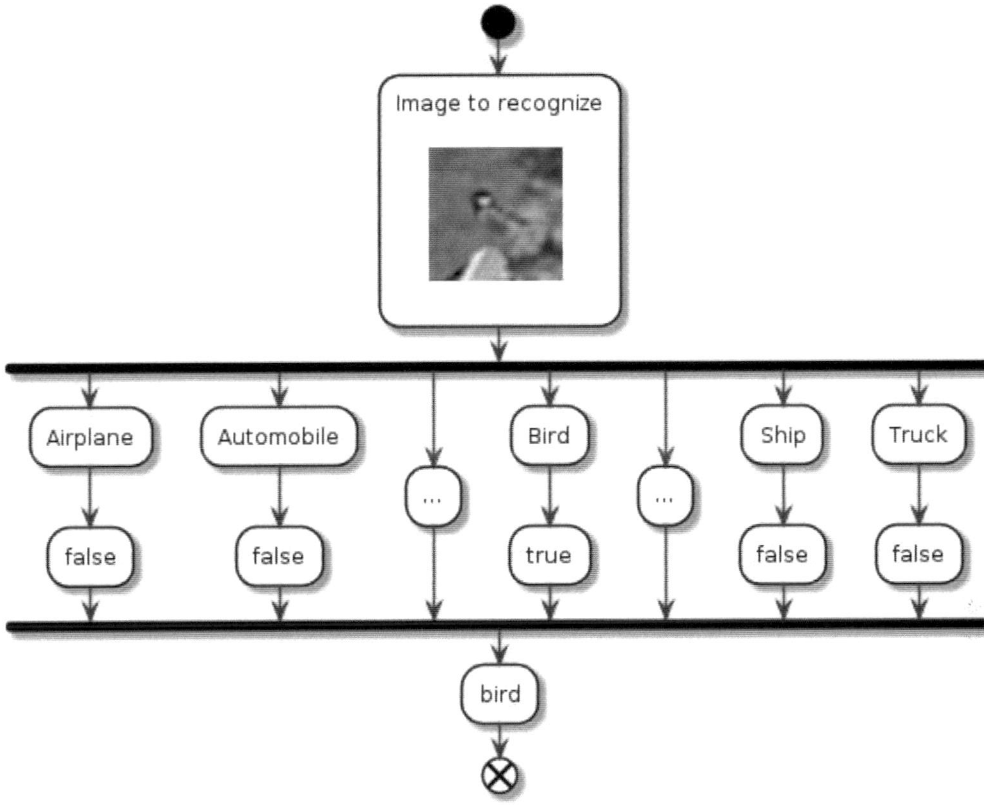

Figure 1. Diagram of 2CNN method based on CIFAR-10 dataset. First, we trained 10 2CNN models which can recognize only one label and can give output "true" or "false". Next, we can compare results from all 2CNNs and get final output

3. EXPERIMENTS

We tested our solution with CIFAR-10 data set, but the concept may be used on any kind of data. We compared two different CNN models with our solution. One is simple model (our own concept) and one is Fractional Max-Pooling model (state-of-the-art for that data set).

We tested our concept in classic way. First, we trained models in traditional way, next prepare database to be able to test our solution, and finally we trained 2CNN models.

We showed our results in detail below and compare them with each other.

3.1 Prepare Database

We used CIFAR-10 data set to test our models, but we needed to prepare it in a specific way. We generated 10 separate data sets for each class (like airplane, automobile, etc.). To do that for each class we copied all images belonging to a chosen class and set a label for them to 1/true (positive examples) and all other images and set them as 0/false (negative examples). Because of that there were 10 classes in our original data-set. We had unbalanced data set with 1:9 (1:number of classes - 1) ratio for false label.

To get better balanced data we copied images with "true" label additional 8 times (number of classes - 2) to our training set. Other - probably a little better option - would be to modify all additional images by changing hue, contrast, brightness, saturation or flip image horizontally. We didn't use that technique with generating additional images, because we would like to be able to contrast with original models – based only on the original data-set.

After that procedure we had properly balanced data. We did that procedure for both training and testing (without adding additional images) datasets - modifying testing-set was done only for checking accuracy of single 2CNN model. Final step was mixing images with training set. When we test general model with multi true/false models we used original CIFAR-10 testing set (without any modification).

3.2 Model based on Simple CNN

First, we trained typical CNN model to have good reference to our concept. This is regular CNN, where as outputs we have 10 values which sum up to 1(after Soft Max function). That model has 76.80% accuracy.

Next, we created 10 models for each class in the way described in the previous section. We can see these models in detail in figure 2. These models are based on simple CNN, we changed only outputs neurons, so we had two neurons (true or false). Each model had its own database based on procedure described above.

We achieved similar accuracy using 2CNN models - 78.74%. We presented confusion matrix in table 1 and information about precision, recall and f1 score in table 2.

All models were training with the same parameters. We used 50 epochs and batch size equal to 32.

Table 1. Confusion matrix for our 2CNN models using simple models

		0	1	2	3	4	5	6	7	8	9
airplane	0	**852**	9	19	25	6	0	11	6	60	12
automobile	1	16	**875**	1	20	1	2	15	3	29	38
bird	2	83	1	**561**	109	50	41	115	19	16	5
cat	3	28	7	19	**683**	40	102	87	11	16	7
deer	4	17	1	16	82	**727**	18	95	28	15	1
dog	5	15	5	17	172	31	**688**	37	24	8	3
frog	6	5	0	14	37	4	4	**928**	3	4	1
horse	7	19	0	12	81	36	28	13	**799**	4	8
ship	8	43	13	2	14	1	2	7	0	**904**	14
truck	9	26	40	3	32	2	3	11	1	25	**857**

```
batch_size = 32
num_classes = 2
epochs = 50

x_train = numpy.array(img_train);
x_test = numpy.array(img_test);

y_train = numpy.array(labels_train);
y_test = numpy.array(labels_test);

# Convert class vectors to binary class matrices.
y_train = keras.utils.to_categorical(y_train, num_classes)
y_test = keras.utils.to_categorical(y_test, num_classes)

model = Sequential()
model.add(Conv2D(32, (3, 3), padding='same', input_shape=x_train.shape[1:]))
model.add(Activation('relu'))
model.add(Conv2D(32, (3, 3)))
model.add(Activation('relu'))
model.add(MaxPooling2D(pool_size=(2, 2)))
model.add(Dropout(0.25))

model.add(Conv2D(64, (3, 3), padding='same'))
model.add(Activation('relu'))
model.add(Conv2D(64, (3, 3)))
model.add(Activation('relu'))
model.add(MaxPooling2D(pool_size=(2, 2)))
model.add(Dropout(0.25))

model.add(Flatten())
model.add(Dense(512))
model.add(Activation('relu'))
model.add(Dropout(0.5))
model.add(Dense(num_classes))
model.add(Activation('softmax'))

opt = keras.optimizers.rmsprop(lr=0.0001, decay=1e-6)
model.compile(loss='categorical_crossentropy', optimizer=opt, metrics=['accuracy'])

x_train = x_train.astype('float32')
x_test = x_test.astype('float32')

model.fit(x_train, y_train, batch_size=batch_size, validation_split=0.1, epochs=epochs, shuffle=True)

scores = model.evaluate(x_test, y_test, verbose=1)
```

Figure 2. The 2CNN model based on the simple CNN

Table 2. Confusion matrix for our 2CNN models using custom models

name		**precision**	**recall**	**f1-score**
airplane	0	0.77	0.85	0.81
automobile	1	0.92	0.88	0.90
bird	2	0.84	0.56	0.67
cat	3	0.54	0.68	0.61
deer	4	0.81	0.73	0.77
dog	5	0.77	0.69	0.73
frog	6	0.70	0.93	0.80
horse	7	0.89	0.80	0.84
ship	8	0.84	0.90	0.87
truck	9	0.91	0.86	0.88
avg / total		0.80	0.79	0.79

3.3 Model based on Fractional Max-Pooling

We did similar steps for model based on Fractional Max-Pooling. First, we trained model for all 10 classes and we achieved 85.94% accuracy. Next, we trained our 10 2CNN models based on Fractional Max-Pooling. We achieved 84.35% accuracy for our method.

We presented confusion matrix in table 3 and information about precision, recall and f1 score in table 4.

Table 3. Confusion matrix for our 2CNN models using Fractional Max-Pooling

		0	1	2	3	4	5	6	7	8	9
airplane	0	**866**	5	26	8	9	5	4	7	31	37
automobile	1	9	**916**	0	3	1	3	4	2	16	45
bird	2	38	3	**736**	46	43	23	43	25	12	30
cat	3	18	4	37	**690**	40	99	32	16	14	47
deer	4	11	1	29	30	**835**	17	27	24	5	21
dog	5	8	2	17	90	30	**778**	12	22	5	33
frog	6	4	1	12	26	19	16	**894**	3	4	21
horse	7	9	0	15	20	30	31	5	**876**	2	9
ship	8	23	6	7	7	3	4	5	2	**918**	22
truck	9	19	29	5	5	2	2	4	3	18	**913**

Table 4. Confusion matrix for our 2CNN models using Fractional Max-Pooling

name		**precision**	**recall**	**f1-score**
airplane	0	0.86	0.87	0.86
automobile	1	0.95	0.92	0.93
bird	2	0.83	0.74	0.78
cat	3	0.75	0.69	0.72
deer	4	0.83	0.83	0.83
dog	5	0.80	0.78	0.79
frog	6	0.87	0.89	0.88
horse	7	0.89	0.88	0.89
ship	8	0.90	0.92	0.91
truck	9	0.78	0.91	0.84
avg / total		0.84	0.84	0.84

All models were trained with exactly the same parameter. We used 60 epochs and batch size equal to 64. This is a reason why we didn't achieved accuracy for models with 10 classes as big as in state-of-the-art model of CIFAR-10.

4. CONCLUSION

Our method seems to get similar results compared to the classic method - see table 5. But the 2CNN method has additional advantages.

Adding a new label to be recognized is much easier than in classic approach. In a classic situation if we want to add a new label we need to modify the whole network and retrain all weights. It may happen that the images, which were classified correctly after that procedure will be misidentified. The traditional CNNs have also limited capacity, so if we want to add too much labels, it may happen that we will need to change all hyper-parameters in a network and we would lose all the previous work. In our method, adding a new label is independent of previous 2CNN models, so we can avoid above problems.

We can also easily remove labels without changes in previous 2CNN models. It is impossible in traditional CNN models.

Updating traditional neural networks is also problematic. If we want to add more images in a training process we need to modify the whole network even if we only have new images from one class. It is necessary to add images carefully and to try to keep them balanced - evenly distributed for all labels. In our method is not a problem, but an advantage. If we have a lot of new images for one class we only need to re-train one 2CNN model responsible for this class.

Using 2CNN method we can easily modify any part of the global network. If we see that our network misidentifies two classes, for example a dog and a cat, then we can re-train only these two 2CNN models giving additional "true" and "false" examples of images.

There are also disadvantages. First, our method generates a lot of parameters, usually by n if we consider n as a number of labels. The second disadvantage is that we need to pass a single image over the all 2CNN models, so it takes more time than in a classic approach. Also, initial generation and training of all 2CNN models take much more time.

Table 5. Comparison of accuracy for classic and 2CNN model

Base model	**Accuracy for classic method**	**Accuracy for 2CNN method**
Custom	76.80%	78.74%
Fractional Pooling	85.94%	84.35%

5. SUMMARY

We proposed a new way of using CNNs. The main modification comparing to the classic method is to prepare a separate CNN for each label, which we want to recognize. Each single CNN (we called them 2CNN) gives as an output only two neurons. These two neurons are called by us as "false" (not fit to label) or as "true" (fit to label).

We did experiments by comparing our models with a classic approach. Experiments are based on CIFAR10 dataset. The results are show in table 5. The main advantage of using 2CNN method is an additional possibility to add, remove or improve labels. These operations are very easy to apply and do not require re-training of the whole network.

We plan to further work with this idea in the future. We hope the 2CNN method can give the possibility of detecting the images that are not described by the given labels (open space problem).

ACKNOWLEDGMENTS

This paper is supported by Młoda Kadra Grant 0402/0146/17.

REFERENCES

Goodfellow, I., Bengio, Y., Courville, A., & Bengio, Y. (2016). *Deep learning* (Vol. 1). Cambridge: MIT press.

Graham, B. (2014). Fractional max-pooling. *arXiv preprint arXiv:1412.6071.*

He, K., Zhang, X., Ren, S., & Sun, J. (2015). Delving deep into rectifiers: Surpassing human-level performance on imagenet classification. In *Proceedings of the IEEE international conference on computer vision* (pp. 1026-1034).

He, K., Zhang, X., Ren, S., & Sun, J. (2016). Deep residual learning for image recognition. In *Proceedings of the IEEE conference on computer vision and pattern recognition* (pp. 770-778).

Hoi, S. C., Sahoo, D., Lu, J., & Zhao, P. (2018). Online Learning: A Comprehensive Survey. *arXiv preprint arXiv:1802.02871.*

Howard, A. G. (2013). Some improvements on deep convolutional neural network based image classification. *arXiv preprint arXiv:1312.5402.*

Krizhevsky, A., Sutskever, I., & Hinton, G. E. (2012). Imagenet classification with deep convolutional neural networks. In *Advances in neural information processing systems* (pp. 1097-1105).

Li, Z., & Hoiem, D. (2017). Learning without forgetting. *IEEE Transactions on Pattern Analysis and Machine Intelligence.*

Russakovsky, O., Deng, J., Su, H., Krause, J., Satheesh, S., Ma, S., ... & Berg, A. C. (2015). Imagenet large scale visual recognition challenge. *International Journal of Computer Vision*, *115*(3), 211-252.

Szegedy, C., Zaremba, W., Sutskever, I., Bruna, J., Erhan, D., Goodfellow, I., & Fergus, R. (2013). Intriguing properties of neural networks. *arXiv preprint arXiv:1312.6199.*

Szegedy, C., Vanhoucke, V., Ioffe, S., Shlens, J., & Wojna, Z. (2016). Rethinking the inception architecture for computer vision. In *Proceedings of the IEEE Conference on Computer Vision and Pattern Recognition* (pp. 2818-2826)

Zeiler, M. D., & Fergus, R. (2014, September). Visualizing and understanding convolutional networks. In *European conference on computer vision* (pp. 818-833). Springer, Cham.

FULL MODEL SELECTION IN HUGE DATASETS THROUGH A META-LEARNING APPROACH

Angel Díaz Pacheco and Carlos Alberto Reyes-García
Instituto Nacional de Astrofísica, Óptica y Electrónica (INAOE), Computer Science Department
Luis Enrique Erro No.1, Santa María Tonantzintla, Puebla, 72840, Mexico

ABSTRACT

One of the main concerns in the pattern recognition field is enhancing the predictive accuracy of the classification algorithms. While some efforts are focused in the development of new algorithms, another approach is centered in the search of the combination of data preparation techniques, a subset of features and, the selection of the adequate learning algorithm with its hyper parameters tuned. This approach is known as Full Model Selection (FMS) and because of the high search space, this paradigm is largely unexplored especially in large size datasets. In this work, the use of the meta-learning approach is suggested as a way to solve the FMS problem in huge datasets and retain the knowledge gained of each analysis performed which would be lost in another way.

KEYWORDS

Big Data, Meta-Learning, Model Selection

1. INTRODUCTION

The lowering cost and the development of new technologies has made possible the generation of unprecedented scales of information, just in 2014, 2.5 quintillions of Bytes of information were daily created. This means that 90% of the data in the world was created in an interval of two years (Wu et al., 2014). This information could be considered just as expenditure in disk storage or can be turn into a valuable asset through their analysis and one of the main trends in this field is the use of pattern recognition techniques. However, the choice of an appropriate learning algorithm is not a trivial task. In that same spirit, the Full Model Selection (FMS) paradigm attempts to find the combination of a feature subset, data preparation techniques and the classification algorithm that obtains the lowest misclassification rate. Each solution in a search algorithm for FMS represents a series of transformations in the dataset. Such transformations, the number of solutions found during the search and the time employed in this search process makes to FMS paradigm not to be the first choice to select the best model for a dataset of large size. In the literature, the model selection problem has been addressed through different search techniques as in Escalante et. al (2009), where the FMS was faced with a Particle Swarm Optimization (PSO) algorithm using the Balanced Error Rate (BER) of the two-fold cross validation as fitness parameter. Thornton et al. (2013) used Bayesian sequential optimization techniques for the search of models and hyper-parameters optimization with the available algorithms in WEKA. In Lessmann et al. (2006) a genetic algorithm was employed for the hyper-parameter tuning of the SVM algorithm, while Bansal & Sahoo (2015) proposed the use of the bat algorithm for solving FMS. The previous approaches show that the search of models is a time expensive process and none of them offers the mechanism to take advantage of the knowledge gained in previous analysis. This last factor is not insignificant, because the model selection problem never ends and it could be very useful to gain some insights from previous tasks that can be used in a current search. This approach is known as meta-learning and the main concept behind it is to employ the knowledge acquired from previous similar problems to recommend one or more techniques successfully applied, now for the new dataset under analysis (Campos et al., 2016). Several works have been proposed for the use of knowledge of past analysis and meta-learning in recommendation, ranking and prediction of the performance of classification algorithms and other techniques in new problems. Kaloussis & Hilario (2001) proposed the use of meta-learning in order to provide a rank with the performance of the evaluated classifiers. Reif et al. (2012) proposed a hyper-parameter optimization genetic algorithm for the algorithms Random Forest and SVM. The meta-dataset consisted of 15 meta-features and as target, a file with the hyper-parameters of the best individual found is employed. In Campos et al., (2016) the use of meta-learning was proposed in order to recommend the best segmentation algorithm (a model selection task). A meta-dataset was made for each segmentation algorithm with a binary label (Suitable/ Not suitable). In FMS a single model is comprised by a combination of the previously mentioned factors and therefore there are a huge number of models. For this reason, building a meta-dataset for each one is not feasible. In this work the use of a non-supervised learning technique (k-NN) is proposed in order to move the FMS problem from huge datasets to smaller and easy to handle meta-datasets. This paper is organized as follows: section 2 describes some background aspects to understand this work, section 3 describes our approach to solve the FMS problem in huge datasets through the use of meta-learning, section 4 is for the experiments and results and in the section 5 are the conclusions and future work.

2. THEORETICAL FRAMEWORK

In order to make this work as self-contained as possible, crucial aspects as full model selection and the MapReduce framework will be detailed in this section.

2.1 Full Model Selection (FMS)

Full model selection is the combination of several factors in order to obtain the lowest classification error for a given dataset. An attempt of a formal definition is given in **Eq. 1.** Given a set of learning algorithms *A*, data preparation techniques *P*, and feature selection algorithms *F*, the goal of the FMS is to determine the combination of algorithms: $a^*_{wA} \in A$ (a machine learning algorithm with an specific configuration in its hyper-parameters values), $p^* \in P$ and $f^* \in F$ with the lowest misclassification rate, which is estimated over the dataset *D* and this dataset is split in two disjoint partitions ($D^{(i)}_{train}$ and $D^{(i)}_{validation}$ for $i = 1,2,...,k$). Misclassification rate is calculated with the loss function $L(a^{(j)}_{wA}, p^j, f^j, D^{(i)}_{train}, D^{(i)}_{validation})$, training the algorithm a_{wA} in the partition $D^{(i)}_{train}$, and evaluated in the partition $D^{(i)}_{validation}$. The data partitions are previously transformed by *p* and *f*.

$$a^*_{wA}, p^*, f^* \in \arg\min L(a^{(j)}_{wA}, p^j, f^j, D^{(i)}_{train}, D^{(i)}_{validation}) \quad a^{(i)} \in A, p^{(i)} \in P, f^{(i)} \in F, w_A \in W_A \tag{1}$$

2.2 The MapReduce Framework and Big Data

Due to its size, it is not easy to handle datasets that cannot be loaded into main memory of a personal computer. The traditional algorithms to process those datasets cannot be used (due to very large computing times or the algorithms inability to handle such datasets), therefore it is necessary to employ new tools and technologies as the MapReduce paradigm (Dean & Ghemawat, 2004). MapReduce enables the parallelization and distribution of big scale computation, required to analyze large datasets. This programming model was designed to work over computing clusters and it works under the master-slave communication model. The design of MapReduce considers the following fundamental principles: 1) Low-Cost Unreliable Commodity Hardware. The MapReduce framework is designed to run on large clusters of commodity hardware. 2) Extremely Scalable Cluster. The nodes can be taken out of service with almost no impact to keep the MapReduce jobs running. 3) Fault tolerant. The MapReduce framework applies straightforward mechanisms to replicate data and keep processes running in case of failures. In MapReduce a computing task is specified as a sequence of stages: map, shuffle and reduce that works on a dataset $X = \{x_1, x_2, \ldots, x_n\}$. The map step applies a function μ, to each value x_i to produce a finite set of key-value pairs (k, v). To allow for parallel execution, the computation of function $\mu(x_i)$, must depend only on x_i. The shuffle step collects all the key-value pairs produced in the previous map step, and produces a set of lists, $L_k = (k; v_1, v_2, \ldots, v_n)$ where each of such lists consists of all values v_i such that $k_i = k$ for a key k assigned in the map step. The reduce stage applies a function ρ to each list $L_k = (k; v_1, v_2, \ldots, v_n)$, created during the shuffle step, to produce a set of values $y_1, y_2, \ldots, y_n$. The reduce function ρ is defined to work sequentially on L_k but should be independent of other lists L_k, where $k' \neq k$ (Goodrich, Sitchinava & Zhang, 2011). A widespread definition of Big Data describes this concept in terms of three characteristics of information in this field: **Volume, Velocity** and **Variety** (Tlili & Hamdani, 2014) referring to the huge quantity, the high speed of generation and the different formats of the information. Despite being an extended definition, is little ambiguous and do not provides rules to identify a huge dataset. Therefore, in this work we propose an alternative definition but related to the model selection problem. For our definition we propose that a huge dataset for the model selection problem must accomplish two rules: 1) The dataset size is big enough that at least one of the considered classification algorithms in their sequential version cannot process it. 2) The dataset size is defined by their file size considering the number of instances (I) and features (F) as long as I » F.

3. META-LEARNING TO SOLVE THE FMS PROBLEM

As previously established, the meta-learning approach makes use of the gained knowledge in solved problems (pre-processing techniques employed, learning algorithm with lowest error, algorithm employed for feature selection, among others) in order to suggest potential solutions to the current problems under analysis. In order to use that knowledge, it is essential to characterize the analyzed datasets. With this in mind we propose the use of some of the most popular meta-features employed in several works in the use of meta-learning, those meta-features are in Table 1.

Table 1. Meta-features employed in this work

Type of meta-feature	Meta-feature
Simple	Proportion of attributes with outliers Number of continuous attributes Number of discrete attributes Proportion of examples and number of attributes
Statistical	Mean absolute correlation coefficient Standard deviation ratio Bhattacharyya distance Mean skewness Mean kurtosis Fisher discriminant ratio
Information theory	Mean mutual information Noise-signal ratio Mean entropy

The meta-features are divided in 3 groups: simple features, statistical properties and information theory properties. The first group comprises simple features of the dataset. The second group is for statistical properties that describe dataset as the skewness and kurtosis. Finally, the third group describes the dataset in terms of the information theory measures as the entropy and the mutual information. The second key element in meta-learning is the algorithm that will be used as meta-learner. The choice of such algorithm strongly depends to what is expected to get of the meta-learning module: Estimated performance of an algorithm, suggestions of potential solutions, ranking of the performance of a set of algorithms, suitability or unsuitability of an algorithm to a problem, etc. As mentioned early in this document, the FMS problem can not be turned into a supervised meta-learning (classification or regression) problem. Therefore, in the interest to obtain a list of the best models for the dataset at hand, suggested through meta-learning, we used the well known k-NN algorithm (Fix & Hodges, 1951). This algorithm used for both classification, regression and ranking problems is based on the Euclidean (among others) distance between a test sample and the specified training samples (Leif, 2009). The final essential element in the meta-learning approach is the creation of a meta-dataset and, therefore, a FMS analysis and the extraction of the meta-features on a group of datasets ought to be performed. This may seem a major drawback of our approach, but the time employed to analyze a group of small datasets is much smaller in comparison with the time required for just one huge dataset and it is also important that those analyses can be performed employing a regular PC. Taking into consideration the need to analyze both small and huge datasets, we employed the PSMS (Particle Swarm Model Selection) algorithm proposed by Escalante et al. (2009) but developed under the MapReduce paradigm. This algorithm for FMS is based on the PSO algorithm which is a population-based search algorithm inspired by the behavior of biological communities that exhibit both individual and social behavior (Escalante et al., 2009). Every particle of PSMS is encoded in a 16-dimensional vector as follows: In position 1 the fitness of the potential models is stored. Position 2 allows to determine which operation will be done first: data-preparation or feature selection. Position 3 indicates if the data-preparation step will be done. Positions 4 to 6 are parameters for the data-preparation step (method identifier, parameter 1 and parameter 2). Position 7 determines if the feature selection step will be done. Positions 8 and 9 are for the feature selection step (Method identifier and number of features to be selected respectively). Positions 10 to 16 are for the machine learning algorithm construction. A set of particles $S = \{x_1^t, x_2^t, \dots, x_m^t\}$ is called a swarm. Every particle has a related velocity value that is used to explore the search space and the velocity of such particle at time t is as follows $V_i^t = \{v_{i.1}^t, v_{i.2}^t, \dots, v_{i.16}^t\}$ where $v_{i.k}^t$ is the velocity for dimension k of particle i at time t. The search trajectories are adjusting employing the following equations:

$$v_{i,j}^{t+1} = W \times v_{i,j}^t + c1 \times r1 \times \left(p_{i,j} - x_{i,j}^t\right) + c2 \times r2 \times \left(p_{g,j} - x_{i,j}^t\right) \quad (2)$$

$$x_{i,j}^{t+1} = x_{i,j}^t + v_{i,j}^{t+1} \quad (3)$$

From the previous equations $p_{i,j}$ is the value in the dimension j of the best solution found so far, also called personal best. $p_{g,j}$ is the value in the dimension j of the best particle found so far in the swarm. Regarding to $c1$, $c2 \in \mathbb{R}$, are constants weighting the influence of local and global best solutions, and $r1, r2 \sim U[0,1]$ are values that introduces randomness into the search process. The inertia weight W controls the impact of the past velocity of the particle over the current one, influencing the local and global exploration. As in the original work, the inertia weight is adaptive and specified by the triplet $W=(w_{start}, w_f, w_{end})$; where w_{start} and w_{end} are the initial values of W, w_f indicates the fraction of iterations in which W is decreased. W is decreased by $W\text{-}w_{dec}$ from the first iteration where $W=w_{start}$ to the last iteration where $W=w_{end}$ and $w_{dec} = w_{start}\text{-}w_{end}/Number\_of\_iterations$. As mentioned above a meta-dataset was constructed by analyzing several small datasets by extracting the meta-features in Table 1 and employing as target a file with the best models found by PSMS in each one of the employed datasets. Each one of the PSMS particles represents a potential model for the dataset under analysis and the algorithms 1 to 3 are employed to evaluate/construct the PSMS particles and the potential models suggested through meta-learning that were used in bigger datasets and for that reason, the MapReduce paradigm is employed. In order to provide short and concise information, the central algorithms (under the Apache Spark 1.6 framework) to evaluate the particles of PSMS, that is feature-selection, data-preparation and calculate the error classification are shown next. For greater ease of understanding the algorithms are commented (the comments are denoted with the symbols "// or /* */").

Algorithm 1: Data preparation

```
DataPrep(DataSet,particle)
Return(DataSet.map(row->row.toArray.map(col->Transform(col,particle))))
/*Transform function is applied to every column of each row in the
RDD*/
End
```

Algorithm 2: Feature Selection

```
FeatSelection(DataSet,particle)
 numFeat = particle(9)
 rankRDD = DataSet.map(row->RankingCalculation(row))
 /*RankingCalculation function obtains the ranking of the features */
 reducedRDD = rankRDD.map(row->getF(row,numFeat)) /*function getF is
applied to rankRDD and returns a reduced dataset */
Return(reducedRDD)
End
```

```
Algorithm 3: Classification

Classification(DataSet,particle)
 kFolds=createFold(DataSet,NumFolds=2)/*createFold function
  creates an RDD for k-Fold Cross validation */
  error=kFolds.map{
  case(Training,Validation)/*dataset is separated in
  Training and Validation */
  model = createModel(Training, particle)/*creates a model
  PredictedTargets=Validation.map(Instance->
  model.predict(Instance.features))/*Performs predictions in
  validation set */
  accuracy= getAcc(PredictedTargets,Validation.targets)
  //Obtains the accuracy in each fold
  error = 100-accuracy
 Return(error) }
  meanError=error.sum/error.length
 Return(meanError)
End
```

4. EXPERIMENTS AND RESULTS

To evaluate our approach, we experimented with the datasets shown in Table 2. The datasets "Synthetic 1" and "Synthetic 2" were created using the tool for synthetic datasets generation in the context of ordinal regression: "Synthetic Datasets Nspheres" provided in Sánchez-Monedero et al. (2013). Despite of have been developed for ordinal regression, the tool can be properly adjusted for traditional binary or multi-class problems and provides the mechanism to control the overlaps and classes balance. The remaining datasets were obtained from the UCI (Dua & Karra, 2017) and from the Libsvm project (Fan, 2018).

Table 2. Datasets used in the experiments

Dataset	Data points	Attributes	Samples by class	Type of variables	File size
RLCP	5,749,111	11	(5728197;20915)	Real	261.6 MB
KDD	4,856,150	41	(972780;3883369)	Categorical	653 MB
Synthetic 1	200,000,000	3	(100000000;100000000)	Real	5.5 GB
Higgs	11,000,000	28	(5170877;5829123)	Real	7.5 GB
Synthetic 2	49,000,002	30	(24500001;24500001)	Real	12.7 GB
Epsilon	500,000	2000	(249778;250222)	Real	15.6 GB

Another major feature of the aforementioned datasets is its intrinsic dimension. The intrinsic dimension (ID) is the minimum number of parameters needed to represent the data without information loss (Lombardi et al., 2011) The id of the employed datasets was estimated with the "Minimum neighbor distance estimator" (MNDE) (Lombardi et al., 2011) and the "Dimensionality from angle and norm concentration" (DANCO) estimator (Ceruti et al., 2012). The importance of the "ID" estimation on each dataset is made in order to get evidence that the datasets in Table 1 represents different computational problems and, therefore, our approach have the capacity to deal with a wide range of problems and in the context of this work also with datasets of different sizes. In the next table the calculated intrinsic dimension using the aforementioned estimators is shown.

Table 3. Intrinsic dimension of the datasets

Dataset	MNDE	DANCO
RLCP	2	2
KDD	1	1
Synthetic 1	3	3
Higgs	12	15
Synthetic 2	22	28
Epsilon	160	78

In order to obtain a statistical power of 90%, 44 replications of each experiment for every dataset were performed (The number of replications depends on the statistical test performed and the number of methods contrasted pursuing to obtain a statistical power of 90%). Each replication was performed with a particular random sample of the data points with different random samples among replications. For each experiment, the dataset was divided in two disjoint datasets with 60% of the data samples for the training set and 40% for the test set. With the FMS analysis performed by PSMS to small datasets, a meta-dataset was built. To each instance (this means a dataset described by its meta-features) corresponds a file with the best particles found in the search. Because choosing a single model is not a trivial task, the MapReduce-based PSMS version and our meta-learning approach use a set of solutions to build a final model in the form of a weighted ensemble. PSMS use the 30 best models found during the search and the meta-learning approach use the best model of the "k" nearest (k=30) instances in the meta-dataset. The stopping criteria of PSMS was to complete 50 iterations with a swarm size of 30 (this means 1500 particles evaluated during a search). In Table 4 the mean classification error obtained by the meta-learning approach and PSMS is shown. From the mean errors of both approaches, it can be seen that the meta-learning approach had the lowest errors in three datasets (RLCP, KDD and Epsilon) and PSMS in the remaining three (Synthetic 1, Higgs and Synthetic 2). A t-test was performed, in order to find significant differences in the performance of both methods, in Table 5 are the results.

Table 4. Mean classification error obtained in the test dataset by PSMS and our meta-learning approach over 44 replications. The best results are in **bold**

Dataset	PSMS	Meta-learning
RLCP	0.052±0.001	**0.004±0.003**
KDD	0.166±0.148	**0.030±0.004**
Synthetic 1	**15.862±0.004**	15.863±0.003
Higgs	**28.299±0.057**	31.046±0.246
Synthetic 2	**6.681±0.005**	6.683±0.003
Epsilon	54.008±0.926	**31.476±1.740**

Table 5. t-statistic obtained from the Student's t-test. The critical values at the 95% confidence level are 2.016 with 43 d.f. Cases that exceed the critical value (absolute value) are considered as a difference that is statistically significant at the fixed level and are in **bold**

Dataset	t-statistic
RLCP	**-101.624**
KDD	**-6.097**
Synthetic 1	-0.409
Higgs	**75.282**
Synthetic 2	-0.216
Epsilon	**-73.078**

From the results in table 5, it can be seen that the meta-learning approach obtains significant differences in those datasets where it got the best performance (RLCP, KDD and Epsilon) and there are no important differences in two of the three datasets where the meta-learning is not the best method (Synthetic 1 and 2). Though the meta-learning performance is not the best in the dataset Higgs, the intrinsic dimension of the datasets shows that the meta-learning approach has the capacity to deal with different problems (Epsilon is the hardest in the comparative with an ID of 160/78) and with a wide range of datasets sizes. On the other hand, the MapReduce-based PSMS version explored through a higher number of potential solutions (1500) before to build the final model, while the meta-learning approach employ just 30 models to do that. Our approach was also tested against the kernel k-NN algorithm proposed by Yu et al. (2002), but developed under MapReduce and a grid search algorithm (with an exploration of 1500 possible solutions) also developed under the MapReduce paradigm (Apacheorg, 2017). The results are shown in Table 6, the statistic test (an ANOVA test) is shown in Table 7.

Table 6. Mean classification error obtained in the test dataset by the Meta-learning approach, K-NN (K=9,999) and the grid search, over 20 replications. The best results are in **bold**

Datasets	Meta-learning	Grid search	K-NN
RLCP	0.004±0.003	**0.001±0.000**	0.500±0.098
KDD	0.029±0.004	**0.001±0.000**	19.535±0.261
Synthetic 1	**15.863±0.003**	17.011±0.120	50.088±0.028
Higgs	31.019±0.292	**30.955±0.228**	46.916±0.408
Synthetic 2	**6.683±0.003**	22.152±0.541	50.126±0.115
Epsilon	31.581±2.287	**29.664±0.174**	50.673±3.323

The results in table 6 shown that the best algorithm in the comparative is the grid search and the second best is our approach. In order to obtain a statistical power of 90% in an ANOVA test, 20 replications were performed. The statistical test shown that in two (RLCP and KDD) of the four datasets where the grid search was the best method, there were no significant differences compared against meta-learning. In the datasets Synthetic 1 and Synthetic 2, the meta-learning was the best approach with significant differences in the performance. That means that in four of the six datasets in the comparative, the meta-learning approach is the best or as good as the best method. In the remaining two datasets (Higgs and Epsilon) the best method was the grid search. Despite these results, is remarkable that the meta-learning approach has the capacity to solve the FMS problem in huge datasets, moving the effort of the search of models from big datasets to small meta-datasets. Although the effort required by the meta-learning approach is considerable, it is small in comparison with the effort of the complete search and the performance of the meta-learning approach can still be refined using the suggestions as an initial swarm in PSMS.

Table 7. F-statistic obtained from the ANOVA test and q-values from the Tukey HSD test. The critical values at the 95% confidence level for the ANOVA test are 3.16. The critical values at the 95% confidence level for the Tukey HSD test are 3.44. Cases that exceed the critical value are considered as a difference that is statistically significant at the fixed level and are marked with an asterisk (*)

Datasets	Anova F	Meta-Learning vs Grid search	Meta-learning vs K-NN
RLCP	**740.762***	0.216	**47.032**
KDD	**68112.252***	0.660	**451.710**
Synthetic 1	**2747339.519***	**99.734**	**2919.500**
Higgs	**30350.798***	**56.137**	**269.740**
Synthetic 2	**21784.864***	**97.925**	**290.130**
Epsilon	**496.368***	**3.675**	**36.620**

5. CONCLUSION

The full model selection paradigm is useful to improve the predictive accuracy of the existent machine learning algorithms. The use of this paradigm is restrictive due to the higher computing time needed to analyze a dataset and, the larger the dataset the more the computing time. In order to face that problem, this work proposed the use of meta-learning to find the most adequate models to a dataset, transforming a big search problem in a small meta-dataset analysis. This paradigm has the benefit of storing the knowledge acquired in each analysis that, would be lost in another way. The experimental results shown that our propose method can outperform the complete search with a well known method for full model selection (PSMS). It is also important, that the performance of the meta-learning paradigm can be improved using it as an initial swarm of the aforementioned algorithm for FMS. As a future work, the performance of the meta-learner algorithm (k-nn) will be contrasted against other methods.

ACKNOWLEDGEMENT

The first author is grateful for the support from CONACyT scholarship no. 428581.

REFERENCES

Alexandros K., H. Melanie, 2001, Model selection via meta-learning: a comparative study, *International Journal on Artificial Intelligence Tools* 10 (04) (2001) 525–554.

Apacheorg (2017), 'Ml tuning: model selection and hyperparameter tuning', http://spark.apache.org/docs/latest/ml-tuning.html.

Bansal, B., & Sahoo, A. (2015, March). Full model selection using Bat algorithm. *In Cognitive Computing and Information Processing (CCIP)*, 2015 International Conference on (pp. 1-4). IEEE.

Campos G. F., S. Barbon, R. G. Mantovani, A meta-learning approach for recommendation of image segmentation algorithms, 2016, *in: Graphics, Patterns and Images (SIBGRAPI), 2016 29th 310 SIBGRAPI Conference* on, IEEE, 2016, pp. 370–377.

Ceruti, C., Bassis, S., Rozza, A., Lombardi, G., Casiraghi, E., Campadelli, P.: Danco, (2012), Dimensionality from angle and norm concentration. *arXiv preprint arXiv*:1206.3881 (2012)

Dean, J. & Ghemawat, S. (2008), 'MapReduce', *Communications of the ACM* 51(1), 107–113.

Dua, D. and Karra Taniskidou, E. (2017). UCI Machine Learning Repository [http://archive.ics.uci.edu/ml]. Irvine, CA: University of California, School of Information and Computer Science.

Escalante H. J. , M. Montes, L. E. Sucar, Particle swarm model selection, *Journal of Machine Learning Research* 10 (Feb) (2009) 405–440.

Fix, E., Hodges, J.L. Discriminatory analysis, nonparametric discrimination: Consistency properties. *Technical Report 4, USAF School of Aviation Medicine*, Randolph Field, Texas, 1951.

Goodrich, M. T., Sitchinava, N. & Zhang, Q. (2011), Sorting, searching, and simulation in the mapreduce framework, in '*International Symposium on Algorithms and Computation*', Springer, pp. 374–383.

Leif E. Peterson, (2009), K-nearest neighbor. *Scholarpedia*, 4(2):1883.

Fan, R. (2018). LIBSVM Data: Classification, Regression, and Multi-label. Retrieved April 17, 2018, from https://www.csie.ntu.edu.tw/~cjlin/libsvmtools/datasets/

Lessmann, S., Stahlbock, R., & Crone, S. F. (2006, July). Genetic algorithms for support vector machine model selection. *In Neural Networks, 2006*. IJCNN'06. International Joint Conference on (pp. 3063-3069). IEEE.

Lombardi, G., Rozza, A., Ceruti, C., Casiraghi, E., Campadelli, P.,(2011), Minimum neighbor distance estimators of intrinsic dimension. In: *Joint European Conference on Machine Learning and Knowledge Discovery in Databases*. pp. 374–389. Springer (2011)

Reif M., F. Shafait, A. Dengel, 2012, Meta-learning for evolutionary parameter optimization of classifiers, *Machine learning* 87 (3) (2012) 357.

Sánchez-Monedero, J., Gutiérrez, P.A., Pérez-Ortiz, M., Hervás-Martínez ,(2013), C.: An n-spheres based synthetic data generator for supervised classification. *In: International Work-Conference on Artificial Neural Networks*. pp. 613–621. Springer (2013).

Thornton, C., Hutter, F., Hoos, H. H., & Leyton-Brown, K. (2013, August). Auto-WEKA: Combined selection and hyperparameter optimization of classification algorithms. *In Proceedings of the 19th ACM SIGKDD international conference on Knowledge discovery and data mining* (pp. 847-855). ACM.

Tlili, M., & Hamdani, T. M. (2014, August). Big data clustering validity. *In Soft Computing and Pattern Recognition (SoCPaR)*, 2014 6th International Conference of (pp. 348-352). IEEE.

Yu, K., Ji, L. & Zhang, X. (2002), 'Kernel nearest-neighbor algorithm', *Neural Processing Letters* 15(2), 147–156.

Wu X., X. Zhu, G.-Q. Wu, W. Ding, Data mining with big data, *IEEE transactions on knowledge and data engineering* 26 (1) (2014) 97–107.

AN INCREMENTAL LEARNING SYSTEM FOR ONLINE KNN CLASSIFICATION: APPLICATION TO NETWORK INTRUSION DETECTION

Ahmed Riadh Baba-Ali
University of Science and Technology of Algiers, Algeria (USTHB)

ABSTRACT

In this paper, we describe an incremental learning system based on the KNN classification algorithm (K Nearest Neighbor). Our approach uses an incremental learning paradigm since the used knowledge is improved over time, in contrast to the offline learning paradigm, where the learning is done once for all at the beginning. The incremental learning ability is attractive for problems with changing environments such as network intrusion detection where new and previously unknown attacks appear overtime. This kind of problems needs a continuous adaptation of the system's knowledge. Our system has been tested with live data coming from a real network under state of the art attacks. The results, showed that our approach is faster with a substantial smaller error rate and also a smaller false negative (FN) error rate compared to the classical KNN.

KEY WORDS

Incremental Learning, Classification, KNN, Network Intrusion Detection System

1. INTRODUCTION

For the purpose of intrusion detection, network, events such as packets or flows are classified with supervised classifiers such as neural networks, support vector machine (SVM), Decision Rules, decision trees etc (Axelsson S., 2000). Among them, KNN classifiers are also successfully used (Deepika D. and Richhariya V. , 2012), (Liao Y. and Vemuri V.R., 2002). With KNN, a training database is used to measure the similarity of each event to classify, with the data contained in the training database. An important property of the KNN algorithm is that they are non parametric. It means that KNN doesn't rely on a model or a concept, but rather on a dataset. This property is important to problems with fast changing environments such as NIDS where new attacks and changes appear overtime. Consequently, it is mandatory for such systems to be able to adapt their own knowledge to possible changes. This important property is called the concept drift adaptation (J. Gama et al , 2013).

2. RELATED WORK

The concept drift has been recognized as an important and a challenging problem. There are several approaches described in the literature to deal with the concept drift: some are based on decision trees, Bayes models, or SVM etc, whereas some are neighbor based approaches (J. Read et al , 2012).

To deal with concept drift, nearest neighbor (NN) algorithms are based on different approaches in order to prioritize the most recent acquired knowledge which is considered as "more true" than the oldest one. Among the existing approaches, one can cite the time window approach which considers only the instances acquired within a time window. Another approach is called the instance time weighted, where each instance has a weight which is greater when the instance acquisition time is more recent (Zhang P. et al , 2011), (Beringer J. , 2007). To the author's knowledge, none are based on the CNN algorithm that we used in our system. Surprisingly, our approach obtained very promising results, as we will see in the next sections.

Compared to other well known classifiers, neighborhood techniques are attractive thanks to their simplicity and their classification accuracy. However, one of the limitations of the KNN rule is the size of the training set (Suguna N. & Thanushkodi K. ,2010), (Yu W. & Zheng'ou W., 2007). For KNN classification, the size of the training database, is crucial: If the number of training instances is too small, the accuracy of the KNN classifier is not acceptable. But if the training set is too large, the KNN classification running time can be prohibitive. Consequently, the optimal size of the training database is very important and constitutes a difficult problem to solve (Liu H, Motoda H , 2002). This problem has already been addressed in the literature, for many years due to its importance. It is called the instance selection problem (IS) or the prototype selection problem. This problem can be solved in two ways: either by reducing the dimensions of the feature space by using smaller data sets; or by using an improved classification algorithm which can accelerate the calculation time (Shi B., Yi W. & Zhang'ou W., 2007).

Instance selection (IS) is the process of finding representative instances from the data, which can help in reducing the size of the data (Murty M. N., Babu T. R. , 2001). This problem is classified as an NP-hard problem (Zukhba A. V. ,2010), which means that there is no polynomial time algorithm able to find an optimal solution. Existing approximation algorithms can however give acceptable solutions in reasonable time. As a consequence, instance selection algorithms are essentially based on heuristics and metaheuristics:

First: Heuristic algorithms are essentially greedy ones. Examples of such algorithms are: CNN (Hart P. , 1968), CBP (Nikolaidis et al , 2011) etc. Second: Metaheuristic algorithms on the other hand are essentially evolutionary ones. An example of such algorithms is the genetic algorithm which has proven its efficiency in dealing with difficult problems (Gil-Pita R. & Yao X. ,2007), (Aci M., Inan C. & Avci M., 2010).

3. SYSTEM DESCRIPTION

The system includes the following components:

- The KNN classification module
- The instance selection module
- The KNN report validation module
- The incremental Learning module

- KNN classification module is the heart of the whole system since it classifies the incoming events from the network as either normal or attack, using a training database containing labeled data.
- The Instance selection module processes the initial training database, in order to reduce its size by selecting the most meaningful data. This operation is necessary in order to reduce the classification time of each incoming traffic event.
- Thanks to the report validation module, classification outcomes are assessed generally by the network administrators or automatically. Basically, this module corrects the classification errors made by the KNN classification module. It produces a file which contains all the misclassified events produced by the KNN classifier. This file is subsequently used as input data for the next module.
- The last module is the incremental learning module. It processes the previous classification errors in order to update the knowledge database. The goal is to avoid redoing the previously done errors.

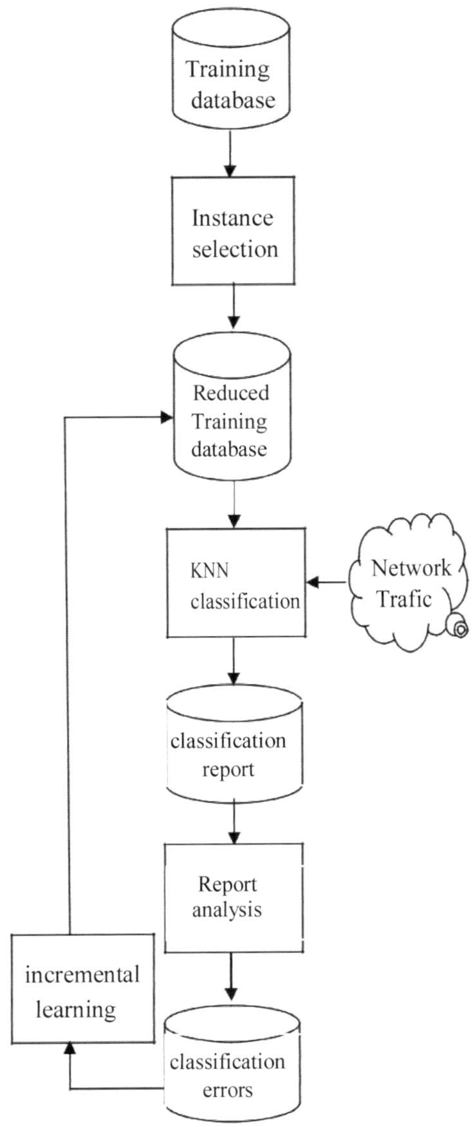

Figure 1. System Components

3.1 The KNN Classification Module

The K-nearest neighbor classification rule (KNN) is a powerful classification method that allows the classification of an unknown instance using a set of classified training instances. The purpose of this algorithm is to classify a new instance according to the classes of the instances of the training set.

Each instance Ii of the training set is composed of inputs and one output, where:
$Ii = < a_{1i}; a_{2i}; \ldots; a_{ji}; c_i >$.

The inputs are the features of the instance:
$(a_{1i}; a_{2i}; \ldots; a_{ji})$
The output is its respective class (c_i).

The class of the unknown instance is found according to the classes of the K most similar instances in the training database. The similarity function is usually a distance function such as the Euclidian distance.

To make a prediction for a test instance, the algorithm first computes its distance to every training instance. Then, it keeps the k closest training instances, where $k \geq 1$ is a fixed integer. The algorithm looks for the most common class among these instances' classes. This class is the predicted class for the test instance. There are two design choices to make: the value of k, and the distance function to use. It is common to select a small and odd an *k* (typically 1, 3 or 5 ...). The 1-NN is the basis of the KNN algorithm. It simply classifies the unclassified instance in the same way as its nearest neighbor.

3.2 The Instance Selection Module

Instance selection is the process of finding the most representative instances from a training dataset (Liu H, Motoda H , 2002). This problem is classified as an NP-hard problem (Zukhba A. V. ,2010), since there is no polynomial algorithm able to find an optimal solution. Existing heuristics can however, give acceptable solutions in a reasonable time. One of the techniques that is used in the selection of instances is the genetic algorithm which belongs to a class of algorithms called evolutionary algorithms. Evolutionary Algorithms (AE) are a family of algorithms belonging to metaheuristic inspired by the theory of the evolution dedicated to solve various problems. These algorithms transform over time a set of solutions for a given problem in order to find the best possible solution. A solution is represented as a chromosome, where each gene corresponds to an instance in the training database. Each gene can contain either a 1 or 0. In the first case, a 1 means that the corresponding instance is selected otherwise it is deleted from the database. We used as fitness, a function which permits to minimize the training database size without degrading the classification accuracy.

$fitness = \lambda_1\ (accuracy) + \lambda_2\ (reduction)$
Where: $\lambda_1 + \lambda_2 = 1$;

These two parameters (λ_1 and λ_2) allow to find a compromise between the two objectives to be achieved. The fitness function includes the two aspects of the problem, leading to solutions that are as satisfactory as possible. More implementation details can be found in (Miloud-Aouidate A., et al, 2013).

3.3 The Diagnostic Validation Module

The outcome of the classification module could have many forms. It could be labeled events such as packets or flows or could be sophisticated alerts issued by an automatic system. These events are labeled, which means that each event is classified as attack or normal. In many ways, each label of the incoming events can be verified. This diagnosis could turn to be true when an event is found as a normal event whereas it has been labeled as normal, it is called a true positive (TP). The second case is that when an event is found as an attack whereas it has been classified as an attack, it is called a true negative (TN). On the other hand, the diagnosis could turn to be false when an event is identified as a normal event whereas it has been classified as an attack, it is called a false negative (FN). The fourth case is when an event is identified as an attack whereas it has been classified as a normal event, it is called a false positive (FP).

The validation of the diagnosis could be done automatically by software such as an alert classifier (Miloud-Aouidate A., et al, 2013) or manually by a person who is generally the network administrator. In fact, after analysis and verification, the network administrator can say that an alert does not correspond to an actual attack, or that a normal event corresponds actually to an attack. In both cases, these false diagnoses are used subsequently to improve the system's knowledge database.

3.4 The Incremental Learning Module

The outcome of the incremental learning is to update the training database used by the KNN classifier. This update is made using the Hart algorithm called, the Condensed Nearest Neighbor Rule or CNN (Hart P., 1968). CNN was one of the first used method for the training dataset size reduction. It permits to select among the corrected predictions the most appropriate knowledge. It eliminates equivalent training instances, especially those that do not add additional information or are redundant.

CNN basically uses a greedy heuristic. Its main advantage is its fast speed along with its good results in terms of reduction rate. On the other hand, one major disadvantage of CNN, is the fact that the algorithm is sensitive to the order of events used to update the training database. However, to the author's point of view, this disadvantage, in the context of incremental learning, is actually an advantage, since the KNN report validation come in a precise temporal order. This order is the time where the report errors have been discovered. Therefore the updates of the training database must be done according to the precise time of the validation, in order to reflect the evolution of the knowledge. This evolution of knowledge is called concept drift adaptation (J. Gama et al , 2013). The concept drift in the network intrusion detection context, may have several meanings. Either that a network security policy has changed, or new threats have been discovered. In this case a quick improvement of the knowledge base is necessary, preferably in real time.

Besides, the speed performance of the Hart algorithm (Hart P. , 1968), makes it suitable for real time learning, and it is compatible with the high throughput of actual networks. In our case the CNN algorithm selects from the updated events, the ones which are the most pertinent updates of the training data.

4. TESTS

The presented tests have been conducted on real data, in order to compare the obtained results with or without the incremental learning concept.

4.1 Used Data

The database contains the descriptions of TCP connections composed of 41 attributes per connection. These connections gather training and testing data collected over about a week of network traffic containing several attacks.

4.2 Results

The results obtained by the instance selection module permits to reduce the training database by 99%. This remarkable result is generally obtained by almost all the instance selection approaches. This result can be explained by the fact that network events are very similar during a short period of time. For example the packets generated by a download, or video or audio stream share many features such as addresses, ports, protocols etc. This important size reduction of the training database, has a proportional impact on KNN classification speed. In fact, the running time is reduced in the same proportion.

The following tests have been conducted in order to demonstrate the efficiency of our approach. We measure the error rate or misclassification rate of the events produced by the KNN module, first without incremental learning and second with the incremental learning. We measure the daily mean error rate over a period of about a month. We conducted the tests for different values of K, varying from 3 to 11. It appears that the optimal value is K=3 (see table 1) since the error at that value, reaches its lowest value. We can see that the error rate is roughly reduced by about a fourth.

Table 1. Comparison of the mean classification error rate

K	1	3	5	7	9	11
Classical KNN	13.75	7.63	10.13	13.73	13.59	13.53
KNN with incremental learning	2.56	2.28	2.33	2.50	2.70	2.80

For K=3, we can see in figure 2, the evolution of the classification error rate over time with (light line) and without incremental learning (dark line). It starts from about 10% and decrease progressively to about 2.33%. This proves that the system is able to learn incrementally from its previous errors, since the error rate decrease regularly over time as shown by the linear tendency line drawn in dashed.

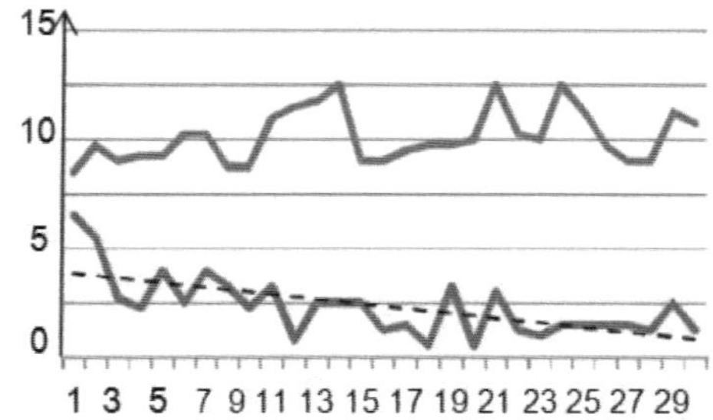

Figure 2. Comparison of classification mean error rate with and without incremental learning vs time

The next tests are similar to the previous ones, with the difference that the FN (false negative) is rather measured. This rate is important since it indicates the number of undetected attacks which are missed by the NIDS. The false positive (FP) in the context of NIDS is relatively less important since it represents the rate of detected false attacks.

Table 2. Comparison of mean classification false negative error rate

K	1	3	5	7	9	11
Classic. KNN	5.85	6.70	9.63	13.62	13.65	13.43
KNN with increment. learning	1.14	1.24	1.25	1.35	1.41	1,42

Table 2, shows a substantial reduction of the false negative error rate. In this case also, we can notice that the error rate decreases regularly, which proves one more time that the system is able to learn from its previous errors.

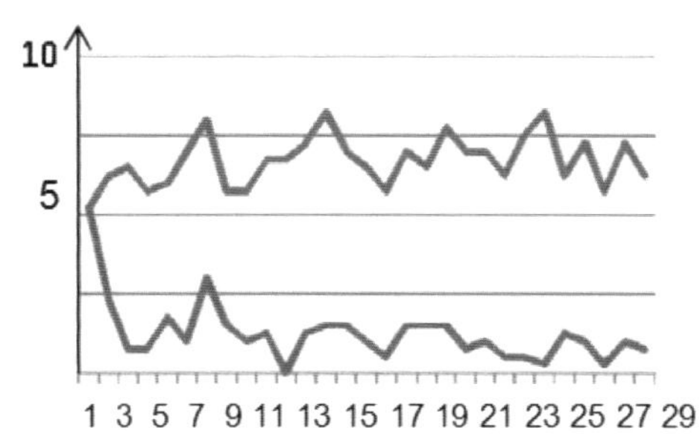

Figure 3. Comparison of mean classification false negative error rate VS time

The last aspect that we studied is the evolution of the training database size. Since the new knowledge is continuously added over time to the training database, the question one can ask, is how evolutes the size of the training database ? Figure 4 shows a constant increase of the database size, of about 2.5% of the input test data size. We conducted the tests for different values of K, varying from 3 to 11. In all cases compared to the initial reduced training database size, the increase is about 20%. Whereas compared to the initial training database without reduction, the increase represents less than 1%.

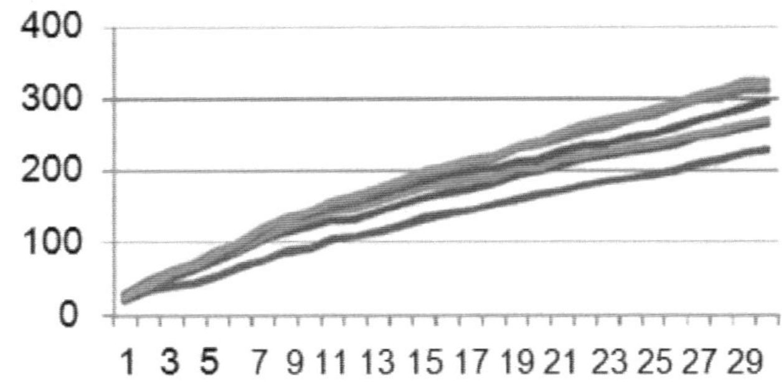

Figure 4. Evolution of the size of the training data base vs time

5. CONCLUSION

Network intrusion detection is an important computer security field. The computational requirements of the field are mainly the classification speed as well as the classification error rate. Our approach has addressed both requirements in the following ways:

Since network speed is an important feature, processing high speed networks has become nowadays mandatory for efficient network security. The instance reduction contributes to reduce the classification running time substantially. KNN classification speed is proportional to the training database size. The smaller the database size, the smaller is the running time. It is important to note that this gain is overshadowed by the incremental learning concept, since it constantly adds new knowledge to the training database. The experiment has shown, that when processing data with the size of the original training database, the added knowledge represents less then 2,5 % of its size. So the advantage obtained by the instance reduction, disappears overtime when the system processes data with more than 40 times its original size. However, even in this case it is possible to run the instance selection module, to reduce the training database size offline.

The tests show also a substantial reduction of the error rate, which has been dropped by a factor of about five. This result is due to the incremental learning process which avoids redoing the same errors by enhancing the training database. Moreover, the false negative error rate has been substantially reduced ranging from fifth to more than tenth. This fact is very important in the intrusion detection context since it represents the proportion of undetected attacks by the system.

The author believes that the simplicity of the approach using robust algorithms such as KNN, CNN and genetic, make it remarkably efficient in terms of speed and accuracy. Moreover it can be applied to other fields such as robotics and control. The author believes also that this approach could provide a robust solution to several challenges facing incremental learning such as autonomous learning, noise and drift differentiation (J. Gama et al , 2013).

REFERENCES

Aci M., Inan C. & Avci M. ,2010. A hybrid classification method of k nearest neighbor, Bayesian methods and genetic algorithm, *Expert Systems with Applications*, 37, pp 5061-5067.

Axelsson S., 2000. Intrusion Detection Systems: A Survey and Taxonomy, *Engineering*, Vol. 52 (99-15), pp.541-554.

Beringer J. ,2007. Efficient instance-based learning on data streams, *intelligent Data Analysis*, vol 11, No 6, pp 627-650

Deepika D. and Richhariya V. , 2012. Intrusion detection with KNN classification and DS-theory, *International Journal of Computer Science and Information Technology and Security*, Vol. 2 (2), pp. 274–281.

Garcia S., Cano J. R. and Herrera F., 2008. A memetic algorithm for evolutionary prototype selection: A scaling up approach, *Pattern Recognition*, Vol. 41, pp. 2693–2709.

Gama J. et al , 2013. A Survey on Concept Drift Adaptation, *ACM Computing Surveys*, Vol. 1, No. 1,: January 2013.

Gil-Pita R. & Yao X. ,2007. Using a Genetic Algorithm for Editing k-Nearest Neighbor Classifiers. *IDEAL 2007*, LNCS, 4881, pp. 1141-1150.

Hart P. , 1968. The Condensed Nearest Neighbor Rule, *IEEE Trans. on Information Theory*, 14, pp. 515-516.

Liao Y. and Vemuri V.R., 2002. Use of K-Nearest Neighbor classifier for intrusion detection, *Computers and Security*, Vol. 21 (5), pp.439–448.

Liu H, Motoda H , 2002. On issues of instance selection, *Data Mining Knowledge Discovery*. Vol. 6 (2), pp.115–130.

Miloud-Aouidate A., et al, 2013. IDS False alarm reduction using an instance selection KNN memetic algorithm, *International Journal of Metaheuristic*, Inderscience, Volume 2(4), pp 333-252.

Murty M. N., Babu T. R. , 2001. Comparison of genetic algorithm based instance selection schemes, *Pattern Recognition*, 34, pp. 523-525.

Nikolaidis et al , 2011. A class boundary preserving algorithm for data condensation, *Pattern Recognition*, 44, pp 704-715.

Read J. et al , 2012. Batch-Incremental versus Instance-Incremental Learning in Dynamic and Evolving Data, *Advances in Intelligent Data Analysis XI*, Volume 7619 of the series Lecture Notes in Computer Science pp 313-323

Suguna N. & Thanushkodi K. ,2010. An Improved k-Nearest Neighbor Classification Using Genetic Algorithm, *International Journal of Computer Science* , Issues, 7, pp. 18-21.

Shi B., Yi W. & Zhang'ou W., 2007. A fast KNN algorithm applied to web text categorization, *Journal of The China Society for Scientific and Technical In-formation*, 26(1), pp. 60- 64.

Yu W. & Zheng'ou W., 2007. A fast KNN algorithm for text categorization, *Proceedings of the Sixth International Conference on Machine Learning and Cybernetics*, Hong Kong, pp. 3436-3441.

Zhang P. et al , 2011. Enabling Fast Lazy Learning for Data Streams, *IEEE International Conference on Data Mining*, ICDM '11, pp 932- 941

Zukhba A. V., 2010. NP-Completeness of the Problem of instance Selection in the Nearest Neighbor Method, *Pattern Recognition and Image Analysis*, 20, pp 484-494.

STOCK PREDICTION USING RANDOMNESS LEVEL OF PRICE FLUCTUATION MEASURED BY THE RMT-TEST

Mieko Tanaka-Yamawaki[1], Yuuta Mikamori[2], and Xin Yang[3]
[1]*Meiji University, 1-21-4 Nakano, Nakano-ku, Toyko, 164-8525 Japan*
[2]*Probizmo Co.,Ltd, Izumo, Japan,* [3]*Taizhou Vocational & Technical College, Zhejiang, China*

ABSTRACT

The degree of randomness in the price fluctuation is shown to be a useful tool to predict the future stock price levels. The RMT-test is employed as a tool to measure the randomness of the price time series of selected stocks in the Tokyo Stock Exchange Market for three years from 2007 to 2009. The result shows that the stock of the highest randomness is a stable stock that belongs to the sector of electric/gas power supply, which turns out to be more profitable than the Nikkei Average Price throughout the following year. This indicates that the suitable stocks to invest under a bear market have higher randomness that belongs to the category of 'defensive' stocks.

KEYWORDS

Randomness, RMT-Test, Eigenvalues of Cross Correlation Matrix, Tick-Wise Stock Price

1. INTRODUCTION

In dealing with various kinds of big data, one first measures various labels to characterize each data, such as the size, data-type, or the time when the data are taken. A good label would greatly reduce the burden of big data analysis. The main purpose of this article is to show the effect of the 'randomness of the time series' as a new label to be added. Although random numbers play important roles in the daily life as well as the various fields of science and many tools exist to measure the randomness of given data sequences, most of them suffer from various types of limitations, such as a rigid restriction on the data type and the size, ambiguous foundations, lengthy manuals, etc. A good and easy-to-use tool to measure the randomness is strongly called for.

Based on the random matrix theory (RMT) (Wigner, 1955; Mehta, 1995; Edelman, & Rao., 2005) applied on the cross-correlation matrix between financial time series (Bouchaud, & Potters, 2000; Plerou, et.al., 2002), the authors have proposed to use the RMT-test, as a new tool to measure the randomness of given data sequences (Yang, et. al., 2011,2012; Tanaka-Yamawaki, et.al., 2012). The qualitative version of the RMT-test is designed to visualizes the randomness degree by comparing the eigenvalue distribution of the cross-correlation matrix of data sequence to its theoretical counterpart derived by means of the random matrix theory (RMT). This is suitable to view intuitively the degree of randomness of real data that are relatively low in randomness .

The quantitative version of the RMT-test represents the degree of randomness by the error represented by the difference between the 6-th moment of the eigenvalue distribution of the correlation matrix and its RMT-theoretical counterpart. This method has been applied to distinguish subtle difference between reputed pseudo random generators, and the physical random generators installed in the super computers. It has also been used to explain the cause of effective criterion to discriminate principal components from the sea of strongly random background. It has also proved to be effective to compare the security levels of Hash functions, by showing that the output of secure SHA-1 has higher level of randomness than the older MD5.

The RMT-test has also been applied to forecast future performance of stocks. Namely an empirical rule stating that "the higher randomness of minute-wise profits of individual stock indicates the better performance compared to other stocks of lower randomness" is shown to hold at least in the period of 2007-2009 in Tokyo market, which was the typical bear market. This rule is further discussed in this article by investigating the real-world price time series found in the period of 1993-1996 in the U.S. market, which was the typical bull market (Yang, et. al., 2013).

The rest of this article is constructed as follows: Firstly, the methods of the qualitative version and the quantitative version of the RMT-Test, including the application to measure the randomness of various random number generators such as linear congruential generators (LCGs), Mersenne Twister, and three different physical generators, is summarized in Section 2. Section 3 is devoted to investigate possible relationship of the degree of randomness of the stock profit time series and its future performance, based on empirical analysis using minute-wise data of Tokyo market in the period of 2007-2009, as well as the corresponding data of U.S. market in the period of 1993-1996. Finally, Section 4 concludes the article by summarizing this work and discussing the remaining problems.

2. THE RMT TEST

2.1 Mathematical Preparation

The method of the RMT-test is outlined as follows. We aim to test the randomness of a long 1-dimensional sequence of numerical data, S.

At the first step, we cut S into N pieces of equal length T, then shape them in an N×T matrix, $S_{i,j}$, by placing the first T elements of S in the first row of the matrix $S_{i,j}$, and the next T elements in the 2nd row, etc., by discarding the remainder if the length of S is not divisible by T. Each piece, $S_i = (S_{i,1}, S_{i,2}, \ldots, S_{i,T})$, is converted to a normalized vector $x_i = (x_{i,1}, x_{i,2}, \ldots, x_{i,T})$ by means of

$$x_{i,t} = \frac{S_{i,t} - \langle S_i \rangle}{\sigma_i} \tag{1}$$

$$\langle S_i \rangle = \frac{1}{T}\sum_{t=1}^{T} S_{i,t} \tag{2}$$

$$\sigma_i = \sqrt{\langle S_i^2 \rangle - \langle S_i \rangle^2} \tag{3}$$

such that every row in the new matrix x has mean=0, variance =1. Since the original sequence S is random, in general all the rows are independent, i.e., no pair of rows is identical.

The cross correlation matrix $C_{i,j}$ between two stocks, i and j, is constructed by the inner product of the two time series, $x_{i,t}$ and $x_{j,t}$,

$$C_{i,j} = \frac{1}{T}\sum_{t=1}^{T} x_{i,t} x_{j,t} \tag{4}$$

thus the matrix $C_{i,j}$ is symmetric under the interchange of i and j.

A real symmetric matrix C can be diagonalized by a similarity transformation $V^{-1}CV$ by an orthogonal matrix V satisfying $V^t=V^{-1}$, each column of which consists of the eigenvectors of C. Such that

$$C v_k = \lambda_k v_k \; (k=1,\ldots,N) \tag{5}$$

where the coefficient λ_k is the k-th eigenvalue and v_k is the k-th eigenvector.

According to the RMT, the eigenvalue distibution spectrum of the cross correlation matrix C of random series is given by the following formula (Sengupta, & Mitra, 1999) called Marcenko-Pastur distribution (Marcenko, & Pastur, 1994)

$$P_{RMT}(\lambda) = \frac{Q}{2\pi}\frac{\sqrt{(\lambda_+ - \lambda)(\lambda - \lambda_-)}}{\lambda} \tag{6}$$

$$\lambda_\pm = (1 \pm Q^{-1/2})^2 \tag{7}$$

valid at the limit of N and T going to infinity, keeping

$$Q = T/N \tag{8}$$

as a constant.

2.2 Qualitative Version of the RMT-Test

The qualitative version of the RMT-Test compares the theoretical curve in Eqs. (6) and (7) and the histogram of eigenvalue distribution of the cross-correlation matrix made by the inner-product of N pieces of time series of length L. The randomness of the time series is high if the histogram matches the theoretical curve, and it is low if they do not match (Yang, X., et. al.,2011).

Examples are shown in Figure 1, where the left figure shows the case of high randomness, in which the solid line shows the theoretical curve in Eq. (1) and the histogram shows the eigenvalue distribution of LCG, and the right figure shows the case of low randomness, in which the minute-wise price of the stock (Kao Corporation) shows a clear protruding from the theoretical curve in Eq. (1).

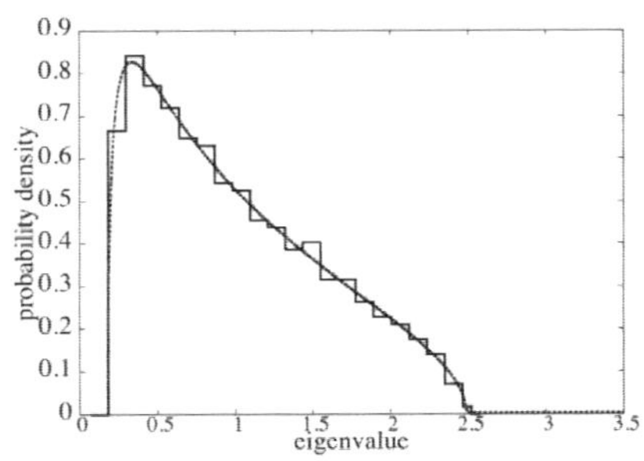

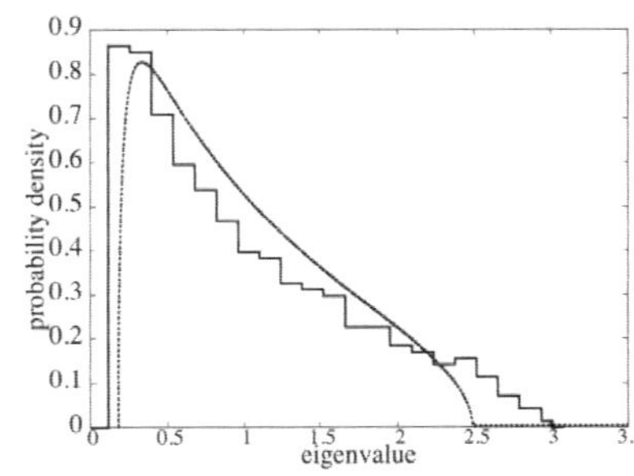

Figure 1. Examples of highly random data (left: LCG) and less random data in the qualitative RMT-Test

2.3 Quantitative Version of the RMT-Test

The quantitative version of the RMT-Test is used to discriminate subtle difference of randomness among good random numbers (Tanaka-Yamawaki,.et. al., 2012). The k-th moment of the eigenvalues

$$m_k^{EXP} = \frac{1}{N}\sum_{i=1}^{N}(\lambda_i)^k \tag{9}$$

is compared to the corresponding theoretical moments derived from P_{RMT} in Eqs. (1)-(3) of the random matrix theory.

$$m_k^{RMT} = \int_{\lambda_-}^{\lambda_+}\lambda^k P_{RMT}(\lambda)d\lambda \tag{10}$$

The theoretical moments up to k=6 can be explicitly obtained as a function of Q=L/N as follows

$$m_1^{RMT} = 1 \tag{11}$$

$$m_2^{RMT} = 1+\frac{1}{Q} \tag{12}$$

$$m_3^{RMT} = 1+\frac{3}{Q}+\frac{1}{Q^2} \tag{13}$$

$$m_4^{RMT} = 1+\frac{6}{Q}+\frac{6}{Q^2}+\frac{1}{Q^3} \tag{14}$$

$$m_5^{RMT} = 1+\frac{10}{Q}+\frac{20}{Q^2}+\frac{10}{Q^3}+\frac{1}{Q^4} \tag{15}$$

$$m_6^{RMT} = 1+\frac{15}{Q}+\frac{50}{Q^2}+\frac{50}{Q^3}+\frac{15}{Q^4}+\frac{1}{Q^5} \tag{16}$$

The quantified criterion of randomness is defined by the deviation of the experimental value of the k-th moment from its theoretical value as

$$\text{Error} = \frac{m_k^{EXP}}{m_k^{RMT}} - 1 \tag{17}$$

The authors have chosen to use the 6th moment (i.e., k=6) in order to define the level of randomness in the RMT-test as the inverse of

$$|\text{Error}| = |m_6^{EXP} - m_6^{RMT}| \tag{18}$$

By using this measure of randomness, the left figure in Figure1 corresponds to |Error| = 0.016 and the right figure corresponds to |Error| = 0.199.

By setting the upper limit of the Error in Eq. (15), we accept the string to be random if

$$|\text{Error}| < \varepsilon \tag{19}$$

and reject it if otherwise.

The quantitative version of RMT-test can be summarized in the following five steps in Table 1.

Table 1. Algorithm of the quantitative RMT-test

Step	Action
1	Prepare a string to be tested and cut it into N pieces of length T, and normalize each piece, $S_i = (S_{i,1}, S_{i,2}, \ldots, S_{i,T})$, to $x_i = (x_{i,1}, x_{i,2}, \ldots, x_{i,T})$ by Eq. (1)-(2) to construct an $N \times T$ matrix $x_{i,t}$ by placing x_i in the i-th row.
2	Construct the correlation matrix, C defined $C_{i,j} = \frac{1}{T}\sum_{t=1}^{T} x_{i,t} x_{j,t}$ in Eq. (4).
3	Obtain the k-th moment m_k^{EXP} for k=1,…,6 from the trace of C^k.
4	Compute the error in Eq. (16) from the ration of m_k^{EXP} and m_k^{RMT}.
5	The string passes the RMT- test if $|\text{Error}| < \varepsilon$ and fails otherwise.

Note that we do not need to solve the eigenvalue problem in Eq. (5) directly but simply obtain the trace (sum of all the diagonal elements)

$$\sum_{i=1}^{N} (C^k)_{i,i} = \sum_{i=1}^{N} (\lambda_i)^k \tag{20}$$

of the matrix of the k-th power C^k of the cross correlation matrix to obtain the k-th moment in the Step 3.

2.4 Determining the Reasonable Range of N and T

It is necessary to determine the reasonable range of N and T before applying the RMT-Test. Because the theoretical formula of the eigenvalue distribution P_{RMT}, as a function of Q=T/N, is derived at the limit of N and T being infinity by keeping the ratio Q=T/N constant, sufficiently large but finite values of N and T are to be chosen for the sake of practical computation. For this purpose, the authors have applied the test on the data taken from the two popular pseudo random number generators, the Linear Congruential Generator (LCG) and Mersenne Twister(MT) (Matsumoto, & Nishimura, 1998), for N=200, 300, 400, 500 at Q=3, and compared the moments up to the 6-th order to the corresponding theoretic formula.

For LCG, the most popular function used as rand() by C-programmers, the following function is employed

$$X_{n+1} = (aX_n + b) \bmod M \tag{21}$$

with a=1103515245, b=12345, M=2147483648.

For MT, the best pseudo-random generator having a very long period 2^{19937}-1, the source code downloaded from the inventor's home pages can be used. By using LCG and MT, experiments for 100 different seeds, such as SEED=1,.., 100, are performed to obtain the average errors. The result is shown in the two figures of Figure 2., by six lines corresponding the 1st to the 6-th moments from the bottom to the top, for LCG (left) and MT (right). In both figures, the errors go down gradually as N increases from 200 to 400, and then become stable after N reaches 500. At N=500, the errors become smaller than 0.3%. Based on this fact, we justify the value N=500 to be large enough (at least for Q=3) to apply our RMT-test.

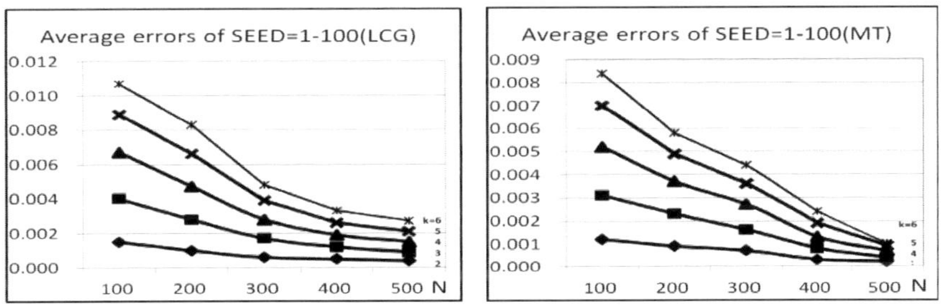

Figure 2. Errors become sufficiently small for both LCG(left) and MT(right) for N > 100

2.5 Choice of Randomness Measure

We have come to the point of discussing the choice of randomness measure ε in Eq.(19) and in Table1. Figure 2 shows that the errors between the experimental moments and its theoretical counterparts do not converge to zero, but gradually reduce to the value less than 0.2-0.4% as N reaches the region of 400-500. Is this because the two pseudo random numbers are not perfectly random, or the RMT formula is not perfectly valid for the finite values of N and T.

In order to answer to this question, the degree of randomness of the physically generated random numbers are employed. Since the case of k=1 is trivial, only the k-th moment for k=2,.., 6 are shown in the rest of this paper. Table 2 summarizes the average values (and the standard deviation in parentheses) of 100 independent experiments for three physical random numbers (Toshiba, Hitachi and Tokyo-Electron) and two pseudo random numbers (LCG, MT). The k-th moment ratio for three physical random numbers by the three physical random numbers are compared to the corresponding results of two pseudo-random numbers, LCG and MT compared to Hitachi or Toshiba. However, those physical generators are basically less stable compared to the pseudo random generators. In other words, pseudo random generators can produce more uniform sequences with high stability. Moreover, they are deterministic and the entire sequence can be reproduced once the SEED is known together with the algorithm. The result in Table 2 tells us that the moment analysis cannot distinguish significant difference.

Table 2. Q=3(T=1500) average (SD) of 100 independent tests of the five random data

k	LCG	MT	Toshiba	Hitachi	Tokyo
2	-.0004(.0010)	-.0004(.0009)	-.0004(.0010)	-.0004(.0010)	-.0004(.0009)
4	-.0018(.0047)	-.0014(.0041)	-.0019(.0046)	-.0019(.0044)	-.0015(.0044)
6	-.0036(.0100)	-.0022(.0085)	-.0033(.0096)	-.0037(.0092)	-.0021(.0093)

Table 3. Q=3 (T=1500) [min.:max.] of 100 independent tests of the five random data

k	LCG	MT	Toshiba	Hitachi	Tokyo
2	[-.0023: .0016]	[-.0026:.0022]	[-.0031:.0032]	[-.0033:.0017]	[-.0029:.0024]
4	[-.0100:.0082]	[-.0103:.0086]	[-.0142:.0143]	[-.0133:.0083]	[-.0123:.0108]
6	[-.0198:.0176]	[-.0183:.0153]	[-.0286:.0277]	[-.0257:.0181]	[-.0226:.0218]

Table 4. Q=6(T=3000) average (SD) of 100 independent tests of the five random data

k	LCG	MT	Toshiba	Hitachi	Tokyo
2	-.0003(.0006)	-.0001(.0006)	-.0002(.0006)	-.0002(.0006)	-.0002(.0005)
4	-.0014(.0028)	-.0006(.0027)	-.0008(.0027)	-.0011(.0028)	-.0007(.0026)
6	-.0026(.0060)	-.0012(.0058)	-.0015(.0058)	-.0020(.0060)	-.0010(.0056)

Table 5. Q=6 (T=3000) [min.:max.] of 100 independent tests of the five random data

k	LCG	MT	Toshiba	Hitachi	Tokyo
2	[-.0018: .0013]	[-.0019: .0011]	[-.0015: .0011]	[-.0016: .0011]	[-.0015: .0010]
4	[-.0083: .0057]	[-.0094: .0046]	[-.0076: .0052]	[-.0074: .0060]	[-.0075: .0045]
6	[-.0165: .0113]	[-.0191: .0087]	[-.0153: .0112]	[-.0143: .0127]	[-.0161: .0084]

Among LCG, MT and the three physical random numbers, in accordance with our qualitative test, by which they all pass the RMT-test and the degrees of randomness are indistinguishable. This fact supports the importance of the qualitative test in Figure 1. We conclude that a given sequence passes the RMT-test if it passes the qualitative test, and the corresponding quantitative test by means of moment analysis gives the error less than a few percent for all the moments for k=1 to 6. We next deal with the examples that fail the RMT-test.

3. APPLICATION TO THE STOCK PREDICTION

It is customary to convert the price time series $p_1, p_2, ..., p_T$ to the log-return time series $r_1, r_2, ..., r_T$

$$r_i = log\ p_{i+1} - log\ p_i \tag{22}$$

in the financial analysis, in order to eliminate the unit/size dependence of different stock prices.

However, this process involves the same p_i for r_i and r_{i+1}. Because of this, the time series of log-returns loose the randomness that existed in the original price time series and a certain pattern specific to the log-return time series emerges. This effect can be eliminated if we take the non-overlapping log-return by giving up the half of the total elements of $\mathbf{r}_i$ (i=even or odd), in exchange of the length of data T to one half of the original. Using this fact, we analyze the randomness of the stock price with non-overlapping log-return series.

Tick data of stocks in TOPIX 500 from 2007 to 2009 per minute satisfying the appropriate conditions are selected and used for analysis. Tick data mean the time series stamped in seconds or minutes which record the information of traded or quoted prices. Since trades or quotes may not occur at every time period, the lengths of the tick data are not fixed. For this reason, some work is required to prepare the fixed-length time series to serve for analysis. The blanks are filled by copying the previous data as long as the added part is less than the 20 percent of the total length in order to calculate equal time correlation of each stock price. As a result, the data length (*L*) and the number of stocks (*N*) are different at each year. The values of *L* and *N* for each year used in this paper are summarized in Table 6.

Table 6. Data used for analysis

year	Data length (L)	Number of stocks (N)
2007	66338	211
2008	66338	240
2009	65945	229

The RMT-test has a free parameter, Q=L/N, to be determined beforehand. The condition required by the RMT is Q>1 and N→∞.

It is known that N > 100 is necessary based on the numerical experiments using pseudo random generators. According to Table 6 the data length in 2009 is 65945= N*L. Suppose N=100 is chosen, then L=659 thus Q=6.59. For N > 100, L < 659 and Q < 6.59. This means Q can be chosen in the range of 1<Q<6.59. Therefore, Q=2,…,6 are the possible integer values for the parameter Q, and the analysis are done for each value of Q and the performance in the following year (January - December, 2010) of the stocks of the highest randomness (H) and the lowest randomness (L) are compared in Figue 3. Only the case of Q=4 exhibits the superiority of H to L throughout the year of 2010. The other values of Q do not show any clear sign of superiority of H.

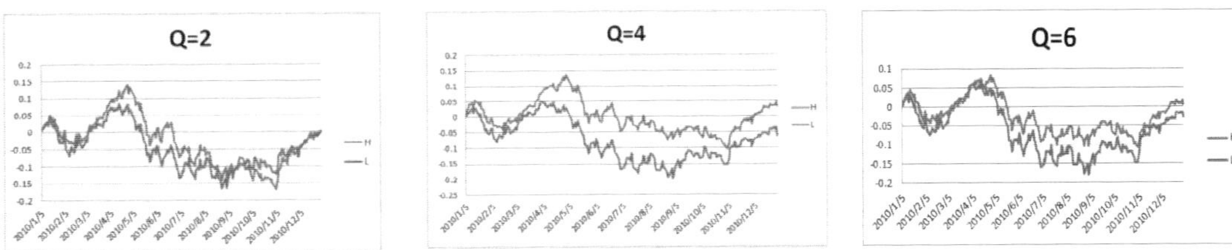

Figure 3. The best Q is 4 to see the superiority of the most random stock(H) over the least random stock(L)

The ranking of randomness in 2007 is shown in Table 7 in which the stock of the highest randomness in 2007 is 9504 in the sector of Electric/Gas. The stock of the lowest randomness in 2007 is 7201 in the sector of Transportation and Equipment. Fig 4 shows the log-return of the top five stocks of code number 9504, 6460,9506,9508,4676 having the highest randomness comparing with the stock of the lowest randomness 7201. As a result, the top five stocks perform better than 7201 and effected very little by the financial crisis. On the contrary, the 7201 which has the lowest randomness in 2007 fell down enormously due to the effect of Lehman shock that occurred in September 2008. Based on this observation, the authors conclude that the stock which has the highest randomness is stable and safe under a bear market.

Table 7. The ranking of randomness by using the tick data of 2007

Rank	Sector	Code	|Error|
1	Electric/ Gas	9504	26.4
2	Machinery	6460	37.6
3	Electric/ Gas	9506	38.2
4	Electric/ Gas	9508	43.3
5	Information & Communication	4676	44.9
	…		
210	Iron and steel	5541	1001.5
211	Transportation Equipment	7201	1209.6

However, the ranking of randomness in 2008 does not show the same tendency as the result of 2007. The reason for this may be viewed as the effect of the Lehman shock occurred in September 2008, which made the rest of this year the period of an abnormal fluctuation of stock price. By amputating the abnormal part and using the data just before the end of August in 2008, it is expected to have the normal condition. The result shown indeed shows the normal features, where the stable stock 9506 in Electric/Gas sector is extracted as the stock of the highest randomness, while a relatively unstable stock 7201 in Transportation and Equipment sector shows the lowest randomness. The result of 2009 also extract the stock 9509 from Electric /Gas sector as the highest randomness stock, and the almost of the top five highest randomness stocks perform better than the lowest randomness stock 8058 from Wholesale Trade sector in the next year. The empirical rule, "high randomness means low risk" also worked in the stock market of 2009. So far, we have seen the empirical rule, "high randomness means low risk" works for 2007-2009 in Japanese market, which was a typical bear (declining) market. A corresponding analysis on the bull (rising) market has been performed by using

S&P index for 1993-1996 in American market. The parameters are chosen to be (L=628;N=157) for 1993, and (L=624;N=156) for 1994, 1995 and 1996, so that we have the best value of Q=4. By evaluating the randomness each year in the period of 1993-1996, we compare the performance of the stock return next year. As shown in Table 8, the average returns of the top 5 stocks in terms of randomness in 1993, 1995, 1995 perform better in the next year compared to the bottom 5 stocks. However, the rule does not hold in 1994. Thus the empirical rule "high randomness means low risk" is satisfied in 3 out of 4 cases.

Table 8. The empirical rule "high randomness means low risk" is tested in the period of the rising market. 1993-1994

	1993-1994	1994-1995	1995-1996	1996-1997
5 most random stocks	**+0.11**	+0.33	**+0.27**	**+0.39**
5 least random stocks	-0.06	**+0.43**	+0.11	+0.24

4. CONCLUSION

In this paper, 'randomness of the time series' is proposed to be used for labelling big data, and this hypothesis is tested by using the real-world stock prices of Tokyo market in the period of 2007-2009. It is shown that the stock of higher randomness indeed performed better than the stock of lower randomness in the following year. Although the period 2007-2009 in Tokyo was a bear (falling) market, the same rule seems to be held in the bull (rising) market, as we tested the period 1993-1996 in American market. However, the method contains many assumptions and free parameters. Further analysis over wider range of data are needed before making more conclusive remarks.

REFERENCES

Bouchaud, J.P., & Potters, M. (2000). *Theory of Financial Risk*, Cambridge University Press.

Edelman, A. & Rao, R. (2005). *Random Matrix Theory*, Cambridge University Press, 1-65.

Knuth, D.E., (1980). *The Art of Computer Programming, Vol. 2: Seminumerical Algorithms*, Addison-Wesley.

Laloux, L., Cizeaux, P., Bouchaud, J.-P., and Potters, M., (1999). Noise Dressing of Financial Correlation Matrices, *Physical Review Letters,* 83, 1467-1470.

Marcenko, V., & Pastur, L. (1994). Distribution of eigenvalues for some sets of random matrices, *Mathematics of the USSR-Sbornik,* 1, 457-483.

Matsumoto, M., & Nishimura, T. (1998). Mersenne Twister: A Dimensionally Equidistributed Uniform Pseudorandom Number Generator, *ACM Transactions on Modeling and Computer Simulation*, 8, 3–30.

Mehta, M. (1995) *Random Matrices,* Academic Press.

Park, S., & Miller, K. (1988). Random Number Generators: Good ones are hard to find, *Communication of ACM,* 31, 1192-1201.

Plerou, V., Gopikrishnan, P., Rosenow, B., Amaral, L.A.N., & Stanley, H.E. (1999). Universal and Non-Universal Properties of Cross-Correlations in Financial Time Series, *Physical Review Letters,* 83, 1471-1474.

Plerou, V., Gopikrishnan, P., Rosenow, B., Amaral, L.A.N., & Stanley, H.E. (2002). Random matrix approach to cross correlation in financial data, *Physical Review E*, 65, 066126.

Sengupta, A.M, & Mitra, P.P., (1999). *Distribution of singular values for some random matrices*, Physical Review E, 60, 3389-3392.

Tanaka-Yamawaki, M., Yang, X., & Itoi, R. (2012). Moment approach for quantitative evaluation of randomness based on RMT formula, *Intelligent Decision Technologies (SIST 16)*, 423-432.

Wigner, E. (1955). Characteristic Vectors of Bordered Matrices with Infinite Dimensions, *Ann. of Math.,* 62, 548–564.

Yang, X., Itoi, R. , & Tanaka-Yamawaki, M. (2012). Testing randomness by means of Random Matrix Theory, *Progress of Theoretical Physics Supplement,* 194, 73-83.

Yang, X., Itoi, R., & Tanaka-Yamawaki, M. (2011). Testing randomness by means of RMT formula, *Intelligent Decision Technologies*, *SIST 10*, 589-596.

Yang, X., Mikamori, Y., & Tanaka-Yamawaki, M. (2013). Predicting the security levels of stock investment by using the EMT-test, *Procedia Computer Science,* 22, 1172-1181.

TOPIC MODELING OF TEXT CONTENT FOR MONITORING THE EMPLOYEE'S EFFICIENCY VIA HIS INTERNET ACTIVITY

Aleksandra Vatian, Sergey Dudorov, Artem Beresnev, Artem Vasilev, Niyaz Nigmatullin, Nikolay Vedernikov, Andrey Stankevich, Natalia Gusarova and Anatoly Shalyto
ITMO University, 49 Kronverksky pr., Saint-Petersburg, Russia

ABSTRACT

In this paper, we investigate the possibilities of topic modeling techniques, namely LDA and ARTM, for monitoring the employee's efficiency via his Internet activity. Our experiments show that use of the ARTM model allows to construct the most accurate and well interpreted reference model of the information search. At the same time, if the employee begins to use inefficient scenarios of behavior, i.e. deviation or drift of information search, then it leads to deviations from the reference model, which can be identified by setting the cutoff threshold for concrete business. Our experiments show that the proposed solution provides a more confident identification of small deviations from the target topic in comparison with other methods, which is especially important in real business. The proposed model can find other applications, for example, parental control and highlighting the scientific articles related to the research topic.

KEYWORDS

Topic Modeling, Regularization, Employee's Efficiency, Coherence, Portrait of Ideal Document

1. INTRODUCTION

Maintenance of the necessary level of employee's efficiency is one of the main tasks of business. In general, it can be measured in two ways: as the amount of units of a product or service that an employee handles in a defined time frame (productivity) or as a ratio of an employee's actual time to perform each unit of service against the theoretical time needed to complete it (actual efficiency). But it is difficult to apply such approach to employees whose activities are connected to information search, in particular, with Internet browsing. For example, if the company is engaged in the development of computer games, then employees shall trace new decisions of competitors. In this case it is useless or even harmful to list the websites allowed or forbidden to visit, because it is unknown, where exactly these decisions will appear.

Any employee selects his own strategy of information search; but the effective employee's strategy leads to the success of the whole business, and vice versa. That is, the effective employee fulfills the information retrieval within the topics that bring success to business. Hence, in order to make a distinction between useful (effective) and useless (ineffective) employees' web-browsing behavior the manager shall compare the behavior of each employee to the behavior of the effective employee.

Deviations from the ideal behavior of an employee in web browsing can be described in two scenarios. In the first scenario the employee fulfills the information retrieval within the useful topics during only a part of working time; the remained working time he devotes to the extrinsic topics. For example, having the topic "Sport" as the main topic for his business he also seeks information about politics. In the second scenario the employee fulfills the information retrieval within the topics of business' interest, but looks for content not strictly on a topic, but with deviations. For example, having the topic "Sport" he looks for information about scandals in private life of athletes.

The first scenario of employee behavior can be tracked by clustering methods. For example, we can separate web-content browsed by the effective (referent) employee and the employee under consideration into clearly defined groups (topics) and then compare these topics. The plethora of solutions is already proposed for this purpose (see Section 2). However, for the second scenario, as a rule it is not possible to build confident clustering, that is, to form clearly shared groups. In this case we need to build an actual reference model of the effective employee behavior and at the same time we need to trace deviations of the behavior of other employees from a reference model. This problem is actively researched today. In our paper, we investigate the possibilities of topic modeling techniques for this purpose, namely the influence of topic models regularization on the discernability of effective and ineffective employees' behavior in web-browsing.

The article is organized as follows. In Section 2, related studies are presented and the research tasks formulated. Section 3 describes the research methodology, in Section 4 are the results of the experiments and their discussion. Section 5 presents the conclusion and a direction of further work.

2. RELATED WORK

Despite already mentioned diversity of the proposed application-oriented solutions, the amount of types of representative variables describing the web user browsing behavior is small. In (Parvatikar & Joshi, 2014) three types of such variables are selected. These are the web structure, the web user session and the web content, but for modeling of user behavior in the modern high-dynamic Internet only the last two types are used.

The web user session is represented as a browsing trajectory, which is a sequence of his relocation among nodes. In order to describe the user's behavior, the time spent on each node (Phoa & Sanchez, 2013) or web log records (Cheng, Yin, Dong, Dong, & Zhang, 2016; Fujimoto, Etoh, Akinaga, & Kinno, 2011; Luo, Wang, Shen, Wang, & Qi, 2017; Parvatikar & Joshi, 2014; Uetsuji, Yanagimoto, & Yoshioka, 2015) are taken into account. But, judging by the literature, the most extensive opportunities for modeling of web-users behavior arise when using the web content as representative variables or when combining this approach with others mentioned above. For example, in (Shah, Verma, & Tiwari, 2018) the authors describe changes in the behavior of the user through the tracing of its personal profile in Twitter and analyzing the content of tweets. In (Boratto, Carta, Fenu, & Saia, 2016) authors use neural word embedding for modeling web-user behavior. In order to take into account the current changes in users' behavior, authors suggest giving more weights to those concepts which are associated with positive evaluation.

In order to identify changes in web-user's behavior of the an ontological approach (Hawalah & Fasli, 2015) is also used. But, as a rule, application of ontological approach requires heavy methodologies and leads to sophisticated technical solutions. To this end, the decisions based on the latent factor revealing are of great interest in modeling user behavior (Bokde, Girase, & Mukhopadhyay, 2015; Zhang, Zheng, & Zeng, 2016). Here, in turn, the approaches connected to topic modeling are estimated as very perspective (see review (Jelodar, Wang, Yuan, & Feng, 2017)).

To the best of our knowledge, the work (Serdyukov, Taylor, Vinay, Richardson, & White, 2011) was one of the first to suggest such approach for modeling employee's behavior; however, other decisions mentioned below can also be easily transformed for this purpose. For example, authors (Moosad, Vinayachandran, & Kumar, 2016) offer rather simple way to find user search preferences from web browsing histories. They store the browsing history of various users in the form of a CSV file and then process it using LDA (Blei, Ng, & Jordan, 2003) for topic modeling. In order to reveal the dynamics of users' interests, they visualize the LDA results for each selected topic in the form of word vector and of the word cloud. However, visualization allows receiving the rather conditional and integrated assessment.

For more exact separation of topics within topic modeling different approaches are offered. A set of authors offer to analyze simultaneously not only the text information generated by users, but also other types of additional information on them, including their position in a semantic community they belong to (see (Nikolenko, Koltcov, & Koltsova, 2017) and a review of related works within). For example, in (Li et al., 2015) a generative model named the author-topic-community is proposed. Each user is associated with a topic distribution as well as with a community distribution. In (Xin, Yang, Xie, & Zhang, 2015; Yin, Cui, Chen, Hu, & Zhou, 2015) more sophisticated structural and temporal representations of social communities are used. But such approaches are rather difficult and require the large volume of versatile information which is not always available in real applications, especially in the case of monitoring of employee's behavior in specific businesses.

The other way is connected to the complication of topic structure. In (C. Wang, Liu, Song, & Han, 2015; Q. Wang, Xu, & Li, 2014) means for constructing a hierarchical structure of topics are suggested. According to the authors, such structure helps to solve both the problem of data sparseness and the topic diversity problem. However, judging by materials of articles, experiments were made on the data sets created by concatenation of separate short texts of tweet tip. Meanwhile, the employee has to deal with extensive texts with internal semantic links, such as articles or monographies. As shown in (Avdeeva et al., 2015), in such texts the semantic hierarchical structure is poorly expressed and, as a rule, it does not match the rigid structure stated in the table of contents.

For surer determining of effective and ineffective employees' web-browsing behavior the method of topic model regularization (Koltcov, Nikolenko, Koltsova, Filippov, & Bodrunova, 2016) is of special interest. In this case the additional criterion is appended to the main criterion of optimization which allows to consider the specifics of the task and available knowledge of data domain. In (Bodrunova, Koltsov, Koltsova, Nikolenko, & Shimorina, 2013; Koltcov et al., 2016; Paul & Dredze, 2014; Vorontsov & Potapenko, 2015) different models on the basis of LDA are described, such as ATAM (ailment topic aspects model), SSLDA (semi-supervised LDA), ISLDA (interval semi-supervised LDA), GLDA (granulated LDA), which allow to improve distinguishability and an interpretation of topics for specific data domains. In (Vorontsov & Potapenko, 2015) authors show that the majority of these models can be provided through uniform approach, called Additive Regularization of Topic Models (ARTM), and they explicitly consider its advantages.

But, to the best of our knowledge, the application of ARTM in order to monitor the employee's behavior during web-browsing was not considered in the literature before. So, we formulate the research tasks of our work in the following way:

- the comparative analysis of the efficiency of topics extraction by various methods of topic modeling;
- building the model of information search for effective and ineffective employee;
- the analyzis of the efficiency and limitations of the proposed solution, especially for estimating the small deviations from the target topic;

3. METHODS AND MATERIALS

3.1 Topic Modeling

The topic model is a model of a collection of text documents which defines to what topic each document of a collection belongs. Let D be a collection of text documents and W be a set (dictionary) of all terms used in D. We suppose that there is a finite set of latent topics T, and each use of the term $w \in W$ in each document $d \in D$ is related to some topic $t \in D$. We suppose that the bag-of-words hypothesis is fair, i.e. we don't consider the interrelation between words in the text. We also suppose that the hypothesis of conditional independence is fair, i.e. emergence of word w on a topic t doesn't depend on the document d: $p(w|t) = p(w|d, t)$. Then

$$p(w|d) = \sum_{t \in T} p(w|t)p(t|d), \quad (1)$$

where $\varphi_{wt} = p(w \in t)$ is the distribution of words in a topic and $\theta_{td} = p(t \in d)$ is the distribution of topics in a document. Thus, in order to create the topic model on D one should find the set of multinomial distributions φ_{wt}, $t \in T$, and θ_{td}, $d \in D$, represented by the matrices $\Phi = (\varphi_{wt})$, $t \in T$, and $\Theta = (\theta_{td})$, $d \in D$ respectively.

In Latent Dirichlet allocation (LDA) model [11] multinomial distributions θ_{td} and φ_{wt} are generated from prior Dirichlet distributions with parameter α for the θ distributions and with parameter β for the φ distributions respectively, and in the simplest case

$$\varphi_{wt} \sim n_{wt} + \beta_w, \quad \theta_{td} \sim n_{td} + \alpha_t. \quad (2)$$

Equations (2) allow to treat the LDA model as "a regularizer by default". The approach named Additive Regularization of Topic Models (ARTM) uses explicit regularizers in the form of

$$R(\Phi, \Theta) = \sum_i \tau_i R(\Phi, \Theta), \quad (3)$$

where τ_i is regularization coefficient. In our work we have used the following regularizers: smooth sparse regularizer for the matrices Φ and Θ, and decorrelating topics regularizer. Smooth sparse regularizers are based on sparseness hypothesis, i.e., each topic is characterized by a small number of terms, and each document belongs to a small number of topics; then matrices $\Phi = (\varphi_{wt})_{W\times T}$ and $\Theta = (\theta_{td})_{T\times D}$ should contain a lot of zeros. Smooth sparse regularizers generalize Dirichlet regularizers as follows:

$$R(\Phi,\Theta) = \beta_0 \sum_{t\in T}\sum_{w\in W} \beta_{wt} \ln \varphi_{wt} + \alpha_0 \sum_{d\in D}\sum_{t\in T} \alpha_{td} \ln \theta_{td} \tag{4}$$

where vectors

$$\beta = \beta_0(\beta_w)_{w\in W},\ \alpha = \alpha_0(\alpha_t)_{t\in T} \tag{5}$$

are hyperparameters of the Dirichlet distributions. Decorrelating topics regularizer assumes that the topic model shall not contain the duplicated or similar topics. The more different topics are the more informative model is. In order to realize this heuristic the following regularizer is used:

$$R(\Phi) = -\frac{\tau}{2}\sum_{t\in T}\sum_{s\in T\setminus t}\sum_{w\in W} \varphi_{wt}\varphi_{ws}, \tag{6}$$

where t and s are the columns of the matrix Φ, τ is regularization coefficient.

In order to evaluate the quality of topic modeling we used the criteria selected in (Li et al., 2015). The perplexity of topic model p(w|d) in collection D is defined as

$$perp\ (D;p) = \exp\left(-\frac{1}{n}\sum_{d\in D}\sum_{w\in W} n_{dw} \ln p(w|d)\right). \tag{7}$$

The coherence of a topic shows that the words which are found nearby in texts appear in the kernel of the topic:

$$coher_t = \frac{2}{k(k-1)}\sum_{i=1}^{k-1}\sum_{j=1}^{k} PMI\left(w_i, w_j\right), \tag{8}$$

where k defines the top-k most probable words of the topic. Following (Li et al., 2015), we estimated the value of coherence for k=10, k=100 and k=$|W_t|$, i.e. coh_{10}, coh_{100} and coh_{kern}. Coherence was calculated as average on all topics and was estimated on the same collection on which the model was built.

3.2 Modeling of Business Situation

In our experiments, we use a collection of documents obtained of the Kos collection[1]. The original dataset contains 686 documents and 12 topics in total, the number of unique words after preprocessing is equal to 6906. Each article is considered as the separate document. For analysis, an easily interpreted theme of the presidential election was chosen as a basic topic for web-browsing.

In order to model the web-browsing of an effective ("ideal") employee, we build a dataset using the following method: randomly select sufficiently large part of the articles from the target topic (namely 343 articles), and 10–20 articles from each of the remaining topics. On the constructed datasets, we train the LDA and ARTM models and obtain the matrices Φ^{LDA}_{ideal} and Θ^{LDA}_{ideal} as well as Φ^{ARTM}_{ideal} and Θ^{ARTM}_{ideal} respectively which characterize the desired result of an effective search. Top-100 values of the matrix Φ^{ARTM}_{ideal} on the target topic, sorted in descending order, we will consider as the reference model ("portrait of ideal document").

To model the web-browsing of an ineffective ("real") employee, we expand the data set with articles from other topics, but in such a way that the target topic remains the most probable. In our case, the resulting dataset contains 12 topics, the number of articles in each topic ranging from 686 to 28. We train the LDA and ARTM models on the resulting dataset obtaining the matrices Φ^{LDA}_{real} and Θ^{LDA}_{real} as well as Φ^{ARTM}_{real} and Θ^{ARTM}_{real}. Then we select randomly from the entire collection articles that did not participate in the training of the ideal

[1] dailykos.com

employee model and for each article we calculate the indicators of its belonging to the topic t of matrix Θ^{LDA}_{real} or respectively Θ^{LDA}_{real} (the "portrait of real document") in the following form:

$$I_t^{LDA} = \sum_w \varphi_{wt}^{LDA} \cdot n_t; \quad I_t^{ARTM} = \sum_w \varphi_{wt}^{ARTM} \cdot n_t \tag{9}$$

where n_t is the number of occurrences of the word w in the article. Comparing the portraits of the ideal and real document, one can judge the deviation of the employee from the target search topic during the web-browsing.

Note that with this approach to modeling, the nomenclature of words in the models of the ideal and real employee is nearly the same. Besides, the target topic is guaranteed to exist in both matrices Θ^{ARTM}_{ideal} and Θ^{ARTM}_{real}, that is, its vocabulary contains practically (within the dispersion of the matrix Φ^{LDA}_{real} and Φ^{ARTM}_{real}) unchanged, although other topics are undergoing changes. These limitations ensure the validity of the above mentioned comparison.

3.3 Data Processing

Python v.2.7 was chosen as basic language due to the richness of its libraries for information collection, parsing of content and topic modeling.

For downloading of all text content of a resource we used the request library[2] which allows sending an HTTP-request to URL-address and receiving HTML-page in the text form. For removing HTML-elements (tags, scripts, and overhead information) the BeautifulSoup library[3] was used. After receiving the cleaned text we preprocessed it linguistically using the library[4]. Stopwords removing was made using standard language means.

For topic modeling, we have chosen the BigARTM library[5] which supports different methods of regularization, i.e. allows to build models of ARTM type (see Section II). This library needs as an input text a certain format which is described in the Vowpal Wabbit resource[6]. We created for each document the auxiliary dictionary, containing for each word of the document the number of its occurrences in the text.

For model training we used the following parameters:

- the approaches of topic modeling – LDA, ARTM (see Section II);
- the number of topics for each approach $|T| = 17$ including $|B| = 5$ background topics.

The settings for the LDA model were as follows:

- a regularized EM-algorithm with smoothing (4) with parameters (5) $\alpha = 0.5$, $\beta = 0.01$;
- for background topics – a uniform smoothing with $\alpha = 0.8$, $\beta = 0.1$.
- for sparsing domain-specific topics – a uniform distribution $\beta w = 1/|W|$.

The settings for the ARTM model were as follows:

- for background topics – a uniform smoothing with $\alpha = 0.2$, $\beta = 0.15$ (see eq. (4));
- for sparsing domain-specific topics $\alpha = -0.45$, $\beta = -0.7$ (see eq. (4));
- for domain-specific topics decorrelation $\tau = 120000$ (see eq. (6)).

4. RESULTS AND DISCUSSION

The results of our experiments are represented in Figures 1–3.

First of all we fulfilled the comparative analysis of efficiency of topics extraction by various methods of topic modeling. Figures 1, a–b, show the advantage of the ARTM model in comparison with the LDA models. We see more than twofold increase of coherence (8) (fig. 1, a) along with very insignificant increase of perplexity (7) (fig. 1, b), that is, more compact and more clearly separable topics are being formed. Thus,

---

[2] http://docs.python-requests.org
[3] https://www.crummy.com/software/BeautifulSoup/
[4] https://www.clips.uantwerpen.be/pattern
[5] http://bigartm.org/
[6] https://github.com/JohnLangford/vowpal_wabbit/wiki/Input-format

this part of our research confirms the results and confirms our successful choice of the regularization parameters.

In the second part of a research we analyze the efficiency of comparing the portraits of the ideal and real document (see part 3.2) using ARTM or LDA models. Fig. 2 shows the values of I_t (9) and their variances for LDA and ARTM models. It can be seen that with increasing of topic probability for the document, the value of I_t^{LDA} in the range of low probabilities increases, but with increasing probability, it practically ceases to change. At the same time, the value of I_t^{ARTM} with the growth of topic probability for the document steadily grows up. This means that the LDA model allows you to identify only the strong deviations of the employee from the basic search topic, but the behavior of the employee during web-browsing within the topics closer to the basic one cannot be controlled. At the same time, the ARTM model allows to control small deviations of the employee from the basic search topic.

This conclusion is confirmed by figure 3, where we show the dependence of I_t^{ARTM} on topic probability for selected documents. For calculations, the original data set (see 3.2) was used, in which the target topic is presented in its entirety. Fig. 3, a, is built on a subsample of documents for which their probability $p(t|d)$ lies in the interval $0 \leq p(t|d) \leq 0.2$, and fig. 3, b, is built on a subsample of documents for which their probability $p(t|d)$ lies in the interval $0.65 \leq p(t|d) \leq 1$). Note that both figures correspond to different fragments of coordinate axes. Fig 3, a, shows that if the documents do not exactly belong to the target topic then the value of I_t^{ARTM} does not rise above 1.3. Vice versa (fig 3, b), if the documents exactly belong to the target topic, then the value of I_t^{ARTM} does not fall below 2.5. This means that between the documents that accurately contain the topic and which do not exactly contain it, a clear boundary can be drawn.

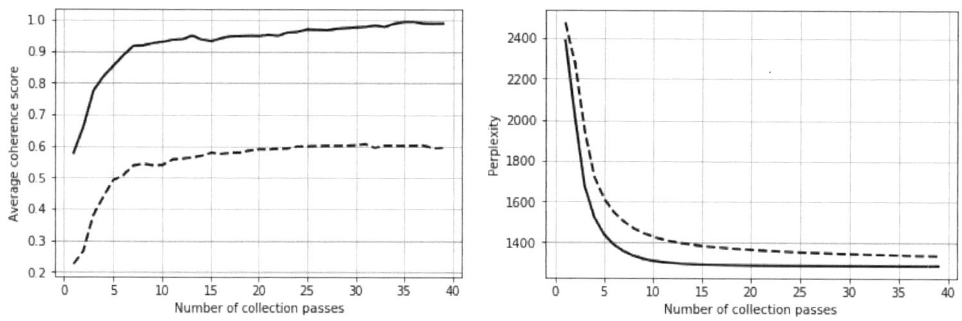

a b

Figure 1. Values of coherence (a) and perplexity (b) for LDA (dotted line) and ARTM (solid line) models

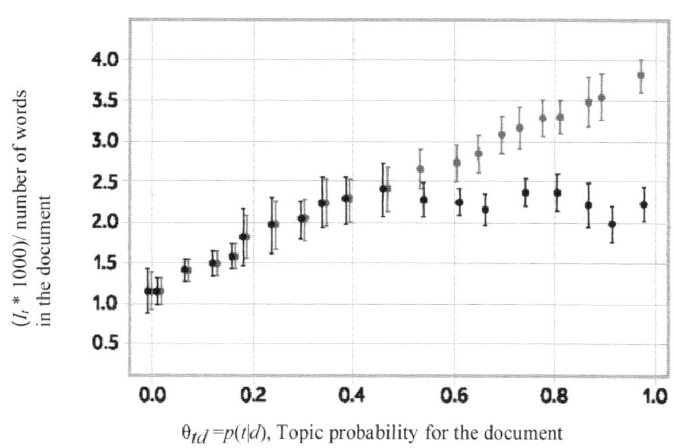

Figure 2. Dependence of I_t on topic probability and its variance for LDA (black lines) and ARTM (gray lines) models

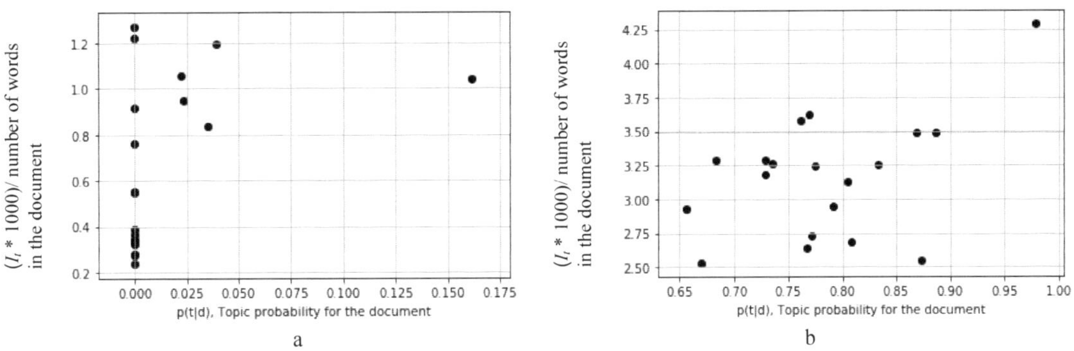

Figure 3. Dependence of I_t on topic probability for ARTM model for different subsamples of documents: (a) with topic probability $0 \le p(t|d) \le 0.2$; (B) with topic probability $0.65 \le p(t|d) \le 1$

5. CONCLUSION

In this paper, we investigated the possibilities of topic modeling techniques for monitoring the employee's efficiency via his Internet activity. Specifically, we investigate the influence of topic model regularization on the discernability of effective and ineffective employees' behavior in web-browsing. Our experiments show that use of the ARTM model allows to construct the more accurate and well interpreted reference model of information search. At the same time, if the employee begins to use inefficient scenarios of behavior, i.e. deviation or drift of information search, then it leads to deviations from the reference model, which can be identified by setting the cutoff threshold for concrete business. Our experiments show that the proposed solution provides a more confident identification of small deviations from the target topic in comparison with other methods, which is especially important in real business.

The proposed solution has the following advantages. The manager can monitor employee's performance dynamically, not waiting for the complete collection of documents, but tracking each newly appearing document separately. The use of a regularizers in thematic modeling makes it possible to build a clearer boundary between documents in which the target topic is not presented, and documents in which it is presented quite clearly. Besides, regularization allows to combine common and stop-words into background topics, thereby further improving the quality of the target topic selection.

We can formulate two limitations on the applicability of the proposed solution. Firstly, the target topic (one or more, depending on the business model) should predominate in the structure of the data set. Secondly, when the business model changes or the new terms appear in the target topic, it is required to re-teach the model. It is easy to see that both restrictions can be easily overcomed in modern business practice.

In addition to monitoring the behavior of the employee in web browsing, the proposed model can find other applications. For example, it can be used in parental control, allowing to assess dynamically the degree of negativity of the content consumed by the child, and (in conjunction with the crawler) to more accurately highlight the scientific articles related to the research topic.

ACKNOWLEDGEMENT

This work was financially supported by the Government of Russian Federation, "Grant 08-08".

REFERENCES

Avdeeva, N., Artemova, G., Boyarsky, K., Gusarova, N., Dobrenko, N., & Kanevsky, E. (2015). Subtopic segmentation of scientific texts: Parameter optimisation. In International conference on knowledge engineering and the semantic web (pp. 3–15).

Blei, D. M., Ng, A. Y., & Jordan, M. I. (2003). Latent dirichlet allocation. Journal of machine Learning research, 3(Jan), 993–1022.

Bodrunova, S., Koltsov, S., Koltsova, O., Nikolenko, S., & Shimorina, A. (2013). Interval semi-supervised lda: Classifying needles in a haystack. In Mexican international conference on artificial intelligence (pp. 265–274).

Bokde, D., Girase, S., & Mukhopadhyay, D. (2015). Matrix factorization model in collaborative filtering algorithms: A survey. Procedia Computer Sci- ence, 49, 136–146.

Boratto, L., Carta, S., Fenu, G., & Saia, R. (2016). Using neural word embed- dings to model user behavior and detect user segments. Knowledge-Based Systems, 108, 5–14.

Cheng, W., Yin, G., Dong, Y., Dong, H., & Zhang, W. (2016). Collaborative filtering recommendation on users' interest sequences. PloS one, 11(5), e0155739.

Fujimoto, H., Etoh, M., Akinaga, Y., & Kinno, A. (2011). User profiling based on latent topic modeling. In Pacific-asia conference on knowledge discovery and data mining (pakdd 2011) (pp. 525–536).

Hawalah, A., & Fasli, M. (2015). Dynamic user profiles for web personalisation. Expert Systems with Applications, 42(5), 2547–2569.

Jelodar, H., Wang, Y., Yuan, C., & Feng, X. (2017). Latent dirichlet allocation (lda) and topic modeling: models, applications, a survey. arXiv preprint arXiv:1711.04305 .

Koltcov, S., Nikolenko, S. I., Koltsova, O., Filippov, V., & Bodrunova, S. (2016). Stable topic modeling with local density regularization. In International conference on internet science (pp. 176–188).

Li, C., Cheung, W. K., Ye, Y., Zhang, X., Chu, D., & Li, X. (2015). The author-topic-community model for author interest profiling and commu- nity discovery. Knowledge and Information Systems, 44(2), 359–383.

Luo, X., Wang, J., Shen, Q., Wang, J., & Qi, Q. (2017). User behavior analysis based on user interest by web log mining. In Telecommunication networks and applications conference (itnac), 2017 27th international (pp. 1–5).

Moosad, A., Vinayachandran, A., & Kumar, P. (2016). Browsing behavioral analysis using topic modeling. In International conference soft computing systems.

Nikolenko, S. I., Koltcov, S., & Koltsova, O. (2017). Topic modelling for quali- tative studies. Journal of Information Science, 43(1), 88–102.

Parvatikar, S., & Joshi, B. (2014). Analysis of user behavior through web usage mining. In Icast–international conference on advances in science and technology.

Paul, M. J., & Dredze, M. (2014). Discovering health topics in social media using topic models. PloS one, 9(8), e103408.

Phoa, F. K. H., & Sanchez, J. (2013). Modeling the browsing behavior of world wide web users. Open Journal of Statistics, 3(02), 145.

Serdyukov, P., Taylor, M., Vinay, V., Richardson, M., & White, R. W. (2011). Automatic people tagging for expertise profiling in the enterprise. In Eu- ropean conference on information retrieval (pp. 399–410).

Shah, B., Verma, A. P., & Tiwari, S. (2018). User interest modeling from social media network graph, enriched with semantic web. In Proceedings of in- ternational conference on computational intelligence and data engineering (pp. 55–64).

Uetsuji, K., Yanagimoto, H., & Yoshioka, M. (2015). User intent estimation from access logs with topic model. Procedia Computer Science, 60, 141– 149.

Vorontsov, K., & Potapenko, A. (2015). Additive regularization of topic models. Machine Learning, 101(1-3), 303–323.

Wang, C., Liu, X., Song, Y., & Han, J. (2015). Towards interactive construc- tion of topical hierarchy: A recursive tensor decomposition approach. In Proceedings of the 21th acm sigkdd international conference on knowledge discovery and data mining (pp. 1225–1234). New York, NY, USA: ACM.

Wang, Q., Xu, J., & Li, H. (2014). User message model: a new approach to scalable user modeling on microblog. In Asia information retrieval symposium (pp. 209–220).

Xin, Y., Yang, J., Xie, Z.-Q., & Zhang, J.-P. (2015). An overlapping semantic community detection algorithm base on the arts multiple sampling models. Expert Systems with Applications, 42(7), 3420–3432.

Yin, H., Cui, B., Chen, L., Hu, Z., & Zhou, X. (2015). Dynamic user modeling in social media systems. ACM Transactions on Information Systems (TOIS), 33(3), 10.

Zhang, Z., Zheng, X., & Zeng, D. D. (2016). A framework for diversifying rec- ommendation lists by user interest expansion. Knowledge-based systems, 105, 83–95.

TECHNOLOGICAL AREAS DETECTION AND CLUSTERING FOR LARGE-SCALE OF PATENT TEXTS

Mustafa Sofean and Hidir Aras
FIZ Karlsruhe, Hermann-von-Helmholtz-Platz 1, 76344 Eggenstein-Leopoldshafen, Germany
http://www.fiz-karlsruhe.de

ABSTRACT

The text of technical field section in patent document displays the technological areas of inventions. Analyzing this text will help patent information professionals searching for related patents, and observe and track trending areas of inventions. This work introduces methods for detecting texts of technical field in unstructured patents texts, extracting terms of technological areas, and identifying semantically meaningful communities/topics for a large collection of patent documents. A hybrid text mining techniques such as machine learning, rule-based algorithm, and heuristics are used to identify the text of technical field section. The most significant technical areas are extracted by applying scalable analytics service that involves natural language processing techniques. Community detection approaches are applied for efficiently aggregating terms of technical areas into communities/topics based on a network graph. Our methods are built on top of big-data architecture to deal with large-scale of patent texts. A comparison to the standard LDA clustering is presented, and the results show that our methods do not share common terms and perform well with real applications.

KEYWORDS

Patent Analysis, Community Detection, Topic Modeling, Big Data, Text Mining

1. INTRODUCTION

Patent documents contain a lot of important valuable knowledge, which can save time for new product development, increase success chance for market, and reduce potential patent infringement. But they are large in quantity, lengthy in space and rich in technique terminology such that they are difficult for human to sift through. A patent document often contains dozens of fields that can be grouped into two categories: First; structured fields (metadata), which are uniform in semantics and format such as patent number, inventor/s, and citation/s, filing date, issued date and assignee/s. Second; unstructured fields, which consist of text content in different length (title, abstract, claims, and the detailed description of the invention). The latter includes the technical field, background, summary, embodiments, and the description of figures and drawings of the invention. Patent classification schemes such as the International Patent Classification (IPC) are assigned by experts to classify the patent documents according to their technology. It is mainly based on a taxonomy, which is a hierarchical structure consisting of sections, classes, subclasses, groups and subgroups, and contains approximately 72,000 categories. Based on IPC codes, many studies have been done to obtain the features or trends of technology development by using patent search and international patent classification (IPC) (Yan et al. 2016). However, these classifications have proved to be quite inconsistent in various aspects because of the complexity and they may not be available for all areas of technology specially the emerging technology areas as we have observed that most of trending areas in computer science domain such as "Deep Learning", "Big Data Cloud", "Blockchain", and "Internet of Things (IoT)" are missing in description of patent classification schema, but they clearly appear in texts of the technical field segment.

The technical field section in patent is a brief paragraph/s, typically one to two sentences long, describing the accurate technological areas to which the invention relates, and appear in detailed description part of patent texts. The clue in this paper is to use the technological information in texts of technical field segment instead of the whole texts in order to discover trending technical areas for an specific topic, as well as indexing texts of technical field segment in separated field in a search index enables the interested actors to easily extract all patent documents that are related to specific technical area/s. Moreover, analyzing texts of technical field segment will be beneficial for the patent information professionals to understand deeply the accurate technical areas which the inventions are related to, discover trends and emerging technologies, and effective for the patent text information retrieval specially to increase the Recall. According to guidelines from patent experts (Trippe, 2015), the patent analysis is performing on a dataset related to a specific topic. However, discovering topics for texts of technical field of inventions by standard topic modeling like LDA (Latent Dirichlet Allocation) is suffering from topics overlap when analyzing a patent dataset related to an accurate topic. The methods in this work do not suffer from topics overlap, and automatically determine the appropriate number of topics, via the adaptation of community detection algorithms on a network graph where vertices are technological areas of the inventions and edges are the relations between them. In this paper, our main contributions are as follows:

- Identification texts of technical field segment from patent texts and extraction all technical areas of inventions.
- We present a large-scale graph-based technical area clustering methods that utilize community detection approaches to aggregate terms of technical areas into communities/topics based on a network graph.
- We develop our methods on top of big-data architecture namely Apache Hadoop and Apache Spark to deal with large-scale of patent texts.
- We show in our experiment results that our methods identify communities/topics without topics overlap, as well as the evaluation results of technological areas are presented.

The remaining of this paper is organized as follows. Section 2 outlines the related works. Section 3 provides our methods and analysis. Section 4 describes our experiments and results. Finally, Section 6 gives the conclusion and outlines the future research.

2. RELATED WORD

Many studies have been conducted on patents, the work in (Abbas. et al., 2015) provides an overview of previous research of text mining and visualization based techniques for patent analysis and a taxonomy that classifies these approaches. However, the prior studies focused on analysis of standard textual fields of patent document such as abstract, claims, and the detailed description of the invention, and did not consider analysis of specific segment of patent texts like texts of technical field segment. Our work extracts technological areas in texts of technical field segment that will be benefit in discovering topics/trends and emerging technologies, and effective for the patent text information retrieval via retrieving patents documents by searching in technical field section instead of full text of patent.

Hu et al. (Jie Hu. et al, 2018) proposed a hierarchical feature extraction model (HFEM) for multi-label mechanical patent classification. They extracted the features from full texts of patents (abstract, claims, and description) instead of focusing on specific segment like technical field. Arunagiri et al., (Arunagiri. et al., 2017) proposed a framework for capturing technology evolution over time by analyzing patent classes network. Leydesdorff et al. (Leydesdorff. et al., 2017) used community detection methods for mapping patent classes. The drawback of analyzing patent classification is the complexity of classification schema and the classification codes are not available for all areas of technology.

Topic modeling has been applied on patent texts (Ankam. et al, 2012., Hongshu. et al., 2015. and Tang. et al., 2012). It has been applied on datasets that contained many different topics. Therefore, applying standard topic modeling like LDA on texts of technical field segment of patents is suffering from topics overlap especially when analyzing a patent dataset that is related to accurate topic. In contrast, the methods in this work do not suffer from this shortcoming, and automatically determine the appropriate number of topics, via the adaptation of community detection algorithms on a network graph.

3. METHODS AND ANALYSIS

Patent analysis benefits many areas of business and can help in getting the know-how of the relevant technological area in order to forecast market needs. World Intellectual Property Organization (WIPO) has developed a guidelines for patent search and analysis to create a Patent Landscape Reports (PLRs) that support informed decision-making, and are designed to efficiently address the concerns associated with making high stakes decisions in various areas of technology, and increasing the related degree of confidence (Trippe, 2015). The basic idea here is to consider ways that analyze patent information to help in business decisions, and these ways start with selecting specific topic that will typically be based on an industry, or technological focus area that is critical to the decision, extract patent documents related to that topic, understanding which organizations own patents, and what technological areas they cover, can have a significant impact on policy making and corporate decision-making. In fact, patent analysis involves a series of steps, including extracting patents from patent repositories, deeply structure and enriches the unstructured parts, extracting the significant information from specific part/s of patent texts, and analyzing the extracted information to infer the logical conclusions. In accordance with these guidelines, the accurate technical information that represents the technical area of subject matter of inventions is extracted from the important sections of text fields of patent. This work analyzes the patent documents that are related to the "information Security and Cryptography" domain. From the databases Patent Cooperation Treaty (PCTFULL) and European Patents (EPFULL), 34340 patents are gathered by using patent classification codes (H04L0009, H04W0012, H04H0060-23, G06F21, and H04W0012-06) that are related to information security topics. In addition to standard topic modeling, we present our methods in this paper in the following subsections.

3.1 Identification Technical Field of Invention

The detailed description texts of the invention include many different sections, namely the technical field, background, summary, embodiments, and the description of figures and drawings of the invention. The text of technical field is a short paragraph/s, with three or four sentences or could be more, which display the technological areas of the described invention. It generally mirrors the wording of the beginning of the independent claim. The aim of technical field section is to guide patent information professionals searching for related patents and understand in depth the accurate technical areas which the inventions are related. The text of technical field segment is also mirror the hierarchies expressed in more patent classification codes. For example, this text "*The invention belongs to the field of communication network, in particular relates to a domain name of the biometrics-based authentication system and method.* " belongs to a new authentication method for the area communication network.

To identify the text of technical field section in patent texts, our significant and scalable segmentation methods are developed for structuring the patent texts into pre-defined sections (Sofean, 2017). The description of the patent text is segmented into semantic sections including technical field by using a hybrid text mining techniques such as machine learning, rule-based algorithm, and heuristics (learning-by-problem-solving pattern). Particularly, our segmentation process was used to classify each patent paragraph in description text of patent into one of several pre-defined semantic sections. The segmentation methods start with extracting a description text from the patent document, and checks if the text is structured by headlines. Then the text is divided into paragraphs, a pre-processing step will take place to remove undesired tokens and apply stemming, a rule-based algorithm will be used to identify the headers, and a machine learning model is used to predict a right segment for each header. For the patent that do not have complete structured segments or do not have any heading at all, heuristic methods will be used. The final step is, identify boundaries of each segment and their related text content.

The evaluation was conducted on three different dataset. The first dataset consists of 100 documents which are randomly selected from European patents. The second dataset consists of 50 patents and randomly selected from German patents. The third dataset is randomly extracted from Japanese and Chinese patents, and consists of 50 patents. The performance of our segmentation methods achieved up to 94% of accuracy.

3.2 Technological Areas Extraction

Natural Language Processing (NLP) processes are performed on the provided texts to automatically extract the most significant technological areas. We started with the removal of duplicates in the collection of documents by selecting only one document from each patent family since there are patents that represent and/or build on the same invention and these patents can also be grouped in so-called patent family (EPO, 2017). In order to avoid analyzing the same invention, a patent family identification process should carry out on overall patents and only one member of each family is considered as representative member of the respective family.

We observed that the most key phrases in technical field are noun phrases. Therefore, a large-scale, efficient, distributed NLP pipeline is built to extract the significant noun terms and phrases for each patent document.

The NLP pipeline is a sequence of stages, each stage performs a process on the text, such as: Sentence Detection (splitting the text into sentences); Tokenization (terms identified by spaces between them); Part-of-Speech tagging (labeling each term in a sentence with its appropriate part of speech such as noun, verb, adjective); Shallow Syntactic Parsing or Chunking (splitting the text of sentence into smaller chunks by noun phrase); Stopword Removal (removing the standard stopwords list customized stopwords list that are general, very frequent and non-significant words such as invention, embodiment, claims, background, disclosure, etc.); Stemming (converting only all plural noun terms to singular ones); and Pruning (ignoring terms that have very low or very high frequency). A lot of technological area terms contain more single words than one word; in this case the words of each technological area are linked via dashes and treated them as single word in our methods, e.g., digital_rights_management and quantum_cryptography. Finally, the output of NLP pipeline is a list of technological areas that represent candidates for further analysis.

3.3 Technological Areas Co-occurrence and Clustering

Patent technological areas clustering task is described as follows: given a set of technological areas, cluster them into groups so that the similar areas are in the same cluster. Let us take an example. Assume a set of areas is given: authentication method, public key, private key, biometric authentication, elliptic curve, and personal authentication. Clearly, the first, fourth, and sixth are related to the authentication, and the other areas are related to public key cryptography. We develop a clustering-based topic modelling algorithm that uses community detection approaches for topic modelling, based on the network graph of texts of technical fields segment in patent domain.

3.3.1 Network Graph Construction

We first introduce some basic notations used in this work. In traditional network theory, V and E denote the set of vertices and edges, respectively, and an undirected graph G = (V, E) is represented as a collection of vertices/nodes V that are connected by a set of edges E. In turn, each edge $e \in E$ is denoted by $e = (\{v_i, v_j\}, w)$, which represents a similarity between nodes v_i and v_j and can be taken as a weight w.

Scalable methods are developed to extract all technological areas in our dataset. To extract the most interesting areas, the first task is applied for counting the number of occurrences each term of technology area, ranking them, and then taking the most frequent ones (hotspots) depending on predefined threshold. A co-occurrence graph for technical areas of information security domain is created by generating a co-occurrence matrix to generally describe how technical areas occur together that in turn capture the semantic relationships between them, since each technical area is treated as a topic (node) and the relationship between two areas (edge) is simply based on co-occurrence statistics which can indirectly represent the semantic information of related areas, and should be above a certain threshold. The weight of edges is created by using statistical measure of occurring two co-areas in a collection of patent documents. To avoid sparsity problem, the weights that are above a specific threshold are considered. Various statistical measures are tested to calculate the values of co-occurrence matrix such as pointwise mutual information (PMI), Chi-Square, and TFIDF (term frequency and inverse term frequency).

3.3.2 Topic/Community Detection

After constructing the network graph in the previous section, we now describe our approach to cluster the technical areas into groups and modelling the topics by using community detection methods. This work mainly focuses on adapting a Smart Local Moving Algorithm (SLM) for this purpose (Waltman et al., 2013). SLM algorithm is used for modularity-based community detection in large networks, and it was shown to be one of the best performing algorithms in a comprehensive survey of community detection algorithms. The first step (iteration) of the algorithm is assigning each node in a network to its own community, the second iteration starts with the community structure obtained in the first iteration of the algorithm. This means that the second iteration allows individual nodes to move between the communities produced in the first iteration. After the second iteration has been completed, the third iteration is using the community structure obtained in the second iteration as input. In this way, more and more iterations of the algorithm can be performed. The iterative approach can be stopped as soon as performing an additional iteration of the algorithm does not result in a modularity increase. Finally, the nodes in the network are assigned to communities. A community is a set of closely related nodes. Each node in a network is assigned to exactly one cluster. The number of communities is determined by a resolution parameter since the higher value of this parameter, the larger the number of communities.

3.3.3 Community/Topic Assignment

This sub section shows our approach to assign each document into related community/topic. In particular, we assign a patent document to a community/topic that has the highest co-occurrence of terms of technical areas in both the patent document and community/topic, where the term in the community/topic is weighted based on its co-occurrence to other terms.

4. EXPERIMENTS AND RESULTS

The methods in this work were developed based on a combination of Apache Hadoop and Apache Spark frameworks. Spark (Zaharia. et al, 2010) was designed as an alternative to Hadoop, capable of performing faster distributed computing by using in-memory primitives. In fact, our methods are integrated into our scalable patent mining and analytics framework that is built on top of big-data architecture and a scientific workflow system for allowing the user to efficiently annotate, analyze and interact with patent data on a large-scale via visual interaction (Sofean. et al, 2018). The framework is based on the Hortonworks Data Platform, which consists of two name nodes and 14 data nodes with 1,8TB of RAM in total.

In particular, all patent documents related to information security domain are extracted into HDFS (Hadoop Distributed File System), a MapReduce-based tool called PatSeg (Sofean, 2017) is developed to identify the texts of technical field segment in each description text of patent and the outputs are stored into NoSQL database. A scalable spark service is developed to identify patent families in order to remove duplicates, and the output is stored in Spark-RDD (Resilient Distributed Dataset), and then a Spark-NLP service is developed to apply NLP methods that are presented in section 3.2 in order to filter the row texts of technical field sections from undesired tokens and extract the most significant technological areas.

We started our experiment by applying Spark Latent Dirichlet Allocation (Spark-LDA) on the output of Spark-NLP task to extract the list of topics. Spark-LDA is integrated with our Spark services and we run the algorithm many times with different values of hyperparameters α (Dirichlet prior topic distribution of each document) and β (word distributions for each topic). It was found that some terms of technical areas are shared between many different topics. For instance, the term "authentication" is shared between five different topics. However, this usually makes it much harder to find more accurate areas such as "fault attack", "biometric authentication", and "access control" that are clearly appearing in our dataset. Also LDA has experimented on sub topics in "Information Security" domain such as cryptography. We found that LDA is suffering much more from topics overlap in case of analyzing texts of technical fields of inventions.

To show the results of our methods in this work, the number occurrence are calculated for each technical area that is extracted by a Spark-NLP service. A Spark-based service is developed to create the network graph for most frequent areas via calculating a co-occurrence matrix. The co-occurrence matrix is computed by counting how two or more technical areas occur together in our corpus. For community detection, the open source codes of Smart Local Moving Algorithm is integrated into our Spark application for clustering network graph into communities/topics, and the community with only one or two technical areas are ignored.

Figure 1 provides the most frequently technology hotspots in the field of information security such as public key and private key cryptography, digital signature, access control, authentication systems, cryptographic algorithms and key management. It also shows more accurate areas such as DRM systems (Digital Rights Management), quantum cryptography, and security with smart cards.

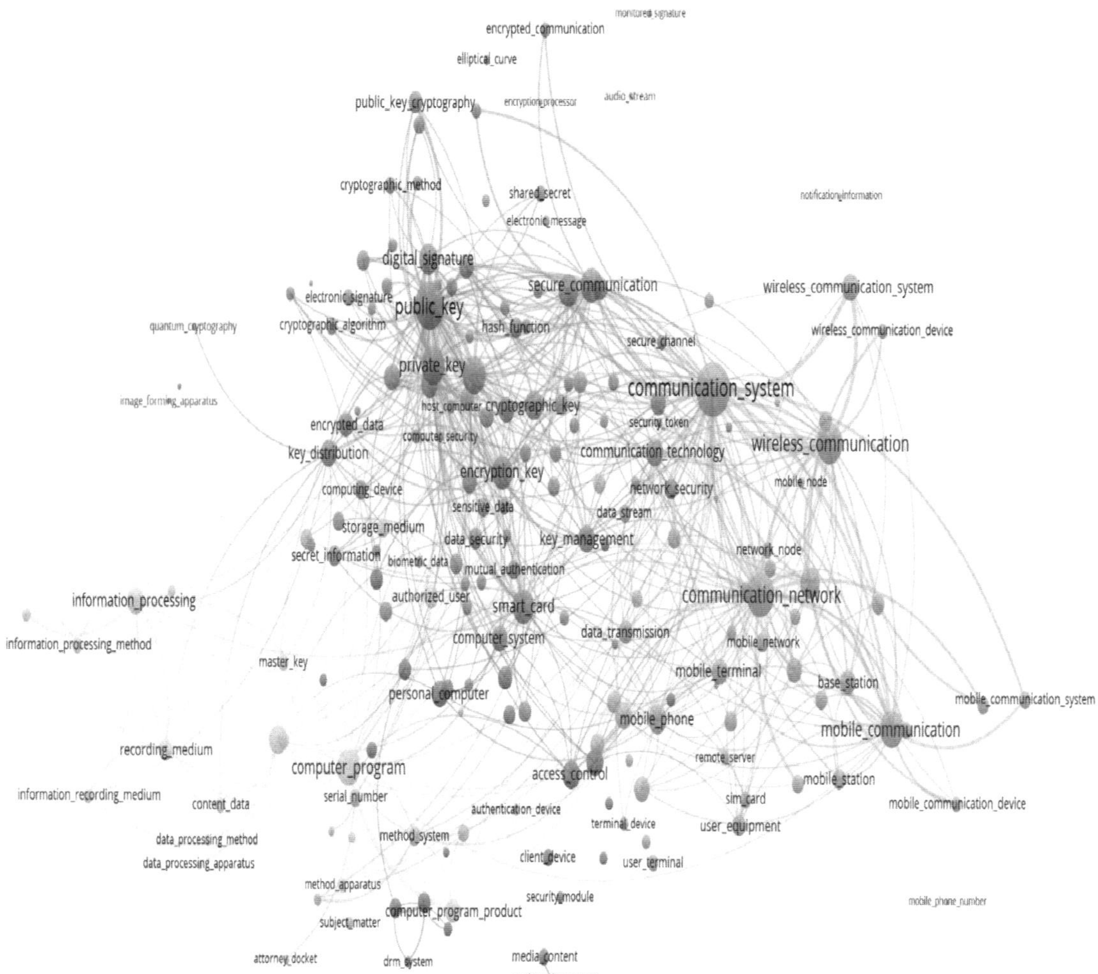

Figure 1. Visualizing hot areas of technology and their relationships

In addition, we show a co-occurrence network of terms (terms of technical areas of inventions or terms related to them) that are grouped together into colored clusters. Each cluster can be seen as a community/topic.

Table 1 only presents five communities/topics from all topics that are discovered by our methods in this work. As shown in the table, all technical areas that related to the topic "public key infrastructure" are grouped in the community 1, community 2 contains all terms that are related to a topic "authentication", community 3 is related to security in mobile communication, community 4 is related to "quantum cryptography", and community 5 is related to "digital right management". Moreover, more promised technical areas appeared in our results such as "security management", "access control", "data integrity", "personal information (privacy)", as well as certain more specific areas have appeared in the results which represent the subject matter of inventions like "one-time password", "fault attack", "biometric authentication", and "single sign-on".

In comparison with standard topic modelling like LDA, our methods do not suffer from topics overlap, and do not require the setting of numerous parameters since are able to automatically determine the appropriate number of topics based on a local maximization of modularity among the network graph of technical areas. In contrast, the standard topic modeling requires setting of numerous parameters and needs much time for training the model specially when dealing with a big data.

Table 1. List of communities/topics

Label	*Detailed Content*
Community 1	public key, digital signature, private key, electronic signature, digital certificate, elliptic curve, electronic transaction, common key, elliptical curve, unique identifier, hash function, public key infrastructure, encrypted message, symmetric key, shared secret, certification authority, public key certificate, public key encryption, public key cryptography, electronic commerce, certificate authority, key generation, modular exponentiation, signature generation, symmetric encryption, prime number, public key infrastructure PKI
Community 2	user authentication, authentication method, authentication system, biometric data, authentication server, biometric authentication, biometric information, personal identification, authentication device, mutual authentication, biometric identification, authentication process, personal identification number, user identification, user authentication method, authentication token
Community 3	mobile terminal, mobile communication, user equipment, telecommunication network, mobile station, mobile communication device, telecommunication system, portable radio, mobile communication system, mobile communication terminal, home agent, mobile communication network, mobile telecommunication packet data, subscriber identity module, mobile communication technology, foreign agent, cellular networ
Community 4	DRM system, digital content, digital management, digital management DRM, digital media, digital protection
Community 5	quantum key, quantum key distribution, quantum cryptography

Moreover, we found that using community detection for topic modeling works well with real applications of patent analysis without sharing terms between communities/topics. For instance, the terms in the community 4 and 5 in the table 1 are related to "DRM" and "quantum cryptography" respectively without any term interference from other communities.

For the evolution of patent technological areas extraction, we independently request three data scientists and one patent expert to provide human judgement on the top (200) returned terms. The judgments about relevant (Like) or irrelevant (DisLike). If there are more than two annotators saying that an extracted technological area is irrelevant, we remove it from the returned list. We used the Precision to measure the ability of our methods to reject any non-relevant technical area in the retrieved set. Therefore, the evaluation is conducted in terms of P@N (Precision for top N results), mean average precision (MAP) (Buckley, 2004).

Table 2. Performance of methods of technological area extraction

Data	*P@50*	*P@100*	*P@150*	*P@200*	*MAP*
Patent Dataset	92%	90%	88%	87%	89%

In more details, we concentrated on precision at top 50, 100, 150, and 200 technological areas retrieved, as well as the mean of the precision scores (MAP). The performance results of the evaluation are presented in the Table 2.

5. CONCLUSION

In this paper we have described our methods for detecting texts of technical field in unstructured patents texts, and extracted technological areas of inventions. We presented a large-scale graph-based technical area clustering methods that utilize community detection approaches to aggregate technical areas into communities/topics based on a network graph of areas of inventions to discover communities/topics for a large collection of patent documents. The methods in this work are developed on top of big-data architecture in order to deal with huge amount of data. A comparison to the standard LDA clustering has been presented, and the results showed that our method do not share common terms and perform well with real patent applications. Our future directions of research will continue to analyze trends in patent domain on the results of community detection methods, and improve the semantic between technological areas of patents by using intelligent algorithms such as word embedding, ontological knowledge and linked data.

REFERENCES

Bowen Yan. et al., 2016. *Measuring technological distance for patent mapping*. Journal of the Association for Information Science and Technology, 68: 423-437. doi:10.1002/asi.23664

Assad Abbas. et al., 2015. *A literature review on the state-of-the-art in patent analysis*, World Patent. Information, 37, pp.3–13

Jie Hu. et al., 2018. *A Hierarchical Feature Extraction Model for Multi-Label Mechanical Patent Classification*. Sustainability, MDPI, Open Access Journal, vol. 10(1), pages 1-22

Arunagiri. et al., 2017. *Exploring Technology Evolution Using Patent Classification: A Case of Cochlear Implant Technology Patents.* International Journal of Innovation and Technology Management. Vol. 14, No. 01

Loet Leydesdorff. et al., 2017. *Mapping Patent Classifications: Portfolio and Statistical Analysis, and the Comparison of Strengths and Weaknesses*. Scientometrics. Volume 112, Issue 3, pp 1573–1591

Suraj Ankam . et al., 2012. *Exploring emerging technologies using patent data and patentclassification.* CHI'12 ACM. Austin, Texas, USA

Hongshu Chen. et al., 2015. *Modeling technological topic changes in patent claims.* Proceedings of PIC MET '15, Portland, OR, USA

Jie Tang. et al., 2012. *PatentMiner: Topic-driven Patent Analysis and Mining*. KDD'12, ACM. Beijing, China.

Anthony Trippe., 2015. *Guidelines for Preparing Patent Landscape Reports. Patinformatics*, LLC, With contributions from WIPO Secretariat.

Mustafa Sofean, 2017. *Automatic Segmentation of Big Data of Patent Texts*. Proceedings of the International Conference on Big Data Analytics and Knowledge Discovery. DaWaK 2017. Springer pp 343-351. Lyon.

EPO, 2017. *Patent Family.* https://www.epo.org/searching-for-patents/helpful-resources/first-time-here/patent-families.html

Ludo Waltman. et al., 2013. *A smart local moving algorithm for large-scale modularity-based community detection.* The European Physical Journal. Springer.

Matei Zaharia. et al., 2010. *Spark: cluster computing with working sets*. HotCloud'10 Proceedings of the 2nd USENIX conference on Hot topics in cloud computing Pages 10-10

C. Buckley. et al., 2004. *Retrieval evaluation with incomplete information.* In SIGIR'2004, ACM, pages 25–32, Sheffield, South Yorkshire, UK

Mustafa Sofean. et al., 2018. *A Workflow-based Large-Scale Patent Mining and Analytics Framework*. Proceedings of 24th International Conference on Information and Software Technologies 2018 (ICIST); Vilnius, Litauen.

A SPECTRAL CLUSTERING-BASED APPROACH FOR SENTIMENT CLASSIFICATION IN MODERN STANDARD ARABIC

Ikram El Karfi, Sanaa El Fkihi and Rdouan Faizi
ENSIAS, Mohammed V University in Rabat, Morocco

ABSTRACT

Thanks to its various applications in a variety of domains, sentiment analysis has attracted a lot of attention in the last couple of years. Therefore, our objective in this work is to propose a spectral clustering-based approach for sentiment classification in Modern Standard Arabic. This class of graph-based algorithms has been widely successful due to its high performance in many contexts where several classical techniques fail. In fact, on the basis of the experiments we conducted on a dataset collected from Goodreads, it was found out that is this approach can automatically extract and identify the polarity of a given text and can, thus, reach higher accuracy compared to other machine learning algorithms. Results of the study have, actually, proven that our approach out performs K-means algorithms by achieving an accuracy rate of 83.13%.

KEYWORDS

Sentiment Analysis, Modern Standard Arabic, Machine Learning, Unsupervised Approach, Spectral Clustering

1. INTRODUCTION

Sentiment Analysis (also known as opinion mining) refers to the computing study of people's sentiments, opinions, evaluations and perceptions towards specific products or services. Today, with the increasing proliferation of social media platforms such as social networks, discussion forums, and peer-to-peer networks, internet users have at their disposal unprecedented reach and power to post their opinions, be they positive or negative, on different brands as well as share their experience with others. The Web has, thus, evolved towards an era in which the online community is likely to have a say on future products and services (Cambria et al, 2017).

Therefore, since online opinions and reviews are likely to have a great effect on the reputation of businesses and on shaping the decisions of many people in a variety of domains, sentiment analysis has been drawing considerable interest from both academia and business in the last couple of years. Its impact has already been felt in various domains, namely business, politics, tourism and health.

Given the potential benefits of sentiment analysis, many research works have focused on this research area. Nevertheless, most of the techniques or solutions that have been put forward in these studies have been tailored to online reviews posted mainly in English and in other Indo-European languages. The number of studies carried out on sentiment analysis in other languages, such as Arabic, is still minimal given that it is morphologically complex. Accordingly, our objective in this paper is to propose a spectral clustering-based approach for sentiment classification in Modern Standard Arabic.

Sentiment or polarity classification is, actually, one of the major tasks of sentiment analysis that aims at classifying a subjective text into two or more polarity classes. In the case of a binary classification, an opinion is identified as being either positive or negative. In a multi-class classification, texts are classified according to the intensity of the expressed sentiment, namely extremely negative, negative, neutral, positive or extremely positive (Lunardi et al., 2016; Collomb et al., 2014).

The remainder of the present paper is structured as follows. Section 2 gives an overview of the major studies on Sentiment Analysis in Arabic. In Section 3 we propose our sentiment classification approach. Section 4 presents the results of this approach and compares them with those of the K-means technique. Finally, conclusions are drawn in Section 5.

2. RELATED WORK

Sentiment Analysis in Arabic is usually conducted by making use of three different approaches: supervised, unsupervised and hybrid. The supervised approaches are based on machine learning algorithms such as Support Vector Machines (SVM), Naïve Bayes (NB), and K-Nearest Neighbour (KNN). The unsupervised approaches use words and their corresponding sentiments while the hybrid combines both supervised and unsupervised techniques (Boudad et al. 2017).

In this respect, Hossam et al. (2015) used an SVM classifier to find the polarity of each sentence in a corpus of 1000 microblogs of different types of data (tweets, products reviews, TV-program comments and hotel reservation). Furthermore, they used Arabic sentiment idioms/saying phrase lexicon to improve the classification process. For their parts, Duwairi et al. (2016) made use of Arabizi dataset that consists of 3206 tweets (1803 positive, 831 negative and 572 neutral). For experimentation purposes, the authors used NB and SVM classifiers. Results of their analysis showed that SVM outperformed NB. However, accuracy did not greatly improve whilst removing stop words and replacing emoticons with their corresponding words. Hadi (2015) investigated the decision tree, NB, KNN and SVM on Arabic Twitter corpus that contains 3700 Arabic tweets (1579 positive, 1374 negative and 747 neutral). The findings revealed that the SVM learning method outperformed all other learning methods with F1-score equals 0.72. Al-Rubaiee et al. (2016) introduced Arabic text classification for Mubasher products. N-gram feature was combined with supervised machine learning algorithms, namely SVM and NB. The best accuracy of SVM was achieved without N-gram feature whilst the best accuracy of NB was attained when combined with N-gram feature. In the same context, Shoukry and Rafea (2015) proposed a hybrid approach to classify Arabic text, especially Egyptian dialect by combining semantic orientation and machine learning approaches. Results showed that considering semantic words occurring after negation terms improved the performance of the hybrid approach by 0.1%. El Makky et al. (2015) presented a subjectivity and sentiment analysis system for Egyptian Arabic tweets. Their proposed system was based on a hybrid approach that combines machine learning and a new Arabic lexicon merging two modern standard Arabic lexica with two Egyptian Arabic lexica. El Ghazaly et al. (2016) compared between SVM and NB algorithms using political Arabic twitter data. The corpus contained 18278 tweets, 11910 positive and 6368 negative. The study displayed good results. F1-score of NB classifier was 0.92 and F1-score of SVM classifier was 0.87. El Naggar et al. (2017) performed sentiment analysis on modern standard Arabic and Egyptian dialectical Arabic tweets. The hybrid algorithm employs lexicon-based and machine learning techniques. Using an emoji lexicon and solving the problems available in Shoukry and Rafea (2015) and El Makky et al. (2015), the results of the proposed hybrid algorithm outperformed the aforementioned systems.

3. PROPOSED APPROACH

In this paper, we propose an unsupervised approach which consists of three main steps which are: (1) the pre-processing step, (2) the vectorization step and (3) the spectral clustering step. Each of these steps is detailed below.

3.1 Preprocessing Step

In this section, we present a detailed description of the pre-processing phase of our proposed approach. This first step aims at cleaning data so as to keep relevant and significant text.

3.1.1 Tokenization

Splitting the given text into tokens is a mandatory step before proceeding any further in the process. Tokens may be words, numbers, punctuation marks or even emojis. For example, "رواية رائعة جداً" contains three tokens that are: "رواية", "رائعة" and "جداً".

3.1.2 Arabic Stop Words

Arabic stop words are words that are frequently used in Arabic texts, but they are useless. This includes items such as "و", "أن", "التي", "هو", and "كيف". Hence, these words have to be filtered out. Nonetheless, even if negation terms are stops words, they removed from the list because when they occur before a sentiment word they usually change its sentiment polarity from positive to negative and vice versa. For example, "رواية تستحق القراءة" and "رواية لا تستحق القراءة", the sentence changed from positive to negative in the presence of the term 'لا'.

3.1.3 Normalization

In this step diacritics are removed and each lengthened word is reduced to its canonical form. For instance, the word "جميــــــــل" (beautiful) is transformed to "جميل" using a regular expression to remove the character "ـ". Moreover, a regular expression is used to remove lengthening; if a character is repeated more than once, the sequence of the repeated characters is replaced by a single instance of that character. The word "جيييييد" (good) will be replaced by "جيد". Then normalize characters such as أ, إ, آ, ٱ transformed to ا by removing the *Hamza,* as shown in Table 1.

This sub-step is very important because it guarantees that terms like قرأ (to read), قارئ (reader) conflate to the same root and not considered as unique words while calculating the frequency.

Table 1. Characters normalization

Character	Normalized character
أ	ا
إ	ا
آ	ا
ٱ	ا
ى	ي
ؤ	ء
ئ	ء
ة	ه

3.1.4 Emojis

All emoticons and emojis are deleted based on a preselected list of the most commonly used emojis. For instance, "جميل جدا ☺" becomes "جميل جدا".

3.1.5 Stemming

ISRI Arabic stemmer (Taghva et al., 2005) is adopted in this step. It is an Arabic stemmer that is similar to Khoja stemmer (Khoja and Garside, 1999). The main difference is that no root dictionary is used. They remove affixes and match patterns from an Arabic patterns and roots list depending on the length of the word then extract the relevant stem. If we take for example the word "تشجيع" the result will be the term "شجع" (to encourage) using PR53 set which contains word "تفعيل" composed by five patterns length and three roots length.

3.2 Vectorization Step

This section details the second phase of the proposed approach. It includes (1) corpus-specific stop words, (2) N-grams and the (3) TFIDF and binary count vectorizer.

3.2.1 Corpus-specific Stop Words

In order to ensure that our approach works in any context we used a corpus-specific stop words technique by ignoring terms that have a document frequency higher and lower than a threshold for the too frequently and too infrequently used terms in the corpus. This step is justified by the fact that, on the one hand, the too frequently words usually refer to a domain of study. As such, they are not relevant to sentiment analysis. On the other hand, the too infrequently used terms do not occur a lot. Therefore, they may be removed without influencing the sentiment polarity.

3.2.2 N-grams

An N-gram is an N-character slice of a longer string (Cavnar and Trenkle, 1994) which means a subsequence of N successive items from a given text. In this work a combination of unigrams, bigrams and trigrams is used to detect any negation in the given text and represent features a as count vector using TF-IDF and Binary count vectorizer. Table 2 gives an example of N-grams of: استمتعت كثيرا بالرواية

Table 2. Example of N-grams of: استمتعت كثيرا بالرواية

N-gram	Text
Unigram (1-gram)	استمتعت
Unigram (1-gram)	كثيرا
Unigram (1-gram)	بالرواية
Bigram(2-gram)	استمتعت كثيرا
Bigram(2-gram)	كثيرا بالرواية
Trigram(3-gram)	استمتعت كثيرا بالرواية

3.2.3 TF-IDF & Binary Count Vectorizer

In this sub-step, we adopted two different approaches to convert a given text into vector space. These approaches are:

- First approach: TFIDF Vectorizer

TF-IDF (Salton and Buckley, 1988) is used to measure the importance of a term throughout the corpus, the weight of a term t_i in a document d_j is

$$w_{ij} = TF_{ij} \times IDF_i$$

where $TF_{ij}$is the frequency of the term $t_i$in the document d_j. With

$$TF_{ij}= w_{ij}|d_j|$$

w_{ij} is the number of occurrences of the term t_i in the $d_j$document

$|d_j|$ is the total number of terms in the document d_j

Besides, the inverse document frequency is given by the next equation

$$IDFi = \log(\frac{|D|}{|\{d_j: t_i \in d_j\}|})$$

Where$|D|$ denotes the total number of documents in the corpus and $|\{d_j: t_i \in d_j\}|$ is the number of documents where the term t_i appears.

- Second approach: Binary Count Vectorizer

It is a binary weighting approach. Here each document is represented as a binary vector; all non-zero counts are set to 1.

3.3 Spectral Clustering Step

The idea of spectral clustering consists in extracting the k eigenvectors of a graph Laplacian corresponding to the k largest eigenvalues that form a lower-dimensional space where points will be linearly separable. In this context, two different partitioning approaches can be used:

- Recursive bi-partitioning: At each iteration, the graph is recursively split into two partition using eigenvector corresponding to the second largest eigenvalue of the normalized Laplacian graph (Shi and Malik, 2005) or Fiedler vector (Biggs, 1998) if not normalized.
- K-ways partitioning: Low-dimensional space is formed using k eigenvectors corresponding to k largest eigenvalues of a normalized Laplacian graph. Then each data point is assigned into one of the k clusters using a standard clustering method such as k-means (Ng et al., 2002; Meila & Shi, 2001).

The computational approach that we have developed to cluster the reviews into positive and negative clusters is based on (Ng et al., 2002) spectral clustering algorithm. The concept is that we consider data as a graph using eigenvectors of matrices derived from the data.

The first step of this above technique is to build a graph based on the data; the graph vertices represent the N data points while the graph edges are weighted based on similarity between vertices.

The affinity matrix (similarity matrix) W of the graph is constructed using the function Laplacian kernel and then the adjacency matrix is calculated. Thus, the function Laplacian kernel is defined as:

$$W = K(x,y) = exp^{(-\gamma \|x-y\|_1)}$$

where x and y are the input vectors, $\|x - y\|_1$ is the Manhattan distance between the input vectors and γ is a scaling parameter of the Manhattan distance.

Moreover, the adjacency matrix *A* is defined by the next equation:

$$A = D - W$$

where *W* is the affinity matrix and *D* is a diagonal matrix where the (*i*, *i*) entry is equal to the sum of the weights on the edges that are adjacent to vertex *i*.

The adjacency matrix of the graph is then normalized using the following formula:

$$A' = D^{-\frac{1}{2}} AD^{-\frac{1}{2}}$$

where *A* is the adjacency matrix of the graph, A' is the normalized adjacency matrix and *D* is the diagonal matrix.

The next step of the spectral clustering approach is to find the eigenvalues and eigenvectors of the normalized matrix that satisfies the following equation:

$$A'\vec{v} = \lambda\vec{v}$$

In order to find *k* clusters, an *N* by *k* matrix is built using the *k* eigenvectors with highest eigenvalues in this case *k* = 2 (positive and negative polarity of a sentiment) and a clustering method is used to cluster the rows. Hierarchical clustering is a method of clustering algorithms that create clusters by merging or splitting them successively. It has been used in many research such as the work reported (Suresh & Raj, 2017). In the agglomerative (bottom-up) method each data point is initially set in a cluster on its own then compute the similarity between two data points and merge them together into one cluster. In a divisive (top-down) method, all the data points are in a single cluster, on each step we recursively split the cluster into two least similar clusters. The adopted method in this work is the agglomerative clustering using cosine similarity function for computing the similarity between two observations.

4. EXPERIMENTS AND RESULTS

In this section, we evaluate the performance of our proposal. In this aim, we compare the latter to the known k-means approach.

Before moving on, note that we have built a corpus from the known website Goodreads (2018). Thus, we have selected 1298 Modern Standard Arabic reviews from Goodreads. Then, we manually annotated the data by 0 (for a negative review) and 1 (for a positive review). Furthermore, to balance our dataset and make a good decision, we randomly choose 648 positive reviews and 646 negative reviews.

Table 3 shows the achieved results of representing features as a count vector of unigrams, bigrams, and tri-grams with gamma equals to 0.29 (see figure 1 to justify the used gamma value; it is the max obtained value). We can see that with Binary Count Vectorizer, unigrams and bigrams we reach the best results, in contrast the best accuracy using TF-IDF was achieved combining TF-IDF with unigrams, bi-grams and tri-grams (up to 83.13%).

Table 3. Performance comparison with γ=0.29

N-gram	Binary Count Vectorizer	TF-IDF
N=1	0.7360	0.7602
N=2	0.6610	0.7697
N=3	0.5195	0.8152

To fix the gamma value, Figure 1 represents the accuracies for each value of gamma generated within the half-open interval [0.01, 0.31] with a step size 0.02. The best results were reached with $\gamma = 0.29$ where the accuracy equals to 83.13%. These results were reached using agglomerative clustering as a last step in spectral clustering algorithm to plot the graph.

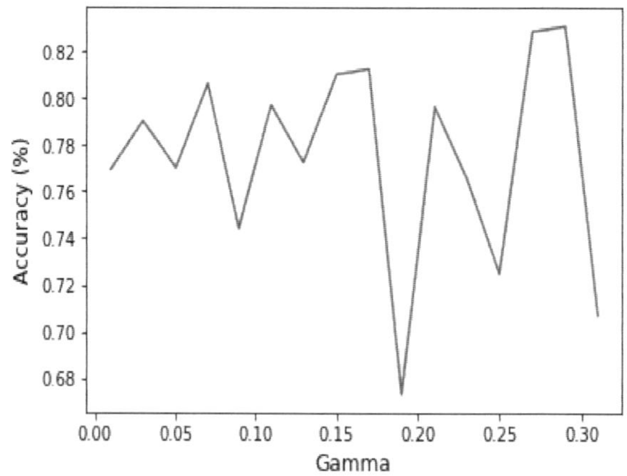

Figure 1. Accuracy results with gamma changing

To compare our algorithm with other unsupervised learning algorithms, we considered the K-means techniques. Figure 2 shows that our algorithm outperforms K-means by achieving 83.13% accuracy while K-means reaches only 64%.

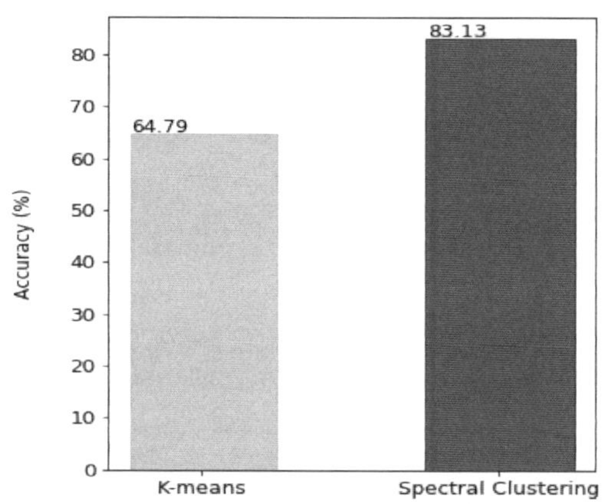

Figure 2. Performance results of the compared approaches

As was mentioned above, our proposal performs better than the k-means approach. This can be justified by the fact that the proposal is based on the eigenvalues and eigenvectors. Furthermore, it was mathematically proven that the latter give accurate results because they allow to discriminate data more efficiently.

5. CONCLUSION

Given the increasing application of sentiment analysis in different languages and in a variety of fields, our objective in this paper was to contribute to the research studies conducted on Modern Standard Arabic, which is a morphologically complex language. In this vein, we put forward an unsupervised approach that is based on spectral clustering so as to classify sentiments as being either positive or negative. On the basis of the experiments that were carried out on data collected from Goodreads, it was noticed that the proposed approach can automatically extract and identify the polarity of an Arabic text and, thus, outperforms K-means by achieving an 83.13% accuracy rate.

REFERENCES

Al-Rubaiee et al, 2016. Identifying Mubasher software products through sentiment analysis of Arabic tweets. *In IEEE, International Conference on Industrial Informatics and Computer Systems (CIICS).* Sharjah, United Arab Emirates

Biggs, N. 1998. Spectral graph theory. *Bulletin of the London Mathematical Society*, vol. 30, no.2, pp.196–223.

Boudad, N., Faizi, R., Thami, R. O. H., & Chiheb, R., 2017. Sentiment analysis in Arabic: A review of the literature. *Ain Shams Engineering Journal.*

Cambria, E. et al, 2017. A practical guide to sentiment analysis. Heidelberg. Springer, vol. 5.

Cavnar W. B., and J. M. Trenkle. 1994. N-Gram Based Text Categorization. *Proceedings of SDAIR-94, 3rd Annual Symposium on Document Analysis and Information Retrieval.*

Collomb, A., et al, 2014. A study and comparison of sentiment analysis methods for reputation evaluation. Rapport de recherche RR-LIRIS-2014-002.

Duwairi, Rehab M., et al. 2016. Sentiment analysis for Arabizi text. *In IEEE 7th International Conference on Information and Communication Systems (ICICS). Irbid, Jordan.*

Elghazaly Tarek et al, 2016. Political Sentiment Analysis Using Twitter Data. Proceedings of the International Conference on Internet of things and Cloud Computing. Cambridge, United Kingdom

El-Makky, N. et al., 2015.Sentiment analysis of colloquial Arabic tweets. The 3rd ASE International Conference on Social Informatic., At Harvard University, Cambridge, MA, USA

El-Naggar Nadine et al, 2017. Sentiment analysis of modern standard Arabic and Egyptian dialectal Arabic tweets. In 2017 Computing Conference. London, UK. pp. 880-887.

Goodreads (2018). Retrieved from https://www.goodreads.com

Hadi et al, 2015. Classification of Arabic Social Media Data. *Advances in Computational Sciences and Technology 8.1*, pp.29-34.

Hossam S. et al, 2015. Sentiment Analysis for Modern Standard Arabic and Colloquial. International Journal on Natural Language Computing (IJNLC), pp.95-109.

Khoja Shereen & Roger Garside, 1999. Stemming Arabic text. Computer Science Department, Lancaster University, Lancaster, UK, http://www.comp.lancs. ac.uk/computing/users/khoja/stemmer.ps

Lunardi, A., et al, 2016. Domain-Tailored Multiclass Classification of User Reviews Based on Binary Splits. *In International Conference on Social Computing and Social Media*. Springer, Cham. pp. 298-309

Meila,M. & Shi,J., 2001. A random walk view of spectral segmentation. *Artificial Intelligence and Statistics*.

Ng, Andrew Y. Michael I. Jordan, and Yair Weiss, 2002. On spectral clustering: Analysis and an algorithm. *In Advances in Neural Information Processing Systems*. pp. 849-856

Salton, G. & C. Buckley. 1988. Term-weighting approaches in automatic text retrieval. *Information Processing & Management*, vol. 24, issue. 5, pp.513–523.

Shi, J., & Malik, J., 2000. Normalized cuts and image segmentation. *IEEE Transactions on pattern analysis and machine intelligence*, *22*(8), pp. 888-905.

Shoukry, A. et al, 2015. A Hybrid Approach for Sentiment Classification of Egyptian Dialect Tweets. *In First International Conference on Arabic Computational Linguistics (ACLing)*. Cairo, Egypt, pp. 78–85.

Suresh H., S Gladston Raj, 2017. A Fuzzy Based Hybrid Hierarchical Clustering Model for Twitter Sentiment Analysis. *International Conference on Computational Intelligence, Communications, and Business Analytics*, Kolkata, India, pp 384-397

Taghva, K. et al, 2005. Arabic Stemming without a root dictionary. Information Science Research Institute. University of Nevada, Las Vegas, USA.

APPLIED MACHINE LEARNING: PREDICTING BEHAVIOUR OF INDUSTRIAL UNITS FROM CLIMATE DATA

Dieter Meiller[1] and Christian Schieder[2]
[1]*East Bavarian Technical University Amberg-Weiden, Kaiser-Wilhelm-Ring 23, 92224, Amberg, Germany*
[2]*BHS Corrugated Maschinen- und Anlagenbau GmbH, Paul-Engel-Straße 1, 92729 Weiherhammer, Germany*

ABSTRACT

The goal of this project was to develop a model and a working prototype for the evaluation of energy consumption of a factory in connection with climate data. The factory produces corrugated card board. This product is very susceptible to climate influences. At the end of the project, it should be clear what options there are for using data from the factory in conjunction with climate data and deriving a correlation between them. The following questions should be clarified: Which possibilities of prognosis and evaluation are there? Which data are needed? How big is the effort?

KEYWORDS

Machine Learning, Virtual Sensor, Climate Prediction, Industry 4.0

1. COURSE OF THE PROJECT

It is assumed that climate has a strong influence on production processes. Humidity and temperature do not only have an influence on the quality of products, but also on the energy consumption of industrial plants. In the project a model for the evaluation of plant data in connection with climate data was developed, which shows the possibilities to derive correlations between these data.

After starting the project, measurements of humidity and temperature values at the production site for corrugated board should be started soon. Data should be recorded for as long as possible and should be measured at intervals of one minute. For this, about ten data loggers were installed on site. We decided to construct complete new data loggers by our own. Reasons were: Commercial data loggers are either very expensive and must be configured extensively, or they are cheap devices that do not meet the requirements. The components for the data logger are: Arduino Pro Mini, a humidity sensor, a real-time clock with better accuracy than the clock on the board, and a NTC thermistor, which has a temperature accuracy of 0.05 degrees Celsius. The housing was made using a 3d printer. Then the data loggers were installed at different places at the factory. The company itself provides the data of the power consumption of single machines for the period of the measurement. After six weeks, the first data were collected, so we could start with our first analysis. The following describes the implementation and results of the data analysis.

2. DATA ENGINEERING

First, the available data sets are described briefly. On the one hand, it is climate data: humidity and temperature values from inside the factory-hall. Then, there are weather data from outside, also temperature and humidity values. Humidity values are measured as relative humidity (RH) in percent (labeled as humidity in the diagrams). Further, we have data sets with values for power consumption (watts) of individual parts of the plant. We analyzed two kinds of data: Long-term (over four months) and short-term (six weeks). In the first step, the data sets were preprocessed. This step was necessary to get data with consistent time frames and without recording errors. For data analysis, we used Python programming language in the Anaconda environment. This free collection of open source libraries offers many opportunities in the field of data engineering and data science. The software is constantly being developed by an active community. Individual processing sessions can be performed in so-called "Jupyter-Notebooks" (Kluyver et al. 2016). All our processing and analysis steps were executed in such notebooks. For pre-processing, several notebooks were created using the Pandas library (McKinney 2011). This library can read data from different sources and offers many possibilities for processing, cleansing, analysis and visualization. In the first step, climate-data were merged with energy-data and brought to a uniform time scale: two-minute intervals in a uniform period. The plot shows the result of a short-time dataset for a single part of the factory (Fig. 1).

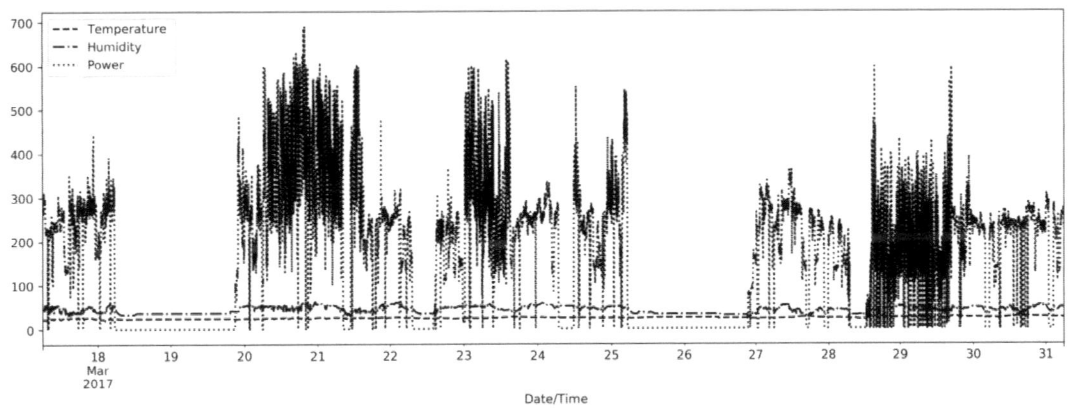

Figure 1. Plot Humidity / Power

3. DATA SCIENCE

The following analysis steps are devoted to the development of a forecast model. For this purpose, methods of machine learning were used. The technical basis was Python library Scikit-Learn (Pedregosa et al. 2011). Basically, a distinction is made between supervised and unsupervised learning. It is possible to use unsupervised learning to analyze climate data (Meiller 2017), but in this paper we focus on supervised learning. The difference is that during supervised learning there is a target size (y) of the data in addition to the individual features of the respective samples. In our case, these are the values for energy consumption. Because the values y are not given as discrete, but as continuous values, we can use regression analysis to predict these values. There is another term to be explained: „virtual sensors“ (Kabadayi et al. 2006). When it is possible to predict values, the model could replace the sensors for measurement. Because there are lots of expensive built-in sensors, this could be an option.

4. DATA PREPARATION

Data analysis and associated modeling was done by an iterative process of experiments. The aim was to have the best possible forecast of energy consumption based on the measured climate data. Different methods of machine learning with different parameters were tested. In addition, the input data has been preprocessed in various ways. Various combinations of possibilities were compared. This process took up most of the data analysis. At the beginning, the data were normalized, so that all data fit in an interval of [0,1]. This step is necessary because energy values are measured in scales other than climate data. After that, the data were split into two parts. The first part of the data (2/3rd) is the training set, the rest are test data. It was taken into account that the data is time-based, so that individual combinations of climate and power measurements have predecessors and successors in time. Therefore, we avoided to pick samples randomly to form training and test data from the original data set. The aspect of transient behavior would be lost as information. In order to be able to map time even better, higher-dimensional data were also generated from initial data (climate data): at each point in time, a vector was generated which represents a time interval around the selected point in time (Kapoor and Bedi 2013). In Fig. 2, the process of feature generation is shown schematically, here with a time window of 80 minutes. The number of features (m) has thus increased from two features (humidity, temperature) to 2 * 80 features. The high-dimensional training data generated in this way then were used as input data for various learning methods.

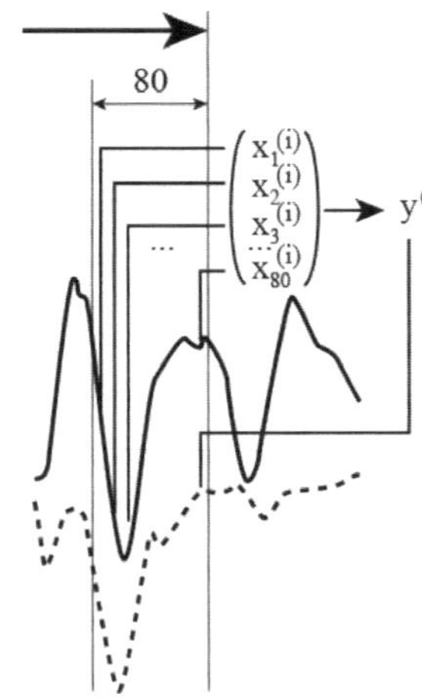

Figure 2. Feature Generation

5. MODEL TRAINING AND EVALUATION

The coefficient of determination(R^2) (see Formula 1) was used as quality measure for success control. It is interesting to know, that there are several definitions of R^2. The definition we used from the scikit-learn library is the same as the R^2_1 definition mentioned in (Kvålseth 1985). It is used to indicate how successful the model is. It compares the values for power consumption $\hat{y}$ estimated by the model from the test climate data with actual values for power from test data y. The values can be a maximum of 1, which would correspond to a match of 100%. Values close to 0 occur when taking constant values as estimated values $\hat{y}$. The estimate can be arbitrarily bad, values smaller than 0 indicate this. Using a multi-layered neural network, values of individual data loggers with current values of specific plant sections were evaluated. The best R^2 of 0.49 resulted from climate data measured on a machine located apart from other machines and its corresponding power data. We conclude that a measurement at a greater distance to the main-plant is more favorable, since there are no extreme fluctuations in temperature and humidity. Afterwards, further learning algorithms and parameters were tested to improve the results. One special preprocessing step was important to improve our results and to produce better visualizations: the smoothing of measured values using a Savitzky-Golay filter (Schafer 2011). The data were interpolated within a window of 351 minutes or less through a third degree curve (Fig. 3).

$$R^2(y,\hat{y}) = 1 - \frac{\sum_{i=0}^{n_{samples}-1}(y^{(i)}-\hat{y}^{(i)})^2}{\sum_{i=0}^{n_{samples}-1}(y^{(i)}-\bar{y})^2}$$

where

$$\bar{y} = \frac{1}{n_{samples}}\sum_{i=0}^{n_{samples}-1} y^{(i)}$$

Formula 1. Coefficient of Determination

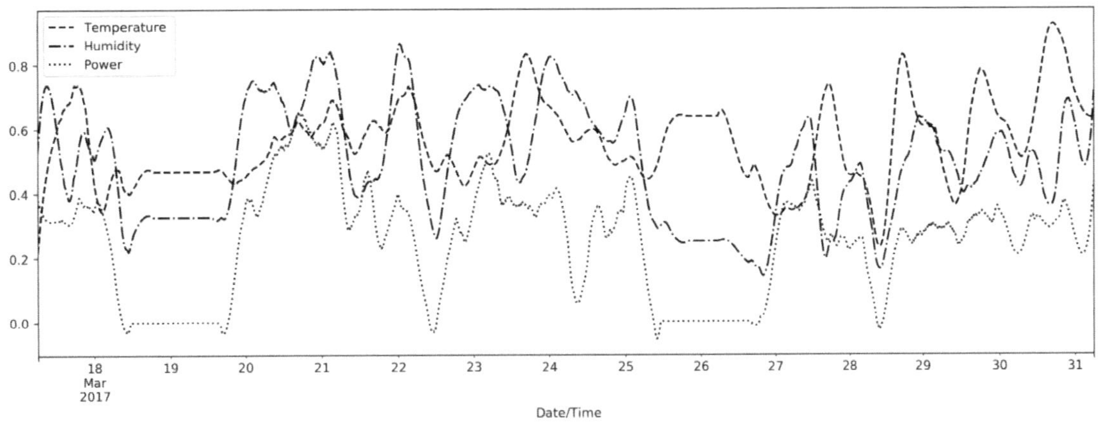

Figure 3. Plot Humidity / Power scaled and interpolated

We paid attention to split training and test data before preprocessing, hence before scaling and smoothing, otherwise information from test data could be leak in training data. In contrast to earlier studies (Radhika and Shashi 2009) (Rao et al. 2012), using the data mentioned to train a support vector machine gave mediocre results (R^2 value of 0.45). A trained neural network regressor gave an R^2 value of 0.58.

Better results of R^2 were produced with a random forest regressor: 0.68. Thus, it seems that using the latter regressor is a better choice than the former for making forecasts. Though, using a gradient boosting regressor produces a R^2 value of 0.71. Finally, after adjusting the alpha value and the number of hidden nodes, the neural network achieved the best value for R^2 of 0.77 (see Fiure 4).

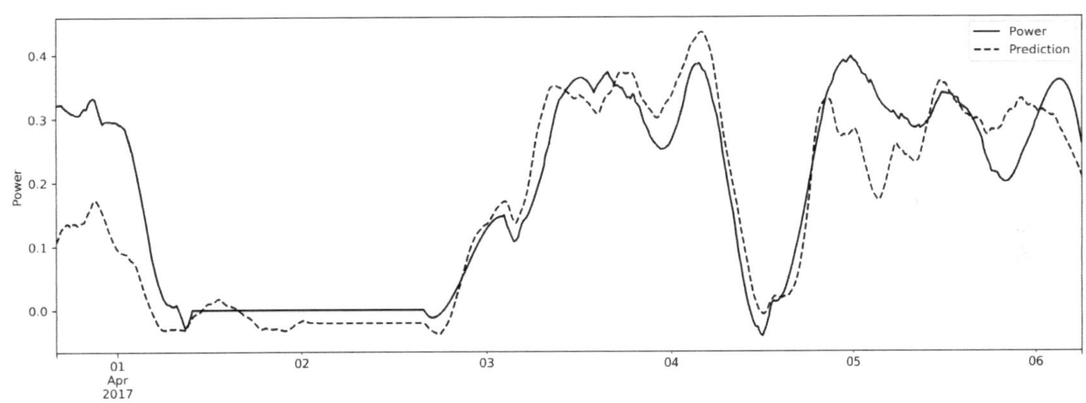

Figure 4. Prediction of power consumption (neural network)

In the next step, the long-term climate data were analyzed. The R^2 value for data from the already mentioned location was 0.4 (see Figure 5).

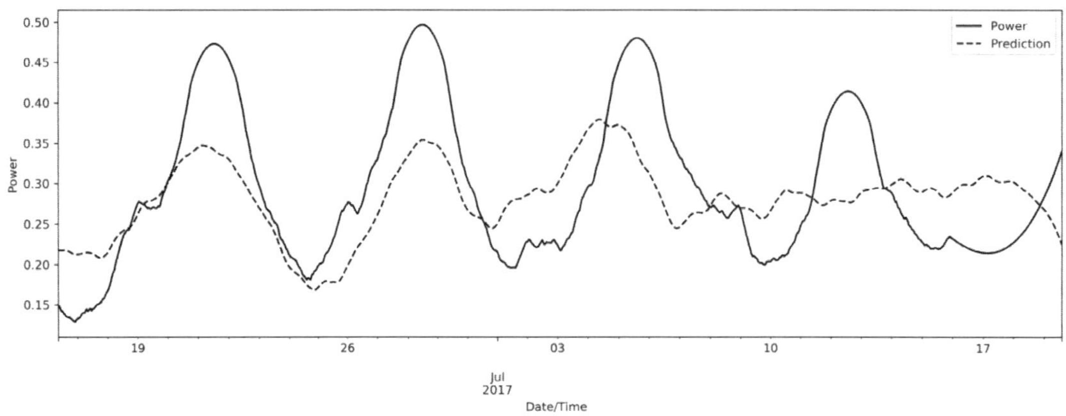

Figure 5. Long term prediction of power consumption

Thus, a short-term estimate with data of three weeks is better than a longer-term one with data of several months. Nevertheless, a trend can be predicted over a longer period of time, since the R^2 value is above 0 and also the curve of the estimated power values shows a similar progression to the actual values in the first days.

In addition to the climate data measured in the hall, weather data from outside the factory were included in the analysis. The R^2 value for predicting power consumption with weather data (two months) using a neural network was even good: 0.76. The curve-progression shows that the power consumption decreases when the humidity of the weather (outside) increases. This could be the proof that high humidity allows a static discharge, which reduces mechanical friction and so power consumption (Mardiguian 2009). Thus, a correlation between weather and power consumption of the system can be determined (Figure 6).

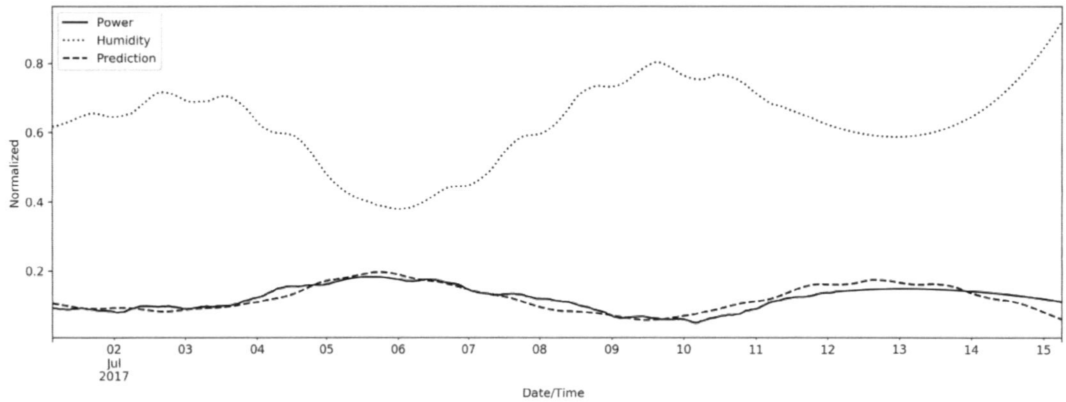

Figure 6. Prediction of power consumption using weather data

Finally, the relationship between the weather outside and the climate in the hall was examined. The input data were weather and climate data over a period of four weeks. As before the data were split into training and test data. It turned out that it is possible from training data to generate a correct estimate of nine days of indoor climate, with an R^2 value of 0.62. The progression of the curve for interior humidity corresponds to the estimated values (Figure 7).

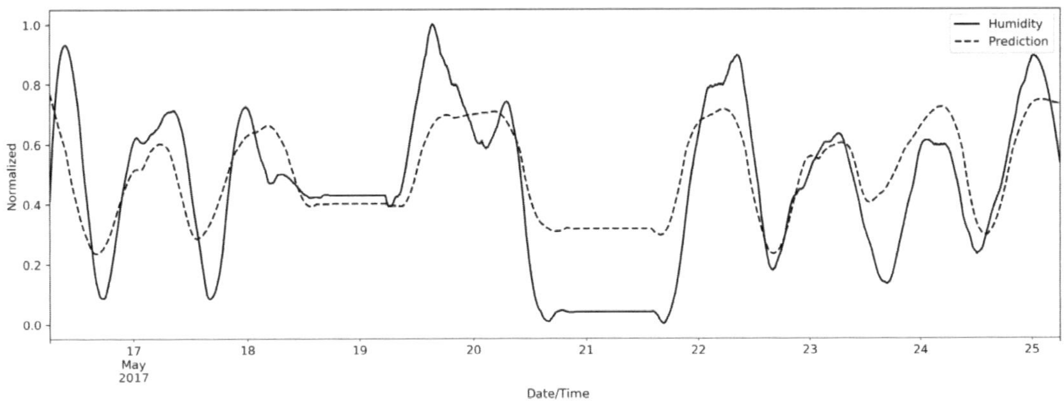

Figure 7. Correlation between weather and climate

Examination of a longer period of three months did not give a good result (R^2 value of -1.78) (Figure 8).

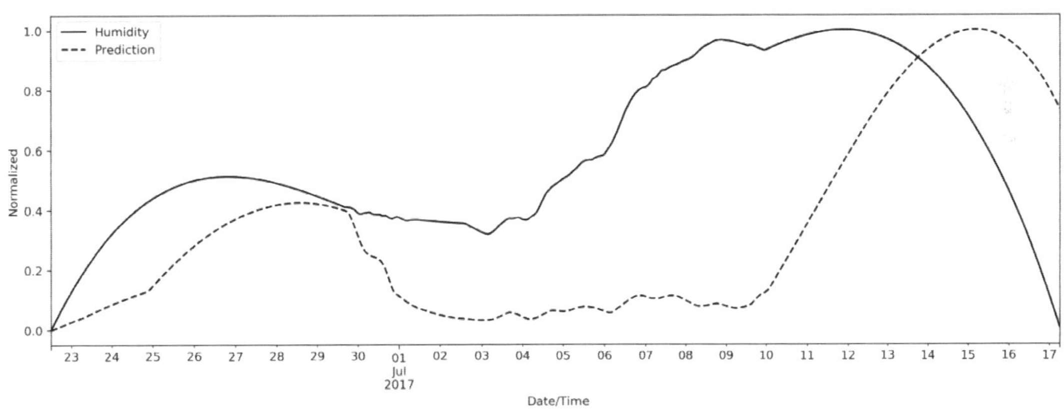

Figure 8. Correlation between weather and climate (long term)

6. CONCLUSION

The project dealt with the evaluation of plant data in combination with climate data in order to prove any correlations. The feasibility of this approach was proved. A correlation between the climatic data in the hall and the power consumption of the system parts could be proven. Weather conditions certainly have an influence on the power consumption of the plant components. For stable and correct forecasts, however, continuous measurements of power consumption should be available. The influence of the weather on the indoor climate could be proven. Short-term forecasts of the indoor climate can be made from existing weather data.

ACKNOWLEDGEMENT

We thank Norbert Städele, Nadine Fröhlich, Andreas Gmeiner, Susanne Kriesche and Florian Schöler-Niewiera for their valuable suggestions.

REFERENCES

Kabadayi, S. et al, 2006. Virtual sensors: Abstracting data from physical sensors. In *Proceedings of the 2006 International Symposium on on World of Wireless, Mobile and Multimedia Networks*, pp. 587-592.

Kapoor, P., and Bedi, S., 2013. Weather forecasting using sliding window algorithm. *ISRN Signal Processing, 2013.*

Kluyver, T. et al, 2016. Jupyter Notebooks-a publishing format for reproducible computational workflows. *In ELPUB*, pp. 87-90.

Kvålseth, T.O., 1985: Cautionary Note About R2. *In The American Statistician.*, Vol. 39, No. 4, pp 279-285.

Mardiguian, M., 2009. *Electro Static Discharge: Understand, Simulate, and Fix ESD Problems.* John Wiley & Suns, Hoboken, New Jersey.

McKinney, W., 2011. pandas: a foundational Python library for data analysis and statistics. *Python for High Performance and Scientific Computing*, Seattle, USA, pp. 1-9.

Meiller, D., 2017: Using Interactive Visual Analytics to analyze influences of climate on industrial production. *In International Conferences Computer Graphics, Visualization, Computer Vision and Image Processing 2017 and Big Data Analytics, Data Mining and Computational Intelligence 2017.* Lisbon, Portugal, pp. 357-358.

Pedregosa, F. et al, 2011. Scikit-learn: Machine learning in Python. *In Journal of machine learning research*, *12*(Oct), pp. 2825-2830.

Radhika, Y, and Shashi, M., 2009. Atmospheric Temperature Prediction using Support Vector Machines. *In International Journal of Computer Theory and Engineering*, Vol. 1, No. 1, pp. 55-58.

Rao, T., Rajasekhar, N., and Rajinikanth, T. V., 2012. An efficient approach for weather forecasting using support vector machines. *In International Conference on Computer Technology and Science (ICCTS) IPCSIT*, Vol. 47, pp. 208-212.

Schafer, R. W., 2011. What is a Savitzky-Golay filter? *IEEE Signal processing magazine*, *28*(4), pp. 111-117.

International Conferences Big Data Analytics, Data Mining and Computational Intelligence 2018;
Theory and Practice in Modern Computing 2018; and Connected Smart Cities 2018

DYNAMIC EPISTEMIC REASONING SYSTEM WITH AWARENESS (DEMO^{+A}) AND ITS LEGAL APPLICATION

Tetsuji Goto[1], Ryo Hatano[2] and Satoshi Tojo[1]
1School of Information Science, JAIST, 1-1 Asahidai, Nomi, Ishikawa, Japan
2 Tokyo University of Science, 2641 Yamazaki, Noda, Chiba, Japan

ABSTRACT

For a software tool of legal reasoning, it is important to describe the prediction about the result of a criminal action, because a crime is often caused by the unpredictability about the result of the defendant. In the court, the judge needs to investigate the predictability and the intention of the agent. Previously, we have formalized the reasoning process of judgment by action model in dynamic epistemic logic (DEL) and have attempted to describe the precedents. However, the prediction in legal cases depends not only on the states of knowledge but also on the limited degree of attention by agents. In this paper, we employ DEL with awareness for multi-agent to represent the predictability and model the typical criminal precedents. We propose a revised semantics of action model with awareness which can define the concrete action models to simulate the agent's considering process. We introduce an extension of model checking program DEMO to include the awareness (we call it DEMO^{+A}). We also present a GUI in this extended program to calculate the updated epistemic model easily and to classify precedents according to degree of prediction. In the end, we simulate the typical cases of criminal law by this newly developed tool and estimated them.

KEYWORDS

Dynamic Epistemic Logic, Action Model, Model Checking, Awareness, Legal Reasoning

1. INTRODUCTION

To determine criminality specified in the Penal Code (1907), at first, the judge examines whether the action of the accused comes under the external elements defined in the Penal Code (Tatbestand)[1] in the court. Then, the judge tries to determine the accused is responsible for the external elements by evaluating whether the accused's action is taken by intent (Mens rea)[2] or by negligence[3] (Oya, 2007; Yamaguchi, 2006). This is greatly influenced by the predictability of the results by the defendant.Thus far, our previous work (Goto & Tojo, 2014) focused on the predictability of the result (external elements) and formalized the reasoning process of judgement by Action Model in Dynamic Epistemic Logic (DEL) , but the frameworks has still been clumsy to describe these affairs. This makes hard to implement a concrete system or use the system in cases where the predictability is a issue. Therefore, we use awareness to explain the degree of intention and extended DEMO (Dynamic Epistemic MOdeling) (von Eijck, 2004) to handle the awareness (Goto & Tojo, 2015). In addition to this extension, we also make easier to set the calculation conditions and to examine the calculated result from GUI, especially to check the degree of intention.

The rest of this paper is organized as follows. First, we recall DEL with awareness (van Benthem, 2006, 2010) and provide our revised semantics in Section 2. Next, we explain our extended DEMO program, called "DEMO^{+A}" that can capture the notion of both knowledge and awareness in Section 3. We also show input/output GUI for DEMO^{+A}. Finally, we simulate some typical precedents which posses a different degree of intention to commit a crime and confirmed the calculated results in Section 4, and conclude with further remarks.

---

[1] The guilty acts or typified criminal acts sometimes called as the objective element of a crime.
[2] A guilty mind or an intention to commit a crime.
[3] A failure to take reasonable care when they act by taking account of the potential harm to other people, sometimes called as delinquency or negligence (Fujiki, 1975).

2. PRELIMINARIES

2.1 Limited Reasoning by Awareness

Awareness logic (Fagin & Halpern, 1988) is an extension of epistemic logic (Hintikka, 1962) and it distinguishes between "implicitly known information"(an agent knows eventually, but is not conscious of) and "explicitly known information"(an agent knows and is conscious of). That is, an agent infers according to his/her "explicit known information" and left "implicit information" as unconscious. Accordingly, awareness logic has the operator A and a formula $A\varphi$ stands for "an agent is aware of φ".

Now, let us recall awareness logic. A language L_A of awareness logic consists of the following vocabulary: a finite set of (atomic) propositional variables Prop, Boolean connectives $\neg$, $\wedge$ and modal operators K and A. The set of formulas of the language L_A is defined as follows:

$$\varphi ::= p \mid \neg\varphi \mid \varphi \wedge \varphi \mid K\varphi \mid A\varphi.$$

where $p \in$ Prop. As usual, $K\varphi$ stands for "an agent knows that φ."

An awareness model is a tuple $M = \langle W, R, \mathbf{A}, V \rangle$ where W is a non-empty set of worlds, $R \subseteq W \times W$ is an accessibility relation, $\mathbf{A} : W \rightarrow P(L_A)$ is an awareness function and V : Prop $\rightarrow P(W)$ is a valuation function. Here, awareness function $\mathbf{A}$ is introduced to return a set of formulas which an agent is aware of in the corresponding knowledge state. An epistemic model is the result of dropping an awareness function from an awareness model. Given any awareness model $M = \langle W, R, \mathbf{A}, V \rangle$ and any possible world $w \in W$, the satisfaction relation $M, w \models \varphi$ is defined as follows:

$M, w \models p$ *iff* $w \in V(p)$,
$M, w \models \neg\varphi$ *iff* $M, w \not\models \varphi$,
$M, w \models \varphi \wedge \psi$ *iff* $M, w \models \varphi$ and $M, w \models \psi$,
$M, w \models K_i\varphi$ *iff* $M, w' \models \varphi$ for all $w' \in W$ with wRw',
$M, w \models A\varphi$ *iff* $\varphi \in \mathbf{A}(w)$.

This language can be extended for the multi-agent system by using the modal operator for multi-agent like K_i, A_i, where $i \in I$ means an agent i of a set of agent I. Concerning the semantics, the model is defined like $M = \langle W, (R_i)_{i\in I}, \mathbf{A}, V \rangle$, where $(R_i)_{i\in I}$ is a relation for agent i and $\mathbf{A} : I \times W \rightarrow P(L_A)$ is an aware function which assigns the formula the agent i is aware of at the state.

2.2 Dynamic Epistemic Logic with Awareness

Van Benthem et al. extended dynamic epistemic logic (Harel, Kozen & Tiuryn, 2000; van Ditmarsch, 2008) to include the dynamics of awareness (van Benthem, 2006, 2010). They defined Action Model (Baltag, 2004) which has a post condition function to update the epistemic state of agents with awareness by an epistemic action.

The syntax of the language L_{DA} of DEL with awareness is based on that L_A of awareness logic. Besides Boolean connectives $\neg$, $\wedge$, and modal operators K and A, the language L_{DA} has actions operators ";" and "[ ]." Given a non- empty finite set I of agents, the set of formulas and the set of actions of this language are defined by simultaneous induction as follows:

$$\varphi ::= p \mid \neg\varphi \mid \varphi \wedge \varphi \mid K_i\varphi \mid A_i\varphi \mid [\alpha]\varphi$$
$$\alpha ::= (E, s) \mid \alpha; \alpha'$$

where $i \in I$, $\alpha; \alpha'$ means a continuous execution of the action α' after α, and (E, s) is an (pointed) action model defined as follows.

Definition 1 (Action Model with Awareness)

An action model with awareness is a tuple $E = \langle S, (R_i)_{i\in I}, Pre, Pos \rangle$ where S is a non-empty finite set of actions, $R_i \subseteq S \times S$ is a relation for agent i, Pre: $S \rightarrow L_{DA}$ is a precondition function, Pos: $I \times S \times P(L_{DA}) \rightarrow P(L_{DA})$ is a post condition function.

Definition 2 (DEL with Awareness)

Given any awareness model M and any possible world $w \in W$, the satisfaction relation $M, w \models \varphi$ is defined as follows:

$M, w \models p$ *iff* $w \in V(p)$,
$M, w \models \neg\varphi$ *iff* $M, w \not\models \varphi$,
$M, w \models \varphi \wedge \psi$ *iff* $M, w \models \varphi$ and $M, w \models \psi$,
$M, w \models K_i\varphi$ *iff* $M, w' \models \varphi$ for all $w' \in W$ with wR_iw'
$M, w \models A_i\varphi$ *iff* $\varphi \in \mathbf{A}(i, w)$,
$M, w \models [(\mathrm{E}, \mathrm{s})]\varphi$ *iff* $M, w \models \mathrm{Pre(s)}$ implies $M \otimes \mathrm{E}, (w, \mathrm{s}) \models \varphi$,
$M, w \models [\alpha; \alpha']\varphi$ *iff* $M, w \models [\alpha][\alpha']\varphi$

where $\mathbf{A}$: $\mathrm{I} \times W \rightarrow \mathrm{P}(\mathrm{L_{DA}})$ returns a set of formulas which an agent i is aware of at the state w and updated model $M \otimes \mathrm{E} = <W', (R_i')_{i \in I}, \mathbf{A}', V'>$ is defined as:

– $W' := \{ (w, \mathrm{s}) \mid M, w \models \mathrm{Pre(s)} \}$,
– $(w, \mathrm{s})\ R_i'\ (w', \mathrm{s}')$ *iff* wR_iw' and $\mathrm{sR_is'}$,
– $\mathbf{A}'(i, (w, \mathrm{s})) := \mathrm{Pos}(i, \mathrm{s}, \mathbf{A}(i, w))$,
– $(w, \mathrm{s}) \in V'(p)$ *iff* $w \in V(p)$.

As for the proof theory of DEL with awareness, Velázquez-Quesada (2011) provided reduction axioms and shown completeness theorem for that. In order to focus our attention on semantics side, we simply follow their results and omit the details.

2.3 Revised Semantics for Action Model with Awareness

As mentioned in the introduction, it is not enough to handle the predictability by the original DEL and it is a good way to do by the DEL with awareness. However the previous semantics of action model with awareness is hard to implement the concrete system, because the post-condition function of the original one map a set of all awareness formulas with a set of all and new awareness formulas, so it is required to define the function for each status respectively. This prevent from defining the general action models like listed in 3.1. And we mean to use this language for the precedents, it is required for an agent to become aware of the rule or causal relation itself. In this section, we provide revised semantics for action model with awareness. We use the same syntax and action model of DEL with awareness as shown in Section 2.2. Then, we also use the same satisfaction relation $M, w \models \varphi$ defined in Section 2.2 where the definition of updated model $M \otimes \mathrm{E} = <W', R_i', \mathbf{A}', V'>$ is revised as follows, using an awareness condition $\mathbf{F}$: $\mathrm{P}(\mathrm{L_{DA}}) \rightarrow \mathrm{L_{DA}}$, which assigns an function to an action point and an awareness condition function Awc: $\mathrm{P}(\mathrm{L_{DA}}) \times \mathrm{P}(\mathrm{L_{DA}}) \rightarrow \mathrm{L_{DA}}$ which returns a formula in $\mathrm{L_{DA}}$ and is defined according to each action model

Definition 3 (Update of knowledge and awareness)

Updated model $M \otimes \mathrm{E}$ is a tuple $<W', (R_i')_{i \in I}, \mathbf{A}', V'>$ where

$W' := \{ (w, \mathrm{s}) \mid M, w \models \mathrm{Pre(s)} \}$,
$(w, \mathrm{s})R_i'(w', \mathrm{s}')$ iff wR_iw' and $\mathrm{s}Ri\mathrm{s}'$,
$\mathbf{A}'(i, (w, \mathrm{s})) := \mathbf{A}(i, w) \cup \mathrm{Awc}(\mathbf{F}(i, \mathrm{s}), \mathbf{A}(i, w))$,
$V'(p) := \{ (w, \mathrm{s}) \in W' \mid w \in V(p) \}$.

In this definition, we assume that the awareness does not disappear immediately after some actions. In the real world, such actions as 'forget' or 'become not aware of' might be taken, but it is better way to begin with this assumption to estimate the effect of limited reasoning by applying the dynamic epistemic logic with awareness. Based on this, we can discuss the intention (e.g., the cause, the causal relation and the prediction about the result) as mentioned in the previous section. According to this assumption, for example, a formula $A\varphi \rightarrow [\mathrm{E}, \mathrm{s}]A\varphi$ becomes valid in this semantics, but is not the case in the original semantics. This implies that our revised semantics is actually different from the original one. Then, to avoid the complexity of increasing the number of states and links, we also assume the accessibility relation is an equivalence relation.

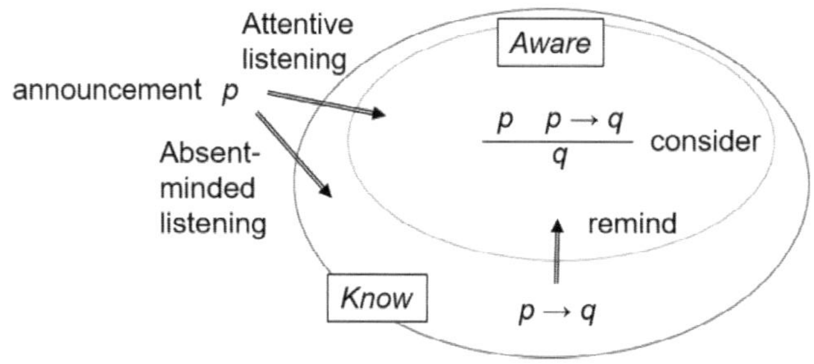

Figure 1. The model of consideration process of an agent

3. IMPLEMENTATION OF DEMO^{+A}

3.1 Modeling and Implementation of Consideration Process

In this section, we introduce a set of concrete epistemic actions into our DEL with awareness. First in Figure 1, we roughly depict our remind/consider actions, where an agent hears an announcement p in an absent-minded way. Also, the agent vaguely recognizes $p \rightarrow q$. In this occasion, the agent becomes conscious of this causality, and by *Modus Pones*[4] the agent comes to be aware of q by a consideration.

Now we distinguish the following epistemic actions.

[remind] if a proposition resides deeply in the agent's mind and he/she is not conscious of it, he/she is reminded it to his/her awareness domain.

[cons] if two premises of *Modus Ponens* reside in his/her awareness domain (aware of them), employ the inference.

> [cons(1)] is a shallow consideration, that is, to apply *Modus Ponens* only once;
>
> [cons(+)] is a deep consideration, that is, to apply *Modus Ponens* recursively and exhaustively, a sufficiently large number of finite times;
>
> [cons(+)] := [cons(1); cons(1); cons(1); . . .].

By these actions, $A_i(\varphi)$ and $A_i((\varphi \wedge \psi) \rightarrow \chi)$ results in $A_i(\psi \rightarrow \chi)$, since $(\varphi \wedge \psi) \rightarrow \chi \leftrightarrow \varphi \rightarrow (\psi \rightarrow \chi)$, by a shallow consideration. If $A_i\psi$ also exists in awareness domain, the agent obtains $A_i\chi$ by a deep consideration.

In addition, we provide two more epistemic actions. Here, we assume that the formulas in awareness domain exist necessarily in knowledge domain (the formulas are known to the agent.).

[abst] if an agent hears announcement φ in an absent-minded way, then φ enters Knowledge domain but not Awareness domain.

[atnt] if an agent hears the announcement φ attentively, φ enters Awareness domain.

3.2 Development of DEMO^{+A}

DEMO (von Eijck, 2004) is a modeling tool for dynamic epistemic logic and programmed in Haskell (Jones, 2002). This system simulates an updating process of an epistemic model, displays an action model and evaluates a formula in these models, and thus DEMO can be used to check our semantic intuitions about what goes on in the belief change.

We extended DEMO to handle the defined language with awareness and call it DEMO^{+A}. The awareness function is added to the original epistemic model as the list of awareness state as a tuple which consists of an agent, a state and a set of formula. The awareness condition function is also added to the action model as the list of a pair of formulas which consists of preceding conditions and a result.

Furthermore, those functions in the original program are replaced with the new corresponding data type, as well as the updating functions to change the awareness states, according to the conditions of the previous awareness state. In addition, we have developed the GUI of input and output for DEMO^{+A} to confirm the calculated result easily.

---

[4] An inference rule: p and $p \rightarrow q$ imply q.

3.3 Implementation of Epistemic Actions

In DEMO^{+A}, for example, Action Model of "Consider" mentioned in the previous subsection are defined as follows (Table 1, "actCons"). In the definition of actCons(agent, p, $p \rightarrow q$), the awareness condition function make the agent aware of q, if he/she is aware of p and $p \rightarrow q$. The other agents do not know the fact that this agent becomes aware of it.

Table 1. Definition of actCons

actCons a	
Action points	0,1 (Underlined number indicates the actual action state.
Precondition	0: φ, ψ
Awareness condition	a 0 :$[\varphi \rightarrow \psi, \psi] \rightarrow \psi$, 1: [ ] j 0:[ ], 1:[ ]
Relation	a[0],[1] j[0,1]
a, j: agent, [ ](blank) in Aware condition: No condition The number in relation [ ] indicates the action which cannot be distinguished.	

The other Action Models ("Hear attentively" , "Hear in an absent-minded way" and "Remind") to describe the actions are also defined and used to define the actions assumed in the considering process model of an agent (Figure 1).

- Shallow consideration cons1 (agt: agent, m: an awareness model) :refer to the Algorithm 1
- Deep consideration cons(+) (agt: agent, m: an awareness model) : repeat cons1 until no new information can be gained.
- Remind remind(agt: agent, m: an awareness model, φ: a formula) := update(m, actRemind(agt, φ))
- Hear Attentively atnt(agt: agent, m: an awareness model, φ: a formula) := update(m, actNotice(agt, φ)
- Hear in an Absent-minded way abst(agt: agent, m: an awareness model, φ: a formula) := update(m, actKnowIm(agt, φ))

Algorithm 1 Shallow consideration

```
Shallow consideration (cons(1) ( agt: agent, m: an awareness model))
Require: i ← agt
    m′ ← m
    while a state unchecked exists in W do
        if p, p → q ∈ A_i at some states and p,q are True at the states and q ∈ A_i then
            m' ← update(m, actCons(p,p → q))
            break
        end if
    end while    ▷ modus ponens can be applied.
m′               ▷ need not be updated
```

3.4 GUI for Input and Output

We developed new GUI of input and output for DEMO^{+A} to set the conditions and to confirm the calculated result easily (Figure 2). We use FLTKHS, which is a Haskell binding to FLTK GUI library. At the beginning of calculation, such items as the propositions (the number of propositions and their description), the common back ground for the defendant and the judge, the individual epistemic actions which change the awareness or knowledge status based on their testimony (These knowledge or awareness is required to be set with their acquiring action ("Hear attentively", "Hear in an absent-minded way" or "Remind"), the defendant's depth of consideration (once (cons(1)) or many times (cons(+))) and the cause and the external elements to calculate the predictability about the external element are required to be set in advance.

Then DEMO^{+A} calculate the final knowledge and awareness status according to the following steps.

1. Create an initial model according to the designated propositions.
2. Update the initial model by the knowledge or awareness of common back-ground for both an accused and a judge by using the defined actions.

3. Update the model which reflects the common knowledge by the actions derived from their testimony of each person respectively.
4. Check the awareness about cause and causal relation of an accused at the actual states from the view point of the judge.
5. Check the awareness about the external element (result) of an accused at the actual states from the view point of the judge.
6. Classify the precedent according to the awareness status about the cause, the causal relation and the external elements.
7. Display the calculated final model.
8. Draw the dot graph of the calculated mod

After calculation of the updated model, DEMO^{+A} can output the predictability, the knowledge status model, the dot-graph and the inference log.

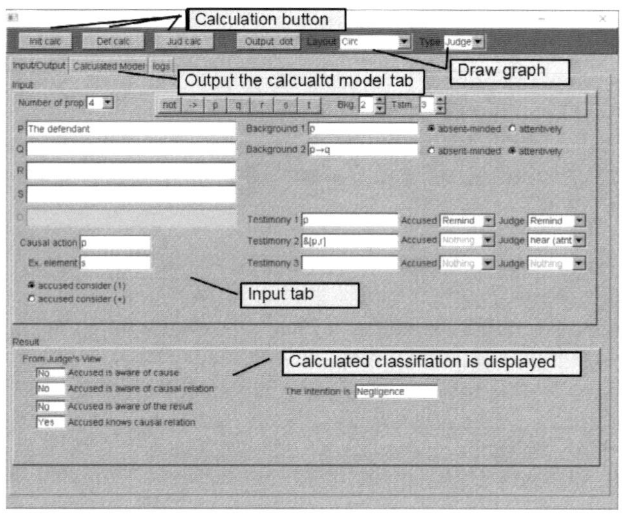

Figure 2. The main screen of DEMO^{+A} and its input/output

4. CALCULATION OF MODELS OF PRECEDENT

4.1 Example

We explain about the calculation of the precedents by DEMO^{+A} using the ex- ample of Case 1. At first, we set the propositions as the following.

p The thing the accused carries is the stimulant.

q The accused return to his country carrying with some things.

r The accused carries the stimulant.

And then we updated the initial knowledge status by their actions according to their testimony.

1. Both the accused and the judge explicitly know the accused carries something.
2. It is commonly but implicitly known that an accused who carries the stimulant shall be punished.
3. The accused reminds that if he carries the stimulant, he shall be punished.
4. The accused considers that this might be the stimulant.
5. The judge reminds that if the accused carries the stimulant, he shall be punished and explicitly knows the thing is the stimulant.
6. The judge considered carefully and repeatedly.

At the final knowledge status where the judge cannot distinguish, the judge is aware of the result but the accused is not.

Including this example, we set the criteria to classify the precedents by observing the result of each calculation of the selected precedent as follows and implemented this classification in our DEMO^{+A}.

Table 2. Classification criteria for precedents

$A\varphi \wedge A(\varphi \to \psi)$	Crime by a deterministic intention
$\neg A\varphi \wedge A(\varphi \to \psi)$	Crime by an indeterministic intention (Willful negligence, Generalized intention, Mistake of cause)
$A\varphi \wedge \neg A(\varphi \to \phi)$	Erroneous recognition of causal relation, Aggravation by result
$\neg A\varphi \wedge \neg A(\varphi \to \psi) \wedge K(\varphi \to \psi)$	Negligence
$\neg A\varphi \wedge \neg A(\varphi \to \psi) \wedge \neg K(\varphi \to \psi)$	Innocence

4.2 Calculation Result

The following typical precedents (Nishida et al., 2008) are modeled and calculated by DEMO^{+A} (Table 3). We attach the results of classification. These results match the judgment of the precedents. This tool may be able to simulate the multi-agent knowledge status where the limited knowledge is available other than the legal cases.

Table 3. Various pattern of precedents

Precedents	Judgment	Calculated result
Case 1: Accused of buying the stolen goods (No. Re238, 1967)	Willful negligence	Willful negligence / Generalized intention
Case 2: The Stimulant Drug Control Law violations (No. A1038, 1998)	Generalized intention	
Case 3: Accused of injury resulting in death case (No. A35, 2003)	Aggravation by result	Aggravation by result / Misunderstand of causal relation
Case 4: Accused of murder by strangulation (No. RE 517, 1923)	Misunderstand of causal relation	
Case 5: Hokkaido University electric scalpel case (No. U219, 1974)	Negligence	Negligence
Case 6: Accused of resulting in death during driving a truck (No. A193, 1986)	Negligence	
Case7: The use of HIV contaminated blood in Teikyo University Hospital (No. WA1879, 1996)	Innocence	Innocence
Case 8: Not the guilty of resulting in death (No. A183, 2002)	Innocence	

5. CONCLUSION

We have defined the consideration process of an agent and defined the concrete epistemic actions with awareness according to our new semantics of action model. By using these actions and modal operator A, we could model the deterministic or indeterministic intention, erroneous recognition of the causal relation, negligence and innocence in the precedents.

We have developed the precedent classification system by implementing the DEL with Awareness in the extended DEMO program (DEMO^{+A}) and a GUI is added to calculate easily. In this GUI, the classification of precedents was dis- played according to the proposed classification criteria. We have also simulated some typical variation of intentions for crime and confirmed the availability for legal cases. Our program can be obtained from our website (http://www.jaist.ac.jp/is/labs/tojo-lab/html/demo.html). We expect the system users to evaluate it, by which we can exert ourselves toward the further development of the rational and formal judgment system.

For further directions, it is considerable to expand the classification method to be applied other than legal cases. In the real world, there are often cases such that the predictability is an issue

ACKNOWLEDGEMENT

The work of the third author was supported by JSPS KAKENHI KIBAN(B) No.17H02258.

REFERENCES

Baltag, A.,. & Moss, L.S. (2004). Logics for epistemic program: *Synthese*, vol.139 Issue 2, pp.165-224.

Eijck, J.V. (2004). Dynamic epistemic modeling: Technical Report. Centrum voor Wiskunde en Informatica, Amsterdam.

Fagin, R., & Halpern, J.Y. (1988). Belief, awareness, and limited reasoning. Artificial Intelligence, 34(1), pp.39-76.

Fujiki, H. (eds.) 1975. *Criminal negligence, a dispute on the old and new negligence theory*. Gakuyoushobou (in Japanese)

Goto, T. and Tojo, S. (2014). Classification of Precedents by Modeling Tool for Ac- tion and Epistemic State: DEMO In:*Proceedings of the 8h International Workshop on Juris-Informatics*.

Goto, T. and Tojo, S. (2015). Predictability of Agent in Legal Cases In:*Proceedings of the 9h International Workshop on Juris-Informatics*.

Harel, D., Kozen, D. & Tiuryn, J. (2000). *Dynamic Logic. Foundations of Computing. Massachusetts*: MIT Press.

Haskell bindings to FLTK GUI toolkit https://github.com/deech/fltkhs

Hintikka, J. (1962). *Knowledge and belief: An introduction to the logic of the two notions*. Ithaca,NY: Cornell University Press.

Jones, S. P. (Eds.). (2002). Haskell 98 Language and Libraries. http://www.haskell.org/onlinereport/

Nishida, N. Yamaguchi, A. Saeki, H. (Eds.) (2008). *The 100 selected precedents of the Penal Code 1*, 6th edit. Yuhikaku (in Japanese).

Oya, M. (2007). *Lecture note on Criminal law: General part*. Seibundo (in Japanese).

Penal Code.(1907.) http://www.japaneselawtranslation.go.jp/law/detail/?id=1960

van Benthem, J., van Eijck, J., & Kooi, B. (2006). Logics of communication and change. In: *Information and Computation* Vol. 204, pp.1620-1662. Elsevier.

van Benthem, J. & Velázquez-Quesada, F.R. (2010). The dynamics of awareness. *Synthese* vol. 177, pp.5-27, Springer.

van Ditmarsch, H. et al. (2008). *Dynamic Epistemic Logic.* Springer.

Velázquez-Quesada, F.R. (2011). A Small steps in dynamics of information. *Thessis,* Institute for Logic, Language and Computation.

Yamaguchi, A. (2006). *Criminal law: General part*. Yuhikaku (in Japanese).

SCENARIO-BASED TESTING METHOD ADAPTATION FOR INFORMATION SYSTEMS TESTING

Anastasija Spakova and Marina Uhanova
Riga Technical University, Latvia

ABSTRACT

Due to the great number of existing testing methods, a problem related to choosing the most appropriate testing method arises. Often the tester has difficulty in choosing the necessary testing method for a particular information system to gain assurance that it implements all of its functions correctly. When testing an information system, it is also important to ensure that the system functions are interacting correctly. Therefore, the paper offers a solution to use scenario-based testing method that provides this aspect. This paper is dedicated to the description of the current situation in relation to scenario-based testing method application for testing information systems, as well as offering a solution of adaptation and usage of this testing method for testing information systems.

KEYWORDS

Scenario-Based Testing Method, Equivalence Partitioning, Boundary Value Analysis, Pairwise Testing

1. INTRODUCTION

User's work with the system is complicated and unpredictable. During system use many things can take place generating defects. Scenario-based testing method presents an opportunity to foresee various situations of user's system usage. This method adaptation for testing information systems becomes a topical task.

For testing information system, it is better to use several methods as each method focuses on a particular aspect to gain the necessary result (Black et al. 2012; Dustin 2002; Kaner et al. 2002). Therefore, scenario-based testing method is combined with other black box test design techniques – equivalence partitioning, boundary value analysis and combinatorial testing method – pairwise testing.

This paper is structured in the following way: the second section gives characterisation and description of scenario-based testing method and examines the problem of using scenario-based testing method. The third section offers a solution to this problem. The fourth section reviews the practical application of the offered solution and summarizes the results. The fifth section includes conclusions and further work.

2. SCENARIO-BASED TESTING METHOD AND PROBLEM OF USING IT

In testing, there are such terms as test scenario and test case. They are developed by the tester so that he would know how to test the system and what functionality needs to be tested. One of the test scenario definitions is the following: "Test scenario is a hypothetical story that is used to help the tester to consider a complicated problem or system" (Kaner et al. 2004b; Kaner et al. 2011; Kaner 2013).

The test case is a complex of test input data, execution provisions and expected results to enable checking the compatibility of the object to be tested for the previously defined requirements (ISTQB Exam certification). In comparison with the test scenario, the test case is oriented to checking a particular system function, whereas the test scenario tests interaction of several functions.

Scenario-based testing method deals with development of test scenarios where the scenario describes a hypothetical situation. System testing with scenarios allows an opportunity to check how the system processes hypothetical situation and gives an opportunity to involve and check common work of many system functions (Kaner 2003).

Scenario-based testing method cannot guarantee high code coverage as all the black box testing, but it can guarantee high coverage level for requirements (Kaner 2010). Scenario-based testing does not intend for systematic test scenario development. It causes difficulties for development of test scenarios. Therefore, the author (Buwalda 2004) offers to solve the following questions:

- How to determine which requirements are covered with test cases/scenarios and which are not?
- How to combine requirements for test cases/scenarios to check them?
- What combination of requirements to make for test cases/scenarios?
- How many test cases/scenarios must be made to cover all the necessary requirements?

The authors of this paper believe that the aforementioned questions will help solving significant problems in writing test scenarios as the main thing is to cover all the functionality with test scenarios and to ensure qualitative testing.

3. PROBLEM SOLVING METHODS

The most important precondition for comprehensive system testing is systematic development of test cases/test scenarios (Grochtmann 1994). Scenarios are usually described with natural language as they are not formal or do not use a structured formal model (Ryser et al. 1999).

The authors of the paper offer to implement classification tree method for developing test scenarios. Classification tree method is a black box test design technique, where test cases are described as classification tree and are developed to execute one input data and/or output data value that represents their own input data/output data class (Black et al. 2012). The structure of classification tree can be seen in Figure 1 (Kruse 2013; Miranda 2011).

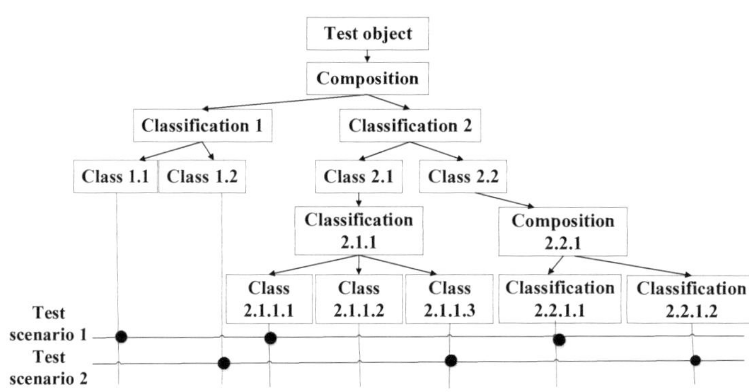

Figure 1. Classification Tree Structure

The essence of the offered testing methodology by using a scenario-based testing method with other testing methods is the following:

1. To begin development of test scenarios, at first scenario-based testing method is used. It means that in a system test objects are distributed to be tested.
2. For every test object must be written a story where it is used in a system, i.e., all the situations where this object is used and how it is used must be written. The story can be positive or negative.
3. Make test item and test condition scheme for a test object by combining all the stories (Figure 2). It means that it is necessary to divide test object functionality to be tested in smaller items that are necessary to be tested. Test scenario is based on an aim or test condition. Test condition is a component or system item that could be tested with one or many test cases or test scenarios, for instance, function, transaction, characteristic or quality, quality attribute or structural element. Test conditions are based on test item specifications' analysis. The task of test conditions is to help the tester understand what is necessary to be

tested. Test item is an individual element that must be tested. Usually there is one test object and several test items. Here the test object is a component or system that must be tested (Black et al. 2012). Test items and test conditions scheme example can be seen in Figure 3.

4. By using equivalence partition, boundary value analysis and pairwise testing, a classification tree is made. From classification tree, test scenarios are made. A fragment of classification tree (Figure 4) based on a scheme of test items/conditions pictured in Figure 3.

Definitions of used testing methods:

- Equivalence partitioning – input data is divided in equivalence classes where only one test value of each class must be tested (Black et al. 2012).
- Boundary value analysis method – checks test values that are located on equivalence class boundaries (Black et al. 2012).
- Combinatorial testing method allows combining input data systematically based on a scheme (Miranda 2011).
- Pairwise testing – is it a combinatorial testing method that checks each pair of parameters in all the possible combinations. The research shows that in majority integration defects show up when interaction between pair of parameters takes place (Black et al. 2012; Grindal et al. 2006; Rice 2006).

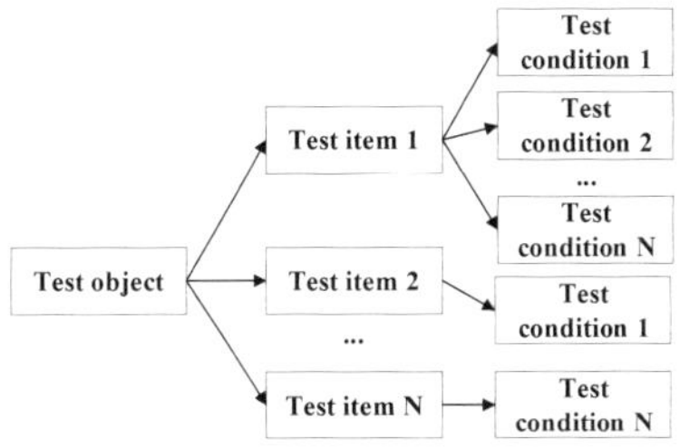

Figure 2. Scheme for Making Test Items/Test Conditions

Figure 3. Test object "Web page" Scheme Fragment of Test Items/Test Conditions

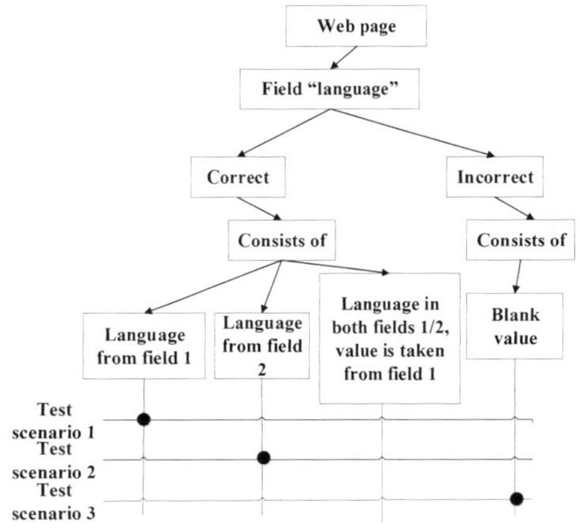

Figure 4. Test Object Classification Tree Fragment of "Web Page"

Figure 5 schematically shows the common test scenario development process. As it can be seen in Figure 5, test object has stories written, test object is divided in test items and test conditions. Based on this distribution, a classification tree is made. For determining classification tree classes equivalence partitioning and boundary value analysis methods are applied.

From classification tree, test scenarios are written by combining test input data/output data classes with pairwise testing method. Figure 5 shows a scheme with one test object, but there can be many test objects in a system where each test object has stories written, every test object is divided in test items and test conditions, every object has a classification tree made and test scenarios written.

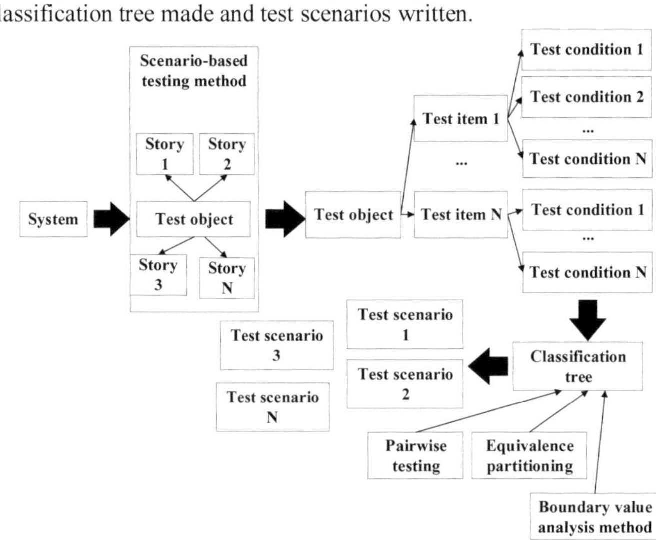

Figure 5. Complete Test Scenarios Making Process and Testing Methods

4. PRACTICAL APPLICATION AND RESULTS

The developed testing approach for making test scenarios was used for real information system testing that is developed by software development company where one of the authors of the paper is employed. One web page of the system was tested. This web page contains 13 elements (fields) where each element was tested.

For assessment of the developed testing approach, the following metrics are used:

- Number of found defects.
- Failure size. Failure size – number of test cases/test scenarios in percentage in a set of test cases/test scenarios that have been unsuccessfully executed due to a defect or that have found a particular defect (Grindal et al. 2006).
- Requirements coverage (RC). It indicates to what extent the requirements are covered with test cases/test scenarios in percentage. This metric can be calculated following the formula in (1) (Software testing 2015).

$$RC = \frac{\begin{matrix}Number\,of\ requirements\\ covered\ with\,test\ scenarios\end{matrix}}{\begin{matrix}Total\ number\\ of\ requirements\end{matrix}} * 100 \quad (1)$$

The acquired testing results by using the developed testing approach are compared with the previous testing results in the company that were acquired in the last testing stages within the time period from 07.2016 to 05.2017. In order to be able to compare the results, the test cases used in the company were analysed and the defects registered in the company were analysed.

58 test scenarios were made: 22 positive and 36 negative test scenarios by using the developed approach. The used approach allowed finding 11 new defects that had not yet been found with the existing test cases

that had been developed in the company as the test scenarios developed within the work framework are more comprehensive, check various input data and their combinations. Whereas the basic test cases are used in the company that check the basic system actions to make sure that the system's main functionality operates properly.

Within the time period from 07.2016 to 05.2017 there were 297 defects found in the system to be tested that are related to the web page which was tested within this work framework and its elements (fields).

To be able to see that the developed testing approach could improve the testing results, the previously registered company's defects (297 defects) were analysed and it was determined whether the developed test scenarios could find them or not. The defects are distributed by priorities: critical, high, average and low (Figure 6).

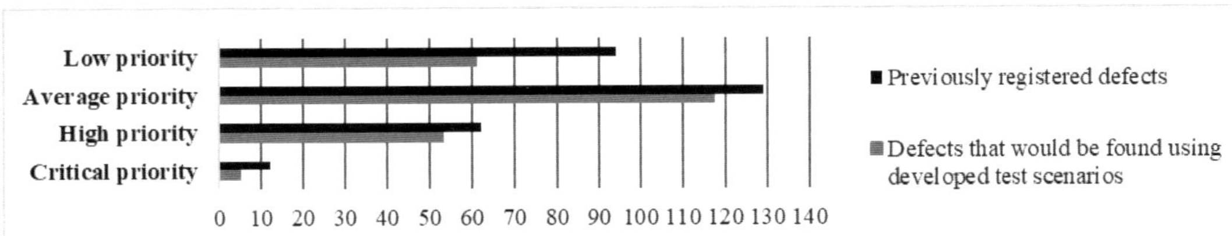

Figure 6. Ratio of Registered and Prevented Defects

From Figure 6 it can be seen that the developed test scenarios are efficient for finding defects of critical, high and average priority. The developed testing approach can also find defects of average priority as not only the most important fundamental test scenarios were executed, but also test scenarios that thoroughly test the functionality by modelling various test scenarios with various input data combinations. Low priority defects are usually not related to system functioning correctness, but the developed test scenarios are more oriented to testing system functionality; therefore, they would not be able to find all or almost all the previously registered defects. For instance, defects reviewed within the company are grammatical errors in texts, cosmetic defects of interface, unnecessary symbol in a text and others.

58 test scenarios were made by using the developed testing approach. In order to compare the results of the requirements coverage, 58 test cases that were made in the company were selected. The test cases were executed in the last three testing stages (55 test cases) and 3 additional test cases were selected. The test cases are also related to the previously mentioned web page which was selected for testing.

The developed test scenarios gave 100% requirements coverage (Table 1) and provided that all the web page functionality that was researched was tested. 100% requirements coverage can be explained with the fact that test scenarios are made based on specification of requirements for every system element, as well as making of test items/test conditions scheme and classification tree helped understand what should be tested and did not allow missing a requirement that should be tested. Requirements coverage for test cases developed within the company is not 100%. It can be explained with the fact that test cases for the web page were written by different testers, as well as this functionality was divided in various test conditions, therefore, some requirements were possibly forgotten to be covered by test cases or it might have happened due to inattentiveness.

Table 1. Requirements Coverage

	Number of requirements covered with test scenarios/test cases	Total number of requirements	Requirements coverage
Test scenarios developed within work framework	135	135	100%
Test cases developed within the company	129	135	95,5%

It is important to mention that if 100% coverage is achieved, it does not mean that the covered functionality is 100% tested. The coverage metric measures only one aspect among many other aspects. For instance, two different test cases can achieve one and the same coverage, but input data of one test case can find the defect, but input data of the other test case can miss the defect (Black et al. 2012). Every requirement must be tested with the maximum number of possible input data sets. The current test cases that were developed within the company cover each requirement with one set of possible input data because the task of these test cases is to test that the developed system function works properly. Whereas the developed test scenarios foresee testing for various input data for one requirement. That is why with the used testing metric it can be seen how many requirements are covered with test cases/test scenarios, but it cannot be precisely said to what extent every requirement had been tested. The web page includes several fields (elements). Every field has its own requirements. Within the framework of this work it is necessary to determine to what extent every field is tested. To determine this, three additional questions are posed:

- How many test scenarios/test cases are made for each field?
- Was positive testing performed for field functionality test and how many test scenarios/test cases were made for field positive testing?
- Was negative testing performed for field functionality test and how many test scenarios/test cases were made for field negative testing?

The more test cases/test scenarios test field requirements the higher is the probability to find any defect for a field that is being tested. The developed testing approach intends for making test items/test conditions scheme, based on the requirements specification and further make classification tree (see Figure 5). Therefore, it can be said that web page field classification tree classes represent various input data and situations to test field requirement or several requirements. Therefore, for determining the number of scenarios, the number of classification tree classes a field has is taken into account (i.e. how much input data or situations are tested for a field). Every class or input data value is regarded as a test scenario. For instance, for the "language" field there are three correct classification tree classes "language from field 1", "language from field 2", "language in both fields 1/2, value is taken from field 1" (Figure 4). Thus, three test scenarios are used for testing the field "language". Total number of test scenarios for each field (element) (positive and negative testing) can be seen in Figure 7.

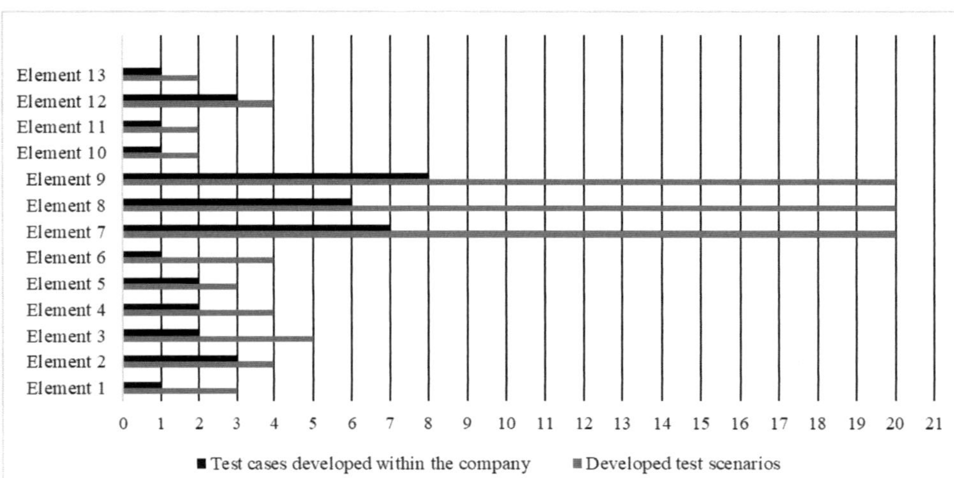

Figure 7. Total number of Test Cases/Test Scenarios for Each Field (Positive and Negative Testing)

The developed test scenarios also provided coverage of every field with a bigger number of scenarios comparing with the test cases that are used within the company.

The more test cases/test scenarios find one and the same defect, the higher possibility to find this defect (Grindal et al. 2006). Thus, to evaluate the developed test scenarios testing metric was chosen – failure size. Failure size is set for each of the 11 found defects (Table 2).

Table 2. Failure Size

Defect No.	Number of test scenarios affected by the defect	Failure size
1.	58	100%
2.	8	13,79%
3.	12	20,69%
4.	8	13,79%
5.	8	13,79%
6.	22	37,93%
7.	22	37,93%
8.	28	48,28%
9.	22	37,93%
10.	12	20,69%
11.	6	10,34%

By analysing the company's test results that were acquired in the last three testing stages within the time period from 07.2016 to 05.2017, the highest number of test cases that is unsuccessfully executed due to one and the same defect or shows one and the same defect is 3 test cases (Table 3).

Table 3. Failure Size in Three Testing Stages

Testing stages	Number of tests cases related to the web page	Failure size for defect related to 3 test cases
First stage	18	16,67%
Second stage	13	23,08%
Third stage	24	12,5%
Total number of test cases in three stages and three additionally chosen test cases	58	5,17%

A conclusion can be made that there is a higher probability for finding defects in developed test scenarios in comparison with company's test cases, as defects that were found by the developed test scenarios with the offered approach, have a higher failure size than defects that were found with company's test cases by testing the web page.

5. CONCLUSIONS AND FURTHER RESEARCH

This paper offers adapting scenario-based testing method for testing an information system by using the solution offered by the authors of the paper to use combination of various testing methods and introduce structure for developing test scenarios. The offered testing methodology is planned to be used for checking laboratory works of students in the study subject "Algorithmization and Programming of Solutions" at RTU FCSIT (Faculty of Computer Science and Information Technology).

Scenario-based testing method does not intend systematic scenario development that is the main factor for providing qualitative testing. The authors of the paper offer combining scenario-based testing method with other testing methods to introduce structure for development of test scenarios. As a result, an approach was developed to test information systems with scenario-based testing method. This approach can be used for testing any information system where functional black box testing is used. As the developed testing approach provides structure for development of testing scenarios, the made test scenarios can be easily modified if any system functionality is modified.

The developed testing approach was evaluated according to metrics (the number of found defects, requirements coverage and failure size) and the acquired testing results were compared to the previous testing results in the company that were acquired during the last testing stages within the period from 07.2016 to

05.2017. To be able to compare the results, the test cases used and defects registered within the company were analysed. It can be concluded that the developed testing approach could find important defects and improve the quality of the system to be tested, as well as bring assurance that the system operates properly and all the functional requirements are tested.

Manual test execution in the system asks for a significant amount of time and attention from the tester not to allow errors in the test execution. Therefore, the next step would be automatization of test scenarios. It is planned to implement the research of possibility of developed test scenario automatization with JUnit and automatize the developed test scenarios.

REFERENCES

Black, R., et al, 2012. *Foundations of software testing: ISTQB certification*. 3rd Edition, Cengage Learning EMEA, Hampshire.

Buwalda, H., 2004. *Soap Opera Testing*. Available at: http://www.testingeducation.org/BBST/testdesign/Buwalda_soap_opera_testing.pdf (Accessed: 1 April 2018).

Dustin, E., 2002. *Effective Software Testing: 50 Specific Ways to Improve Your Testing*. Addison-Wesley.

Grindal, M., et al, 2006. *An Evaluation of Combination Strategies for Test Case Selection*. Available at: http://barbie.uta.edu/~mehra/54_An%20Evaluation%20of%20Combination%20Testing%20Strategies.pdf (Accessed: 31 March 2018).

Grochtmann, M., 1994. Test Case Design Using Classification Trees. *STAR'94*. Washington, USA, pp. 1-11.

ISTQB Exam certification. Available at: http://istqbexamcertification.com/ (Accessed: 30 March 2018).

Kaner, C. and Bach, J., 2004a. *Black Box Software Testing, Part 6 - Scenario Testing*. Available at: http://www.testingeducation.org/k04/bbst6_2004.pdf (Accessed: 30 March 2018).

Kaner, C. and Bach, J., 2004b. *Black Box Software Testing, Part 19 Multi-variable testing*. Available at: www.testingeducation.org/k04/documents/bbst19_2004.ppt (Accessed: 31 March 2018).

Kaner, C. and Fiedler R.L., 2011. *Black Box Software Testing: Introduction to Test Design: A Survey of Test Techniques*. Available at: http://www.testingeducation.org/BBST/testdesign/BBSTTestDesign2011pfinal.pdf (Accessed: 31 March 2018).

Kaner, C., 2003. *What Is a Good Test Case*. Available at: http://www.kaner.com/pdfs/GoodTest.pdf (Accessed: 1 April 2018).

Kaner, C., 2010. *Scenario Testing*. Available at: http://kaner.com/pdfs/CAST2010ScenarioTestingTutorial.pdf (Accessed: 31 March 2018).

Kaner, C., 2013. *An Introduction to Scenario Testing*. Available at: http://www.testingeducation.org/BBST/testdesign/Kaner_ScenarioIntroVer5.pdf (Accessed: 31 March 2018).

Kaner, C., et al, 2002. *Lessons Learned in Software Testing: A Context-Driven Approach*. 1st Edition, John Wiley & Sons, Inc., New York.

Kruse, P.M., 2013. *Enhanced Test Case Generation with the Classification Tree Method*. Free University of Berlin, Berlin.

Miranda, E., 2011. *An Illustrated Introduction to the Classification Tree Method*. Pittsburgh, USA. Available at: http://mse.isri.cmu.edu/software-engineering/documents/faculty-publications/miranda/mirandaclassifcationtreemethodillustrated.pdf (Accessed: 31 March 2018).

Rice, R.W., 2006. *Achieving Test Case Efficiency By Combining Use Case Scenarios And Orthogonal Arrays*. Available at: https://conference.eurostarsoftwaretesting.com/wp-content/uploads/th15-2.pdf (Accessed: 31 March 2018).

Ryser, J. and Glinz, M., 1999, A Scenario-Based Approach to Validating and Testing Software Systems Using Statecharts. *The 12th International Conference on Software and Systems Engineering and their Applications ICSSEA'99*. Paris, France, pp. 1-7.

Software Testing. 2015. Available at: https://software-testing.org/testing/testovoe-pokrytie-test-coverage-kriterii-testovogo-pokrytiya-v-testirovanii-po.html (Accessed: 31 March 2018).

AESTHETIC GRADING: COLOR CORRECTION VIA NEURAL NETWORKS

John Kundert-Gibbs
The University of Georgia, USA

ABSTRACT

Color grading and correction for film and video is a significant and complex aesthetic and technical task that requires a trained operator and a good deal of time. We compare two deep neural network frameworks—a classification network and a conditional generative adversarial network, or cGAN—for quality of their output as potential automated solutions to color correction. Results are very good for both networks, though each has its own problem areas. The classification network has issues with generalizing due to the need to collect and especially to label all data being used to train it. The cGAN on the other hand can use unlabeled data, which is much easier to collect. The cGAN, however, directly changes image pixels, introducing potential damage to the images, so multiple adjustments to the network need to be made to create high quality output. We find that the data labeling issue for the classification network is a less tractable problem than the image correction and continuity issues discovered with the cGAN method, which have direct solutions. Thus we conclude the cGAN is the more promising network with which to automate color correction and grading.

KEYWORDS

Color Correction, Generative Adversarial Neural Network

1. INTRODUCTION

While color correction—also known as color grading—is a relatively invisible task for viewers, it is nonetheless supremely important to the professional look of a finished film or video. Color correction, in essence, takes the raw footage from a video/film shoot and adjusts elements—such as exposure, contrast, black point, white point, and blue-orange cast[1]—to achieve a higher quality and more uniform look for takes shot under different lighting conditions and on different days. The task requires a good deal of operator expertise, time, and expensive equipment, and thus costs a large amount of money—upwards of $10,000US for an independent film ("Pricing Indy Feature", 2015). Thus color correction can be a significant cost to a small film (or even a large budget one). Even more critically, the expertise involved in performing the task of color grading is beyond the abilities or budget of most amateur filmmakers, YouTube producers, home video makers, and so on. For such people, color grading is something akin to voodoo, and thus amateur videos look… amateur: elements like color, contrast, and black point are not adjusted properly, and there is little continuity between shots.

For both professional and amateur filmmakers an automated solution to color correction would be most welcome, both for cost savings and for the very ability to have a "one click" solution to this complex and time-consuming task. While the 'artistic' task of correcting color to please the human eye, as well as to hide discontinuities in coloring for different shots, is at the same time precise, subtle, aesthetic, and fuzzy (i.e., not deterministic), and thus seems an unlikely domain for computers, we show here that color grading/correction can be learned and executed well by either of two different neural network architectures. In essence, a color grader makes a number of traceable, quantitative steps to achieve the artistic goals of creating an intended look and to hide the variations between shots in a film. These steps from an input (uncorrected) image to an output (corrected) image can in fact be learned by neural networks, both as a classification problem via a classification network, and as a generative problem via a conditional generative adversarial network. In both cases, the networks produce excellent results, though each has some issues.

[1] Most professional video is shot using a log format, so color correction/grading also includes running footage through a CLUT (Color Look-Up Table). This is a well established automated task and is thus outside the scope of this paper.

2. BACKGROUND AND ASSET COLLECTION

Though deep neural networks have been studied since the 1980s (Hinton, 1989, Olshausen, 1997), improvements in computer speed, GPU speed, and better algorithms by the early 2000s generated a renaissance in deep neural net research (Hinton, 2006, Benegio, 2007). It was, however, a deep neural net winning the Imagenet 2012 competition (Krizhevsky, 2012) that saw the beginning of a veritable flood of research into this field. From understanding words (Mikolov, 2013), to image recognition (Ciresan, 2012, Zisserman, 2014), to image caption generation (Vinyals, 2015), to colorizing black and white images (Reinhard, 2001, Iizuka, 2016, Zhang, 2016), deep neural networks have, in well under a decade, become the go-to AI architecture for numerous tasks that people once considered beyond computer AI ability. It is the combination of precision (of feature recognition, for example) with the 'human' quality of understanding large-scale semantic elements in images (Chen, 2015, Gatys, 2016) that is particularly important to the project of color correction. In previous work we explored the semantic issue of image-based recall (IBR) (Kundert-Gibbs, 2017) by building off a classification network (Vedaldi, 2016, Vedaldi, 2017b), so this type of network is an obvious contender for color correction, which bears some underlying similarities to IBR. In addition, we examine the relatively newly developed conditional generative adversarial network, or cGAN (Mirza, 2014), modifying the network described in (Isola, 2017) to work on the color correction problem. The two network architectures have complementary advantages and disadvantages, discussed below.

As with most neural network problems (and indeed modern AI as a whole), asset collection is a significant issue. Neural networks prefer large data sets, and classification networks require labeling—their major disadvantage compared to cGANs, which can learn in a semi-supervised setting (Radford, 2015). Film, fortunately, produces an almost limitless number of frames (still images which make up a movie), and thus data can be produced. There are, however, two issues: one is that one needs matched sets of uncorrected and corrected images to train on; the second is that, at least for classification networks, these images must be labeled somehow. For our initial work, we needed a small-to-medium-sized data set of at least 10,000 uncorrected images, each of which needed to have a corresponding corrected image as well as proper labeling to indicate the issue with the uncorrected image.

Josh Kundert-Gibbs, professional cinematographer and color grader, was able to provide us with properly adjusted and logged sample images in the following manner. He properly color graded a number of shots—mostly "talking heads" from a documentary he was shooting—providing 675 frames broken down as follows: 15 different "shots" (one person talking) of 45 frames each. This set of images is "correct" in the sense that Kundert-Gibbs deems them to be so—an artistic judgment, obviously. While the judgment is artistic/aesthetic, many of the elements of good color correction, such as hiding the variability of shots, and "not too green," can be determined fairly effectively, if qualitatively, by looking at the group of shots. Beyond this, the value judgment that the shots look "good" according to a professional's opinion is something that knowledge engineers are familiar with: inputs and outcomes are often somewhat fuzzy when learning from big data (McClean, 2000, Wood, 1989). For these reasons, though "properly color graded" is an opinion by one individual, it is a professional opinion and thus can be respected for our training/testing data set. To provide the 'uncorrected' (or detuned) images, at our direction Kundert-Gibbs then created a number of carefully controlled incorrect images as follows. He took the 675 'perfect' images and detuned them via Davinci Resolve (color grading software), creating 24 sets of images (675 in each set to match the perfect set), each of which sets has one and only one element detuned in a controlled manner. For example, he adjusted each of the 675 'perfect' images to make the green channel one of three levels too high (say 33%, 66%, or 100% too high). Each of these detuned images is labeled with the error (e.g., OneLevelTooGreen001.png) so that a classification network can judge its success or failure in classifying the problem with the image. In total, Kundert-Gibbs produced 24 sets of detuned images, each with a single problem area, creating a detuned database of 16,200 incorrect images. Though we did not need labeled images for the cGAN tests, we utilized the same set of data in order to compare the quality of the output versus the classification network under the same training circumstances.

3. EXPERIMENTAL SETUP

As noted above, we simultaneously explored two options for our work: one to classify color correction errors via a classification network; the other to generate 'perfect' images that would be able to fool a discriminator network as it compared the generator's output with the target (corrected) image. These two paths are fundamentally different in their approach. The classification network's goal is to identify what is wrong with the image (e.g., 33% too much orange, or black point set 66% too low) and return the result, allowing a user—or an automated plug-in extension—to adjust settings on a color grading program. The cGAN, on the other hand, actually changes input pixels to generate an entirely new output image that will (hopefully) fool the adversarial discriminator network into thinking its output is in fact the target image. The primary advantage of the cGAN is that it can utilize any set of corrected/uncorrected image pairs (of which there are a vast supply), while the primary concern with this network is that it will do damage to the image, reducing the quality of the output. An image, for example, might have its green cast adjusted properly by the cGAN, but the generator network might insert random noise into the image, or, worse, insert large-scale artifacts into the image. In these cases, the output images will be sub-optimal, likely to the extent that a viewer will notice the problems. The primary advantage of the classification network is that it will "do no harm." In other words, given that it is a classification network, it will only tell a program/user which adjustments to make to fix a given problem (e.g., if the image is two levels too orange, the output would tell the plug-in to turn the orange level down two levels). The primary disadvantage for the classification network is that it requires massive amounts of labeled data, which is not only time-consuming but an extremely challenging task. In our case, for example, we made 24 singular de-tuning adjustments to our 'perfect' images (black point 66% too high, etc.). This only accounts for one grading issue at a time, however. What happens when there are two issues simultaneously? Or when there is an unknown mix of issues? This problem can make generating properly labeled outputs for classification extremely challenging, as a color grader might make dozens of adjustments to get an image to look right to her. Thus without a large and varied amount of correctly labeled images to train on, the classifier might not generalize well. While our concerns for each network are significant, they are, interestingly, complementary: where one network might have difficulties (e.g., inserting artifacts into an image), the other should do well in that area.

For both networks, we randomly selected approximately 2/3 of the 16,200 images for training, with about 1/6 for testing, and 1/6 held out for validation. For our classification network, we utilized matconvnet, an open source convolutional neural network construction system built to run within MATLAB Vedaldi, 2017a), modifying the fast VGG classification network included in the package. For our conditional generative adversarial network, we modified the open source pix2pix cGAN that is built on the torch convolutional neural network framework (Isola, 2017b, http://torch.ch). For both networks, our interest was primarily in low frequency issues, like color casts or issues with contrast, as shown in Figure 1. Therefore we adjusted the parameters of each network to be more attuned to low frequency issues as opposed to the more usual concern researchers have with high frequency elements of images (e.g., feature detection). Though CNNs have traditionally been trained primarily to deal with the high frequency aspects of images, they worked very well for our focus on low frequency issues.

For the classification network our two main concerns were the ability of the network to classify often subtle and low frequency issues, and how well the network would generalize beyond the training data. To increase chances for a network that would work on a large class of images, we used a very low learning rate, and inserted up to three dropout layers (placed after the last three batch-normalization layers) with up to 80% dropouts on each of these layers to reduce the network's tendency to over-train rapidly. For the cGAN, a significant concern was preserving high frequency detail while correcting large-scale, low frequency image issues. We tried several methods, some of which addressed the problem well. One of the reasons Pix2Pix was a good starting point for us is that the scripts utilize both patch and Euclidean error metrics, which account for feature matching and also per-pixel distance errors. Though it tends to produce blurrier images than the L1 (absolute distance) measure used by (Isola, 2017a), we used MSE (mean squared error) metrics to more drastically penalize rogue pixels in the output images. We also adjusted patch size and metrics for penalizing mismatched patches. Adjusting the network helped deal with unwanted, transient pixels and patches that would come across as flickers in a moving image, with the caveat that the individual images looked slightly softer due to these more draconian error metrics. As our ultimate goal is to produce color corrected image sequences (video), rogue elements are unacceptable as they result in poor quality output, while there are ways to deal with softer images. In addition, we modified our cGAN to read in multiple frames of a video sequence at once by increasing the dimensionality of our tensor by one degree, accounting for a temporal dimension. Adding a fourth dimension to the tensor creates a X by Y by F by 3 (by batch size) tensor where F is the number of frames in a clip. While this addition increased memory requirements, training on sequential frames allowed the cGAN to learn to generate multiple frames that all look alike, which is critical to image continuity for video.

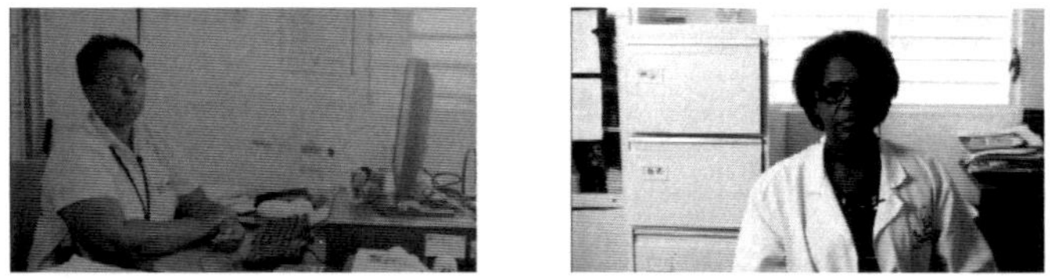

Figure 1. Two source images showing the low frequency nature of color correction issues. The left image has its white point set 100% too low, while the right image has its contrast set 100% too high

4. RESULTS

After adjustments and multiple training runs, both of our networks were able to produce excellent results, though each has its own shortcomings. Section 4.1 discusses results for the classification network while 4.2 discusses results for the conditional generative adversarial network.

4.1 Classification Network

For our classification network, optimal results for the training data was found very quickly, within 30 epochs of retraining the modified VGG-f network. In fact, in many cases classification confidence was at or nearly 100% for the correct problem classification, as shown in Figure 2. For the trained network, nearly all errors made were in neighboring classifications. For example, the network might predict that the white point was 66% too low, whereas the ground truth was that it was 33% too low. As this misclassification is qualitatively nearly correct, we factored these near misses into our results in addition to completely correct results. As Table 1 shows, error rates on validation data was exceptionally low. The error rate was so low, in fact, that we feared the network was over-trained, as was borne out by subsequent experiments.

Figure 2. Correct classification that the source image's contrast is 33% too high. Note that the confidence in the result is 100%

Table 1. Error rates on validation set, including correct and nearest neighbor errors in classification of image problems

	Correct Classification	Nearest Neighbor	Total
Number of Images	2,699/2746	46/2746	2745/2746
Percentage	98.3%	1.6%	100.0%

Figure 3. The network fails to generalize to images with multiple color correction issues. The network predicts four points too orange, with 100% confidence, while the true issues are two points too blue plus two points too green

When we attempted to run the network on images with two classes of problems at the same time, and also on images with unspecified problems, the network failed to generalize properly, as shown in Figure 3. We thus adjusted our training methodology, most notably inserting three dropout layers after the last three batch normalization layers, with up to 80% dropouts. Though this slowed training down considerably it did not resolve the underlying issue of network generalization to other images.

4.2 Conditional Generative Adversarial Network

Our cGAN with larger patches, MSE error metrics, and a high degree of weight given to the MSE portion of the loss function also produced very good, high quality results. As shown in Figure 4, not only is a sample output image nearly indistinguishable from the target (ground truth) image, if one subtracts the pixel values of the two images the result is nearly black, indicating that each pixel in the output image is extremely close to the value of the target image.

Two significant issues pertain to the cGAN solution. First is that high frequency elements of the images are very slightly blurred, as expected due to our highly weighted MSE factor in error accumulation. Though MSE did very well correcting for outlying pixels or groups of pixels, this comes at the cost of a slight blurring or softening of the image. Fortunately there is a simple solution to this problem: oversampling. This technique, which is used in many disciplines, including video games, blows up images beyond 100% before performing convolutional tasks on them. In our case, we doubled both the X and Y dimensions of our validation images (2X oversampling, which quadruples image size) while running the cGAN on them. After processing, we reduced the scale back to the original size. As the cGAN is effective at running on images larger than what it is trained on (see Isola, 2017a), the larger image size did not prove to be a problem for the network. Figure 5 shows the same image run at 100% per dimension versus 200% per dimension. While the difference is subtle, there is a distinct sharpening of edge detail in the oversampled image. We can also, of course, train on oversampled data, though this requires more memory and time for the training.

The second issue with the cGAN is more pernicious: as each image is run through the network individually, spurious pixels or patches can appear in one image that disappear in the next. While examining an individual image these rogue elements are often nearly invisible, but with a moving image sequence the changes between each image can produce a flickering appearance that is distracting. The left-hand side of Figure 6 shows a (greatly exaggerated) problem, while the right-hand side shows one solution: frame blending. Frame blending, as its name suggests, takes information from surrounding frames and averages pixel values between them. While each frame becomes softer using this method, the moving video image, at 24 or 30 frames per second, is markedly improved and the individual image softness is not apparent.

Our other solution to the moving picture issue was, as discussed above, to increase the dimensions of our data tensor to read in image sequences, creating a temporal dimension. By having the cGAN effectively train on a four dimensional 'image'—X, Y, image number, color channel—it learned to generate sequences of images with little variation between them. Due to memory constraints we were limited to 18 images per sequence, but this number of frames was effective at producing minimal variation between frames. One interesting find was that flipping random images within the sequence actually worked better than keeping them all in their original horizontal configuration. Figure 7 shows a portion of an image sequence (with random flipping), indicating that this solution creates consistent images over a sequence.

Figure 4. cGAN output, left, compared to the target image, center. Right is the difference between the two images (via difference layer mode in Photoshop). The nearly black result shows that most pixels have nearly the same value (the image on left is an unusually poor output, used to show some difference between the two images)

Figure 5. The cGAN run on a standard sized image (100% in X and Y), on top, versus a 2X oversampled image (200% in X and Y), on bottom. A blown up portion of the image is shown here in order to show fine detail

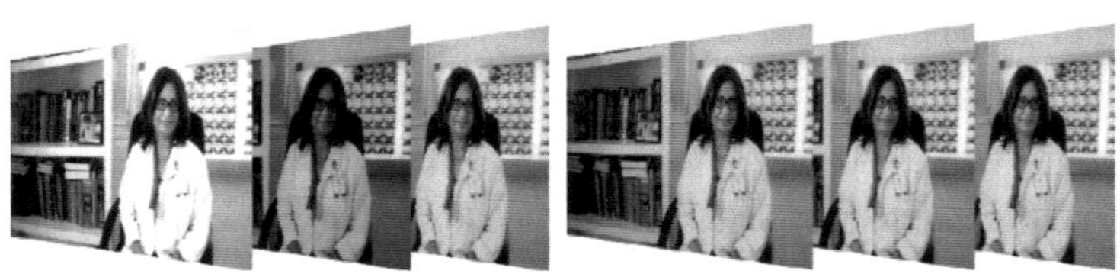

Figure 6. Multi-frame differences produce a flickering effect, left (greatly exaggerated for clarity), while frame blending, right, smooths out frame-to-frame differences to produce a more pleasing sequence of images

Figure 7. Training the cGAN on image sequences as a group produces a more consistent look. Left is the uncorrected input, middle the cGAN output, and right, the corrected target image. Note the random image flipping in the sequence

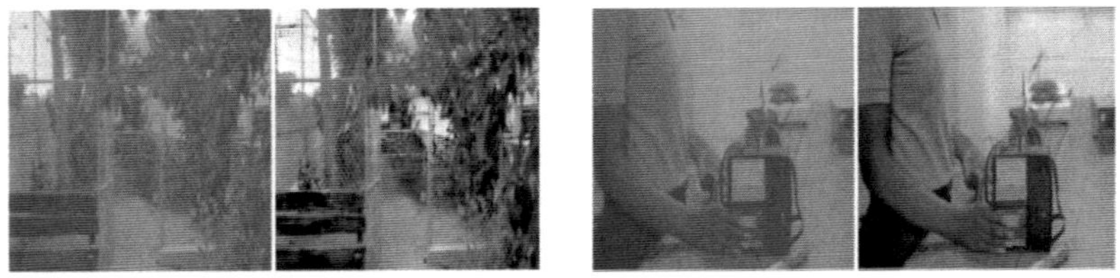

Figure 8. Given totally new types of input images, the cGAN produces high quality results. Original uncorrected images are on the left, while corrected output images are on the right

Finally, the cGAN generalizes well. Given image types the network has not trained on at all, as in Figure 8, the network produces good quality results, indicating that even with a small data set to train on, it already generalizes to a larger class of uncorrected images. With a larger, more diverse training set the quality of output should improve even more.

5. DISCUSSION AND CONCLUSION

Both the classification and the cGAN networks produce very high quality results. Comparatively speaking, the classification system's main shortcoming—its issue with generalizing beyond a labeled data set—is likely to be a more significant issue than the two problems the cGAN has—smoother details and rogue elements in each image that change per image (creating image flicker). The only really effective way to create a more robust classification network is to accrue, and more problematically, properly label all images. Labeling is not only time consuming but also highly challenging as any number of subtle corrections can be performed by a color grader while working on an image. How one would effectively label the range of problems being corrected for any real-world image is something that could perhaps be solved by keystroke recording software, but then the number of classification categories could grow into the thousands or tens of thousands, massively increasing training time and likely reducing the effectiveness of the network as a whole.

The cGAN's issues, on the other hand, have already been partially addressed even with the limited initial data set used. Edge softening is a non-issue, as oversampling (followed by image reduction after processing) has already been added to our scripts, and works very effectively to sharpen edges and other high frequency elements in the images. Working with images larger than those trained on is also not a problem, as there have been few issues noted in our tests. Furthermore, with more time and resources, training can easily be done on larger images, almost certainly improving results further. Image-to-image variance is the big problem with the cGAN. We tried two solutions to this problem, each of which had a positive effect. First was to post-process the image sequences using frame blending. This works well, but there can still remain subtle flickers, and unfortunately the individual images get somewhat smoother and blurrier, which while generally undetectable for a viewer, is nonetheless a reduction of overall quality and fidelity to the source images. Second was to add a temporal dimension to our image data tensor. This addition, while increasing memory load on the CPU/GPU system, allows for image sequences to be corrected as a unit, creating a correction to the overall sequence rather than to individual frames. One other potential solution is to modify our code to include temporal convolution as in (Ji, 2013), though it is not obvious that this will produce better results than the image sequence modification we have implemented.

Both our classification network and our conditional generative adversarial network were trained to produce high quality output on the data we gave them. Our opinion is that between the two, the cGAN system is more suited to further research, as collecting unlabeled image pairs is relatively easy and straightforward, and as the issues still outstanding are tractable.

Though color correction is considered an aesthetic task, both of our neural networks learned the basics of the task using only a few thousand images. We believe that with further training on larger, more diverse data sets, our cGAN network in particular can provide a practical solution to a complex, time-consuming, artistic task with which every film/video producer has to contend.

REFERENCES

Bengio, Yoshua and Yann LeCun (2007). Scaling learning algorithms towards AI. Bottou, L. and Chapelle, O. and DeCoste, D. and Weston, J. (Eds), *Large-Scale Kernel Machines*, MIT Press.

Chen, L.C., et al (2015). Semantic image segmentation with deep convolutional nets and fully connected crfs. In *ICLR*, 2015.

Ciresan, Dan, Ueli Meier, and Jürgen Schmidhuber (2012). Multi-column deep neural networks for image classification. Computer Vision and Pattern Recognition *CVPR* 2012. pp. 3642-3649.

Gatys, L.A., A.S.Ecker, and M.Bethge (2016). Image style transfer using convolutional neural networks. *CVPR*, 2016.

Hinton, Geoffrey E. Deterministic Boltzmann learning performs steepest descent in weight-space (1989). *Neural Computation* 1.1, pp. 143-150.

Hinton, Geoffrey E., and Ruslan R. Salakhutdinov (2006). Reducing the dimensionality of data with neural networks. *Science* 313.5786, pp. 504-507.

Iizuka, S., E. Simo-Serra, and H. Ishikawa (2016). Let there be Color!: Joint End-to-end Learning of Global and Local Image Priors for Automatic Image Colorization with Simultaneous Classification. *ACM Transactions on Graphics (TOG)*, 35(4).

Isola, Phillip, et al (2017a). Image-to-Image Translation with Conditional Adversarial Networks. *CVPR* 2017.

Isola, Philip, et al. (2017b). Pix2Pix. Retrieved 15/11/2017, from https://github.com/phillipi/pix2pix.

Ji, Shuiwang, et al (2013). 3D Convolutional Neural Networks for Human Action Recognition. *IEEE Transactions On Pattern Analysis and Machine Intellegence* Issue No. 01 - Jan. (vol. 35). pp. 221-231.

Krizhevsky, Alex, Ilya Sutskever and Geoffrey E. Hinton (2012). ImageNet Classification with Deep Convolutional Neural Networks. *NIPS* 2012.

Kundert-Gibbs, John (2017). Image Based Content Retrieval via Class-Based Histogram Comparisons. *Lecture Notes in Electrical Engineering, Vol. 449: IT Convergence and Security 2017, Vol. 1*, Ed. Kim, J. Kuinam, Hyuncheol Kim, Nakhoon Baek. Singapore, Springer Nature, pp. 3-10.

McClean, Sally, Bryan Scotney and MaryShapcott (2000). Using background knowledge in the aggregation of imprecise evidence in databases. *Data & Knowledge Engineering* Volume 32, Issue 2, pp. 131-143.

Mikolov, et al (2013). Efficient Estimation of Word Representations in Vector Space. *NIPS* 2013.

Mirza, M., and S. Osindero (2014). Conditional generative adversarial nets. *arXiv preprint arXiv:1411.1784.*

Olshausen, Bruno A., and David J. Field (1997). Sparse coding with an overcomplete basis set: A strategy employed by VI? *Vision Research* 37.23, pp. 3311-3326.

Pricing Indy Feature (2015). Retrieved 20/04/2018, from http://www.liftgammagain.com/forum/index.php?threads/pricing-indy-feature.4324

Radford, A., L. Metz, and S. Chintala (2015). Unsupervised representation learning with deep convolutional generative adversarial networks. *arXiv preprint arXiv:1511.06434.*

Reinhard, E., et al (2001). Color transfer between images. *IEEE Computer Graphics and Applications*, 21:34–41.

Vedaldi, Andrea, Karel Lenc and Joao Henriques (2016). Oxford Geometry Group VGG CNN Practical: Image Regression Practical. Retrieved on 15/6/2016 from http://www.robots.ox.ac.uk/~vgg/practicals/cnn-reg/index.html#part-35-learning-a-larger-model-using-the-gpu.

Vedaldi, Andrea, et al (2017a). MatConvNet: CNNs for MATLAB. Retrieved 1/6/2015 to 25/10/2017, from http://www.vlfeat.org/matconvnet.

Vedaldi, Andrea and Andrew Zisserman (2017b). Oxford Geometry Group VGG Convolutional Neural Networks Practical. Retrieved on 15/1/2017 from http://www.robots.ox.ac.uk/~vgg/practicals/cnn/index.html#part1-4.

Vinyals, Toshev, Bengio, and Erhan (2015). Show and Tell: A Neural Image Caption Generator. *CVPR* 2015.

Wood, Kristin L., and Erik K. Antonsson (1989). Computations with Imprecise Parameters in Engineering Design: Background and Theory. *ASME Journal of Mechanisms, Transmissions, and Automation in Design* Volume 111, Number 4, pp. 616-625.

Zhang, Richard, Phillip Isola and Alexei A (2016). Efros. Colorful Image Colorization. Retrieved on 13/11/2017 from http://richzhang.github.io/ colorization/resources/colorful_eccv2016.pdf.

Zisserman, Arxiv (2014). Very Deep Convolutional Networks for Large-Scale Image Recognition. *ILSVRC* 2014.

IDENTIFYING A GAME-THEORETIC TRANSITION THRESHOLD ON HYPERBOLIC NETWORKS

Christine Marshall[1], James Cruickshank[2] and Colm O'Riordan[1]
[1]*Discipline of Information Technology, National University of Ireland, Galway*
[2]*School of Mathematics, National University of Ireland, Galway*

ABSTRACT

In this work we explore agent based simulations of The Prisoner's Dilemma on a set of hyperbolic random geometric graphs, ranging from unconnected to fully connected graphs. Hyperbolic random geometric graphs share many features with real world complex networks, having power law degree distribution, short path lengths and high clustering. We find that as we increase the number of edges in the graphs, there is a clear transition, above which defection spreads to all nodes in the graph, below which the graphs are resistant to defection. We use a game-theoretic approach, based on the Prisoner's Dilemma, to model diffusion in the network, and our analysis of global graph properties at the threshold offers some insight into structural properties which might facilitate or inhibit the spread of defection in the network.

KEYWORDS

Game Theory, Hyperbolic Random Geometric Graphs, Transition Threshold, Diffusion Processes, Complex Networks

1. INTRODUCTION

Hyperbolic random geometric graphs share many features of real world complex networks, such as having a power law degree distribution; they are sparse, highly clustered, with short diameter and average path length. Simulating network processes on these graphs may offer insights into processes in complex real world networks, such as diffusion in the internet graph.

The processes we are examining are game-theoretic, using the spatial and evolutionary form of the Prisoner's Dilemma, where agents with an assigned strategy of cooperation or defection are attached to each node and play the game with their connected neighbours over several generations. At the end of each round of games, all nodes adopt the strategy of their best scoring neighbour. In this way, the long term evolution of strategies can be determined. In the standard form of the Prisoner's Dilemma game, the dominant strategy is defection. Game theorists are interested in circumstances under which cooperation persists. In our previous research, comparing game-theoretic outcomes on the Erdős-Rényi model of random graph and random geometric graphs created in the Euclidean and hyperbolic plane, we observed that defection spread rapidly on the Erdős-Rényi model and also in the hyperbolic model. This latter result was unexpected, as it had been anticipated that the tree like structure of the hyperbolic graph would allow for resistant clusters. However, that work was restricted to a small sample of graphs, all with the same selected edge density, to allow direct comparison between the graphs. In this work, we simulate Prisoner's Dilemma on a set of hyperbolic graphs of increasing edge density from 0 to 1. Our motivation, as we increase the number of edges in the graphs, is to determine if there is a transition threshold above which defection completely spreads and below which cooperation is robust. We then analyse the changing pattern of global graph properties as edge density increases and compare this with our threshold to see if we can identify any particular structural features which might inhibit or facilitate the spread of defection.

Our methodology involves creating hyperbolic graphs of varying average degree, measuring global graph properties and then embedding the game of the Prisoner's Dilemma on the set of graphs to determine how the spread of defection evolves over time. On each graph of 1000 nodes, we simulate the game of the Prisoner's Dilemma 1000 times, choosing a different node each time as the sole defector seed amongst 999 cooperators, to observe spatial effects on the adoption of strategy.

Section 2 provides related information about random graph models and game theory, in section 3 and 4 we outline our experimental design and results respectively, our conclusions are summarized in section 4.

2. BACKGROUND

2.1 Hyperbolic Networks

Random Geometric Graph models were created to model situations where physical distance between nodes is an issue, such as the transmission of pathogens from tree to adjacent tree in a forest. In computer science, these models are frequently used to model wireless ad-hoc and sensor networks (Benezit, 2010), where proximity between nodes defines network connections. They can be used to model connectivity, the capacity of a network, potential outages, and "other fundamental limits on wireless networks" (Haenggi, 2009). They also have applications for determining barrier coverage in wireless sensor networks (Kumar, 2007), the use of gossip algorithms to study information exchange (Boyd, 2006) and sampling-based path planning algorithms in robotics research, where the ensuing data structures share similar features to geometric graph models (Karaman, 2011).

Hyperbolic random geometric graphs are created by distributing points in a hyperbolic space and connecting those that lie within a specified hyperbolic distance. The negative curvature of the hyperbolic plane means points within a hyperbolic disc are not uniformly distributed, the hyperbolic model has more "room" than the Euclidean disc. As the radius of a Euclidean disc increases, the circumference increases linearly; in a hyperbolic disc, the circumference increases exponentially. This tends to give a fish eye view to nodes within the disc, with central nodes appearing to be closer, while outer nodes are exponentially distant. The resultant graphs typically display a tree like structure, with central hub nodes and leaf nodes towards infinity at the boundary.

Hyperbolic random geometric graphs have been used to explore structural properties and processes in complex networks, such as clustering (Candellero, 2014) and navigability. Krioukov et al. (2010) have proposed that these models have potential for modelling the internet graph, which they suggest has an underlying hyperbolic geometry. Recent work by Papadopoulos et al. (2010) has developed a tool to map real world complex networks, such as the Autonomous Systems internet, to a hyperbolic space using the hyperbolic geometric model. Figure 1 shows a snapshot of internet connectivity produced by CAIDA, the Center for Applied Internet Data Analysis, with selected Internet Service Providers coloured separately (Barabási 2018). This image clearly shows the tree like and highly clustered structure of the internet graph. Random graph models have been used extensively in game-theoretic applications, using strategic games such as the Prisoner's Dilemma to model the spread of cooperation and defection in networks (Buesser, 2012).

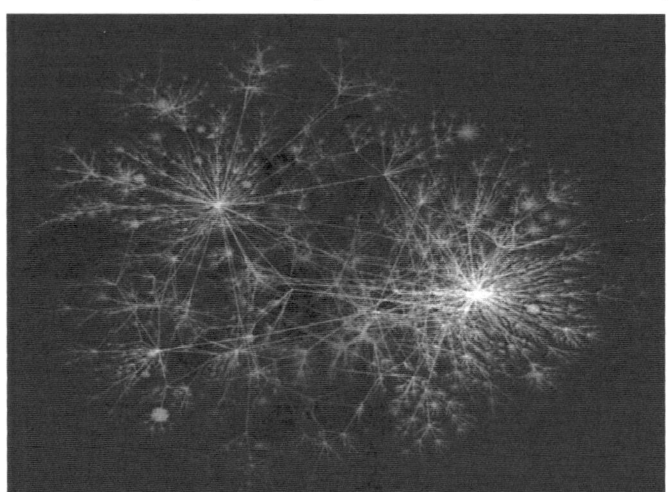

Figure 1. The Topology of the Internet, produced by CAIDA, (in Barabási, 2018)

2.2 Game Theory

Game theory is the study of strategic decision making in interactions between independent intelligent individuals (Myerson, 1991). Classical game theory involves determining the optimal strategies in competitive situations where individuals, or groups of individuals, can choose a strategy of cooperation or defection (Von Neumann, 1944). The game of the Prisoner's Dilemma nicely captures this choice, using a payoff matrix to determine scores. There are four possible outcomes in the simplest form of the game, dependent on the strategies of the players (Axelrod, 1984); the generalised payoff matrix is shown in Table 1

Table 1. Generalised Payoff Matrix for Prisoner's Dilemma Game, where $S < P < R < T$

	Cooperate	Defect
Cooperate	R,R	S,T
Defect	T,S	P,P

If the row player cooperates and the column player defects, the row player has a sucker payoff S whereas the column player receives a temptation payoff T indicated by the top right hand cell. The dilemma arises as both players are better off cooperating and receiving a higher combined reward score R yet there is a temptation for an individual to defect and receive the maximum score T, despite the risk of a lower combined punishment score P if both players defect. In fact, the dominant strategy for a player is to defect, with Nash equilibrium of defection by both players.

In computer science, game theory is used extensively in the study of multi-agent systems, which are computerized systems of autonomous independent agents. Computational models are created in which the agents are “attached” to nodes in a graph model. Each node is then assigned a strategy and their behaviour is observed. Spatial game theory involves interactions between connected neighbours and is ideally suited to modelling as a network (Nowak, 2006; Langer, 2008). Key questions involve whether the spatial structure affects the adoption of particular strategies, such as recent interest in the robustness of cooperation (Nowak, 2012). Evolutionary game theory is a development where the strategies of individuals may evolve over time (Maynard Smith, 1982). This approach uses Darwinian concepts for the evolution of species, such as the concept of natural selection where small individual genetic variations allow for the “survival of the fittest” species in competition for resources. Games can be simulated using computational models of evolutionary processes such as survival of the fittest. The mechanism for this learning involves assigning a strategy to each individual; each individual's score is based on their interactions with other players and on the relevant values in the payoff matrix. At the end of each round, a proportion of the individuals adopts the strategy of higher scoring players and therefore learns to adopt a successful strategy over time. Perc et al. (2013) provided a review of evolutionary dynamics on structured graphs, which adds to our understanding of the dynamics of pro-social cooperative behaviour in human populations. The graphs compared were lattices, complex networks and co-evolutionary models and the authors suggest that work on the dynamics of group interactions benefits from blending methods from statistical physics, network science and evolutionary game theory. Ezaki and Masuda (2017) investigated a special case of the Prisoner's Dilemma game on networks using reinforcement learning, finding that network reciprocity occurs if and only if the benefit significantly outweighs cost, relative to the number of neighbours of a node. Embedding games on random geometric graphs is a relatively recent development and has been used to model processes such as agreement dynamics in wireless sensor networks (Beveridge, 2013) and investigating the links between spatial distribution and social dynamics in opinion formation (Zhang, 2014).

3. EXPERIMENTAL DESIGN

Our experiments involve creating hyperbolic random geometric graphs with varying edge density from 0 to 1, analysing global graph properties and then observing the effect of graph topology on game-theoretic processes by embedding the game of Prisoner's Dilemma on the graphs.

3.1 Graph Creation

In this research, hyperbolic random geometric graphs are created using the model outlined by Krioukov et al. (2010) This approach situates the graph in a disc of radius R. Nodes in the graph have polar coordinates (r, θ) and are positioned by generating these coordinates as random variates; edges are created between pairs of nodes where the hyperbolic distance between them is less than the radius R of the disc of interest, varying R from 0 to 12, at which point it becomes a fully connected graph.

All graphs are created with 1000 nodes and with increasing distance parameters from 0.1 to 12 in increments of 0.1, with 20 graphs created at each distance parameter. The global graph properties for each graph were analysed and the mean values for these 20 graphs were recorded. The properties of interest are the degree distribution, diameter and average shortest path; betweenness, closeness and degree centralisation; transitivity and network average clustering coefficients.

3.2 Simulation of the Prisoner's Dilemma

In these simulations, graphs of 1000 nodes are utilised. A population of agents playing the game of the Prisoner's Dilemma is embedded on each graph to observe any changes in the ratio of cooperation to defection that may arise. An agent is assigned to each node, with a predefined starting strategy. In this experiment we adopt the spatial form of the game, where each node plays against all of their connected neighbours. At the end of each round of games, scores are normalised and all nodes adopt the strategy of their highest scoring connected neighbour. The payoff matrix for our simulations is shown in Table 2.

Table 2. Payoff Matrix for Prisoner's Dilemma Game

	Cooperate	Defect
Cooperate	3,3	0,5
Defect	5,0	1,1

In this research, we are particularly interested in observing the effects that any structural differences might have on this process. For each graph model, we assign one agent as the sole defector amongst 999 cooperators and observe the impact that the initial defector node has on the spread of defection or robustness of cooperation; simulated over 100 generations. This is repeated in turn for all nodes in the graph. The results are then compared and analysed.

4. RESULTS

In this section, we describe our results obtained from simulating the Prisoner's Dilemma game on hyperbolic random geometric graphs of varying average degree. Our results show an identifiable game-theoretic transition threshold; graph properties at this threshold are presented.

4.1 Game -Theoretic Transition Threshold

Figure 2 shows the game-theoretic outcomes at equilibrium on hyperbolic random geometric graphs created with varying average degree. Complete defection is shown in red and persistent cooperation in blue. The horizontal axis represents outcomes from all 1000 simulations on the same graph, each with a different defector seed. Each row contains average data at equilibrium obtained from simulations on 20 graphs at each distance parameter, sorted from least to most defection at equilibrium. For clarity, the heat map has been truncated at an average degree of 40 edges per node, out of a possible 999 edges per node.

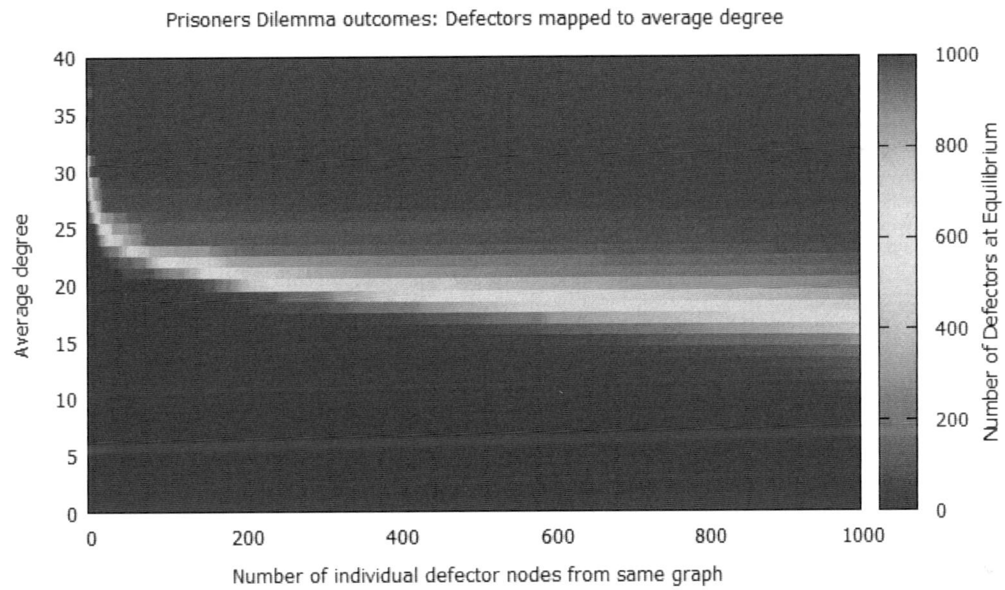

Figure 2. Heat map showing Prisoner's Dilemma outcomes on hyperbolic graphs created with varying average degree

The heat map shows a clear transition from the robustness of cooperation below an average degree of 15 edges per node to the complete adoption of defection above an average degree of 38 edges per node. This threshold lies between the distance parameters of 1.5 and 4, within the blue lines on the following charts.

4.2 Graph Properties at Threshold

The properties of interest are component size, path length, centralisation measures and clustering. The graphs become minimally connected at distance 3, this equates to an average degree of 19 edges per node. As we are only interested in the spread of strategy in a connected graph, this critical point has been marked on the charts with a red line, and we are particularly interested in the zone between the red line and the rightmost blue line.

4.2.1 Component Size

Figure 3 shows the size of the largest component mapped to distance parameter R. In the following charts, the zone of interest is between the red line and the rightmost blue line. The blue lines mark the boundaries of the transition threshold from the persistence of cooperation, below a distance parameter $R = 1.5$ and the complete adoption of defection above 4. This equates to an average degree of between 15 and 35 edges per node. The red line marks the point at which all nodes are reachable by a path from any node.

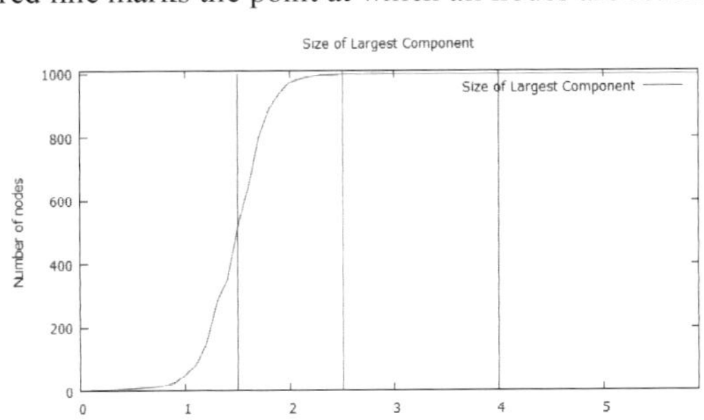

Figure 3. Size of giant component at varying distance parameter R

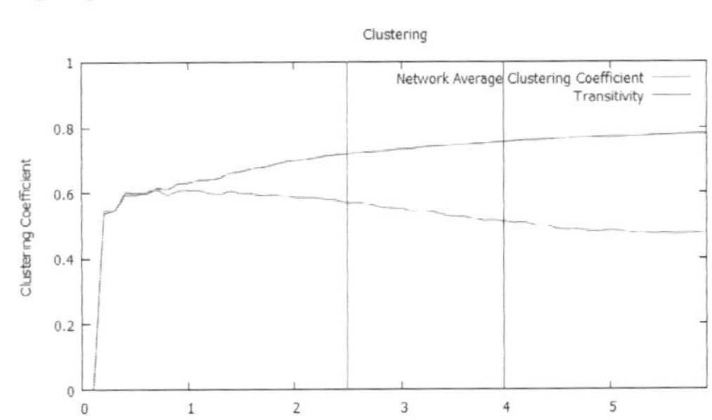

Figure 4. Clustering coefficients, values in the range 0 - 1

4.2.2 Network Average Clustering Coefficient and Transitivity

Clustering coefficients are a measure of the extent to which network nodes cluster together. The local clustering coefficient of a node represents the extent to which a node's neighbours are interconnected. In a friendship network this represents the extent to which friends of a node are friends of each other (Watts, 1998). The network average clustering coefficient is the average of the local clustering coefficients over all nodes in the graph. Transitivity describes the links between triples of nodes. A fully transitive relationship is represented by a closed triple, where the "friends of my friends are my friends" (Snijders, 2011). A potentially transitive relationship is represented by an open triple, where one of the links is missing. Figure 4 shows the network average clustering coefficients and transitivity measures at varying distance parameter. For all significant distance parameters, the graphs display high clustering. At the transition threshold there is a marked and increasing variation between the two measures, with transitivity decreasing significantly. Interestingly, this is in marked contrast to typical values in the Erdős-Rényi model of random graph. Those graphs display low clustering and both clustering measures are practically indistinguishable

4.2.3 Diameter and Average Shortest Path

The shortest path between any pair of nodes in the graph is the least number of edges between those nodes. The average shortest path length is the average of all the shortest paths in the graph. The diameter is the longest of these shortest paths and represents the "width" of the graph. Figure 5 shows greater adoption of defection as diameter and average shortest path length decrease.

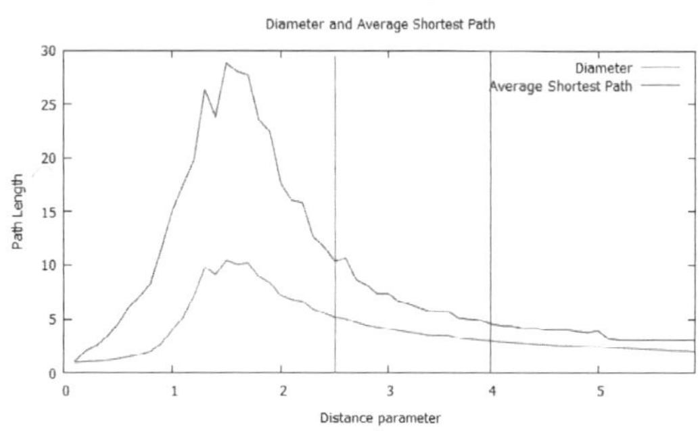

Figure 5. Diameter and average shortest path at varying average degree

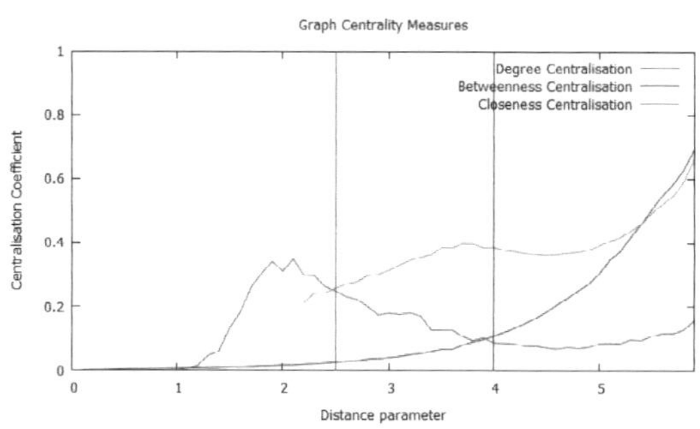

Figure 6. Degree, betweenness and closeness centralisation

4.2.4 Degree, Betweenness and Closeness Centralisation

Centrality measures determine how central, or important, a node is. If such a measure is applied to the whole graph it is known as centralisation. A high centralisation score represents a skewed centrality distribution, whereas a low centralisation score represents a graph where most nodes are in a similar centrality range. Figure 6 displays comparisons of the three centralisation measures, mapped to increasing distance parameter R All the centralisation values are in the range [0, 1]. Degree centrality measures the node degree. Nodes with high degree centrality may refer to hubs which may be effectively targeted for network disruption or to facilitate information flow. The hyperbolic graphs display low skew for degree centralisation in the transition zone, reflecting the low level of variance in node degree throughout each graph. Betweenness centrality is calculated by proportionally determining the number of times a node appears on the shortest paths between all possible pairs of nodes. A node with a high betweenness centrality score can represent a "brokerage" role in a network, as information between sub networks has to pass through this node. Low betweenness centralisation means that all nodes within a graph are equally likely to be on the shortest paths between all pairs of nodes. The graphs display decreasing betweenness centralisation as the tendency to defection increases. Closeness centrality describes the situation where a node is closely linked to important nodes, whilst not necessarily having high betweenness or degree centrality. Nodes with high closeness centrality are close to the action and may have influence out of proportion to their number of connections, either by receiving information or being able to widely disseminate information. Closeness centrality is calculated by finding the length of the average shortest path between a node and all other nodes in the graph. The graphs display increasingly skewed closeness centralisation within the transition zone, indicating an increasing degree of disparity in individual node centrality scores.

5. CONCLUSION

Our main contribution in this research is an investigation of a game-theoretic transition threshold in the hyperbolic model, looking at structural and abstract properties at the threshold to determine if there are any identifiable patterns which affect the outcomes. Our experiments show that as we increase the number of edges in the set of graphs from 0 to a fully connected graph, there is a distinct game-theoretic threshold in the hyperbolic random geometric graphs. Below this threshold, cooperation is robust and after it there is no resistance to the spread of defection. This threshold occurs at an edge density between 0.15 and 0.35, which in our graphs of 1000 nodes equates to an average degree of between 15 and 35 edges per node, out of a possible 999 edges per node in a fully connected graph. Whilst the hyperbolic graphs at the threshold are relatively sparse, sparsity is also a feature of many real world complex networks.

At the threshold, closeness centralisation increases, meaning that there is increasing disparity in centrality values for individual nodes in the graphs. All of the minimally connected graphs have a high level of clustering but the variance between the two measures increases as defection becomes more likely, with transitivity decreasing, meaning that inter-connections in the neighbourhood of a node decrease. These matters show potential for applications in network science, particularly in modelling the internet graph. The hyperbolic graph appears to be a useful model for the internet graph and for modelling processes on the network, such as the flow of data. Our work also offers insights into the vulnerability to attack of real world complex networks, for example identifying potential targeting of nodes with high closeness centrality, which might not have as much security as nodes with high degree.

Future work might involve a form of intelligent selection of nodes to inhibit or enhance the spread of defection on a network, based on an analysis of global graph properties. The set of graphs display distinct patterns of global graph properties at and around the threshold; this suggests that some correlation exists between these properties and outcomes in the Prisoner's Dilemma game.

Using these global graph properties, it may therefore be possible to target defection at nodes which are top ranked for these properties, or perhaps select these nodes to abstain from the game, and observe the effect that this has on outcomes. Hub nodes (nodes with high degree centrality) are often regarded as being influential in networks. The changing patterns of centrality measures at the game-theoretic threshold suggest that other centrality measures may have greater influence in these networks and suggest that we may be able to target nodes which are top ranked for specific centrality measures to facilitate or disrupt the spread of defection.

ACKNOWLEDGEMENT

This research was supported by the Irish Research Council Postgraduate (Government of Ireland) funding.

REFERENCES

Axelrod, R. (1984), *The Evolution of Cooperation*, Basic Books, Inc., New York.

Barabási, A.L, (2018), '*The topology of the Internet*' [image], Available at: http://networksciencebook.com/chapter/4#universality [Accessed 3 July 2018].

Bénézit, F., Dimakis, A. G., Thiran, P. & Vetterli, M. (2010), 'Order-optimal consensus through randomized path averaging', *Information Theory*, IEEE Transactions on 56(10), 5150–5167.

Beveridge, A., Dudek, A., Frieze, A., Muller, T. & Stojakovic, M. (2013), 'Maker-breaker games on random geometric graphs', *arXiv* preprint arXiv: 1309.5759.

Boyd, S., Ghosh, A., Prabhakar, B. & Shah, D. (2006), 'Randomized gossip algorithms', *IEEE Transactions on Information Theory* 52(6), 2508–2530.

Buesser, P. & Tomassini, M. (2012), 'Evolution of cooperation on spatially embedded networks', *Physical Review E* 86(6), 066107.

Candellero, E. & Fountoulakis, N. (2014), 'Clustering and the hyperbolic geometry of complex networks', *Lecture Notes in Computer Science* (including subseries Lecture Notes in Artificial Intelligence and Lecture Notes in Bioinformatics) 8882, 1–12.

Ezaki, T. & Masuda, N. (2017), 'Reinforcement learning account of network reciprocity', *PLOS ONE* 12(12), 1–8.

Haenggi, M., Andrews, J. G., Baccelli, F., Dousse, O. & Franceschetti, M. (2009), 'Stochastic geometry and random graphs for the analysis and design of wireless networks', *IEEE Journal on Selected Areas in Communications* 27(7), 1029–1046.

Karaman, S. & Frazzoli, E. (2011), 'Sampling-based algorithms for optimal motion planning', *The International Journal of Robotics Research* 30(7), 846–894.

Krioukov, D., Papadopoulos, F., Kitsak, M., Vahdat, A. & Boguñá, M. (2010), 'Hyperbolic geometry of complex networks', *Physical Review E* 82, 036106.

Kumar, S., Lai, T. H. & Arora, A. (2007), 'Barrier coverage with wireless sensors', *Wireless Networks* 13, 817–834.

Langer, P., Nowak, M. & Hauert, C. (2008), 'Spatial invasion of cooperation', *Journal of Theoretical Biology* 250(4), 634–641.

Maynard Smith, J., 1982. *Evolution and the Theory of Games,* Cambridge University Press.

Myerson, R. B. (1991), *Game Theory: Analysis of Conflict*, The President and Fellows of Harvard College, USA.

Nowak, M. A. (2006), *Evolutionary dynamics*, Harvard University Press.

Nowak, M. A. (2012), 'Evolving cooperation', *Journal of Theoretical Biology* 299, 1–8.

Papadopoulos, F., Psomas, C. & Krioukov, D. (2015), 'Network mapping by replaying hyperbolic growth', *Networking*, IEEE/ACM Transactions on 23(1), 198–211.

Perc, M., Gómez-Gardeñes, J., Szolnoki, A., Floría, L. M. & Moreno, Y. (2013), 'Evolutionary dynamics of group interactions on structured populations: a review', *Journal of the Royal Society Interface* 10(80), 20120997.

Snijders, T. A. (2011), 'Statistical Models for Social Networks', *Annual Review of Sociology* 37, 131–153.

Von Neumann, J. & Morgenstern, O. (1944), *Theory of Games and Economic Behavior*, Vol. 2.

Watts, D. J. & Strogatz, S. H. (1998), 'Collective dynamics of 'small-world' networks.', *Nature* 393, 440–442.

Zhang, W., Lim, C., Korniss, G. & Szymanski, B. (2014), 'Opinion dynamics and influencing on random geometric graphs', *Scientific Reports*, 4, p.5568.

EXPERIMENTAL ANALYSIS OF SPURIOUS TIMEOUT DETECTION METHODS WITH LTE HANDOVER EMULATION

Toshihiko Kato, Masahito Moriyama, Ryo Yamamoto and Satoshi Ohzahata
University of Electro-Communications, 1-5-1, Chofugaoka, Chofu, Tokyo 182-8585, Japan

ABSTRACT

In this paper, we describes the performance evaluation of the well-known spurious timeout detection methods, Eifel, DSACK, and F-RTO, through experiments with the network emulator imitating handovers over LTE (Long Term Evolution) networks. Specifically, the emulator supports to insert the time-variant delay and packet loss in packet streams. By taking account of the lossless handover in LTE, this paper shows the results for the cases only the delay spike is inserted, and both delay spike and packet loss are inserted. In the former case, the three methods show the similar performance, but in the latter case, the performance of Eifel is worse than the others.

KEYWORDS

TCP, Spurious Timeout, Eifel, DSACK, F-RTO, LTE

1. INTRODUCTION

Modern wireless and mobile networks, such as IEEE 802.11 WLANs (Wireless LANs) (IEEE, 2016) and the 4G LTE (Long Term Evolution) wide area mobile network (Sesia et al., 2011), establish high speed and high quality data communication. Although previous wireless networks suffering from packet losses invoked by bit errors, modern wireless networks provide rich capabilities recovering from packet losses in their MAC (media access control) protocols. Moreover, the LTE protocols provide lossless handover functions that avoid packet losses even during handover changing the base stations called eNodeBs. So, it is possible that upper layer protocol modules over LTE networks do not experience packet losses during not only communication via one eNodeB but also handover between two eNodeBs.

Instead, during a handover, upper layer protocols over LTE, such as TCP and UDP, encounter sudden increase of delay, i.e., *delay spike*, in the order of seconds. Although it is highly possible that there are no packet losses during this large delay, TCP will retransmit a packet by timeout caused by this delay, and the timeout is not effective, i.e., *spurious*. The spurious timeout invokes unnecessary decrease of congestion window (*cwnd*) and reduces the TCP throughput. In order to detect the spurious timeout and recover unnecessary decrease of cwnd, several methods are proposed and implemented. Among them, the Eifel algorithm (Ludwig and Katz, 2000), (Ludwig and Reyer, 2003), the DSACK based algorithm (Blanton and Allman, 2004), and F-RTO (Sarolahti et al., 2003), (Sarolahti et al., 2009) are standardized as RFCs (requests for comments) by IETF (Internet Engineering Task Force) and implemented in several operating systems. So far, several papers discussed the performance of the spurious timeout detection methods, but many of them are using simulation, and the detailed performance evaluation is not reported over the LTE network.

In this paper, we show the results of performance evaluation through experiments using Linux PCs and the network emulator that provides time-variant delay and packet losses. We compare the Eifel algorithm, DSACK based algorithm, and F-RTO under the conditions that there is only delay spike, which supposes the LTE lossless handover, and that there are delay spike and some packet losses, which supposes some packet losses during handover. The rest of paper consists of the following section. Section 2 shows related work on the TCP spurious timeout detection methods and TCP performance evaluation. Section 3 describes the experimental conditions including the network emulator we implemented. Section 4 gives the results of performance evaluation, and section 5 concludes this paper.

2. RELATED WORK

2.1 Survey on Spurious Timeout Detection Methods

Table 1 shows examples of spurious timeout detection methods proposed so far. These methods are summarised as follows.

The Eifel algorithms relies on the TCP timestamp option. If retransmission timer expires, a TCP sender retransmits the oldest unacknowledged segment and remembers the timestamp of this segment. When an ACK segment is returned after the timeout, it compares the timestamp echo reply value in the ACK segment with the remembered timestamp value. If the echo reply is earlier than the timestamp value, then the sender recognises that the timeout was spurious. The DSACK based algorithm modifies the TCP SACK (selective acknowledgment) option's rule so as to allow the first SACK components to indicate the duplicate data segments. When a TCP sender receives an ACK segment, it compares the ACK number of the TCP header and the first component of SACK option. If the ACK number is larger, it means that the data segments corresponding to the first SACK component is received duplicated. In this case, the retransmission is considered as spurious. F-RTO does not rely on any TCP options. When a retransmission timer expires, a TCP sender enters the slow start phase and retransmits one data segment. When an ACK segment is returned for the retransmission, the sender sends two new, i.e., not previously transmitted, data segments. If the ACK segment received following these data segments responds to the new data, that is, if it is a new ACK, then the sender recognizes that the timeout was spurious. Those three methods are currently standardized as RFCs and implemented widely. In this paper, we focus on them.

Table 1. Comparison of Existing Spurious Timeout Detection Methods

name	option	RFC	detection time	modification
Eifel	Timestamp	RFC 3522	< RTT	Tx/Rx
DSACK based	SACK	RFC 3708	> RTT	Tx/Rx
F-RTO	N/A	RFC 5682	> RTT	Tx
STODER	N/A	N/A	< RTT	Tx
E-RTO	SACK	N/A	< RTT	Tx/Rx
ER-SRTO	Timestamp	N/A	< RTT	Tx/Rx
ECN based	IP ECN nonce bit	N/A	< RTT	Tx/Rx
SnR	N/A	N/A	< RTT	Tx
Delay Injection	Mobile protocols	N/A	N/A	Rx
WiTracer	Timestamp	N/A	< RTT	Tx/Rx

The STODER algorithm (Tan et al., 2005) exploits TCP repacketization to detect spurious timeouts. If a TCP sender detect the retransmission timer expiry, it retransmits a data segment which is *k*-bytes smaller than the original segment. It detects the spurious timeout, if the ACK segment after the timeout has the ACK number more than the last byte retransmitted. In the E-RTO algorithm (Lee and Kwon, 2006), a TCP sender transmits a new data segment on retransmission timeout, instead of the oldest unacknowledged segment. If the ACK segment for the new data segment acknowledges all of the outstanding data, then the timeout is considered as spurious. It also uses the SACK option in order to handle packet losses during the delay spike. If the TCP sender receives a duplicate ACK with SACK option, then it aggressively retransmits unSACKed segments. The ER-SRTO algorithm (Cho et al., 2008) also intends to detect packet losses during delay spike and to conduct efficient recovery. As for the spurious timeout detection, it uses the same approach with the Eifel algorithm. After that, if duplicate ACKs are received, it tries to retransmit outstanding data segments aggressively. The retransmission of the E-RTO and ER-SRTO algorithms might be too aggressive compared with the normal TCP fast retransmit. The ECN (Explicit Congestion Notification) nonce based algorithm (Welzl, 2008) uses the ECN nonce code point in the IP datagram header. The ECN capable sender sets the

ECN nonce code point to 1 for original data segments, a value called ECN(1), and 0 (ECN(0)) for retransmitted data segments. ACK segments include the corresponding Nonce Sum field in TCP header, which allows the TCP sender to discriminate whether the retransmission was spurious or not. The SnR (Sprit-and-Retransmit) algorithm (Wen and Yeung, 2010) is similar with the STODER algorithm and its key idea is to split the retransmitted data segment into two smaller ones. A TCP sender detects the spuriousness when it receives an ACK segment with larger ACK number than the sequence number of the segment retransmitted at first.

The methods so far use an approach that a TCP sender detects the spuriousness by an ACK segment with some information, and that it resets the congestion control event if the timeout was spurious. In contrast, there are two proposals that increase delay intentionally when handover occurs (Klein et al., 2004), (Ahn et al., 2012). They focus mainly on the download data transfer to mobile nodes. Mobile nodes check the delay increase or the invocation of handover procedure, and inject delays to returning ACK segments. WiTracer (Hu et al., 2013) is a relatively new proposal that combines the congestion identification by use of RTT threshold, in the sender side, and the opportunistic recovery in the sender and receiver sides. The congestion identification relies on the timestamp option to detect RTT for every segment. As for the opportunistic retransmission, a sender invokes retransmission for a single duplicate ACK, and a receiver allows the spurious data reception for every other data or after a specific time period.

2.2 Studies on Performance Evaluation of TCP Over Wireless Networks

There are some studies on the performance evaluation of TCP over wireless networks. (Park and Chung, 2010) is an example of simulation-based study on TCP behavior over wireless multi-hop networks. It focuses on spurious fast retransmit recovery as well as spurious timeout retransmission, and indicates that spurious fast retransmit occurs more frequently when the number of hops is small.

On the other hand, other studies report the results of experiments using actual mobile nodes and actual wireless networks. (Kohlwes et al., 2005) shows the performance evaluation over the UMTS (Universal Mobile Telecommunications System) 3G network. It reports that RTT is fairly stable, and that spurious retransmissions were extremely rare. It concludes that no performance benefit was observed for the Eifel and F-RTO algorithms. (Li et al., 2015) and (Li et al., 2017) discuss TCP behaviors in the high speed (> 200 Km/h) mobility cases, in HSPA+ (high speed packet access plus) and 3G/4G, respectively. They show that a number of packet losses and connection shutdowns, but do not discuss about the effects of spurious timeout detection methods. In contrast, we use an actual Linux PC as a terminal and introduce a network emulator providing time-variant delay and packet losses, which are derived from the performance evaluation of a real TCP communication over an LTE network in Japan. We discuss the behaviour of spurious detection methods actually introduced in the Linux operating system.

3. EXPERIMENTAL CONDITIONS

3.1 Network Emulator for LTE Handover

As a network emulator that provides delay and packet losses, NetEm (Jurgelionis et al., 2011) and Dummynet (Carbone and Rizzo, 2010) are adopted widely. They are used in the middle of communicating nodes and can insert delay and packet losses, according to the specified parameter values and distributions. However, these values and distributions are static throughout a measurement run.

Figure 1 shows an example of delay performance measured in a Japanese LTE network, when a mobile node moving by a train in Tokyo area communicates with a server located in our lab. The horizontal axis is the time elapsed and the vertical axis RTT. This result is measured by PING where a mobile node sends ICMP Echo request packets with 500 byte data in the interval of 0.01 sec. The mobile node and the server synchronized the system clock by NTP (Network Time Protocol). The red line shows the one way delay from the mobile node to the server, and the green line indicate the one way delay in the reverse direction. This result indicates that the delay was normally small but there were several delay spikes during the measurement run. Although there were several packet losses, the timing was random, some were in the periods with small delay and others were during the delay spikes.

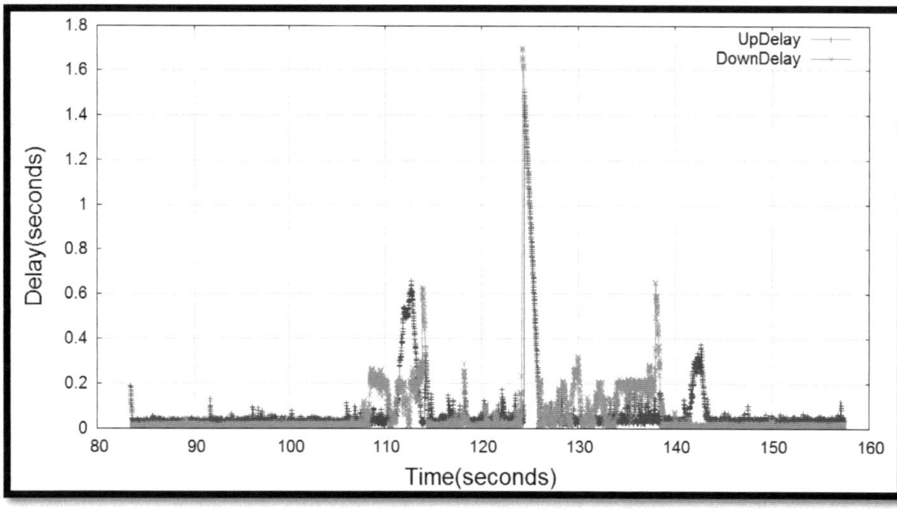

Figure 1. An example of Delay Measurement in an LTE Network using a Node Moving around on a Train in Tokyo Area

In order to emulate the LTE handover as shown in Figure 1, we have developed a network emulator with the following functions.

- The network emulator supports the time-variant delay and packet loss rate. The delay and packet loss rate are given by a table as shown in Figure 2(a). It specifies the elapsed time (*pTime*) from the time handling the first packet by the emulator. The delay (*pDelay*) is the time period in which a packet arriving at the emulator at time *pTime* is queued in the emulator. Similarly, the loss rate (*pLoss*) is the packet loss rate which a packet arriving at time *pTime* suffers from. For the timing not specified in the table, the delay and loss rate are interpolated linearly as shown in Figure 2(b). It should be noted that the delay and loss rate can be changed sharply by specifying different values for the same elapsed time.
- When a packet arrives at the emulator at time *t*, where *t* is between *pTime*[*i*] and *pTime*[*i*+1], it is assigned *delay* as given in Eq. (1). At the outgoing port in the emulator, the packet is queued for the period of *delay*.

$$delay\ at\ t = \frac{pDelay[i+1] \times (t - pTime[i]) + pDelay[i] \times (pTime[i+1] - t)}{pTime[i+1] - pTime[i]} \quad (1)$$

In the case of Figure 2, packets arriving at the emulator during 10,000 msec to 11,460 msec are transmitted in a very short period during 15,000 msec and 15,010 msec.

elapsed time: *pTime* (msec)	delay: *pDelay* (msec)	loss rate: *pLoss* (1/100 %)
0	50	0
10000	50	0
10000	1500	100
11460	50	100
11460	50	0
20000	50	0

(a) parameter setting for emulator

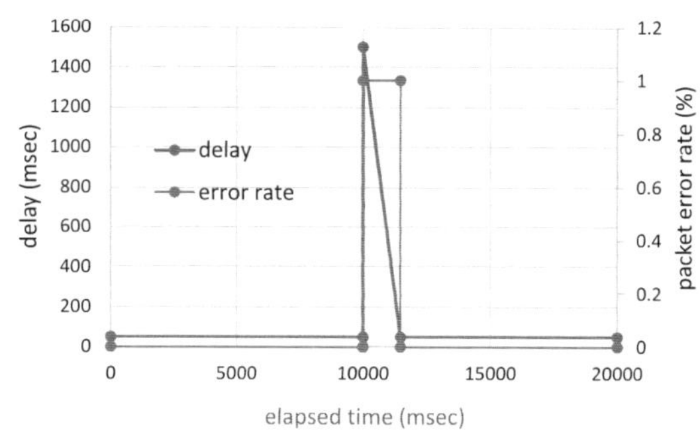

(b) delay and packet loss rate provided by emulator

Figure 2. Delay and Packet Loss Rate Added at Emulator

- As for the packet loss rate, a packet arriving at time *t*, which is similar with above, is assigned the packet loss rate given by Eq. (2). When the packet is being transmitted from the emulator, it is discarded with this possibility.

$$loss\ at\ t = \frac{pLoss[i+1] \times (t - pTime[i]) + pLoss[i] \times (pTime[i+1] - t)}{pTime[i+1] - pTime[i]} \quad (2)$$

  This mechanism is implemented using the Linux kernel function `random32()`, which generates a random number in the uniform distribution. The modulus of this random number with 10,000 is calculated (`random32()%10000`). If *loss* for this packet is smaller than the modulus, this packet is discarded at the outgoing port.

- We implemented the network emulator by modifying the source code of NetEm.

3.2 Experiment Configurations and Parameters

Figure 3 shows the network configuration we used in the experiment. Two PCs are connected by Gigabit Ethernet via the network emulator described above. In the sender side, the packet transmission speed is limited to 10 Mbps with the traffic control (`tc`) command supported by the Linux operating system. In this experiment, the delay and packet loss are inserted only in the direction from the sender to the receiver. In order to analyze the results in detail, the transmitted packets are captured at the output port of the sender, and the cwnd value is monitored in the sender by use of the tcpprobe function in Linux (Linux Foundation, 2016). As for the delay and packet loss rate used in the emulator, we used the setting shown in Figure 2. The congestion control algorithm used in the sender is TCP Reno.

4. RESULTS OF PERFORMANCE EVALUATIONS

4.1 Experiment with Delay Spike Only

Figure 4 shows the results of performance evaluations when only delay spike is added at elapsed time 10 sec. The figure gives the time variation of the sequence/ACK numbers and cwnd for Eifel, DSACK, and F-RTO. The horizontal axis of graphs is the elapsed time, zooming up the duration between 10 sec. and 13 sec. The vertical axis is the sequence and ACK numbers counted in Megabyte and cwnd counted in packets. From the graphs indicating the cwnd values, there are some differences among three methods. F-RTO works best among the three. It can detect the spurious timeout and return to the previous cwnd value very quickly. In the case of Eifel, the spurious timeout can be detected quickly and cwnd is recovered to the value before the timeout, but after that, cwnd is halved and then increases to the previous value. Among three methods, DSACK is poor. The cwnd is reduced to one packet and then it goes up following the slow start and congestion avoidance procedures. This is an ordinal step after timeout, and so it can be said that no steps for spurious timeout detection are working.

However, since RTT after the delay spike is small in this experiment, those differences in the cwnd behaviors are not reflected to the behaviors of sequence/ACK numbers. The increase situations of cwnd shown in Figure 4 (a), (c), and (e) are similar for the three methods. So, it can be said that Eifel, DSACK, and F-RTO work well in the LTE lossless handover.

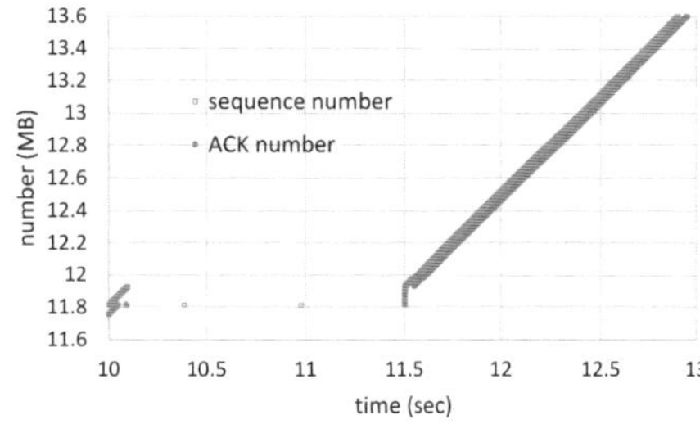

(a) sequence number and ACK number for Eifel

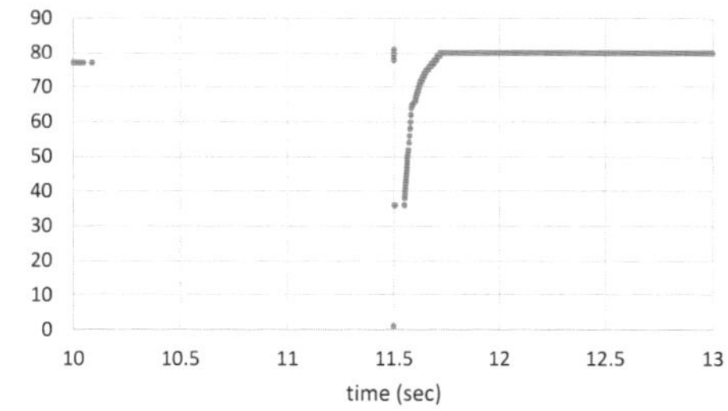

(b) cwnd (in packets) for Eifel

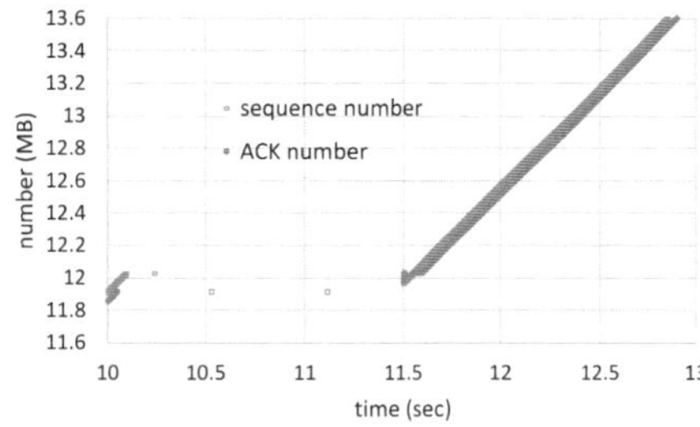

(c) sequence number and ACK number for DSACK

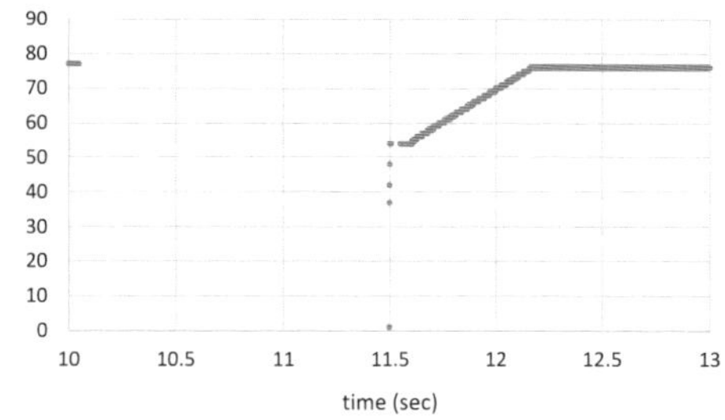

(d) cwnd (in packets) for DSACK

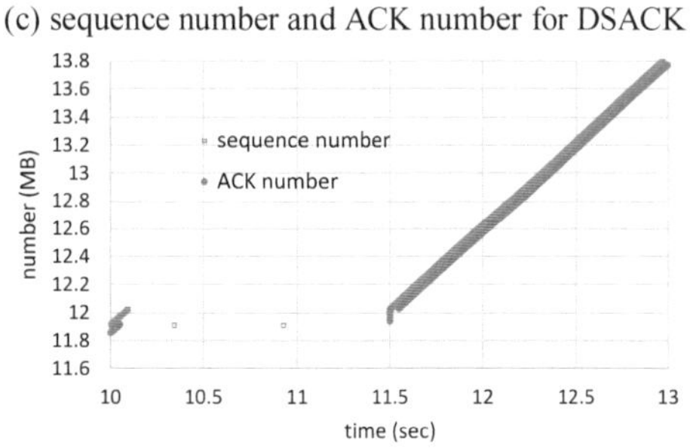

(e) sequence number and ACK number for F-RTO

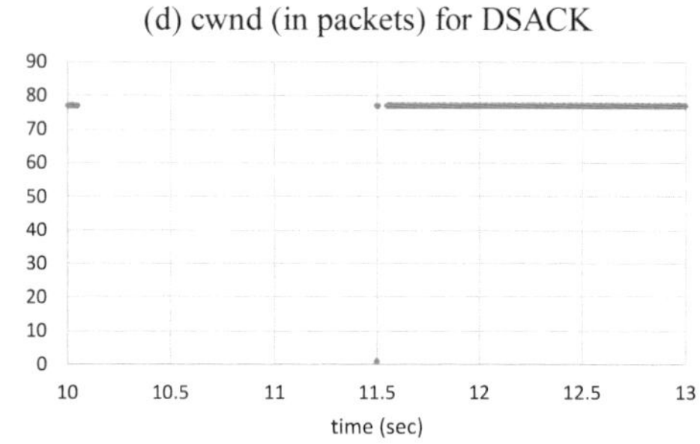

(f) cwnd (in packets) for F-RTO

Figure 4. Sequence/ACK Numbers and cwnd vs. Time with Delay Spike Only

4.2 Experiment with Delay Spike and Packet Loss

Next is the case that packet losses are associated with the handover. Figure 5 shows the time variation of the sequence/ACK numbers and cwnd for three methods. The specification of graphs are similar with Figure 4. In this case, we focus on the elapsed time between 10 sec. and 20 sec. because there are packet losses in this time frame. Since packet losses are provided by stochastic means in our emulator, we performed three measurement runs for each method. Three runs for individual methods provided similar results, and Figure 5 shows one of them for an individual method.

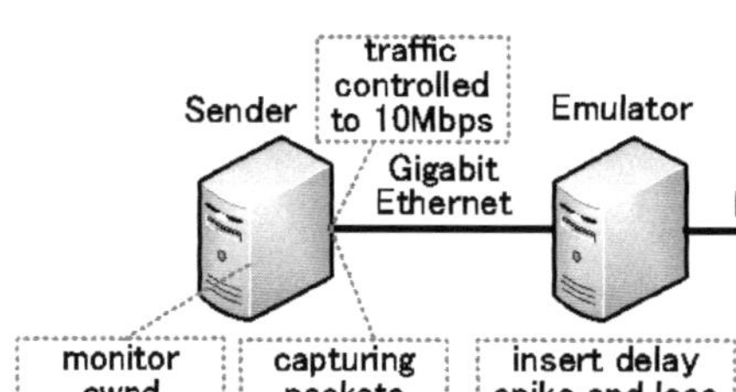

Figure 3. Network Configuration of Experiment

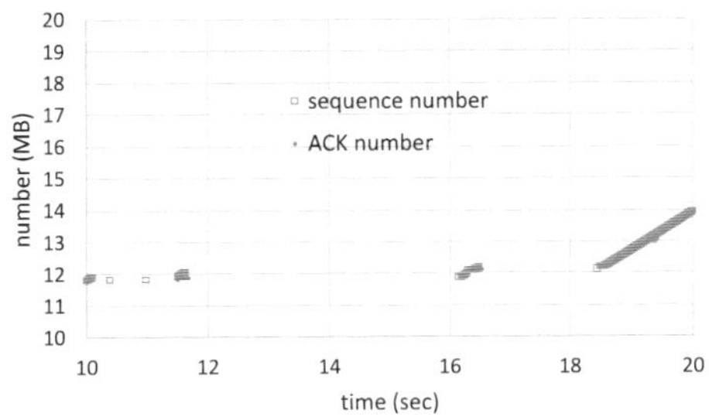

(a) sequence number and ACK number for Eifel

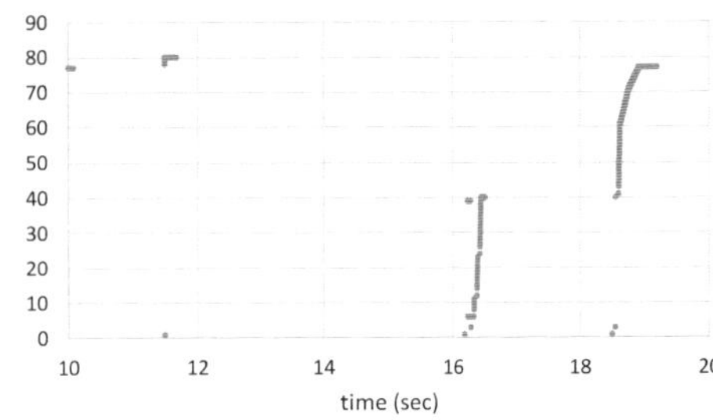

(b) cwnd (in packets) for Eifel

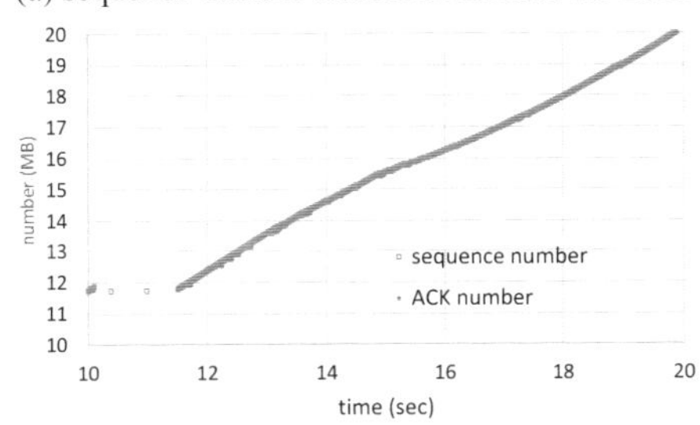

(c) sequence number and ACK number for DSACK

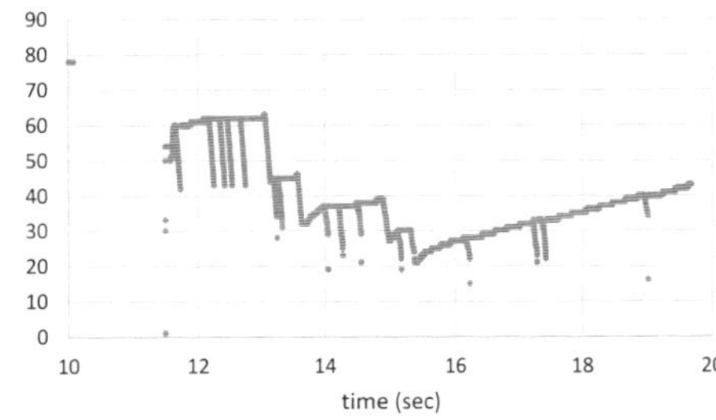

(d) cwnd (in packets) for DSACK

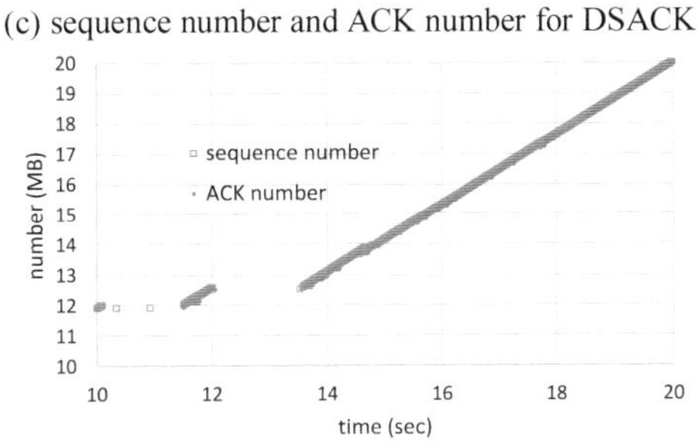

(e) sequence number and ACK number for F-RTO

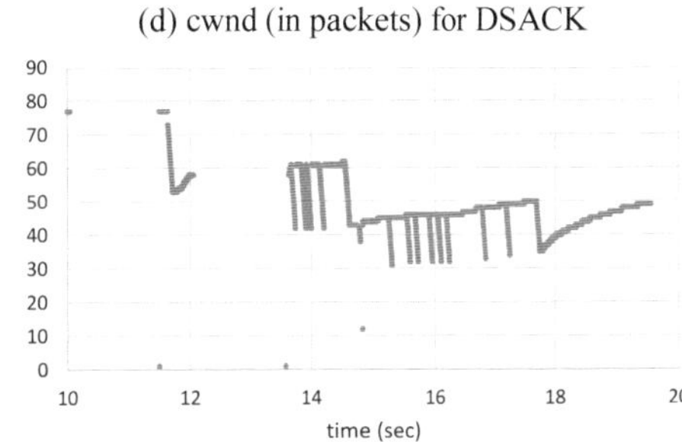

(f) cwnd (in packets) for F-RTO

Figure 5. Sequence/ACK Numbers and cwnd vs. Time with Delay Spike and Packet Loss

In this case, Eifel provided worst performance among the three methods. After the delay spike, there are some timeout retransmissions and they provide large time gaps in data transmission. On the other hand, DSACK and F-RTO provide better performance than Eifel. Although the F-RTO experiment has one timeout retransmission after delay spike, the total transmitted bytes during 10 sec. and 20 sec. are similar for DSACK and F-RTO. These results says that Eifel can detect the spurious timeout effectively, but cannot handle retransmissions efficiently. On the other hand, the SACK option used in DSACK and the new data transmission used in F-RTO seem to be effective for handling retransmissions as well as spurious timeout detection.

5. CONCLUSIONS

In this paper, we presented the results of performance evaluation for TCP spurious timeout detection methods supposing LTE handovers. We adopted a way to use real communicating nodes with introducing a network emulator that provides time-variant delay and packet loss, a delay spike and packet losses during the delay, to imitate LTE handovers. We implemented this network emulator over NetEm, a widely used freeware network emulator.

We conducted experimental measurements for Eifel, DSACK, and F-RTO, wide spread methods standardized by IETF, in the conditions with delay spike only and with delay spike and packet losses. When only the delay spike is inserted, the three methods work well similarly. When the packet losses are added with delay, the performance of Eifel is poorer than DSACK and F-RTO.

ACKNOWLEDGEMENT

The authors thank Dr. M. Nomoto, Mr. K. Ohata, and Mr. R. Fujiyama for their efforts in the early stage of this project, especially the implementation of the network emulator described in Section 3 and the performance evaluation of delay characteristics of an LTE network given in Figure 1.

REFERENCES

Ahn, W., Gwak, Y., and Kim, Y., 2012. A Low-Complexity Delay Injection Algorithm For Improving TCP Performance During LTE Intra Handover. *International Conference on Information Network 2012*, pp. 177-181.

Blanton, E. and Allman, M., 2004. *Using TCP Duplicate Selective Acknowledgement (DSACKs) and Stream Control Transmission Protocol (SCTP) Duplicate Transmission Sequence Numbers (TSNs) to Detect Spurious Retransmissions*. IETF RFC 3708.

Carbone, M. and Rizzo, L., 2010. Dummynet Revisited. *ACM SIGCOMM Comput. Commun. Rev.*, vol. 40, issue 2, pp. 12-20.

Cho, I., Han, J., and Lee, J., 2008. Enhanced Response Algorithm for Spurious TCP Timeout (ER-SRTO). *International Conference on Information Networking, 2008 (ICOIN 2008)*, pp. 1-5.

Hu, C., Yang, X., Fan, M., and Zhao, P., 2013. WiTracer: A Novel Solution to Improve TCP Performance over Wireless Network. *2013 9th International Wireless Communications and Mobile Conputing Conference (IWCMC)*, pp. 450-455.

IEEE Std 802.11-2016, 2016. *IEEE Standard for Information technology – Part11: Wireless LAN medium Access Control (MAC) and Physical Layer (PHY) Specifications*.

Jurgelionis, A., Laulajainen, J., Hirvonen, M., and Wang, A., 2011. An Empirical Study of NetEm Network Emulation Functionalities. *20th International Conference on Computer Communications and Networks (ICCCN)*, pp. 1-6.

Klein, T., Leung, K., Parkinson, R., and Samuel, L., 2004. Avoiding Spurious TCP Timeouts in Wireless Networks by Delay Injection. *IEEE Global Telecommunications Conference, 2004 (GLOBECOM '04)*, pp. 2754-2759.

Kohlwes, M., Riihijarvi, J., and Mahonen, P., 2005. Measurements of TCP Performance over UMTS Networks in Near-Ideal Conditions. *2005 IEEE 61st Vehicular Technology Conference*, vol. 4, pp. 2235-2239.

Lee, M. and Kwon, O., 2006. E-RTO: An Enhanced TCP Retransmission Timeout Algorithm using SACK option. *2006 IEEE Wireless Communications and Networking Conference (WCNC 2006)*, pp. 74-79.

Li, L., et al., 2015. A Measurement Study on TCP Behaviors in HSPA+ Networks on High-Speed Rails. *2015 IEEE Conference on Computer Communications (INFOCOM)*, pp. 2731-2739.

Li, L., et al., 2017. A Longitudinal Measurement Study of TCP Performance and Behavior in 3G/4G Networks over High Speed Rail. *IEEE/ACM Trans. on Networking*, vol. 25, no. 4, pp. 2195-2208.

Linux Foundation, 2016. *Linux Foundation Wiki, Trace: tcpprobe*. https://wiki.linuxfoundation.org/networking/tcpprobe.

Ludwig, R. and Katz, R., 2000. The Eifel algorithm: making TCP robust against spurious retransmissions. *ACM SIGCOMM Comput. Commun. Rev.*, vol. 30, issue 1, pp. 30-36.

Ludwig, R. and Reyer, M., 2003. *The Eifel Detection Algorithms for TCP*. IETF RFC 3522.

Park, M. and Chung, S., 2010. A Simulation-based Study on Spurious Timeouts and Fast Retransmits of TCP in Wireless Networks. *2010 Third International Joint Conference on Computational Science and Optimization*, pp. 273-277.

Sarolahti, P., Kojo, M., and Raatikainen, K., 2003. F-RTO: an enhanced recovery algorithm for TCP retransmission timeouts. *ACM SIGCOMM Comput. Commun. Rev.*, vol. 33, issue 2, pp. 51-63.

Sarolahti, P., Kojo, M., Yamamoto, K., and Hata, M., 2009. *Forward RTO-Recovery (F-RTO): An Algorithm for Detecting Spurious Retransmission Timeouts with TCP*. IETF RFC 5682.

Sesia, S., Toufik, I., and Baker, M., 2011. *LTE – The UMTS Long Term Evolution, From Theory to Practice, Second Edition*. A John Wiley & Sons, Ltd., Publication.

Tan, K., Zhang, Q., and Zhu, W., 2005. STODER: a robust and efficient algorithm for handling spurious retransmit timeouts in TCP. *IEEE Global Telecommunications Conference, 2005 (GLOBECOM '05)*, pp. 3692-3696.

Welzl, M., 2008. Using the ECN Nonce to detect Spurious Loss Events in TCP. *IEEE Global Telecommunications Conference, 2008 (GLOBECOM '08)*, pp. 1-6.

Wen, Z. and Yeung, K., 2010. On Detection Algorithms for Spurious Retransmissions in TCP. *2010 IEEE Wireless Communications and Networking Conference (WCNC 2010)*, pp. 1-6.

A CRITICAL REVIEW ON REFERENCE ARCHITECTURES AND MODELS FOR HIGHER EDUCATION INSTITUTIONS

Felix Sanchez-Puchol[1], Joan A. Pastor-Collado[2] and Baptista Borrell[3]
[1]Open University of Catalonia (UOC) & SEIDOR SBS Services, Barcelona (Spain)
[2]Technical University of Catalonia (UPC), Barcelona (Spain)
[3]SEIDOR SBS Services, Barcelona (Spain)

ABSTRACT

Enterprise Reference Architectures (ERAs) and Reference Models (RMs) have emerged over the last years as relevant instruments for improving the quality and effectiveness of Enterprise Architecture (EA) practice. Whilst a wide variety of different ERAs and RMs have been proposed for different industries and types of business, only few of them have been devoted to the Higher Education (HE) sector. In this paper, we critically review and compare 19 existing ERAs and RMs targeted to the HE domain on the basis of a common set of 12 definitional attributes. In so doing, we contribute to the existing body of knowledge by providing a unified, structured and comprehensive catalog of these abstract EA artifacts, aiming to create awareness on their potential practical utility and to increase their visibility, transparency and opportunity for their practical use by different HE stakeholders. Hence, the proposed catalog is expected to be useful both for practitioners and researchers by providing a panoramic view of rather ready-to-use existing ERAs and RMs for HE. Moreover, and by specifying their main scope, coverage and extend of knowledge captured, the catalog can be a valuable tool for guiding HE stakeholders on making better-informed decisions on the selection of suitable architectural artifacts for being conveniently adapted or applied in their different EA practices conducted at their respective institutions.

KEYWORDS

Enterprise Reference Architectures, Reference Models, Enterprise Architecture, Higher Education, Critical Review

1. INTRODUCTION

Enterprise Architecture (EA) is currently considered as one of the main key instruments for Information Systems (IS) managers to cope with tensions between business demands and IS needs (Kotusev et al., 2015; Niemi and Pekkola, 2017). Over the last years, and as a specific type of EA artifact, Enterprise Reference Architectures (ERAs) and Reference Models (RMs) have emerged as relevant instruments for providing common understanding among different stakeholders, and for improving the effectiveness of EA practices as well as the quality of architectural designs (Timm, 2018; Niemi and Pekkola, 2017). Whilst a wide variety of heterogeneous ERAs and RMs have been proposed for different classes of enterprises and business domains, only a few of them have been designed to be specifically applied in Higher Education Institutions (HEIs), in which EA adoption has been considered as a complex and cumbersome issue (Luftman and Kempaiah, 2007; Syynimaa, 2015; JISC, 2009). Therefore, there still is a clear need to develop and foster "*the feasibility of formalized frameworks and components of EA specifically tailored to suit the structure of HEIs*" (Oderinde, 2010, p.7). The current relevance of the topic has been recently noticed by several different authors, stressing for example, the potential of EA practices and tools as facilitators for developing effective internal quality assurance systems in HE institutions (Olsen and Trelsgård, 2016, p.808; Barata and Cunha, 2017). These complex systems have become nowadays a critical artefact for institutional HE governance, in the case of Europe due to the new regulatory reforms introduced by the Bologna Process (Manatos et al., 2017).

Aiming to bridge such gap, in this paper we extend our previous preliminary work (Sanchez-Puchol and Pastor-Collado, 2017; Sanchez-Puchol et al., 2017) by critically reviewing and comparing existing ERAs and RMs for HE. In so doing, we aim to contribute to the existing body of knowledge by (i) creating awareness on the IS community about the potential practical relevance of such abstract models, and (ii) by providing a well-structured catalog of existing artifacts in order to facilitate their visibility, transparency and potential practical use for both practitioners and professionals in the HE sector.

2. BACKGROUND

As a starting point for the paper, in this section we introduce the concepts of ERA and RM. Although these terms tend to be sometimes used interchangeably, several nuances might be highlighted in each case.

On the one hand, RAs have been defined by Lankhorst (2014) as "*standardized architectures that provide a frame of reference for a particular domain, sector or field of interest (...) provid[ing] a common vocabulary, reusable designs and industry best practices*". RAs leverage the reuse of knowledge by identifying, grouping and abstracting common features of a particular domain in an unique and a product/vendor-independent model, which in turn, acts as a reference for all the specific models of such domain (Cloutier et al., 2010, p.19; Angelov et al., 2012). As abstract artifact models (i.e. models of classes of objects), RAs should be conveniently specialized (i.e. instantiated) in order to obtain the model of a particular solution architecture (Lankhorst, 2014; Clottier et al., 2010). Describing architectures has proven to be difficult, and therefore, they need to be conveniently documented and structured into manageable pieces, each one of which addresses a number of facets configuring the architecture (Greefhorst et al. 2006, pp.103–109). For instance, a RA can be characterized as a bundle or package of multiple architectural assets, which may include, among others: best practices, (architectural) design principles and reusable patterns, vocabularies, glossaries, technical standards as well as different conceptual models representing the targeted architectural or class-of-objects domain (Cloutier et al., 2010; Lankhorst, 2014; Kotzampasaki, 2015).

On the other hand, RMs can be viewed as one of the core elements of a RA, since they particularly detail the specific scope and the level of specialization of the information provided (i.e. features, knowledge, etc.) to consider the scoped domain. In other words, RMs bring to table a clear and simple (usually on-a-single-page) view of the domain of interest, which can be then conveniently adjusted to suit better the particular needs of the RM's user. Thus, RMs are generic conceptual models focussed on specific aspects of a certain problem – i.e. function, information, process, etc. – that formalize a set of generally accepted practices and encapsulate knowledge to be reused later in a particular application domain (Fettke and Loos, 2007). For instance, RAs tend to inherently be layered and partitioned artifacts as they usually incorporate more than just one RM, representing several (disjoint) partial views of a whole domain. Unfortunately, and due to their abstract and generic nature, not all existing RAs incorporate specific consistency patterns or viewpoints showing the interactions, dependencies and relationships among objects represented in each of their RM.

Lastly, ERAs emerge as a particular subtype of RAs, when the targeted domain is set to a "class of enterprises" (Timm, 2018, p.209). Hence, they still encompass a high level of abstraction, but to a lesser extent than a RA. ERAs have been defined as "*a generic EA for a class of enterprises, that in a coherent whole of EA design principles, methods and models which are used as foundation in the design and realization of the concrete EA that consists of three coherent partial architectures: the business architecture, the application architecture and the technology architecture*" (ten Harmsen van der Beek et al., 2012, p.99). ERAs and RMs for HE represent the subset of those artifacts tailored for being used in HE contexts.

3. RESEARCH APPROACH

Based on a previous literature review undertaken by the authors (Sanchez-Puchol et al., 2017), a total of 19 artifacts (6 ERAs and 13 RMs) were identified, and were critically analysed and classified. For simplicity purposes, in the remaining of the paper we will refer to them as Reference Enterprise Architecture Models (REAMs) for HE, regardless of their concrete nature as ERAs or RMs.

Table 1. Higher Education RAs and RMs Analyzed in this Paper

#	Artefact Name	Abbreviator	Type	Bibliographic base references	State
1	Hoger Onderwijs Referentie Architectuur	HORA	ERA	(SURF, n.d., 2013b; a)	Active
2	ITANA Reference Architecture for Teaching and Learning	RATL	ERA	(ITANA Working Group, 2012; Abel et al., 2013)	Active
3	CAUDIT Enterprise Architecture Commons for Higher Education	CAUDIT	ERA	(CAUDIT, 2016, 2017)	Active
4	The TIER (Trust and Identity) Reference Architecture	TIER	ERA	(TIER-Data Structures and APIs Working Group, 2016)	Active
5	Cloud Computing Architecture for Higher Education	CLOUD	ERA	(Pardeshi, 2014; Mircea and Andreescu, 2011)	Unknown
6	Common Enterprise Architecture in the Norwegian HE sector	NOR-EA	ERA	(Bergh-Hoff et al., 2015; Olsen and Trelsgård, 2016)	Ongoing (estimated)
7	Colombian Higher Education Enterprise Architecture	CHE^2A	RM	(Llamosa-Villalba et al., 2015, 2014)	Active (estimated)
8	Charles Sturt Univ. HE Business Process Reference Model	CSU-BPM	RM	(Charles Sturt University, 2010)	Closed (estimated)
9	HE-IUP Business Process Model	HE-IUP	RM	(Reiner, 2014)	Closed
10	Business Process Reference Model for HE	BPRM-HE	RM	(Svensson and Hvolby, 2012)	Unknown
11	Higher Education Information Systems in Croatia	HE-ISC	RM	(Frackmann, 2007)	Closed
12	The ICOPER (eContent+ Best Practices Network) Reference Model for Outcome-based HE	ICOPER	RM	(Simon et al., 2011; Pawlowski and Kozlov, 2013)	Closed
13	Unified Information Systems Reference Model for HE Institutions	UISRM-HE	RM	(Sanchez-Puchol et al., 2017)	Active
14	e-education Application Framework	eEdSF	RM	(Fagan, 2003)	Closed
15	Univ. of Tras-o-Montes e Alto Douro Multidimensional IS Architecture	UTAD-ISA	RM	(Bessa et al., 2016)	Active (estimated)
16	Reference Model of IS for an Integrated Campus Management	RMIS-ICM	RM	(Bick and Börgmann, 2009)	Closed
17	Reusable Process Model Structure for HE	RPMS-HE	RM	(Van der Merwe, 2005)	Closed
18	Value Chain for Higher Education	VC-HE	RM	(Hutaibat, 2011)	Closed
19	Reference Model of University IT Architecture	UNITA	RM	(Chen, Tang and Li, 2016)	Active (estimated)

The comparative analysis framework (see Figure 1) has been conceived and inspired from previous works devoted to create taxonomies or classifications for similar artifacts, as business RMs (Fettke at al., 2006), EA frameworks (Greefhorst et al., 2006), software RAs (Angelov et al., 2012) or IS maturity models (Mettler, 2011). Following, we provide descriptive information for each attribute configuring the framework. Multiple-values are possible for several attributes, as they have not been defined to be mutually-exclusive in all cases.

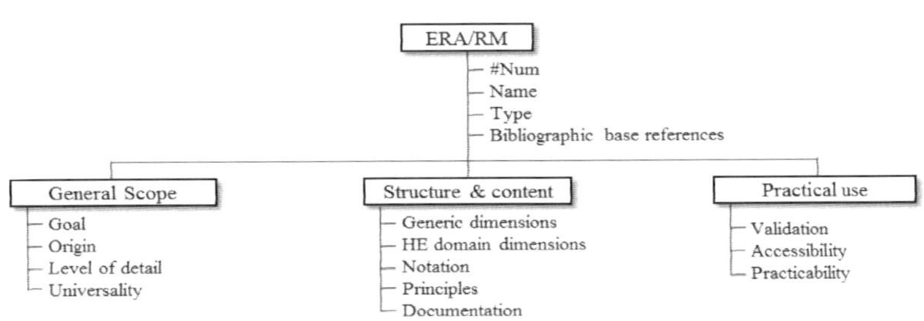

Figure 1. Criteria Framework used in this Paper for Investigating ERA and RMs in HE

- ***Identification***. The identification of the artifact is made by *running numbers* and their original *name* and the *type* of artifact (ERA or RM). *Bibliographic base references* of the sources containing justificatory knowledge and information of the covered models is also provided.

- ***General scope***. According to Cloutier et al. (2010), two main goals can be considered for the intended usage of a RA: *standardization* of specific solution architectures (thus promoting system/component interoperability among them) or design *facilitation* of the specific solution architectures (providing guidelines in the form of generic architectural principles, blueprints, patterns, etc.). The origin attribute reflects whether the artifact has its source from *academia* or *practice*. Similarly to (Greefhorst et al., 2006), the level of detail reflects the concreteness and extent of information captured by the artefact. We consider three possible levels of detail, namely, *detailed, semi-detailed and aggregated*. Finally, the universality attribute reflects the generalizability of the particular artefact in terms of a HE system, which can be at *general* level, at *regional or national* level or at the *particular* scope of a unique HE settlement.
- **Structure and content.** The structure and content of a REAM can be inspected from the point of view of the generic domain levels of an EA− that is, *business* (i.e. processes, capabilities), IS (*data* and *applications*) and *technology* (Kotusev et al., 2015)− as well as from HE-oriented dimensions focussed in its main missions, that is, *teaching and learning*, *research and development*, *support services* and *third mission* (Manatos et al., 2017). In line with Angelov et al. (2012), the level of formalization regarding the content representation presented by an REAM is covered by the notation attribute. Three operational values are possible, *unformal* (by means of natural language or an ill-defined graphical notation), *semi-formal* (using a well-defined notation, as UML or Archimate) or *formal* (based on a formal architecture specification language, strictly defining the semantics of the artifact). We also consider the explicit inclusion of *architectural principles* and the type of documentation available, in terms of a well-structured *specification*, a *wiki/website*, or an alternative form of *documental/textual support* (de Boer et al., 2011).
- **Practical use.** The practical utility of REAMs is assessed by considering three attributes. First, and regarding evaluation, we looked for the existence of usage evidences (i.e. *tested* vs *unclear*) of the operationalization of the artifact aiming to ensure or demonstrate (in some way or another) its practical utility or relevance. Next, the accessibility to the artifact is analyzed on the basis of three possible values, namely whether it is *free* for use (no barriers to accessing to the whole contents or existing documentation of the model), *restricted* (existence of some type of barrier for accessing the artifacts' documentation or any kind of license limiting its practical use) or *charged* (limited access to the model to an audience by means of a fee payment). Finally, we have reviewed whether the information provided by the artifact contains practical recommendations for how to use it in a situational HE context, in terms of *guidelines, basic recommendations,* or contrarily, if such information remains *unclear*.

4. MAIN FINDINGS AND RESULS

Results of the critical analysis performed on the uncovered REAMs are presented in Table 2. Collectively, it can be concluded that there is a plethora of heterogeneous artefacts, conceived with different scope and focus, and with different levels of granularity and detail. Both researchers and practitioners can take advantage of the presented catalog to choose those REAMs that suit better for their concrete EA tasks derived from their duties in their HE contexts. In terms of completeness, we must clearly highlight the potential of the Dutch's national HORA RA, which can provide support for a lot of activities and goals from a very holistic perspective. Similarly, the CAUDIT RA also ranks well is terms of completeness. However, it seems that it provides much less practical support information than HORA and is very focussed on the business and data domain dimensions of an EA. There is also a good variety of different business process-oriented and application-oriented RMs, but they tend to be defined at a very aggregate level of detail, which may complicate its applicability as they would have to be much customized. Finally, we must point up that we found evidence on the existence of an initiative devoted to the development of a Norwegian national HE RA. Nonetheless, we were not able to find clear evidence on its core structural components, and therefore, we only could partially evaluate it. Our suspicion is that it still is an on-going initiative.

We concentrate now on the particular level of the attributes considered by the framework. With regard to the *general scope* attributes, our analysis reveals a relatively good balance in terms of the goal and the origin of the artifacts. Unfortunately, the identification of REAMs goals and their associated target audience becomes sometimes difficult, as developers do not tend to explicitly state it. Also, a tendency towards academic-oriented RMs as well as a great heterogeneity in the detail level of the uncovered REAMs can be appreciated.

Table 2. Analysis and classification of REAMs for HE

Artefact		General scope						Structure and content														Practical use					
Name	Type	Goal		Origin		Det.	Univ.	Generic EA dimensions				HE domain dimensions				Nota-tion	Princi-ples		Documen-tation			Valida-tion		Acces-sibility	Practica-bility		
		Standardization	Facilitation	Academia	Practice	Level of detail (type of)	Universality (type of)	Business	Data	Applications	Technology	Teaching & learning	Research & development	Support services	Third mission	Notation type	Explicitly included	Not transparent	Specification	Wiki/website	Documental/textual sup.	Tested	Unclear	Accessibility issues	Concrete guidelines	Basic recommendations	Unclear
HORA	ERA	■		■	■	D	R	■	■	■	□	■	■	■		S	■		■	■			■	F	■		
RATL	ERA		■		■	S	G	■	■			■		■		S		■		■			■	F		■	
CAUDIT	ERA	■		■	■	D	R	■	■			■	■	■	□	S		■			■		■	R			■
TIER	ERA		■		■	S	G			■	■			■		F		■		■			■	F		■	
CLOUD	ERA		■	■		A	G			□	■	□	□	□		U		■			■		■	F		■	
NOR-EA [1]	ERA	■			■	A	R	–	–	–	–	–	–	–	–	–	■				□		■	F	–	–	–
CHE²A	RM	■		■	■	S	R	■				■	□	■		U	□				■	□		R		■	
CSU-BPM	RM		■		■	D	P	■				■	■	■		S		■		■	■		■	F	■		
HE-IUP	RM		□	■	■	A	G	■				■	■	□		U		■		■	■		■	F			■
BPRM-HE	RM	□		■		A	G	■				■				S		■			■		■	F			■
HE-ISC	RM	□			■	A	R	□		□		□		□		U		■			■		■	F			■
ICOPER	RM		■	■	■	D	G	■		□		■				S	■		■			■		F	■		
UISRM-HE	RM		■	■		S	G			■		■	■	■		S	■				■		■	F			■
eEdSF	RM	□		■		A	G			■		□		□		U		■			■		■	F			■
UTAD-ISA	RM		□	■		S	P			■		■		■		S		■			■		■	F			■
RMIS-ICM	RM		■	■		A	G			■		■		■		U		■			■		■	F			■
RPMS-HE	RM	□		■		A	G	■				■		□		S		■			■	□		F	■		
VC-HE	RM	□		■		A	G	■				□	□	□	□	U		■			■		■	F			■
UNITA	RM		□	■		A	G				■	□		□		U		■			■		■	F			■

Legend

[1] Partially evaluated (still under development)

Level of detail: D Detailed | S Semi-detailed | A Aggregated

Notation type: F Formal | S Semi-formal | U Unformal

■ Full coverage | □ Suggested or basic coverage | – Not evaluated

Level of universality: G General | R Regional/National | P Particular

Accessibility issues: F Free | R Restricted | C Charge

Finally, we also detect a pattern regarding the articulation of some kind of (public) HE sector-oriented interoperability initiatives, grounding on the establishment of a common abstract national REAM (for example, HORA in the Nederlands, NOR-EA in Norway or CHE2A in Colombia). Such reference models need to be next adopted and conveniently instantiated by each HE institution, according to its own context. On the one hand, institutions could benefit of positive economic effects derived from decreasing costs due to model reusability, shortest life-cycle modelling times for developing solution EAs or an increase of the quality of EA models (Olsen and Trelsgård, 2016; Timm, 2018). On the other hand, administrations could benefit from costs reductions due to economies of scale and resource sharing – IS shared service provision across all HE. All these benefits, may justify the economic investments devoted to the REAM's conception.

In terms of *content and structure* attributes, we detect a lack of artifacts addressing technology-oriented issues, as we only were able to find 4 REAMs addressing these in some way. This finding can be considered as consistent with the existing literature on EAs, in which technology domain layers tend to be considered as less application-domain dependent than others. In this sense, we also observe a notable lack of REAMs addressing business processes and activities related with the third-mission of a HE institution. As expected, the main focus tends to be on the teaching and learning processes as well as their respective support processes. On the other hand, architectural principles (as another key component of reference artifacts) should be much more clearly made explicit by developers of these models. A tendency towards the use of semi-formal and unformal notations is also appreciated, which should be interpreted as a sing in favour of the artefact's simplicity, facilitating their understandability by different potential HE stakeholders. Finally, as only 6 of the 19 investigated models have either a dedicated web/wiki page or are alternatively disseminated through a formal specification report, we interpret the availability of detailed documentation of a REAM as a certain sign of rigor in the process development of the artifact.

Lastly, and in terms of *practical use* attributes, our analysis reveals a notable lack of support of the investigated artifacts in terms of applicability. We believe that there is a clear need for developing more easily applicable and practice-oriented REAMs for HE, providing more additional details on how and why to apply them. On the other hand, we also appreciate a general lack of evidences for testing or demonstrating the utility and value of such abstract artifacts in real scenarios, even in those cases being originated from practice. In this sense, several of those REAMs are no more than just simple and basic descriptive conceptual models. In this line, developing for HE in a more transparent and scientifically theoretically-sound procedure would help in providing more empirical evidence on the value of such models. We must highlight at this point, however, that in those cases in which the REAM is developed through joint collaborative efforts (consortiums) engaging a great number of representative stakeholders and participating organizations involved in the HE industry itself – as for the case of HORA, CAUDIT, NOR-EA RATL, TIER or even CHE^2A – it should be considered that their reliability and universality is implicitly validated by all those key users and stakeholders involved in the consortium's development teams. Finally, we note that all the investigated models are freely accessible, but CAUDIT's RA use is restricted by a creative commons license. Whilst this finding may seem up to a point surprising, the social nature inherent to HE should be considered here. Under this context, we understand that REAMs are not produced to be monetarized by means of payment fees or usage licences. Contrarily, they are poised to benefit to as many as possible HE institutions (and interested) parties through their effective application in practice – they are a means, not a goal in themselves–. Hence, their simplicity and understandability should be promoted to the maximum extent.

5. CONCLUSIONS

In this paper, we set out to examine the status-quo of REAMs targeted to the HE domain. Based on a series of attributes characterizing their general scope, structure, content and practical use, we critically review in a comparative style a total of 19 existing abstract models. The framework presented aims to be a primer approach for classification, and therefore, new attributes may be considered in future extensions. For example, an additional quality dimension might be considered in order to evaluate the support offered by the investigated REAMs in terms of integrity, security, maintainability or even scalability. Further research should also be focalized on providing additional empirical evidence on the utility and value of REAMs in real HE contexts. Finally, the subjectivity on the attributes considered for analysis as well as the particular evaluation granted by the authors to each one of them may be considered as the main limitation of the paper.

ACKNOWLEDGEMENT

This work is supported by the Industrial Doctorates Program of the Generalitat de Catalunya (2014 DI 077).

REFERENCES

Abel, R., Brown, M. and Suess, J., 2013. A New Architecture for Learning. *EDUCAUSE Review*, 48(5), pp.88–102.

Angelov, S., Grefen, P. and Greefhorst, D., 2012. A framework for analysis and design of software reference architectures. *Information and Software Technology*, 54(4), pp.417–431.

Barata, J. and Cunha, P.R., 2017. Synergies between quality management and information systems: a literature review and map for further research. *Total Quality Management & Business Excellence*, 28(3–4), pp.282–295.

Bergh-Hoff, H., Sørensen, C.-F., Garshol, J.E., Jakobsen, B.H.M., Vangen, G.M., Pettersen, Ø.D. and Hansen, J., 2015. *ICT Architecture Principles for the Norwegian Higher Education Sector*. September 3, 2015. Uninett. Available at https://www.uninett.no/sites/default/files/ict_architectural_principles.pdf.

Bessa, J., Branco, F., Costa, A., Martins, J. and Goncalves, R., 2016. A multidimensional information system architecture proposal for management support in Portuguese Higher Education: The University of Tras-os-Montes and Alto Douro case study [In Portuguese]. *Proceedings of the 11th Iberian Conference on Information Systems and Technologies*. Gran Canaria, Canary Islands, Spain, pp.1-7.

Bick, M. and Börgmann, K., 2009. A Reference Model for the Evaluation of Information Systems for an Integrated Campus Management. *International Conference EUNIS 2009*. Santiago de Compostela, Spain.

de Boer, R., Schijvenaars, T. and Oord, E., 2011. Referentiearchitecturen in de praktijk. Delen van architectuurkennis in een stelsel van semantische wiki's [In Dutch]. *Via Nova Architectura Magazine*, October 2011, pp.1–14.

CAUDIT, 2016. Enterprise Architecture Commons for Higher Education. *CAUDIT. Council of Australian University Directors of Information Technology*. Available at https://www.caudit.edu.au/EA-Framework (Accessed 28/04/2018).

CAUDIT, 2017. CAUDIT Higher Education EA Reference models roll out to 147 universities - and counting!. *CAUDIT. Council of Australian University Directors of Information Technology*. Available at https://www.caudit.edu.au/news/caudit-higher-education-ea-reference-models-roll-out-147-universities-and-counting (Accessed 7/06/2018).

Charles Sturt University, 2010. Higher Education Process Reference Model. *Charles Sturt University - Work Process Improvement*. Available at http://www.csu.edu.au/special/wpp/resources/reference-model (Accessed 14/04/2018).

Chen, S., Tang, Y. and Li, Z., 2016. UNITA: A Reference Model of University IT Architecture. *Proceedings of the 2016 International Conference on Communication and Information Systems*. Bangkok, Thailand, pp.73–77.

Cloutier, R., Muller, G., Verma, D., Nilchiani, R., Hole, E. and Bone, M., 2010. The Concept of Reference Architectures. *Systems Engineering*, 13(1), pp.14–27.

Fagan, M.H., 2003. Exploring e-education applications: a framework for analysis. *Campus-Wide Information Systems*, 20(4), pp.129–136.

Fettke, P. and Loos, P. eds., 2007. *Reference Modeling for Business Systems Analysis*. IGI Global.

Fettke, P., Loos, P. and Zwicker, J., 2006. Business Process Reference Models: Survey and Classification. In: C.J. Bussler and A. Haller, eds., *Business Process Management Workshops: BPM 2005 International Workshops, BPI, BPD, ENEI, BPRM, WSCOBPM, BPS, Nancy, France, September 5, 2005*. Springer Berlin Heidelberg, pp.469–483.

Frackmann, E., 2007. *Higher Education Information Systems. Proposal for an overall Concept for Higher Education Information Systems in Croatia*. Agency of Science and Higher Education. Available at http://forum.azvo.hr/cd/LinkedDocuments/Higher_Education_Information_Systems.pdf.

Greefhorst, D., Koning, H. and Vliet, H. van, 2006. The many faces of architectural descriptions. *Information Systems Frontiers*, 8(2), pp.103–113.

ten Harmsen van der Beek, W., Trienekens, J. and Grefen, P., 2012. The Application of Enterprise Reference Architecture in the Financial Industry. In: S. Aier, M. Ekstedt, F. Matthes, E. Proper and J.L. Sanz, eds., *TEAR 2012 and PRET 2012 Proceedings*. Springer Berlin Heidelberg, pp.93–110.

Hutaibat, K.A., 2011. Value Chain for Strategic Management Accounting in Higher Education. *International Journal of Business and Management*, 6(11), pp.206–218.

ITANA Working Group, 2012. Reference Architecture for Teaching and Learning. *ITANA Wiki*. Available at https://spaces.internet2.edu/display/itana/Reference+Architecture+for+Teaching+and+Learning (Accessed 10/04/2018).

JISC, 2009. *Doing Enterprise Architecture: Enabling the agile institution*. Version 1.1 March 2009. Available at /http://www.jisc.ac.uk/media/documents/techwatch/jisc_ea_pilot_study.pdf.

Kotusev, S., Singh, M. and Storey, I., 2015. Investigating the usage of enterprise architecture artifacts. *Proceedings of the 23rd European Conference on Information Systems*. Münster, Germany, pp.1–12.

Kotzampasaki, M., 2015. *Design of a process for the selection of an enterprise reference architecture.* (Master thesis). Technische Universiteit Eindhoven. Available at http://repository.tue.nl/5a6b604a-0a72-4465-99d1-a3758565f32.

Lankhorst, M., 2014. *The Value of Reference Architectures*. Bizzdesign Blog. Available at http://blog.bizzdesign.com/the-value-of-reference-architectures (Accessed 20/04/2018)

Llamosa-Villalba, R., Carreño, L.T., Paez, Q.A.M., Delgado, Q.D.J., Barajas, A.B. and Sneyder, E.G., 2015. Enterprise architecture of Colombian Higher Education. *2015 IEEE Frontiers in Education Conference*. El Paso, US, pp.1–9.

Llamosa-Villalba, R., Delgado, D.J., Camacho, H.P., Paéz, A.M. and Valdivieso, R.F., 2014. Organizational Leadership Process for University Education. *11th International Conference on Cognition and Exploratory Learning in Digital Age.* Porto, Portugal, pp.119–126.

Luftman, J. and Kempaiah, R., 2007. An Update on Business-IT Alignment: "A Line" Has Been Drawn. *MIS Quarterly Executive*, 6(3), pp.165–177.

Manatos, M.J., Sarrico, C.S. and Rosa, M.J., 2017. The integration of quality management in higher education institutions: a systematic literature review. *Total Quality Management & Business Excellence*, 28(1–2), pp.159–175.

Mettler, T., 2011. Maturity assessment models: a design science research approach. *International Journal of Society Systems Science*, 3(1–2), pp.81–98.

Mircea, M. and Andreescu, A.I., 2011. Using Cloud Computing in Higher Education: A Strategy to Improve Agility in the Current Financial Crisis. *Communications of the IBIMA*, pp.1–15.

Niemi, E. and Pekkola, S., 2017. Using enterprise architecture artefacts in an organisation. *Enterprise Information Systems*, 11(3), pp.313–338.

Oderinde, D., 2010. Using Enterprise Architecture (EA) as a Business-IT Strategy Alignment for Higher Educational Institutions (HEIs). *Proceedings of UK Academy for Information Systems Conference*. Oxford, UK, pp.1-10.

Olsen, D.H. and Trelsgård, K., 2016. Enterprise Architecture Adoption Challenges: An exploratory Case Study of the Norwegian Higher Education Sector. *Procedia Computer Science*, 100(2016), pp.804–811.

Pardeshi, V.H., 2014. Cloud Computing for Higher Education Institutes: Architecture, Strategy and Recommendations for Effective Adaptation. *Procedia Economics and Finance*, 11, pp.589–599.

Pawlowski, J.M. and Kozlov, D., 2013. Analysis and Validation of Learning Technology Models, Standards and Specifications: The Reference Model Analysis Grid (RMAG). In: K. Jakobs, ed., *Innovations in Organizational IT Specification and Standards Development.* IGI Global, pp. 223-240.

Reiner, M., 2014. *Improvement of Business Process Management in Higher Education institutions.* Erasmus-Multilateral. Education, Audiovisual & Culture Executive Agency (EAC-EA).Final Report, public part. Available at: http://eacea.ec.europa.eu/LLp/project_reports/documents/erasmus/ECUE/eras_ecue_518035_fr.pdf

Sanchez-Puchol, F. and Pastor-Collado, J.A., 2017. A First Litrature Review on Enterprise Reference Architectures. *Proceedings of the 11th Mediterranean Conference on Information Systems (MCIS)*. Genova, Italy, pp.1–12.

Sanchez-Puchol, F., Pastor-Collado, J.A. and Borrell, B., 2017. Towards an Unified Information Systems Reference Model for Higher Education Institutions. *Procedia Computer Science*, 121, pp.542–553.

Simon, B., Pulkkinen, M., Totschnig, M. and Kozlov, D., 2011. *The ICOPER Reference Model for Outcome-based Higher Education.* eContentplus, July 2011. Available at http://www.icoper.org/results/deliverables/D7-3b.

SURF, 2013a. *Hoger Onderwijs Referentie Architectuur. Implementatiehulpmiddelen* [In Dutch]. Project Regie in de Cloud. Versie 1.0: SURF. Available at https://www.archixl.nl/files/HORAImplementatiehulpmiddelen10.pdf.

SURF, 2013b. *Hoger Onderwijs Referentie Architectuur. Referentiemodellen* [In Dutch]. Project Regie in de Cloud. Versie 1.0: SURF. Available at https://www.archixl.nl/files/HORAReferentiemodellen10.pdf.

SURF, n.d. Hoger Onderwijs Referentie Architectuur [In Dutch]. *Hoger Onderwijs Referentie Architectuur*. Available at: https://hora.surf.nl/index.php/Hoofdpagina (Accessed 28/04/2018).

Svensson, C. and Hvolby, H.-H., 2012. Establishing a Business Process Reference Model for Universities. *Procedia Technology*, 5(2012), pp.635–642.

Syynimaa, N., 2015. Modeling the Dynamics of Enterprise Architecture Adoption Process. In: S. Hammoudi, L. Maciaszek, E. Teniente, O. Camp and J. Cordeiro, eds., *Enterprise Information Systems*. Springer International Pub., pp.577–594.

TIER-Data Structures and APIs Working Group, 2016. The TIER Reference Architecture (RA). Available at https://spaces.internet2.edu/pages/viewpage.action?pageId=98306902 (Accessed 01/04/2018).

Timm, F., 2018. An Application Design for Reference Enterprise Architecture Models. In: R. Matulevičius and R. Dijkman, eds., Advanced Information Systems Engineering Workshops. Springer International Pub., pp.209–221.

Van der Merwe, A.J., 2005. *Towards a reusable process model structure for higher education institutions*. (Doctoral thesis) University of South Africa. Available at http://uir.unisa.ac.za/handle/10500/653.

WEB ACCESSIBILITY OF THE CYPRUS ISLAND HIGHER EDUCATION INSTITUTION LIBRARIES

Ümit İlhan[1], Kaan Uyar[1] and Erkut İ. İşeri[2]
[1]*Computer Engineering, Near East University, ZIP: 99138, Nicosia/TRNC, Mersin 10, Turkey*
[2]*Electrical and Electronic Engineering, Near East University, ZIP: 99138, Nicosia/TRNC, Mersin 10, Turkey*

ABSTRACT

This paper evaluates the degree of web accessibility offered by higher education institution libraries of the Turkish Cypriots-controlled area and Greek Cypriots-controlled area part of the Cyprus Island. The accessibility evaluation was carried out using online automated programs to verify compliance with the Web Content Accessibility Guidelines 2.0 (WCAG 2.0) Level AA published by the World Wide Web Consortium (W3C). The results allow concluding that no academic library website in the Cyprus Island is error free.

KEYWORDS

Web Accessibility, Academic Library, Cyprus Island

1. INTRODUCTION

People with disabilities have the same needs as non-disabled people in using the web. Library resources including online services should be provided for all the people without any discrimination. Unfortunately, people with disabilities are not typically considered as a regular internet user group by most of the web developers and hence don't give any consideration about their needs in web designing process. Evidently it is the duty of the web developers and library administrators to be sensitive about the online services usability that will ease the life of people with disabilities.

The United Nations (UN) Convention on the Rights of Persons with Disabilities (CRPD) and its Optional Protocol (A/RES/61/106) was adopted on 13 December 2006 and entered into force on 3 May 2008 (Un.org, 2006). The States that signed and ratified the Convention bound by the obligations that it establishes. Based on the Article 4 of this convention on General Obligations, Article 9 on Accessibility, Article 24 on Education and Article 30 on Participation in cultural life, recreation, leisure and sport the States (including their educational institutions) shall take all appropriate measures to ensure that those persons with disabilities enjoy access to library buildings and services including online resources.

World Wide Web Consortium (W3C) is the sole developer and administrator of the web standards. The inventor of WWW and the director of W3C, Tim Berners-Lee said "The power of the Web is in its universality. Access by everyone regardless of disability is an essential aspect". W3C Web Accessibility Initiative (WAI) sets the guidelines of web accessibility standards and provides resources to keep the web accessible for all groups of people including those having certain disabilities. WAI define the web accessibility as "websites, tools, and technologies are designed and developed so that people with disabilities can use them". The W3C Web Content Accessibility Guidelines (WCAG) 2.0 and WAI Accessible Rich Internet Applications Suite (ARIA) define the current guidelines about web accessibility (W3.org, 2018).

The European Commission has adopted the WCAG 2.0 compliance level AA, by the ratification of the UN Convention on the Rights of Persons with Disabilities and its Optional Protocol in 2010 (Ec.europa.eu, 2018). In the United States of America (USA), web accessibility is governed by Section 508 of the 1998 Rehabilitation Act federal law (Section508.gov, 2018).

There are several published studies that discuss the web accessibility including the academic library web pages. Lilly and Van Fleet analyzed accessibility of the academic library home pages representing Yahoo!'s list of the "100 Most Wired Colleges" (2000). Spindler analyzed the accessibility of 188 web pages of college and university libraries in the USA (2002). Providenti evaluated web accessibility of the Kentucky's academic libraries (2004).Web accessibility of the 33 Kentucky academic library web sites data that collected in 2003 were compared to data collected in 2007 by Providenti and Zai (2007). Comeaux and Schmetzke follow up on earlier study at the web sites of all 56 university libraries and library schools (2007). Comeaux and Schmetzke presented the accessibility of 56 North American academic library web sites between 2002 and 2012 (2013). Craven collected expert opinions to creating accessible webpages for the library and information professionals (2008). Caballero-Cortes, Faba-Perez and de Moya-Anegon analyzed the accessibility of the Spanish and American university libraries (2009). Ferreir and Cianconip analyzed the accessibility of Brazilian university libraries (2011). Video and web-based tutorials created by libraries from 71 USA public universities were reviewed by Clossen and Procesfor accessibility and usability by disabled people (2017).

In this study all higher education institution libraries of the whole of Cyprus Island are subjected to investigation to measure the degree of accessibility of their web sites. The following section shows the list of higher education institution libraries and their locations in Cyprus Island. The research methodology is covered in Section 3, Section 4 presents the research outcomes of the tests carried out and finally the conclusions is presented.

2. HIGHER EDUCATION INSTITUTION LIBRARIES IN CYPRUS ISLAND

Cyprus is an island located on the north east of Mediterranean Sea. The island is de facto partitioned into two main areas. The one on the North is under of the Turkish Cypriot administration and the one on the South is under the Greek Cypriot administration. The whole of the island is a part of European Union (EU) territory but North is kept outside the EU's customs and fiscal territory. North and South administrations have ratified the UN CRPD in 2010 (Mahkemeler.net, 2010) and 2011 (Mlsi.gov.cy, 2011) respectively.

In this study the library websites of the 38 Cyprus Island higher education institutions that their website home pages accessibility evaluated by İşeri, Uyar and İlhan (2017) were analyzed. The total 15 of these institutions, 6 from North and 9 from South either do not have the library websites or are not at all accessible. Such institutions are listed in Table 1 in this work, web accessibility of the 23 library websites are evaluated. The higher education institution names that carries an asterisk (*) in Table 1 are the foreign higher education institutes having campuses in Cyprus Island.

Table 1. The Library Websites of the Higher Education Institutions in Cyprus Island

No	Name in English	Area	Library URL
1	Cyprus International Univ.	North	ciu.edu.tr/en/academic/library
2	Cyprus Science Univ.	North	kiu.edu.tr/kutuphane
3	Eastern Mediterranean Univ.	North	library.emu.edu.tr
4	European Univ. of Lefke	North	eul.edu.tr/en/life-in-eul/services/library
5	Final International Univ.	North	final.edu.tr/m-15-kampus-ve-servisler/a-115-kutuphane/a-369-genel-bilgiler
6	Girne American Univ.	North	library.gau.edu.tr
7	Near East Univ.	North	library.neu.edu.tr
8	Univ. of Kyrenia	North	library.kyrenia.edu.tr
9	Anadolu Univ. Nicosia Campus*	North	kdm.anadolu.edu.trr
10	Istanbul Technical Univ. TRNC Campus*	North	kutuphane.itu.edu.tr
11	Middle East Technical Univ. North Cyprus Campus*	North	library.metu.edu.tr
12	C.D.A. College	South	cdacollege.com/library
13	City Unity College Nicosia	South	cityu.librarika.com
14	College of Tourism and Hotel Management	South	cothm.ac.cy/library
15	CTL Eurocollege	South	ctleuro.ac.cy/en/library/general-information
16	Cyprus Institute of Marketing	South	library.cima.ac.cy
17	Cyprus Univ. of Technology	South	library.cut.ac.cy
18	European Univ. Cyprus	South	euc.ac.cy/en/about-us/library

19	MKC City College	South	citycollege.ac.cy/en/page-id/521
20	Neapolis Univ. Paphos	South	nup.ac.cy/learning-resources
21	Univ. of Cyprus	South	library.ucy.ac.cy/en
22	Univ. of Nicosia	South	library.unic.ac.cy
23	Univ. of Central Lancashire*	South	uclancyprus.ac.cy/en/uclan-cyprus/library1/

3. RESEARCH METHODOLOGY

In this study 3 freely available, real-time, on-line tools TAW, WAVE and EIII Page Checker are used to evaluate web accessibility of the library website homepages of Cyprus Island higher education institutions.

3.1 TAW

Test de Accesibilidad Web (TAW) is a tool based on WCAG 2.0 (Tawdis.net, 2018). The accessibility issues founded by TAW fall in three categories: "problems", "warnings", and "not reviewed" of the principles: Perceivable (P), Operable (O), Understandable (U) and Robust (R). TAW declared that for the "warnings" a human review is necessary. For the "not reviewed" condition a complete manual check is needed.

3.2 WAVE

Web Accessibility In Mind (WebAIM) is a non-profit organization based at the "Center for Persons with Disabilities" at Utah State University (Webaim.org, 2018). WAVE accessibility evaluation tool is developed by WebAIM. WAVE tests the sites in compliance with WCAG 2.0 and ARIA. WAVE analysis reports the result of the test under six categories that contains the errors, alerts, features, HTML5 and ARIA, structural elements, and contrast errors. One disadvantage may be that it does not show the guidelines which used during the test.

3.3 EIII Page Checker (Tingtun Accessibility Checker)

The European Internet Inclusion Initiative (EIII) Page Checker (Tingtun Accessibility Checker) contains tools that test the accessibility of webpages. Also the EIII PDF Checker tool contains accessibility test of the PDF documents. The tests employed are based on WCAG 2.0 standards (Checkers.eiii.eu, 2018). The grading of the EIII Page Checker is given in Table 2.

Table 2. EIII Page Checker Grading

Score (range)	Grade	Explanation of grade
100	A	No tests failed
95-99	B	A few tests failed
85-94	C	Some tests failed
70-84	D	Many tests failed
0-69	E	Most tests failed

4. RESEARCH RESULTS

The selected web accessibility evaluation tools, WAVE, TAW and EIII Page Checker are employed on the 23 websites of the higher education institution libraries of Cyprus Island. The evaluation process with three different tools carried out simultaneously on three personal computers with similar configurations using the same internet service provider and in the same time frame on 7 March 2018. The homepage of each library website was tested. The home is the most important page of a website in terms of accessibility, and if the home page is not accessible, the users will have difficulty to connect to the rest of webpages on the site.

Table 3 contains the numerical data from the evaluation performed with TAW. The higher education institutions that library websites have the most problems are Girne American University with 276 problems, followed by Eastern Mediterranean University and Near East University. The higher education institutions that library websites have fewer problems are City Unity College Nicosia with only 2 problems, followed by CTL Eurocollege and College of Tourism and Hotel Management. Cyprus International University library website has the most warning, followed by Final International University and Cyprus University of Technology library websites. The unverified problems that require to be interpreted manually by human experts are varying between 14 and 17 for all institution libraries. Results of the TAW evaluation are plotted in Figures 1a, 1b and 1c as main, warning and unverified problems respectively.

Table 3. TAW Analysis Results

		Problems					Warnings					Not Reviewed				
No	Name in English	P	O	U	R	Total	P	O	U	R	Total	P	O	U	R	Total
1	Cyprus International Univ.	50	6	18	28	102	76	341	24	407	848	3	7	5	0	15
2	Cyprus Science Univ.	2	2	0	51	55	41	25	0	167	233	4	7	6	1	15
3	Eastern Mediterranean Univ.	189	21	2	6	218	333	2	6	0	341	4	8	5	0	17
4	European Univ. of Lefke	23	20	1	9	53	47	63	6	133	249	4	7	5	0	16
5	Final International Univ.	19	4	2	100	125	40	42	6	437	525	4	7	8	0	16
6	Girne American Univ.	152	11	53	60	276	122	69	108	26	325	4	6	5	0	15
7	Near East Univ.	67	13	13	44	137	179	10	36	22	247	4	7	4	0	15
8	Univ. of Kyrenia	63	10	13	42	128	174	10	36	22	242	4	7	4	0	15
9	Anadolu Univ. Nicosia Campus*	51	15	12	16	94	82	33	30	18	163	4	7	5	0	16
10	Istanbul Technical Univ. TRNC Campus*	46	6	14	30	96	87	71	18	97	273	3	7	4	0	14
11	Middle East Technical Univ. North Cyprus Campus*	13	0	2	3	18	18	10	6	46	80	4	7	5	0	16
12	C.D.A. College	18	0	5	16	39	30	2	6	0	38	4	8	5	0	17
13	City Unity College Nicosia	0	0	0	2	2	16	12	12	70	110	4	5	7	1	17
14	College of Tourism and Hotel Management	4	1	0	8	13	224	9	0	107	340	4	7	5	1	17
15	CTL Eurocollege	2	0	3	3	8	0	9	6	0	15	4	8	4	0	16
16	Cyprus Institute of Marketing	62	11	29	29	131	35	16	0	44	95	3	7	5	0	15
17	Cyprus Univ. of Technology	38	25	12	30	105	33	40	24	197	394	3	6	5	0	14
18	European Univ. Cyprus	33	26	10	16	85	69	79	24	1	173	4	6	5	0	15
19	MKC City College	55	11	1	7	74	128	15	0	37	180	4	7	5	1	17
20	Neapolis Univ. Paphos	16	3	5	8	32	8	42	18	23	91	4	7	5	0	16
21	Univ. of Cyprus	9	8	4	45	66	127	21	6	44	198	4	7	6	0	17
22	Univ. of Nicosia	35	23	10	13	81	277	27	18	268	590	4	6	4	0	16
23	Univ. of Central Lancashire*	9	14	2	4	29	16	61	6	53	139	3	6	5	0	14

The EIII Page Checker results evaluated with scores expressed out of 100 and assigned with a letter grade shown in Table 4. None of the evaluated website has passed from all the tests, only 18% have failed the few tests, 13% have failed some of the tests and 71% of the websites has failed from most of the tests. The average EIII Page Checker score of the evaluated library webpages is 79.85 where the minimum score is 49.17 and the maximum score is 97.44. College of Tourism and Hotel Management library webpage has the highest score, followed by City Unity College Nicosia and Cyprus Science University library webpages. The higher education institution that has the lowest score is C.D.A. College. Library website of the Cyprus International University could not be analyzed with EIII Page Checker. Figure 2 shows the EIII Page Checker scores of the evaluated websites.

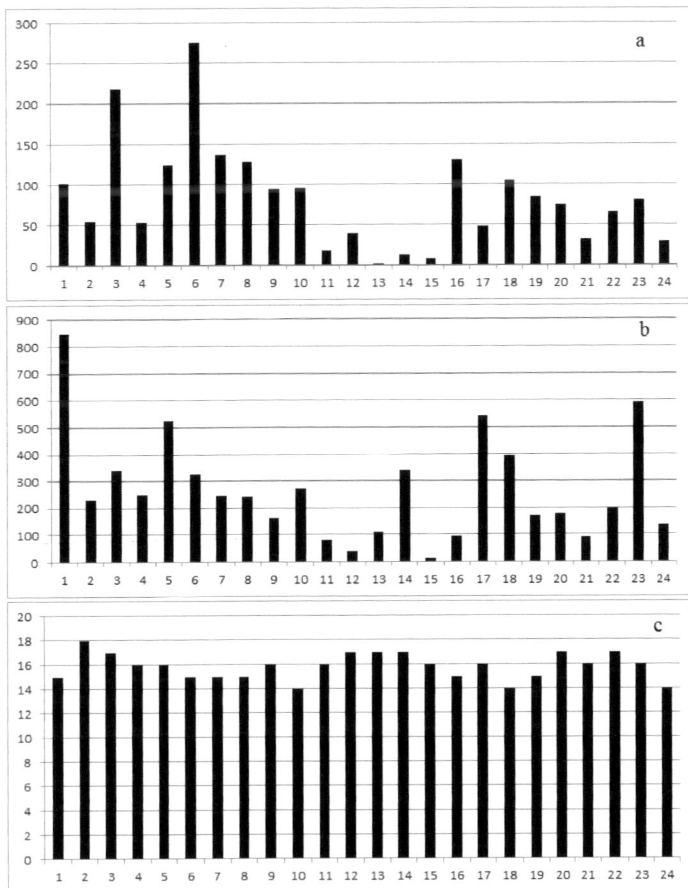

Figure 1. TAW Results. Institutions with (a) Main Problems; (b) Warnings; (c) Unverified Problems of Web Accessibility

Table 4. EIII Page Checker Analysis Results

No	Name in English	Score	Grade
1	Cyprus International Univ.f	-	-
2	Cyprus Science Univ.	96.33	B
3	Eastern Mediterranean Univ.	74.95	D
4	European Univ. of Lefke	92.13	C
5	Final International Univ.	69.58	E
6	Girne American Univ.	72.88	D
7	Near East Univ.	59.49	E
8	Univ. of Kyrenia	56.69	E
9	Anadolu Univ. Nicosia Campus*	77.16	D
10	Istanbul Technical Univ. TRNC Campus*	83.11	D
11	Middle East Technical Univ. North Cyprus Campus*	96.19	B
12	C.D.A. College	49.17	F
13	City Unity College Nicosia	97.19	B
14	College of Tourism and Hotel Management	97.44	B
15	CTL Eurocollege	78.14	D
16	Cyprus Institute of Marketing	79.21	D
17	Cyprus Univ. of Technology	82.90	D
18	European Univ. Cyprus	84.79	C
19	MKC City College	79.55	D
20	Neapolis Univ. Paphos	83.22	D
21	Univ. of Cyprus	79.53	D
22	Univ. of Nicosia	70.80	D
23	Univ. of Central Lancashire*	93.25	C

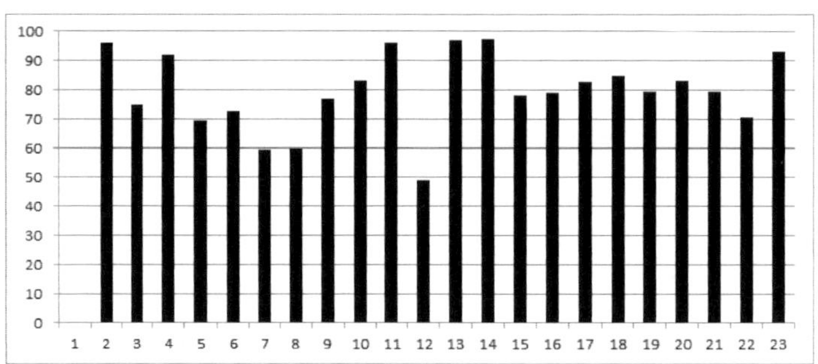

Figure 2. EIII Page Checker Scores of the Evaluated Websites

The results of WAVE evaluation for each library website under six categories are shown in Table 5. According to the WAVE evaluation results of the higher education institution library homepages, the College of Tourism and Hotel Management and City Unity College Nicosia have the lowest error with only one error followed by Cyprus Science University and Middle East Technical University with two errors. Higher education institutions with the highest number of errors are Girne American University, followed by University of Nicosia and Cyprus University of Technology. Final International University and CTL Eurocollege library websites has only one contrast error. The European University of Lefke has the worst contrast error results, followed by Girne American University and European University Cyprus. Figure 3 shows the number of contrast errors and main errors.

Table 5. WAVE Analysis Results

No	Name in English	Errors	Alerts	Features	Structural Elements	Html 5 and ARIA	Contrast Errors
1	Cyprus International Univ.	36	23	11	23	0	32
2	Cyprus Science Univ.	2	15	4	43	90	8
3	Eastern Mediterranean Univ.	37	11	20	25	0	22
4	European Univ. of Lefke	24	32	5	67	45	56
5	Final International Univ.	17	19	0	9	18	1
6	Girne American Univ.	62	15	20	20	1	54
7	Near East Univ.	37	26	1	24	0	38
8	Univ. of Kyrenia	33	26	1	24	0	38
9	Anadolu Univ. Nicosia Campus*	30	21	5	20	0	38
10	Istanbul Technical Univ. TRNC Campus*	12	22	19	30	4	6
11	Middle East Technical Univ. North Cyprus Campus*	2	0	6	12	0	3
12	C.D.A. College	12	1	0	9	0	4
13	City Unity College Nicosia	1	6	5	6	2	13
14	College of Tourism and Hotel Management	1	12	4	10	38	15
15	CTL Eurocollege	11	95	0	28	9	1
16	Cyprus Institute of Marketing	38					
17	Cyprus Univ. of Technology	48	31	16	38	9	6
18	European Univ. Cyprus	39	18	7	74	0	49
19	MKC City College	17	9	8	73	0	12
20	Neapolis Univ. Paphos	10	36	11	58	5	9
21	Univ. of Cyprus	12	4	5	11	0	25
22	Univ. of Nicosia	59	17	39	25	86	13
23	Univ. of Central Lancashire*	15	11	3	35	2	4

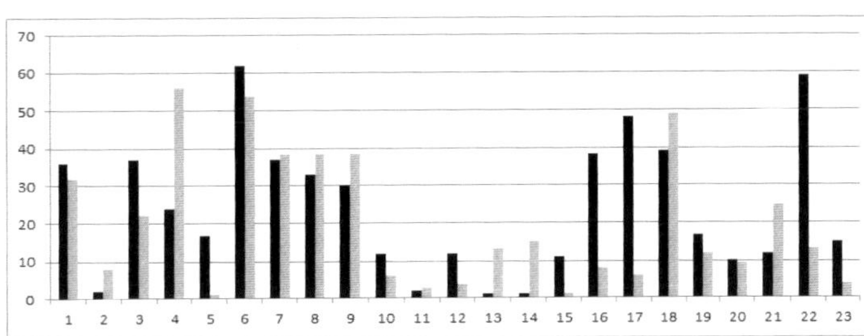

Figure 3. WAVE Analysis Results: Main Errors (black) and Contrast Errors (Grey)

5. CONCLUSION

This study aimed at creating awareness about the degree of accessibility of the Cyprus Island higher education institution library websites based on the international standards. All listed websites failed one or more tests based on WCAG 2.0 Level AA guidelines. Even the most basic standard needs of people with disabilities that identified by the WAI are not met. All websites in general are not satisfactorily accessible by the people with disabilities.

Technical guidelines and the use of web site accessibility tests only used to help to identify the problems for the web developers. Library administrators and website developers should give priority to designing web pages in accordance with the standards listed in WCAG 2.0 guidelines during their website development procedure. There should be some involvement of people with disabilities themselves in design and testing process to ensure that they have the correct access features on the web sites.

REFERENCES

Caballero-Cortes, L., Faba-Perez, C. and de Moya-Anegon, F. (2009). Comparative accessibility assessment of Web spaces in Spanish and American university libraries. *Investigacion Bibliotecologica*, 23(47), pp. 45-66.

Checkers.eiii.eu, (2018). *European Internet Inclusion Initiative Page Checker website.* [online] Available at: http://checkers.eiii.eu/ [Accessed 7Mar. 2018].

Clossen, A. and Proces, P. (2017).Rating the Accessibility of Library Tutorials from Leading Research Universities. *Portal: Libraries and the Academy*, 17(4), pp. 803-825.

Comeaux, D. and Schmetzke, A. (2007).Web accessibility trends in university libraries and library schools. *Library Hi Tech*, 25(4), pp. 457-477.

Comeaux, D. and Schmetzke, A. (2013).Accessibility of academic library web sites in North America Current status and trends (2002-2012).*Library Hi Tech*, 31(1), pp. 8-33.

Craven, J. ed. (2008).*Web Accessibility: Practical Advice for the Library and Information Professional.* Facet Publications, London.

Ec.europa.eu, (2018). *European Commission, Web Accessibility.* [online] Available at: http://ec.europa.eu/ipg/standards/accessibility/index_en.htm [Accessed 14 Feb. 2018].

Ferreira, G.A. and Cianconip, R.D. (2011). Accessibility by the Visually Impaired and Blind People in University Libraries on the Web. *Informacao & Sociedade-Estudos*, 21(2), pp. 151-163.

İşeri, E.İ., Uyar, K. and İlhan Ü. (2017). The accessibility of Cyprus Islands' Higher Education Institution Websites.*Procedia Computer Science*, 120, pp. 967-974.

Lilly, E.B. and Van Fleet, C. (2000). Wired but not connected: accessibility of academic library home pages.*The Reference Librarian*, 32(67-68), pp. 5-28.

Mahkemeler.net, (2010). *Engellilerin haklarına ilişkin sözleşmenin onaylanmasının uygun bulunmasına ilişkin (onay) yasası", Sayı: 38/2010.* [online] Available at: http://www.mahkemeler.net/birlestirilmis/38-2010.doc [Accessed 24 Feb. 2018].

Mlsi.gov.cy, (2011). *Convention on the Rights of Persons with Disabilities and Related Issues (Ratification) Law of 2011, N.8 (III) / 2011.* [online] Available at: http://www.mlsi.gov.cy/mlsi/dsid/dsid.nsf/dsipd08_en/dsipd08_en?OpenDocument[Accessed 24 Feb. 2018].

Providenti, M. (2004). Library web accessibility at Kentucky's 4-year degree granting colleges and universities.*D-Lib Magazine*, 10(9). [online] Available at: www.dlib.org/dlib/september04/providenti/09providenti.html [Accessed 18 Feb. 2018].

Providenti, M. and Zai, R. (2007). Web accessibility at Kentucky's academic libraries.*Library Hi Tech*, 25(4), pp. 478-493.

Section508.gov, (2018). *GSA Government-wide Section 508 Accessibility Program website.* [online] Available at: http://ec.europa.eu/ipg/standards/accessibility/index_en.htm [Accessed 14 Feb. 2018].

Spindler, T. (2002). The Accessibility of Web Pages for Mid-Sized College and University Libraries.*The Reference Librarian*, 42(2), pp. 149-154.

Tawdis.net, (2018). *TAW Web accessibility and W3C standardization services.* [online] Available at: https://www.tawdis.net/ [Accessed 7Mar. 2018].

Un.org, (2006). *United Nations Convention on the Rights of Persons with Disabilities.* [online] Available at: https://www.un.org/development/desa/disabilities/convention-on-the-rights-of-persons-with-disabilities.html [Accessed 14Feb. 2018].

W3.org, (2018). *World Wide Web Consortium Official Website.* [online] Available at: https://www.w3.org [Accessed 14 Feb. 2018].

Webaim.org, (2018). *Web Accessibility In Mind website.* [online] Available at: https://webaim.org/ [Accessed 7Mar. 2018].

DETECTION AND PREVENTION OF CREDIT CARD FRAUD: STATE OF ART

Imane Sadgali, Nawal Sael and Faouzia Benabbou
Laboratory of Modeling and Information Technology
Faculty of Sciences Ben M'SIK, University Hassan II, Casablanca, Morocco

ABSTRACT

Credit card fraud is qualifies as the most critical financial fraud. Financial institutions are forced to continually improve their fraud detection systems, but with technological development, fraudsters use technology to commit their crimes easily. In recent years, several studies have used machine learning and data mining techniques to find solutions to this problem. In this article, we propose a state of the art on various techniques of fraud, as well as detection and prevention techniques proposed in the literature such as clustering, classification and regression. The purpose of this study is to identify the techniques and methods that give the best results so far.

KEYWORDS

Fraud Detection, Financial Fraud, Machine-Learning, Credit Card

1. INTRODUCTION

Credit card fraud is an expensive problem for many financial institutions, that why they use a variety of fraud prevention models to address this problem. However, fraudsters are adaptive, and over time, they conceive several ways of intruding such protectives models. Despite the best effort of financial institutions, law enforcement and government, financial fraud continues to grow. Fraudsters today can be a very inventive, intelligent and fast fraternity.

This paper seeks to carry out comparative analysis of credit card fraud detection techniques, like machine-learning techniques that plays an important role in fraud detection, as it is often applied to extract and uncover the hidden truths behind very large quantities of data. Also, many modern techniques for detecting fraud are continually involves and applied to many areas due to the remarkable lift of fraud which effects on financial field in each year. Our objective is to point out their strength and weaknesses and also to identify the open issues of credit card fraud analysis.

The rest of this paper is organized as follows. Section 2 contains a definition and types of credit card fraud, Section 3 present techniques implemented for credit card fraud detection, Section 4 present review of related work. In Section 5 detailed our comparative study of implemented techniques and discussed the results. Finally, we conclude and propose our future work in Section 6.

2. CREDIT CARD FRAUD

2.1 Definition

The credit card fraud is a fraudulent transaction by an unauthorized person for his personal interest and the authorized cardholder and the card provider are totally unaware about the transaction in the moment of its realization (Askari, 2017) Credit card transactions data are mainly characterized by an unusual phenomenon. Both legitimate transactions and fraudulent ones tend to share the same profile. Fraudsters learn new ways to mimic the spending behaviour of legitimate card (or cardholder). Thus, the profiles of normal and fraudulent behaviours are constantly dynamic (Carcillo, 2017).

2.2 Types of Credit Card Fraud

Credit card fraud, in the literature, is essentially of two types: application and behavioural fraud (Zeager, 2017). Application fraud is where fraudsters obtains new cards from issuing companies using false information or other people's information (Bhattacharyya, 2011). Behavioural fraud can be of four types (Shaji, 2017):

- Mail theft fraud: occurs when fraudsters intercept credit cards in mail before they reach cardholders or pilfer personal information from bank and credit card statements
- Stolen/lost card fraud: happens when fraudsters get hold of credit cards through theft of purse/wallet or gain access to lost cards.
- Counterfeit card fraud: Card holders information is obtained through a variety of ways, such as employees stealing information through unauthorized 'swipers', 'phishing' scams, or through intrusion into company computer networks.
- 'Card holder not present' fraud: when credit cards details are used remotely to conduct fraudulent transactions through mail, phone, or the Internet.

3. RELATED WORK

Various Fraud Detection techniques has been proposed in the past years, each one, has advantages and shortcomings. In this section, we present works, sorted by fraud detection techniques.

Self-Organization Map (SOM), Neural Network (NN), Rules Induction (RI) : SOM is a neural network technique but used as unsupervised learning. SOM allows users to visualize data from high to low dimension. In 2008, Quah and Sriganesh. proposed, for real-time fraud detection, a new and innovative approach; it makes use of self-organization map, Neural Networks and rules induction (Quah, 2008). In 2014, Olszewski proposed a method of the detection threshold setting based on SOM (Olszewski, 2014).

Association Rules (AR), Fuzzy Association Rules (FAR) / Fuzzy Logic (FL), Iterative Dichotomiser 3 (ID3) : We use FL for representing the cognitive uncertainties, measuring the intensity of the truth values for unquantifiable measures or probabilistic measures within the range of 0 and 1. Aso, in 2009, Sanchez (Sanchez, 2009) propose a novel methodology based on using AR and FAR to detect credit card fraud. Askari proposed fraud detection algorithm based on Fuzzy-ID3 (Askari, 2017) in 2017.

Dempster Shafer Theory (DST), Naïve Bayes (NB): DST or evidence theory is a general framework for reasoning with uncertainty, the role of DST is to combine evidences from the rules R1and R2 and compute an overall belief value for each transaction. Suvasini (Panigrahi, 2009) investigated a fusion approach using Dempster–Shafer theory and Bayesian learning.

Cost-sensitive decision tree (CSDT): CSDT is an induction algorithm developed to identify fraudulent credit card transactions. In the well-known decision tree algorithms, the splitting criteria are either insensitive to costs and class distributions or the cost is fixed to a constant ratio In 2013, Sahin developed a methodology for fraud detection using decision tree and showed that this cost-sensitive decision tree algorithm outperforms the existing methods (Sahin, 2013).

Aggregation : Transaction aggregation is found to be advantageous in many but not all Circumstances. Whitrow developed a framework for transaction aggregation, using a variety of classification methods and a realistic cost-based performance measure (Whitrow, 2009).

Support Vector Machines (SVM): SVM use a linear model to implement nonlinear class boundaries by mapping input vectors nonlinearly into a high-dimensional feature space. In the new space, an optimal separating hyperplane is constructed. In 2011, Bhattacharyya evaluated two advanced data mining approaches, support vector machines and random forests, together with the well-known logistic regression (Bhattacharyya, 2011).

Genetic Algorithm (GA), Scatter Search(SS) : GA is an inspired from natural evolution, randomly generated rules are considered as an initial population. SS is an evolutionary algorithm, which shares some common characteristics with the GA. Duman suggested a novel combination of the two well-known meta-heuristic approaches, namely GA, SS. This method was applied to real data and very successful results were obtained (Duman, 2011).

Artificial neural network (ANN), Multilayer Perception Algorithm (MPL)/ Parenclitic Network (PN) : ANN were first created with the purpose to imitate the behavior of the human brain. MPL is an artificial neural network and is a non-parametric estimator that can be used for classifying and detecting intrusions. PN a network reconstruction technique that allows highlighting the differences between one instance and a set of standard. In 2017, Mubalaik proposed an ANN-MPL multilayer perception (Mubalik, 2017), based on implementation of well-known machines learning techniques, it helps to anticipate and quickly detect fraud. Zanin proposed hybrid data mining / complex network, classification algorithm, able to detect illegal instances in a real card transaction data set (Zanin, 2017).

Artificial Immune Recognition System (AIRS), Cloud Computing (CC) : AIRS both self/non-self cells and detector cells are represented as feature vectors. In order to reduce redundancy. In 2012, Halvaiee developed a novel model for credit card fraud detection using AIS and introduced a new model called AIS-based Fraud Detection Model (AFDM), which increase the accuracy up to 25%, reduce the cost up to 85%, and decrease system response time up to 40% compared to the base algorithm (Halvaiee, 2014).

Density based spatial clustering of applications with noise (DBSCAN), Hidden Markov Model (HMM), Logistic Regression (LR) : DBSCAN is a density based clustering algorithm which can be used to filter out outliers and discover clusters of arbitrary shapes. HMM it differs from the normal statistical Markov model by having invisible states, but each state randomly generates one of the visible states. LR is a type of generalized linear model. In 2016, Dai developed a hybrid framework with Big Data technologies (Dai, 2016).

K-nearest neighbor (KNN), Outlier detection (OD) : KNN works extremely well in credit card fraud detection systems using supervised learning techniques. OD is used to detect unusual behavior of a system using a different mechanism. Malini implemented KNN algorithm and outlier detection methods to optimize the best solution for the fraud detection problem (Malini, 2017).

Synthetic Minority Over-sampling Technique (SMOTE), Gaussian Mixture Models (GMM), LR : SMOTE is used to balance the class ratio by generating synthetic instances of fraudulent transactions (N. Chawla, Bowyer, Hall, and Kegelmeyer, 2002). GMM is used to segment the distribution space of continuous attributes as a means to find possible adversarial strategies. In 2017, MF Zeager developped a game theoretical adversarial learning approach in order to model the fraudster's best strategy, using a logistic regression classifier as the fraud detection mechanism (Zeager, 2017).

NEURO-FUZZY INFERENCE SYSTEM (NFIS): This technique allows utilizing the advantage of both neural networks and fuzzy inference system. In 2017, S. Shaji developed a model of a hybrid of neural networks along with fuzzy inference to improve the efficiency of fraud detection process (Shaji, 2017).

Active learning (AL), Highest Risk Querying (HRQ) : AL, which can be considered as a specific instance of semi-supervised learning (Settles, 2010) (Chapelle, 2009), is to select unlabeled training samples which, once labeled, can improve the accuracy. F. Carcillo, investigated the combination of semi supervised and active learning techniques in the context of streaming fraud detection (Carcillo, 2017) in 2017.

Invariant Diversity (ID): ID is based on the concept that the more generic an attribute is, the more diversity will be seen on transactions associated with that attribute. In 2017, R. Laurens, proposed ID as a unique way of combining the strength of both generic and specific correlation, tested on real online merchant transactions and it managed to find several instances of previously undetected fraudulent transactions (Laurens, 2017).

CARDWATCH (CW): CW is based on a neural network, consists of five main modules: Global Constants, Graphical User Interface, Database Interface, and Learning Algorithm Interface. Aleskerov proposed this technique for credit card fraud detection and shown a good rate for detection (Aleskerov, 1997).

4. A COMPARATIVE STUDY

In this section, we will analyse the contribution of each technique and its effectiveness, in order to find a promising combination for future work.

4.1 Criteria

In our comparative tables, we regroup and synthesize most used criteria in anterior credit card fraud detection works in order to have most complete comparison:

- Fraud Type:
  - Online (O): fraud of e-commerce transaction.
  - Merchant (M): fraud when transaction is done from in point of service of a merchant.
  - All (A): all type of fraud even from ATM.
- Real time: parameter show if the technique bellow is able to run in real time.
- Accuracy: a validation parameter of precision (TP+TN)/(TP+FP+TN+FN)
- True positive: the rate of fraudulent case, which is a fraud.
- Dataset size
- Dataset type: particular, standard or generic.
- Parameters: describe which attributes will be considered by the fraud detection model: transaction amount, transaction location, merchant type (MCC), transaction type …
- Observations: limitations (-) and contributions (+) of the technique

TP: true positive / TN: true negative / FP: False positive / FN: False negative

4.2 Comparative Study

In this paragraph, we present three tables, for each type of fraud, we give a summary of techniques in past work and observations belong this study.

Table 1. Contributions and limitations of ML techniques applied to online credit card frauds

Technique	Real time	Validation		Data set		Parameters	Observations	Reference
		Accuracy (%)	TP (%)	Size	Type			
SOM +NN + RI	R	NA	NA	over 200 million customers	P	Branch code of the transaction, account number, currency of transaction, terminal reference, transaction amount, payee account number, debit or credit	+Clustering helps in identifying new hidden patterns in input data. +the filtering of transactions for further review reduces the overall cost as well as processing time.	(Quah, 2008)
DST + NB	R	NA	98	NA	G	Transaction amount, billing address, shipping address, inter-transaction time gap.	+ Architecture has been kept flexible so that new rules using any other effective. technique can also be included at a later stage.	(Panigrahi, 2009)
GA + SS	NR	NA	NA	100,000 fraudulent	P	NA	+ Bank Management should increase the monitoring capacity if they want to face less losses due to fraud.	(Duman, 2011)
SOM	NR	100	NA	10,000 accounts of selected credit card (1.01.2005 - 1.03.2005)	P	Transaction Amount Location Time of Transaction	+ high-dimensional data projected onto a 2-dimensional space can be easily. analysed and interpreted even by a non-expert.	(Olszewski, 2014)
DBSCAN+ HMM + LR	R	NA	NA	5 dataset, 10,000 ,.. 1,000,000 within one year.	G	Each transaction consists of 20 payment attributes.	-should allocate ore computing resources to streaming Detection Layer and Batch Training. Layer to improve the overall performance during real system deployment.	(Dai, 2016)

NFIS	R	NA	NA	contains 20 attributes and 1000 instances	S	20 attributes	- The training time required for the proposed system increases as the number of samples increases. + time taken for testing after the initial training is very less.	(Shaji, 2017)
ID	R	NA	NA	9,547 transactions	P	Device attributes (IP address, device attributes, device information)	+ can detect transactions that were previously undetected using a common rule-based approach.	(Laurens, 2017)

Table 2. Contributions and limitations of ML techniques applied to merchant credit card

Technique	**Real time**	**Validation**		**Data set**		**Parameters**	**Observations**	**Reference**
		Accuracy (%)	**TP (%)**	**Size**	**Type**			
AR + FAR	R	NA	NA	12,107 transactions	P	Product type, place of purchase, purchaser's age, purchaser's sex, years account held, no-money-down purchase, purchase in maximum instalments, purchase period	+The applied methodology overcomes the difficulties of minimum support and confidence, optimizes the execution times, reduces the excessive generation of rules, and helps make the results more intuitive, thereby facilitating the work of fraud analysts.	(Sanchez, 2009)
PN+ ANN + MPL	NR	NA	NA	Transactions 01-2011 →12-2012.	P	Transaction size, Time since last transaction, Last transaction size, Average transaction size, Average time between transactions, Same shop, hour of the day	+the addition of parenclitic features to the raw data set enhance the obtained results, with the error dropping from a 19:2 to a 12:23%.	(Zanin, 2017)

Table 3. Contributions and limitations of ML techniques applied to all credit card frauds

Technique	**Real time**	**Validation**		**Data set**		**Parameters**	**Observations**	**Reference**
		Accuracy	**TP (%)**	**Size**	**Type**			
RF + AG	NR	NA	NA	175million transactions 1.1million transactions	P	Amount, type (e.g. payment, refund, balance enquiry), merchant type (where applicable, e.g. supermarket), channel (e.g. ATM or POS terminal) and verification mode (e.g. chip and PIN, magnetic stripe etc.)	+ The aggregation period has a major impact upon the performance of classifiers for fraud detection. +SVM is capable of detecting the fraudulent activity at the time of transaction.	(Whitrow, 2009)
SVM + AG	NR	NA	NA					
LR + AG	NR	NA	NA					
KNN+ AG	NR	NA	NA					
SVM	NR	95,30	NA	2420 fraudulent transactions	G	Posting date, Account number, Transaction (type, Date), Currency, Merchant (Code, Name, City, Country), Foreign Txn (Amt), Local Txn Amt, Acquirer reference, E-commerce	+ While sensitivity, and accuracy decreased with lower proportions of fraud in the training data, precision showed an opposite trend. + works well with linear data for credit card fraud detection.	(Bhattacharyya, 2011)
RF	NR	90,80	NA					
LR	NR	94,20	NA					

AIS	N R	80	88*	640 361 total transactions	P	Card number, Merchant ID, Location ID, Country Code, MCC, Account, Date, Fraudulent, fraud type, entry mode	+ three mechanisms (new transaction representation and variable width r-contiguous bit matching algorithm, vaccination process and memory cell evolution process) significantly improve the performance of the AIS.	(Wong, 2012)
SVM	N R	NA	90.0	978 fraudulent records 22 million normal transactions	P	NA	-We cannot use misclassification cost without incorporating the class distribution or an impurity measure in cost calculations. +Cost-sensitive decision tree approaches to be used in credit card fraud detection and show that it outperforms the models built using the traditional data mining methods such as decision trees, ANN and SVM.	(Sahin, 2013)
CART	N R	NA	83,1					
CSDT	N R	NA	92.1					
AIRS + CC	N R	NA	83*	3.74% fraudulent transactions	P	Amount FN Amount TP	+improving memory cell generation improves the detection rate. +Changing distance function, performs better regarding FP.	(Halvaiee, 2014)
DT	N R	91,03	NA	NSL-KDD dataset [34]	S	NA	+ Reduce the complexity of host based analysis engines. - Tend to rely on the innate logging and monitoring capabilities of the server.	(Mubalik, 2017)
NB	N R	99,02	NA					
ANN+ MPL	N R	99,47	NA					
SVM	N R	98,8	NA	NSL-KDD	S	NA	+NSL-KDD dataset show that it is a best candidate data set to simulate and test the performance of IDS. +Correlation, based Feature Selection method for dimensionality reduction, reduces the detection time and increase the accuracy rate.	(Dhanabal, 2015)
NB	N R	74,9	NA					
KNN+ OD	N R	NA	NA	NA	P	NA	+OD works fast and well on online large datasets. +KNN can suit for detecting fraud with the limitation of memory.	(Malini, 2017)
FL+ ID3	N R	89	NA	NA	P	Branch code of the transaction, account number, currency of transaction, terminal reference, transaction amount, payee account number, debit or credit, transaction time stamp	+reduce the irrelevant processing so that the detection can be done in optimal time.	(Askari, 2017)

SMOTE + GMM + LR	R	84	NA	86 million transactions in one year	P	Current balance of account, Merchant category code, Total number of authorizations, transaction amount, Authorization outstanding amount, Average daily authorization amount, Plastic issue duration, Point of sale entry method, flag Recurring authorization), Approximate distance of customer's home from merchant	+ able to mimic an adversary's learning and thought processes. + giving the credit card company the ability to pre-emptively react to the changing transaction strategies.	(Zeager, 2017)
AL + HRQ	R	NA	NA	12 million transactions	P	NA	+ increase the fraud detection accuracy by up to five percent.	(Carcillo, 2017)
CW	R	NA	85	323 transactions	G	amount of money time passed since last purchase of the same category	+ The system is easily extensible and able to work directly on a large variety of commercial databases.	(Aleskerov, 1997)

4.3 Synthesis and Discussion

From tables above, we can observe that, practically, almost all of techniques focus on online fraud, because it considered as the most critical and spreader fraud in credit card fraud. Complex networks can be used as a way to improve data mining models; they may be integrated as complementary tools, in order to improve the clustering rates obtained by classical data mining algorithms. Huge challenge in several works was the imbalanced dataset, the use NSL-KDD dataset, show that it is a best candidate data set to simulate and test the performance of IDS.

As can be seen, the detection of credit card fraud uses several ML techniques, especially those of artificial intelligences and combines them with optimization techniques such as aggregation. But, the majority of these techniques give a result based on a particular dataset, which is itself characterized by unbalanced data.

Results based on accuracy, reveal that, SOM Clustering helps in identifying new hidden patterns in input data, outperforms other techniques and works well in real time. We found that OD and FL work fast and well on online large datasets, while NN requires a high computing power for learning and functioning, which makes it makes it unfit to operate in real time. In addition, we observe that, NFIS's training time required for the proposed system increases as the number of samples increases but time taken for testing after the initial training is very less. For parameters of the ML techniques, the most used one are: transaction amount and time of transaction.

5. CONCLUSION AND FUTURE WORK

In this study, we investigated the ML techniques for credit card fraud. We analyse the latest articles in this field, and made a comparative table, to evaluate the strength and weakness of each technique, and to show the most and efficient used techniques.

In our future work we will focus on continuing the study of credit card fraud to improve current algorithms, we wish to propose a hybrid model that is both able to handle imbalanced dataset and the real-time problem, to have a response during the financial transaction runtime, with an improved accuracy.

REFERENCES

Adewumi.O and Akinyelu.A, 2016, A survey of machine-learning and nature-inspired based credit card fraud detection techniques, Springer, International Journal of System Assurance Engineering and Management, Volume 8, Supplement 2, 937–953.

Aleskerov.E, fieisleben.B and Rao.B, 1997, Cardwatch A Neural Network Based Database Mining Systern for Credit Card Fraud Detection, IEEE, Computational Intelligence for Financial Engineering (CIFEr), 220-226.

Askari.S and Hussain.A, 2017, Credit Card Fraud Detection Using Fuzzy ID3, IEEE, Computing, Communication and Automation (ICCCA), 446-452.

Atkeson.C.G, Moore.A.W and Schaal.S, 1997, Locally weighted learning for control, Artificial Intelligence Review 11, 1–5.

Bhattacharyya.S, Jha.S, Tharakunnel.K and Westland.J.C, 2011, Data mining for credit card fraud: A comparative study, Elsevier, Decision Support Systems, Volume 50, Issue 3, p602-613.

F.Carcillo, Le Borgne.Y, Caelen.O and Bontempi.G, 2017, An Assessment of Streaming Active Learning Strategies for Real-Life Credit Card Fraud Detection, Springer, International Journal of Data Science and Analytics, 1–16.

Chapelle.O, Scholkopf.B, and Zien.A, 2009, Semi-supervised learning (chapelle, o. et al., eds.; 2006)[book reviews], IEEE Transactions on Neural Networks, vol. 20, no. 3, 542–542.

Chawla.N.V, Bowyer.K.W, Hall.L.O, and Kegelmeyer.W.P. 2002, SMOTE: synthetic minority over-sampling technique, Journal of artificial intelligence research, 16, 321-357.

Dai.Y, Yan.J, Tang.X, Zhao.H and Guo.M, 2016, Online Credit Card Fraud Detection: A Hybrid Framework with Big Data Technologies, IEEE, Trustcom/BigDataSE/ISPA, 1644-1652.

Dhanabal.L and Dr.Shantharajah.S.P, 2015, A Study on NSL-KDD Dataset for Intrusion Detection System Based on Classification Algorithms, International Journal of Advanced Research in Computer and Communication Engineering, Vol. 4, Issue 6, 446-452.

Duman.E and Ozcelik.H, 2011, Detecting credit card fraud by genetic algorithm and scatter search, Elsevier, Expert Systems with Applications, Volume 38, Issue 10, 13057-13063.

Halvaiee.N.S and Akbari.M.K, 2014, A novel model for credit card fraud detection usingArtificial Immune Systems, Elsevier, Applied Soft Computing, Volume 24, 40-49.

Jin.Y, Rejesus.R.M and Little.B.B, 2005, Binary choice models for rare events data: a crop insurance fraud application, Applied Economics Volume 37, Issue 7, 841–848.

Laurens.R, Jusak.J and Zou.C, 2017, Invariant Diversity as a Proactive Fraud Detection Mechanism for Online Merchants, IEEE Global Communications Conference.

Li.C, Poskitt.D.S and Zhao.X, 2016, The Bivariate Probit Model, Maximum Likelihood Estimation, Pseudo True Parameters and Partial Identification, http://business.monash.edu/econometrics-and-business-statistics/research/publications, 2-34.

Malini.N and Pushpa.M, 2017, Analysis on Credit Card Fraud Identification Techniques based on KNN and Outlier Detection, IEEE, Advances in Electrical, Electronics, Information, Communication and Bio-Informatics (AEEICB), Third International Conference.

Mubalik.A (Mubarek) and Adali.E, 2017, Multilayer Perception Neural network technique for fraud detection, IEEE, Computer Science and Engineering (UBMK), International Conference, 383-387.

Olszewski.D, 2014, Fraud detection using self-organizing map visualizing the user profiles, Elsevier, Knowledge-Based Systems, Volume 70, 324-333.

Panigrahi.S, Kundu.A, Sural.S and Majumdar.A.K, 2009, Credit card fraud detection: A fusion approach using Dempster–Shafer theory and Bayesian learning, Elsevier, Information Fusion, Volume 10, Issue 4, 354-363.

Quah.J and Sriganesh.M, 2008, Real-time credit card fraud detection using computational intelligence, Elsevier, Expert Systems with Applications, Volume 35, Issue 4, 1721-1732.

Sahin.Y, Bulkan.S and Duman.E, 2013, A cost-sensitive decision tree approach for fraud detection, Elsevier, Expert Systems with Applications, Volume 40, Issue 15, 5916-5924.

Sanchez.D, Vila. M.A, Cerda.L and Serrano. J.M, 2009, Association rules applied to credit card fraud detection, Elsevier, Expert Systems with Applications, Volume 36, Issue 2, Part 2, 3630-3640.

Settles.B, 2010 , Active learning literature survey, University of Wisconsin, Madison, vol. 52, no. 55-66, 11. [23]. J.Shaji, Panchal.D, 2017, Improved Fraud Detection in e-Commerce Transactions, IEEE, Communication Systems, Computing and IT Applications (CSCITA), 121-126.

Tavallaee.M, Bagheri.E, Lu.W and Ghorbani.A, 2009, A Detailed Analysis of the KDD CUP 99Data Set, IEEE, Computational Intelligence in Security and Defense Applications (CISDA).

Whitrow.C, Hand. D. J, Juszczak.P, Weston.D and Adams. N. M, 2009, Transaction aggregation as a strategy for credit card fraud detection, Springer, Data Mining and Knowledge Discovery, Volume 18, Issue 1, 30-55.

Wong.N, Ray.P, Stephens.G and Lewis.L, 2012, Artificial immune systems for the detection of credit card fraud: an architecture, prototype and preliminary results, Information Systems Journal, Volume22, Issue1, 53-76.

Zanin.M, Romance.M, Moral.S and Criado.R, 2017, Credit card fraud detection through parenclitic network analysis, arXiv; 1706.01953v1, 1-8.

Zeager. M.F, Sridhar.A, Fogal.N, Adams.S, Brown. D.E, and Beling. P.A, 2017, Adversarial Learning in Credit Card Fraud Detection, IEEE, Systems and Information Engineering Design Symposium (SIEDS), 112-116.

JOB SIMULATION FOR LARGE-SCALE PBS BASED CLUSTERS WITH THE MAUI SCHEDULER

Georg Zitzlsberger, Branislav Jansík and Jan Martinovič
IT4Innovations, VSB-Technical University of Ostrava, Czech Republic

ABSTRACT

For large-scale High Performance Computing centers with a wide range of different projects and heterogeneous infrastructures, efficiency is an important consideration. Understanding how compute jobs are scheduled is necessary for improving the job scheduling strategies in order to optimize cluster utilization and job wait times. This increases the importance of a reliable simulation capability, which in turn requires accuracy and comparability with historic workloads from the cluster. Not all job schedulers have a simulation capability, including the Portable Batch System (PBS) resource manager. Hence, PBS based centers have no direct way to simulate changes and optimizations before they are applied to the production system. We propose and discuss how to run job simulations for large-scale PBS based clusters with the Maui Scheduler. For validation purposes, we use historic workloads collected at the IT4Innovations supercomputing center, and demonstrate the viability of our approach. We are confident that our approach is also transferable to enable job simulations for other computing centers using PBS.

KEYWORDS

High Performance Computing (HPC), Simulation, PBS, Maui Scheduler, Job Scheduling

1. INTRODUCTION

For large-scale High Performance Computing (HPC) centers with a wide range of different projects and heterogeneous infrastructure, efficiency is an important consideration. Depending on the computing center and its objectives, efficiency comprises the optimization of the utilization of the available systems, or minimization of the wait times for users' jobs.

HPC centers continually strive to improve efficiency. Unconfirmed changes and experiments involving live production systems are not justifiable due to an increased risk of undesirable performance effects, such as job congestion or starvation of jobs, unexpected job scheduling behavior for users, etc., or simply because of a lack of comparability as usage patterns of users change with projects. This problem has already been addressed by HPC job schedulers and resource managers by adding simulation capabilities (e.g. Slurm Simulator (Trofinoff, and Benini, 2015), Maui Scheduler (Adaptive Computing, 2014), LSF (IBM, 2016)). However, not all solutions used today offer a simulator, which is also the case for PBS Professional (Altair, 2018). It hence does not allow the analysis of changes to the job scheduler configuration or effects of node reservations before deployment to the live system.

There exists a large range of simulation frameworks for HPC and grid systems. For research purposes, simulators like SimMatrix (Wang, 2014), GridSim (Buyya, and Murshed, 2002), and SimGrid (Casanova, et al., 2014) are widely used to study the effects of large-scale systems. Whilst SimMatrix demonstrated better resource usage than GridSim and SimGrid, and is capable of simulating Exascale level systems (Wang, et al., 2013), it was only validated against real systems of up to 4096 cores with artificial tasks. Another simulator is Alea (Klusáček, and Rudová, 2010), which is based on the GridSim toolkit. It is validated with real workloads (Klusáček, and Chlumský, 2016) for approximately 5,200 CPU cores, containing 102,657 jobs over a span of 4 months. However, all of the above are only toolboxes, and require a manual implementation of the job scheduling algorithms to approximate an existing system. They are also not a suitable in situ replacement for the scheduling algorithms of HPC job management systems.

The Slurm Simulator is an extension of the HPC scheduler Slurm, originally developed by A. Lucero (Lucero, 2011) and improved further by S. Trofinoff and M. Benini. As such, Slurm based systems have the advantage of making use of the simulation capabilities directly. The Slurm Simulator has been validated for large-scale simulations of real workloads from TACC (Simakov, et al., 2017) with 6,400 nodes over 12 weeks.

For LSF based systems, simulations are so far only capable of predicting the start times of jobs. However, further plans to develop simulation capabilities have been announced (Ding and Li, 2017).

The Maui Scheduler (MS in the following) has existed since the 1990s, and even though there is no active development anymore it is open source, mature and highly configurable. Its simulation capability has already been used to analyze HPC workloads (Jackson, et al., 2000). Optionally, it can also be applied as a meta-scheduler to replace the job scheduling components of HPC resource managers like PBS (Bode, et al., 2000) and TORQUE (Advanced Computing, 2018). This allows the simulation and the job management system to use the same scheduling algorithms and configurations.

We use the MS to complement PBS with the analysis of historic workloads of large-scale clusters. To show the viability of MS for larger systems we describe the configuration and changes to approximate the behavior of the PBS job scheduler for a non-trivial 2 PetaFLOP/s system. We furthermore discuss the results and problems we faced whilst using real workload data of that system.

The paper has two main sections. Section 2 describes how to approximate an existing PBS configuration using an additive job priority formula with MS. Section 3 discusses MS simulation results with a real workload from a large-scale PBS based cluster. With the summary of our results in section 4, we also point out current limitations.

2. USING MS IN A PBS ENVIRONMENT

PBS and MS are independent solutions with different configuration options and philosophies. Hence, there is no direct mapping of a PBS configuration to a MS equivalent. PBS supports various job-scheduling policies like First In First Out (FIFO), resource allocation rules, by resource consumption, by time slots, and by priority. MS on the other hand supports a wide range of job priority factors, e.g. job credentials, fairshare usage, requested resources, etc.

Due to the wide range of possible configurations, we concentrate on a PBS setup, using the job priority formula as an additive term. We furthermore consider a PBS configuration without preemption, with strict ordering for priorities, neither round robin nor by queue selections, and no sorting of jobs or nodes. Without loss of generality, we are confident that for many other practical configurations of PBS an approximate MS setup exists. For example, MS supports FIFO based scheduling directly and offers Quality of Service (QoS) attributes to honor different resource categories in addition.

In the following, we explain how to map the PBS job priority formula and workloads to MS. We also discuss how to simulate node and system downtimes with MS.

2.1 PBS Job Scheduling Configuration for MS

If PBS uses priority based scheduling, a formula describes the computation of the job execution priorities. This kind of job scheduling by PBS is freely configurable yet it follows the principles of job priorities, fairshare, eligible time and backfilling. In the following we describe such terms and how to map them to MS.

2.1.1 Job Priorities

As an example, the priority p of a job can be defined as shown in Equation 1 by using a job priority formula. The priority of the queue (class for MS) a job is submitted to is q, w is the job wait time in seconds, and f is the fairshare priority. Equation 2 shows an example of a fairshare priority definition.

$$p(q, f, w) = 1{,}000 * q + \frac{f}{1{,}000} + \frac{w}{864{,}000} \qquad [1] \qquad\qquad f = 10^6 * \left(1 - \frac{u_p}{u_t}\right) \qquad [2]$$

In the above example, the queue priority has a weight of 1,000 to dominate the other terms. The fairshare term is used to give users of a specific project (i.e. account for MS) a higher priority to users of another account in the same queue, if their usage of resources had been lower in the past. It considers the ratio of a project's usage u_p to the total usage u_t and applies a weighting to set it as the second most prioritized term.

The wait time term favors one job over others within the same queue and with the same fairshare value, should they have been waiting longer. The eligible time has the lowest weight in the formula and is noticeable only for long wait times with over 10 days (864,000 s). The weights are examples. PBS supports more coefficients (Altair PBS Works, 2011), such as job priority and resource usage depending on the number of CPUs, memory, wall time, and CPU time.

For MS, the closest equivalent to the job priority formula are the job priority factors (Supercluster R&D Group, 2002). They group into the categories: job credentials, fairshare usage, requested job resources, current service levels, target service levels, and consumed resources. There are further subcategories to access finer grained metrics, e.g. users or groups of the job credentials, and queue time of the current service level.

MS considers all such (sub-)categories as weighted additive terms. Using Equation 1 we can express an analogous priority setup in MS using the following priority categories and subcategories[1]:

```
...
Priority += CREDWEIGHT[864000] * CLASSWEIGHT[1000] * J->C->Priority[q]
Priority += FSWEIGHT[8640000] * FSACCOUNTWEIGHT[1] * dAccountFS[f]
Priority += SERVICEWEIGHT[1] * QUEUETIMEWEIGHT[1] * QUEUETIME[w]
```

Assigned coefficients and variables are in brackets. All other unused weights MS offers are set to zero. Variables `J` and `C` denote a job and its class. Differences of the current fairshare value to a target in the range of [0...100] are expressed as `d*FS` (in the example for accounts only). The initial value for `Priority` is zero and accumulated over all categories, to result in the final job priority.

2.1.2 Queue Priorities and Constraints

Real systems typically have different queues for various purposes, like offering express queues to give short jobs a higher priority in order to minimize wait times, or have dedicated service queues with the highest global priority. Use of those queues can be subject to constraints. Constraints can be limitations of the available nodes for a specific queue, job, or user.

In MS, queue priorities are set via `CLASSCFG[q] PRIORITY=X`, with `q` specifying the queue name and `X` as its priority. Further attributes `MAXNODE=A`, `MAXNODEPERJOB=B` and `MAXNODEPERUSER=C` are available to limit the maximum number of available nodes globally (`A`), per job (`B`) or per user (`C`), respectively.

2.1.3 Fairshare

Fairsharing, if enabled, avoids the starvation of jobs of less active users caused by power users submitting large amounts of jobs. The fairshare configuration can be set in MS via `*CFG[DEFAULT] FSTARGET=X`, for each partition, such as `USERCFG` or `ACCOUNTCFG` for user or account based fairshare, respectively. The target for the fairshare `X` is the usage in percent per partition. According to Equation 2, fairshare is among projects only, with a target of 100%. Thus, the MS equivalent would be `ACCOUNTCFG[DEFAULT] FSTARGET=100`. The variable `f` is the computed fairshare difference provided directly by MS. In MS, the computation of the fairshare difference can be parameterized by interval and decay factor (PBS' half-life setting), fairshare policy, and depth. The closest MS configuration to the default PBS fairshare would be:

```
FSPOLICY      DEDICATEDPS    # CPU time
FSDEPTH       1              # 24 h half-life...
FSINTERVAL    24:00:00
FSDECAY       0.50
```

It defines a 24h half-life, using dedicated processor seconds (**`DEDICATEDPS`**) as a resource usage indicator corresponding to PBS' `cput` metric. Only one fairshare window (**`FSDEPTH 1`**) is considered.

2.1.4 Backfilling

In addition to priority based scheduling, resources for which no suitable scheduled reservation exists can be used for backfilling. This allows lower priority jobs to fill up idle resources as long as their reservations do not delay any higher priority jobs. In contrast to MS, PBS does not have different backfilling policies. We assume that *FIRSTFIT* (Jackson, et al., 2001) is the closest approximation. It dispatches jobs as they fit on the remaining resources without any exhaustive search. In addition, the number of jobs for backfilling can be limited, which is typically considered together with the reservation depth to limit the number of reservations.

---

[1] The formulas are documented in the Maui Administrator's Guide (Supercluster R&D Group, 2002)

The tradeoff between more or less reservations with less or more backfilled jobs allows for conservative or aggressive backfilling (Srinivasan, et al, 2002), respectively. An example MS configuration would be:

```
BACKFILLPOLICY FIRSTFIT
BACKFILLDEPTH  3 # Select only 3 jobs for backfilling
RESDEPTH       1 # Only one reservation per node (less conservative backfilling)
```

This resembles a liberal backfilling setup of PBS with a small backfill depth (PBS' `backfill_depth`).

2.2 Using Historic PBS Workloads for MS

A typical PBS based system does not provide simulation workloads in the form required for MS. We briefly describe the PBS data needed for simulations with MS.

2.2.1 Trace Files

MS uses two different trace files, one for the description of the cluster configuration (e.g. `Resource.Trace`) and one for the simulation workload (e.g. `Workload.Trace`). The documentation of their format is in the Maui Administrator's Guide (Supercluster R&D Group, 2002).

A description of the cluster configuration is required for the simulator, so it is aware of available resources. The list of available nodes can be directly queried from PBS via the `pbsnodes` command. The most important data fields for the resource trace file are the node's name, available resources, such as CPU cores, memory, etc., and a list of supported classes.

The workload trace file requires information about submitted jobs, which PBS typically stores in an SQL database[2]. It contains various information of which the following are needed for the simulation: submission, start and end times, requested number of nodes, user provided wall time, selected queue, and the user, group and account IDs. This information is reliable as PBS creates it directly. However, there are rare events of PBS failures or changes applied to the job scheduler itself that might corrupt the data and require validation.

2.2.2 Unexpected Node Downtimes

If a node goes offline unexpectedly, the job scheduler has to reschedule reservations that were made for that node. This cannot take place in advance, as those downtimes are unpredictable. It is also unclear for how long the downtime will last. Hence, the scheduler can only start planning reservations for it again if the node goes back online. On a real system, nodes are considered offline if a hardware defects occur, nodes need to be rebooted with a different configuration, or the load on nodes is high enough to make them appear unavailable. To simulate this effect in MS, the unexpected node offline times are required. Information about node downtimes can be retrieved from the PBS log file.

MS supports reservations but does not have the functionality to replay them as with workload trace files. We hence propose to use MS' `setres`, `releaseres`, `canceljob`, and `schedctl` commands. The simulation advances to the time step to when the node goes offline to place a *user* reservation with infinite duration on it. When advancing further and reaching a time step where that node turns online again, the related reservation is removed. A node only has one of such *user* reservations at a time. We further assume that a failing node terminates its associated job. The following pseudo code shows how to combine these commands:

1. **for** *step* := 1 to *last_step* **do begin**
2. ∀ nodes switching offline between *step* - 1 and *step*:
    a. **`canceljob`**: delete node's job, and
    b. **`setres`**: place unlimited reservation on node
3. ∀ nodes switching back online between *step* - 1 and *step*:
    `releasers`: remove reservation from node
4. **`schedctl`**: advance one time step
5. **end**

2.2.3 Planned Maintenance

A full system (or site-wide) maintenance is typically known weeks in advance and announced to all users in time. Hence such periods are well documented even if not always machine-readable (e.g. in an internal ticket

[2] PBS uses PostgreSQL by default

system). Compared to unexpected downtime, the cluster will become fully idle right before the system maintenance period (ramp down) and continue its normal operation after the downtime.

To simulate planned maintenances, *system* reservations are created for every one of these windows at the beginning of the simulation. This announces them to the scheduler sufficiently ahead of time. For example, the system maintenance for all nodes is created with the following `setres` command starting at 2017-01-29 8:00:00 and lasting 20,000 s: **`setres -s 08:00:00_01/29/2017 -d 20000 ALL`**

3. SIMULATION RESULTS WITH REAL WORKLOADS

We validate our MS configuration with historic workloads from a large-scale PBS based cluster system with a non-trivial configuration. First, we explain the real cluster setup and PBS configuration in terms of job scheduling. Second, we describe the historic workloads that were available and explain their use for MS. Lastly, we discuss early simulation results concerning accuracy and time step resolution.

3.1 Reference Cluster Setup

We use workloads collected from IT4Innovations' Salomon cluster (2 PetaFLOP/s) which uses PBS Professional 13.1. As of writing, it is ranked 87th in the Top500 list (Top500, 2017). Its nodes contain two Intel Xeon E5-2680v3 processors with 24 cores and 128 GB of memory in total. The entire cluster has 1,008 nodes, of which 432 are equipped with two Intel Xeon Phi 7120P coprocessors in addition. The job scheduling system does not offer node sharing, and as such only assigns entire nodes to a job (multiple of 24 cores/tasks).

Users submit jobs to selected queues and specify the type of nodes. Eligibility for using a queue depends on the queue type, wall time of the job and free project resources (accounting). Certain restrictions apply to the queues as shown in Table 1. For the simulation, queue imposed wall time constraints are not relevant since the real system rejects jobs with wall time violations. Historic workloads contain no such rejected jobs.

PBS uses the job formulas shown in Equation 1 and 2 (IT4Innovations, 2018). The configuration of fairshare is account based with a half-life of 168h (`FSINTERVAL 168:00:00`). Liberal backfilling is used with a maximum of three jobs per cycle (`BACKFILLDEPTH 3`). The simulation required an individual increase of `RESDEPTH` to account for node downtime reservations with one *user* and multiple *system* reservations by week.

Table 1. Queues and Constraints of the Salomon Cluster

Queue name	Number of nodes	Priority q	Maximum wall time	MS configuration
`qexp`	1,006 + 2 dedicated (max. 8 per user, max. 32 total)	150	1h	`CLASSCFG[dexp] PRIORITY=150 MAXNODE=32 MAXNODEPERUSER=8`
`qprod`	1,006	0	48h	`CLASSCFG[qprod] PRIORITY=0`
`qlong`	576 (max. 256 total)	0	144h	`CLASSCFG[qlong] PRIORITY=0 MAXNODE=256`
`qmpp`	1,006	0	4h	`CLASSCFG[qmpp] PRIORITY=0`
`qfree`	1,006 (max. 752 total)	-1,024[3]	12h	`CLASSCFG[qfree] PRIORITY=-1024 MAXNODE=752`
`qmic`	2 * 432	0	24h	`CLASSCFG[qmic] PRIORITY=0`
`SERVICE`	1,008	512	N/A	`CLASSCFG[SERVICE] PRIORITY=512`

3.2 Historic Workloads for the Simulation

For the simulation, we used three different data sources: job information from PBS stored in an SQL database for all submitted jobs, logs from PBS for unexpected node downtimes, and a list documenting the planned system maintenance downtimes.

For the job information in the SQL database, we found that less than 1% of all job records had incorrect information or were subject of system changes. As such, we removed them from the workloads. We used a

[3] Negative priorities require Maui's `ENABLENEGJOBPRIORITY TRUE` and `REJECTNEGPRIOJOBS FALSE`

50 week simulation window in 2017 and consecutively enumerated the jobs by assigning job IDs in ascending order by submission time.

Unexpected node downtime information is currently an approximation as there is no standardized source as with submitted jobs. We parsed the PBS logs to reconstruct the unplanned offline times, which showed good results but still had spurious false positives. Fortunately, planned maintenance had been well communicated to users, and consequently information is readily available and accurate.

Simulation results are available within the `simstat.out` file created by MS for each simulation run. In addition to the workload trace, it contains the job execution and end times. From those, it is possible to derive cluster utilization and job wait times.

3.3 Changes Applied to MS

To enable MS to simulate a cluster the size of Salomon (1,008 nodes, 24,192 cores), with a peak of approximately 60k jobs in the queues, some defaults need to be changed. For properly sized buffers we increase `MAX_MTASK` and `MMAX_JOB` to 32,768 and 80,000 respectively. In addition, `MAX_PRIO_VAL` needs to change from 10^9 to 10^{12} to account for the extended priority value range (compare Equation 1 and Table 1).

To simulate historic workloads, it is beneficial if the simulator uses the exact timestamps of each job. By default, MS will use the current time for the first job of the simulation (relative time). We have applied modifications to MS so it uses the absolute timestamp as provided in the workload trace. This helps to identify timeframes in the past easily.

3.4 Results

In the following, we highlight the initial results from our simulation runs. We compare the simulations against the real system's behavior in terms of accuracy. We do so on a week-by-week basis but prepend the preceding week as a warm-up phase. Furthermore, we explain the impact of the simulation's time step resolution.

3.4.1 Accuracy of the Simulation

For demonstration purposes, we selected week 7 because it contains one system maintenance period, and a large amount of unexpected downtimes. As shown in Figure 1 (left), the simulation shows similar utilization to the real workload. It is visible that during the warm-up week 6 (gray area) the utilization of the cluster builds up and follows the real utilization in week 7 (within day 46 et seq.).

Around the system maintenance period (green area), both the simulation and the real system show a ramp down of utilization. This is typical for a system shutdown, as queued jobs will not fit in the remaining time before all nodes go offline, according to the wall time specified by the users. At the end of the maintenance, queued jobs are assigned to nodes again. In this example, the backlog of jobs accrued during the downtime is quite low, which results in a lower cluster utilization (<80%) directly after the maintenance period.

Unexpected downtimes (red area) reduce the total number of nodes on the system, which is visible by the utilization adjusting accordingly. Even though most of the unexpected downtimes happen early during the warm-up week, their effect is already visible. The node downtimes during the system maintenance period are also visible in red, but have no effect since there is a *system* reservation overlapping them.

Furthermore, Figure 1 (right) compares the wait times of jobs between the real workload and the simulation. Every data point is one executed job, colored depending on the used queue. The wait time is the difference between the execution and submission time of a job. It is visible that especially for the job bursts (to queue *qexp*) the patterns are identical and wait times are similar. The patterns result from how jobs are submitted, by which user/account/group, and the queue restrictions. There are also some deviations visible, which result from job dependencies as discussed below.

Figure shows the comparison of the wait times of jobs in detail. It uses Cumulative Density Functions (CDFs) for weeks 6 and 7 for the real and simulated workloads with 5 or 60 s time step resolution. The warm-up phase is excluded. The wait times of the simulation are tentatively lower than for the real system, since the simulation made the assumption of ideal job dispatching where nodes are immediately available.

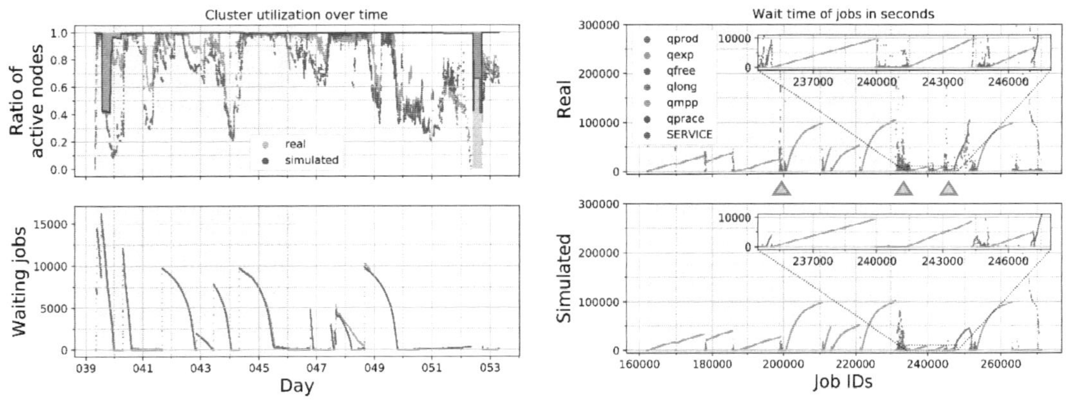

Figure 1. Comparison of a real workload of week 7 with a simulation using a 5 s time step resolution left: real (gray) and simulated (blue) cluster utilization with unexpected node downtimes (red) and a system maintenance period (green); right: job wait times of real (top) and simulated (bottom) workload with jobs from different queues, in ascending order by submission time

This is visible for both weeks using a 5 s time step with errors of week 6 ($\bar{x}$: -52, $\tilde{x}$: 171, σ: 7,557) and week 7 ($\bar{x}$: -2,223, $\tilde{x}$: -10, σ: 21,137). Errors are the differences of the simulated to the real wait times. Using a 60 s time step yields a larger error for both week 6 ($\bar{x}$: 103,386, $\tilde{x}$: 116,932, σ: 53,415) and week 7 ($\bar{x}$: 39,617, $\tilde{x}$: 18,984, σ: 53,245).

In addition, the CDFs for the wait times further show two additional properties of the workloads. First, towards the lower end of the wait times, within the range of 10 to 100 s, the simulation tends to have much lower wait times than the real system. This is due to the ideal job dispatching in the simulation. Second, there are more outliers in the real system, whose wait times are about one order of magnitude larger compared to the simulation. This is mostly due to job dependencies, which, for example, are marked with green triangles in Figure 1 (and Figure below). In the real workload, they show up as vertical spikes. Due to missing job dependency information in the workload data, they are currently simulated as independent jobs.

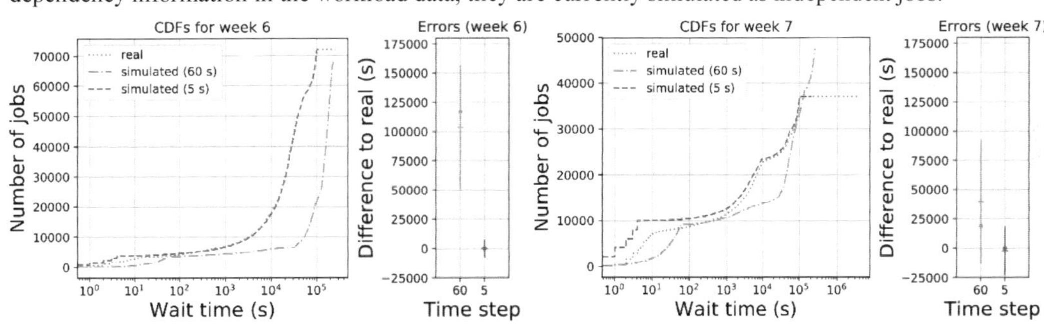

Figure 2. Cumulated density functions (CDF) of job wait times and errors for weeks 6 and 7
For weeks 6 (left) and 7 (right), the CDF for real and simulated workload with 5 and 60 s time steps are shown; errors compared to the real workload is shown with standard deviation σ (range), mean $\bar{x}$ (bar) and median $\tilde{x}$ (dot) for each simulation time step resolution

3.4.2 Time Step Resolution

Jobs submitted to PBS immediately trigger a scheduling event. The historic logs have a resolution of one second, which allows for a fine-grained replay. The MS simulator is capable of handling arbitrary simulation time steps down to a second. However, such a fine-grained resolution increases the simulation time proportionally. For example, the simulation of week 7 took approximately 42h and 239h (in the order of 5 times difference) with a resolution of 5 and 1 s, respectively. Comparing resolutions of 10 to 5 s, the simulation slowdown is about a factor of 2, following the increased time step complexity. The slowdowns with increasing resolutions are not caused by our approach to handling unexpected node downtimes, with placing and removing reservations from nodes. That handling is constant overhead, independent of the time step resolution.

For a shorter time-to-solution, it hence is desirable to reduce the resolution, at the cost of increasing the overall error. Such errors increase as (re-)scheduling only happens at the end of every time step. The time passed during the time step leaves resources idle if jobs finish within that window. When resources remain unused, it increases the risk of congestion, and later jobs might get delayed further (error propagation). Figure shows an example for week 6 (within day 39 et seq.). Even though the node utilization of the simulated system with both 5 and 60 s resolutions are similar, the number of waiting jobs increases in the latter. This results in a gradually increasing wait time for jobs, offsetting the execution time of successive jobs and skewing the results. Therefore, reducing the resolution is not always appropriate, and needs a case-by-case decision. We have found that 5 s time steps offer the best tradeoff between time-to-solution and accuracy. However, some weeks with longer phases of high cluster loads likely require a shorter time step at the cost of an increased simulation time.

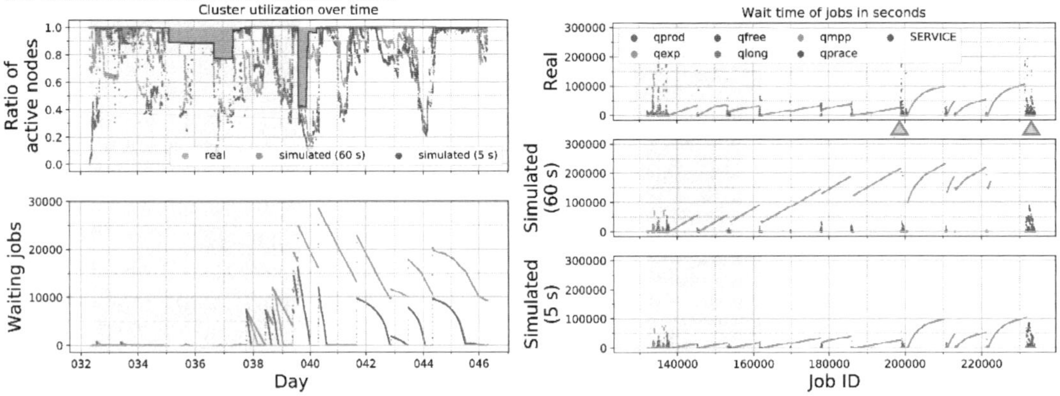

Figure 3. Comparison of a real workload of week 6 with simulations using different time step resolutions left: real (gray) cluster utilization compared to simulations with 60 s (orange) and 5 s (blue) time step resolution; right: job wait times of real (top) and simulated workloads with 60 s (middle) and 5 s (bottom) time step resolution with jobs from different queues, in ascending order by submission time

4. CONCLUSION

We have shown how to approximate non-trivial PBS Professional configurations using an additive job priority formula with different queue priorities and constraints, including fairsharing and backfilling with MS. With this setup, we are able to simulate HPC job scheduling effects with historic workloads from a large-scale 2 PetaFLOP/s cluster, including planned and unplanned node down times. Even though PBS does not have any simulation capabilities, early results suggest MS is a valuable simulation tool for PBS. The quality of approximation is sufficient for analysis of changes to a PBS production system and allows a trade-off between accuracy and time-to-solution by varying the time step resolution. In addition, MS offers the option to replace the job scheduler from PBS, which would further minimize the remaining gaps between simulation and real workloads by using identical configurations for the real system and the simulation.

Limitations currently apply to the quality of historic workloads, such as inconsistent node downtime information, which requires manual validation. In addition, the assumption of idealistic job dispatching is adding a larger error for jobs with a short wall time. Currently missing information about the real dispatching time and job dependencies require improvements to reduce errors further. Whilst it is easy to collect such additional data on a real system, two deficits require an extension of MS itself. The simulation of unexpected node downtime currently uses a simplified approach by terminating the entire job associated to nodes taken offline. This is not always correct and, together with the modeling of job dependencies, MS currently does not have suitable functionalities built-in.

In future projects, we plan to use the discussed simulation framework to study the effects of applying changes to the PBS job scheduler, such as changes of the queue priorities or constraints. Furthermore, we plan to study the effects of job dependencies and different scheduling strategies.

At our *Github* repository (Zitzlsberger, 2018) we provide a *Dockerfile* to build MS with the changes we applied. We also provide the environment we used for our simulations. The environment contains the MS configuration and the resource trace file, as well as an example implementation for handling node downtimes.

ACKNOWLEDGEMENT

This work was supported by The Ministry of Education, Youth and Sports from the Large Infrastructures for Research, Experimental Development and Innovations project "IT4Innovations National Supercomputing Center – LM2015070", as well as by the ERDF in the IT4Innovations national supercomputing center - path to exascale project (CZ.02.1.01/0.0/0.0/16_013/0001791) within the OPRDE.

REFERENCES

Adaptive Computing, 2014, "Maui Scheduler, Release 3.3.1," https://github.com/LabAdvComp/maui/ [06-06-2018].

Advanced Computing, 2018, "Torque Resource Manager," http://www.adaptivecomputing.com/products/open-source/torque/ [06-06-2018].

Altair PBS Works, 2011, "PBS Professional 13.1, Administrator's Guide," https://pbsworks.com/pdfs/PBSProAdminGuide13.1.pdf [06-06-2018].

Altair, 2018, "PBS Works Suite, PBS Professional," https://pbsworks.com/ [06-06-2018].

Bode, B. Halstead, D. M., Kendall, R., Lei, Z., and Jackson, D., 2000, "The portable batch scheduler and the maui scheduler on linux clusters," in Proceedings of the 4th Annual Linux Showcase & Conference - Volume 4, ALS'00, (Berkeley, CA, USA), pp. 27–27, USENIX Association.

Buyya, R., and Murshed M., 2002, "Gridsim: A toolkit for the modeling and simulation of distributed resource management and scheduling for grid computing," Concurrency and Computation: Practice and Experience (CCPE, vol. 14, no. 13, pp. 1175–1220.

Casanova, H., Giersch, A., Legrand, A., Quinson, M., and Suter, F., June 2014, "Versatile, scalable, and accurate simulation of distributed applications and platforms," Journal of Parallel and Distributed Computing, vol. 74, pp. 2899–2917.

Ding, Z. H., and Li, X. Q., 2017, "IBM Spectrum LSF 10 — Taking the guesswork out." https://developer.ibm.com/storage/2016/10/19/ibm-spectrum-lsf-10-taking-the-guesswork-out/ [06-06-2018].

IBM, 2016, "IBM Spectrum LSF, Version 10 Release 1.0, Configuration Reference."

IT4Innovations, 2018, "Job Scheduling," https://docs.it4i.cz/salomon/job-priority/ [06-06-2018].

Jackson, D. B., Jackson, H. L., and Snell, Q. O., 2000, "Simulation based hpc workload analysis," in Parallel and Distributed Processing Symposium., Proceedings 15th International, IEEE.

Jackson, D. B., Snell, Q., and Clement, M. J., 2001, "Core Algorithms of the Maui Scheduler," in Revised Papers from the 7th International Workshop on Job Scheduling Strategies for Parallel Processing, JSSPP '01, (London, UK, UK), pp. 87–102, Springer-Verlag.

Klusáček, D., and Rudová, H., 2010, "Alea 2 – Job Scheduling Simulator," in Proceedings of the 3rd International ICST Conference on Simulation Tools and Techniques (SIMUTools 2010), ICST.

Klusáček, D., and Chlumský, V., 2016, "Planning and metaheuristic optimization in production job scheduler," in Job Scheduling Strategies for Parallel Processing (N. D. Walfredo Cirne, ed.), pp. 1–19, Neuveden.

Lucero, A., 2011, "Slurm Simulator, Slurm User Group Meeting, September 2011."

Simakov, N. A., Innus, M. D., Jones, M. D., DeLeon, R. L., White, J. P., Gallo, S. M., Patra, A. K., and Furlani, T. R., 2017, "A Slurm simulator: Implementation and parametric analysis," in PMBS@SC, vol. 10724 of Lecture Notes in Computer Science, pp. 197–217, Springer.

Srinivasan, S., Kettimuthu, R., Subramani, V., and Sadayappan, P., 2002, "Characterization of backfilling strategies for parallel job scheduling," in ICPP Workshops, pp. 514–522, IEEE Computer Society.

Supercluster R&D Group, 2002, "Maui Administrator's Guide, Maui 3.2," http://docs.adaptivecomputing.com/maui/pdf/mauiadmin.pdf [06-06-2018].

Top500, 2017, "Top500 List," from November 2017, https://www.top500.org/site/50561 [06-06-2018].

Trofinoff, S., and Benini, M., 2015, "Using and Modifying the BSC Slurm Workload Simulator, Slurm User Group Meeting, September 2015," https://github.com/beninim/slurm_simulator/ [06-06-2018].

Wang, K., Brandstatter, K., and Raicu, I., 2013, "Simmatrix: Simulator for many-task computing execution fabric at exascale," in Proceedings of the High Performance Computing Symposium, HPC '13, (San Diego, CA, USA), pp. 9:1–9:9, Society for Computer Simulation International.

Wang, K., 2014, "SimMatrix," https://github.com/kwangiit/SimMatrix/ [06-06-2018].

Zitzlsberger, G., 2018, "Maui simulator configuration and environment for IT4Innovations' Salomon cluster," https://github.com/It4innovations/Maui-Simulation [06-06-2018].

DEVELOPMENT OF A LOW-COST SMART PARKING SOLUTION FOR SMART CITIES

João Fernandes, Carlos Serrão[1] and Nuno Garrido[2]
ISCTE – Instituto Universitário de Lisboa
[1]Information Sciences, Technologies and Architecture Research Center (ISTAR-IUL)
[2]Instituto de Telecomunicações (IT-IUL)
Ed. ISCTE, Av. das Forças Armadas, 1649-026, Lisbon, Portugal

ABSTRACT

The pressure of traffic on modern cities keeps growing. More and more vehicles flow into the city draining the existing parking resources and increasing traffic congestions and fueling the pollution increase. In this paper we present a solution for a low-cost smart parking system and all the software and hardware components that were developed and integrated in a smart parking prototype. The developed prototype is based on Arduino for the sensor network and on the Raspberry Pi for the gateway device. This paper also describes some of the technology aspects used in the communication between the sensors and the gateway – based on the ZigBee protocol. In addition to the hardware part of the prototype, the used backend architecture and the mobile application, that enables the user to find quickly and efficiently a parking spot, are also analyzed in this paper.

KEYWORDS

Smart Parking, Smart Cities, Prototype, Parking, Arduino, Raspberry Pi, Android, iOS

1. INTRODUCTION

Cities' traffic congestion and the increase in the number of the city inflow vehicles are some of the major problems that citizens and city authorities all over the world must face daily. The importance of finding solutions to improve the quality of the city's life has grown in the past years and the use of IT has created a new breed of somewhat intelligent cities – often referred to as smart cities. The concept of "smart" applied to the cities has been regarded as the answer to some of the major city problems and is slowly changing the way we live and interact with our cities. A smart city can be described has "a city that monitors and integrates conditions of all of its critical infrastructures, including roads, bridges, tunnels, railways, subways, airports, seaports, communications, water, power, even major buildings, and that can better optimize its resources, plan its preventive maintenance activities, and monitor security aspects while maximizing services to its citizens" (Chourabi et al., 2012).

For years, parking management systems have been amongst some of the major cities concerns, and some cities have carried out studies on the smart parking concept and what impacts these systems can bring to social, economic, political and environmental issues. However, there have been some problems related to smart parking systems implementation which raised political issues, like the existence of more than one stakeholder which can be a problem in terms of investment management and decision making during the project.

This paper presents an integrated low-cost system based on open hardware and software components tailored for the city needs to monitor and measure, not only the management of the parking areas, but also other environment data such as mobility, temperature and humidity. The developed prototype presented in this paper is considered as proof of concept and a reference for the future implementation of similar system approaches in any city in the world, in a timely and cost-efficient manner. The prototype was designed in a way that it can be used with different architecture or software solutions tailored for parking management systems.

This paper starts by introducing the smart parking topic and its importance in the context of smart cities. Following this section, we present a short overview of current existing smart parking solutions. On the next section of the paper the proposed system is presented as well as the different components and how they are integrated. The tests and results from the developed solution are discussed on the following section and on the final section of the paper we present some conclusions and point out some future work that needs to be accomplished.

2. OVERVIEW OF SMART PARKING SOLUTIONS

"Smart cities deploy various information and communication technology components like radio-frequency identification (RFID), embedded systems, Wi-Fi, WiMax, LTE, ZigBee, machine-to-machine communication (M2M), asset management, energy management, unified communications, and collaboration" (Washburn et al., 2010). Hwaseong Dongtan, in South Korea, is one of the most relevant examples of a smart city that first introduced a global communications network where citizens can interact to get real-time information and, therefore, to prevent crime, control traffic systems and build a smart parking infrastructure.

Different studies on smart parking systems (Thanh Nam Pham et al., 2015) (Giuffrè, Siniscalchi & Tesoriere, 2012) (Idris et al., 2009) mention the need to improve the current parking systems and how these systems can bring benefits to the development of smart cities. The growth of the cities and the increase in the number of vehicles have enabled the development of parking technologies, increasing the need to implement more advanced and intelligent parking systems in metropolitan areas of the cities (Fraifer & Fernström, 2016).

In (Thanh Nam Pham et al., 2015) a proposal is made to create a system like an IoT network that assists drivers on finding a free parking space at the lowest possible cost based on new performance metrics for the calculation of the parking cost, considering the geolocation of the vehicle, the distance between the parking areas and the total number of free slots in the parking lot. If the car park is full, the driver is redirected to another location until he can park the vehicle. Each car park uses WSN (Wireless Sensor Network) (Hancke & Hancke Jr, 2012) technology which monitors the parking lots through RFID (Akyildiz & Kasimoglu, 2004). The system works in real-time and gives the user the choice of the most suitable parking place, sending directions to the destination. Whenever a vehicle enters or exits the park, the data is updated by communicating with the parking lot WSN.

Another solution, presented by SmartParking Systems, consists of an advanced navigation system that signals the availability and directs towards the parking spot closest to the destination chosen by the user (Smart Parking Systems, 2017). The system uses LoRaWAN technology (Adelantado et al., 2017), capable of connecting sensors over long distances, requiring minimal structure while delivering optimal battery life. This offers advantages such as mobility, security and optimized location/positioning, as well as cost savings. A smartphone and tablet application allows the user to see real-time parking spaces and helps drivers to choose the best location without having to move around to check available parking spots. Time wasted in finding available spots is eliminated; the user saves time and the traffic in residential areas is relieved. The user can pay for parking easily using the application that is associated with a credit card.

3. SMART PARKING SYSTEM ARCHITECTURE

The main purpose of this work was to study, design and implement a low-cost smart parking system, using open hardware and open software resources. Figure 1 shows an architectural overview of the system and represents the implementation of the prototype. The architecture of the prototype is divided into four essential components: sensors, gateways, backend and mobile application. These components will be individually analyzed to understand their relevance on the overall operation of the system proposed in this article.

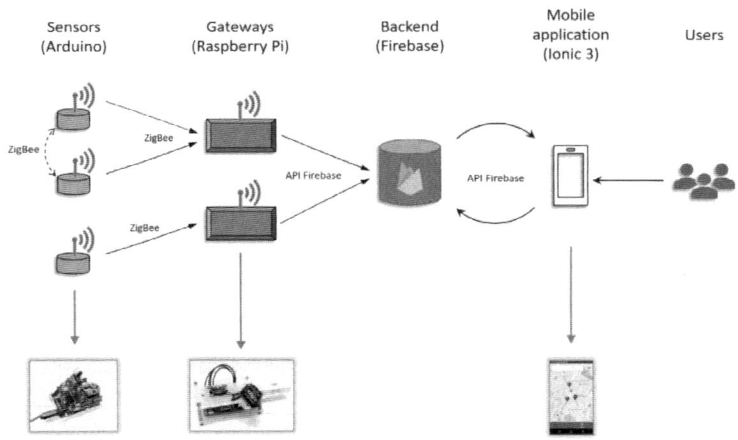

Figure 1. Smart parking system global architecture

The overall smart parking solution integrates a set of hardware components and the necessary software to make them operate in an integrated manner. The following sections of the article will present the different components.

3.1 Parking Sensors

For this prototype, a simple infrared proximity sensor is used for the implementation of the vehicle proximity sensor. This sensor detects the presence of obstacles based on the reflection of infrared radiation emitted by a transparent led and collected by a photoelectric device. It is a basic and low-cost solution used only for prototyping purposes and may not be adequate for use in a final smart parking system, since different things may incorrectly trigger the device and emulate a parked car. This is not a real issue for the smart parking system because one of the objectives was to provide the ability to support any kind of sensor (or groups of sensors) capable of accurately detecting a parked car. The proximity sensor is integrated within an Arduino board to implement the necessary logic switch for the parking sensor.

To implement a wireless communication meshed network between the different parking sensors, XBee was the selected data transceiver used to enable the communication between the different sensors and the gateways using the ZigBee protocol. For the prototype sake all devices were configured as Router (Silicon Laboratories, 2018), due to the existence of only 3 sensors in the sensor network and thus increasing the radius of communication between the sensors and the gateway. Although this configuration is not the most efficient in terms of energy consumption, the sensors energy consumption is extremely low and increasing the range of the sensor relative to the gateway is an important implementation aspect of the system that justifies the followed approach.

The Arduino board integrates the different components of the sensor and enables the communication obtaining the sensor status and sending the data to the gateway. To achieve this, specific software was developed for the Arduino UART controller that allows the initialization of the variables inherent to the proximity sensor and XBee. The remaining global variables are in line with the operation of the software, including the collection and processing of data as depicted in Figure 2.

```
void setup() {
  pinMode(ProxSensor, INPUT);
  Serial.begin(115200);
  xbee.begin(115200);
}
```

Figure 2. Setup function of the Arduino program

In this software, the 'setup()' function is responsible for initialization of the different elements that are part of parking sensor. First, the initialization of the proximity sensor is performed through the 'pinMode' function, which receives as arguments the identifier of where the sensor is connected, and the type of the connected element (in this case, 'INPUT', because the intention here is to obtain the state of the sensor as data input for the Arduino board). After this process, the baud rate (bit per second) of the data transmission is defined.

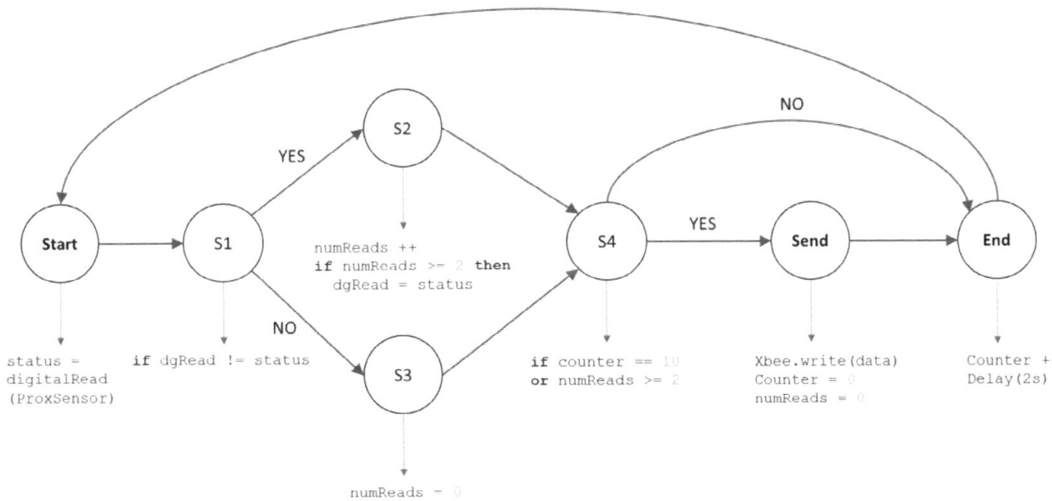

Figure 3. State machine and pseudocode diagram of the Arduino loop function

It is in the looping part of the Arduino software that the collection, processing and sending of data will take place. Figure 3 shows the state machine diagram of the Arduino loop function. The first state is called 'Start' and is responsible for gathering the status of the proximity sensor by calling function 'digitalRead()' and saving it to a 'status' variable. State 'Send' contains the function 'Xbee.write()' which sends the data through the XBee to the gateway. Variables 'counter' and 'numReads' respectively specify a counter for each iteration of the cycle, and the number of readings in which the previous state of the sensor represented by 'dgRead' is different from the current state indicated by the variable 'status'. The goal is to ensure that there are no false detections. 'numReads' must be greater than or equal to 2 (state 'S4'), assuring the first change of status was confirmed by a second iteration of the cycle, thus guaranteeing a true detection. This allows the sensor to respond immediately when sensing a consistent status change while avoiding constantly sending redundant information and thus save energy. The counter can be set to send data every 10 iterations even if there are no state changes, informing the gateway that the sensor is active on the network thus providing fast battery failure detection. The last function of the software implements a delay of two seconds before returning to the first instruction of the cycle, therefore setting the sampling rate of the sensor cell cycle. After connecting all elements, the result of the parking sensor is shown in Figure 4.

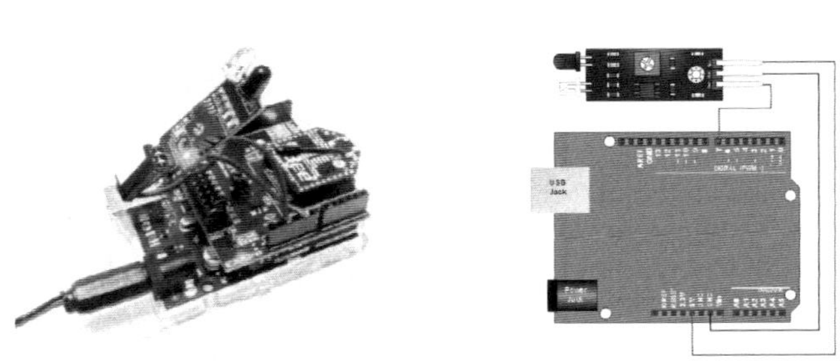

Figure 4. Prototype proximity sensor and IR sensor connection to the Arduino (Vxlabs, 2018)

3.2 Gateway

The gateway is an important component on the system and it will be responsible for allowing the communication of the parking sensors network with the management backend system, through the Internet. The gateway component is composed by hardware and specifically designed software to implement its functionality. Raspberry Pi 3, running on the Raspbian Linux operating system, was the hardware platform selected to implement the gateway prototype. Figure 5 represents the gateway prototype and depicts the connection of the XBee transceiver to the GPIO ports of the Raspberry Pi (Electronics For You, 2016). This will enable the gateway to communication with the neighboring sensor network.

The GPIO ports of the Raspberry Pi are set to use a baud rate of 115200 to connected to the XBee, coherently with the settings of the sensors XBee devices. Since for the backend part of the system, Firebase will be used, on the gateway software the Firebase API needs to be initialized and will be used to send the collected data. It is within the infinite loop shown in Figure 6, that the information from the sensors will be collected from the XBee device. This data will then be transferred to a vector using the '`split()`' method which separates a string from a defined character. The 'if' statement verifies the correct reception of the data and then the information regarding each specific sensor is sent to the database.

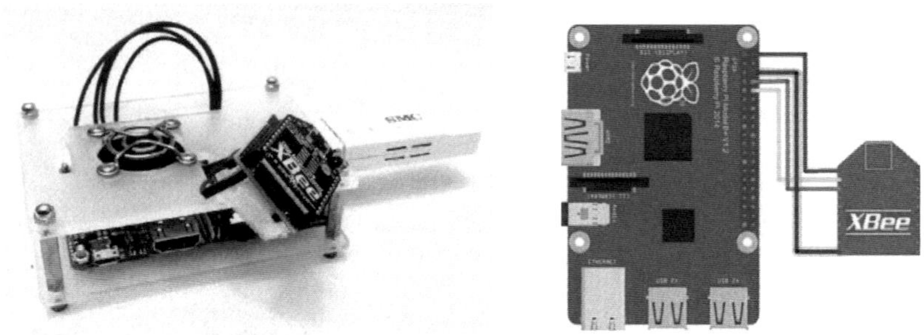

Figure 5. Gateway prototype and connecting of the XBee transceiver to the Raspeberry Pi (Electronics For You, 2016)

```
## Loop
while True:
    dataReceived = str(ser.readline().strip()).replace("b","")
    dataReceived = dataReceived.replace("'","").split(";")
    if dataReceived and len(dataReceived) == 4 and
        dataReceived[0]!= "":
         idS = "s" + dataReceived[0]
         addSensor(sensors, dataReceived)
  sensors[getSensorPosition(sensors,dataReceived[0])].cancelTimer()
         result = firebase.patch("/zonas/"+idZ+"/gateways/" + idG +
"/sensores", {idS: {"id": dataReceived[0],
                   "lat":dataReceived[1],
                   "lng":dataReceived[2],
                   "status":dataReceived[3]}})
  sensors[getSensorPosition(sensors,dataReceived[0])].startTimer()
```

Figure 6. Infinite loop of the gateway side program in Python

3.3 Backend System

For the system to work, the backend part of the prototype is based on the online Firebase platform. This platform was selected because it provides the essential services needed for a faster prototype development, however it may be replaced by any other backend platform if the basic necessary backend services are guaranteed. In the gateway component, authentication is initially performed on Firebase followed by the API initialization, which later allows the use of functions for collecting and sending data to the database. In the configuration of a Firebase project, chunks of code are provided for introduction into the Android, iOS, and Web application projects that allow Firebase API initialization. In the case of the Ionic Framework (used later for the application development), the code for Web applications is withdrawn, as it uses Web technologies for the development of hybrid mobile applications.

3.4 Mobile Application

The final objective of a smart parking solution integrated on a smart city is to provide the necessary tools for citizens to easily and quickly find ways to improve their lives through the usage of affordable technologies. In this specific case, the objective is to provide the end users with a simple tool to access the most convenient parking slot available at a given time. Due to the growing usage of mobile technologies, the best way to bring the solution to the end user is through the development of a mobile application. To produce a mobile application, in a way that it can be usable both on Android and iOS devices, we selected a hybrid mobile development framework - Ionic Framework (Ionic Framework, 2018). After finalizing the design and export of the created project through the Ionic Creator website (Ionic Creator, 2018), the Google Maps library was added to the project scope so that the user could navigate the map in search of parking zones represented by custom markers. Using the mobile application, it is possible to check the number of available spots in a given period represented by a number inserted in the markers of each zone, as shown in Figure 7. This number will be updated depending on the state changing of the sensors for a given zone. Whenever the user presses a marker, he will be taken to another screen that shows in more detail the information about the selected zone, i.e. the list of parking spots and their current state, and information about the parking zone. If the user selects a spot, the screen with the previous map will appear again, but, in this case, the map shows the route from the driver's location to the destination, and this operation can be confirmed or cancelled. There is another way to search for parking zones and it is in the second tab located at the bottom of the screen. The side menu offers completeness to the application, showing the most relevant sections of the application and each one was implemented separately.

All data generated and modified by the user is subsequently updated in the database, where each registered user has a reserved section. This is possible by calling methods implemented in the Firebase API library. During the application execution, information about the parking status in each zone can be updated in real-time, because of the listener implemented that can detect if the database has changed.

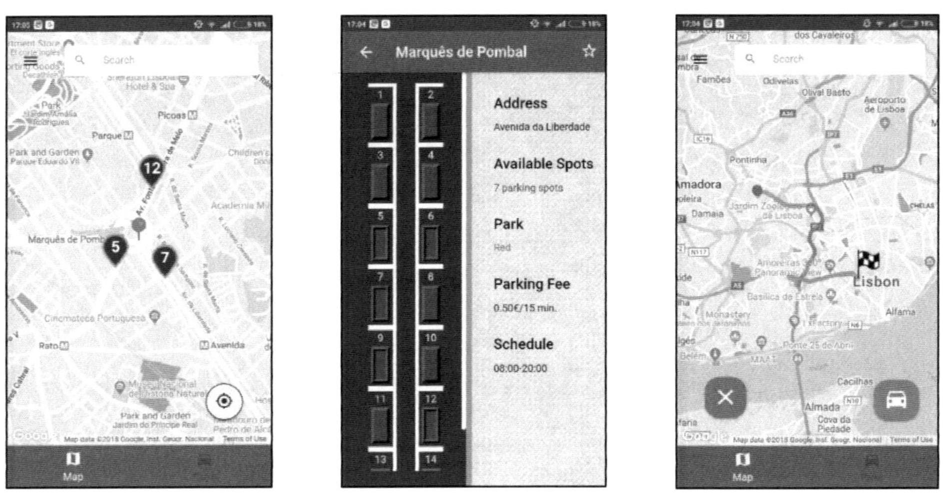

Figure 7. Application prototype layout

4. TESTS AND RESULTS

Through the software console provided for the Arduino's programming and configuration, it is possible to verify that the printed data is consistent with what is intended. The developed Python program works correctly as expected and its operation can be checked in real-time through the Firebase console. During the gateway operation, it is possible to check real-time sensor status changes. All information contained in the database is collected and handled by the application and shown to the user in an organized manner.

The fully functional prototype tested consists of two gateways, three parking sensors and the mobile application installed on an Android device. The gateway on the right side of figure 8 receives information from both sensors, also on the right side of the photo, and the gateway to the left receives information only from the sensor to the left. The intention is to simulate the existence of two active parking zones. One of the gateways is powered by a power bank with photovoltaic cells, which draw power to the lithium polymer rechargeable battery thus presenting a renewable and environmental friendly energy solution. Considering the existence of this method for supplying energy to traffic lights, for example, these devices require a much lower amount of energy, which makes possible the use of renewable energies to power the gateways. The sensors are powered by 9V batteries which are sufficient for the operation of the devices in this prototype environment.

The prototype works as expected and faithfully demonstrates the functionality of the smart parking system. All components interconnect in a consistent way and the data transmitted and subsequently received in the application are coherent and robust. The responsiveness to changes in sensor state is within the minimum standards and ZigBee technology ensures full-time communication between physical components. The range of the sensor network built for the prototype is acceptable although obstacles can negatively influence communication. It was impossible to test the prototype in a real environment; however, the obtained results exceeded the initial expectations for a real-time smart parking management system.

Figure 8. Complete smart parking prototype test setup

5. CONCLUSIONS AND FUTURE WORK

This paper presents a low cost open hardware and software smart parking solution to mitigate the problem of parking in cities and the traffic associated to the search of parking spots. The study of existing systems and the designed prototype built have led to the conclusion that there are advantages in the implementation of a smart parking system in any city, and this concept will be a reality soon that will surely benefit citizens and smart cities.

We present an open solution that allows integration with other components alternative to those chosen for this prototype, which makes it fully scalable. The use of Arduino and Raspberry Pi for parking sensors and gateways, respectively, enables the option to use other types of sensors and data communication methods alternative to those applied during the implementation of the prototype. The use of infrared sensors served as a simple solution for the prototype, but can be easily replaced by a magnetic sensor, specific for the detection of vehicles. This project demonstrates the use of ZigBee technology for the communication between the physical elements of the system. This communication protocol is commonly used in other existing smart parking systems and in other smart cities applications as an appropriate method of communication in terms of energy savings and cost efficiency.

The development of an application that previously reveals the availability of parking spaces in the areas with the highest occupancy and daily demand, could please the citizens, but the issue of reservation of parking spots was not addressed. The integration of smart parking in a city can change the paradigm of traffic and parking as the biggest problems of the cities and improve the solutions and proposals that exist over time.

ACKNOWLEDGEMENTS

This project was partially funded by FCT | UID/MULTI/4466/2016.

REFERENCES

Adelantado, Ferran, Xavier Vilajosana, Pere Tuset, Borja Martínez and Joan Melià. "Understanding the Limits of LoRaWAN." *IEEE Communications Magazine* 55 (2017): 34-40.

Chourabi, H., Nam, T., Walker, S., Gil-Garcia, J. R., Mellouli, S., Nahon, K., ... & Scholl, H. J. (2012, January). Understanding *Smart Cities*: An integrative framework. In System Science (HICSS), 2012 45th Hawaii International Conference on (pp. 2289-2297). IEEE.

Electronics For You. (2016) *XBee interfacing Raspberry Pi Model 2.* Available from: https://electronicsforu.com/electronics-projects/XBee-interfacing-raspberry-pi-model-2/2 [Accessed 15th November 2017].

Fraifer, Muftah & Fernström, Mikael. (2016). Investigation of Smart Parking Systems and their technologies

Giuffrè, T., Siniscalchi, S. M., & Tesoriere, G. (2012). A novel architecture of parking management for *Smart Cities.* Procedia-Social and Behavioral Sciences, 53, 16-28.

Hancke, G. P., & Hancke Jr, G. P. (2012). The role of advanced sensing in Smart Cities. Sensors, 13(1), 393-425

I. F. Akyildiz, I. H. Kasimoglu, "Wireless sensor and actor networks: Research challenges", Ad Hoc Netw., vol. 2, no. 4, pp. 351-367, Oct. 2004.

Idris, Mohd & Y.Y, Leng & E.M, Tamil & N.M, Noor & Razak, Zaidi. (2009). Car Park System: A Review of Smart Parking System and its Technology. Information Technology Journal. 8. 10.3923/itj.2009.101.113

Ionic Creator. (2018) Available from: https://creator.ionic.io/

Ionic Framework. (2018) *Build amazing apps in one codebase, for any platform, with the web.* Available from: https://ionicframework.com/

Silicon Laboratories. (2018) *What is the difference between an end device, a router, and a coordinator?* Available from: https://www.silabs.com/community/wireless/zigbee-and-thread/knowledge-base.entry.html/2012/07/02/what_is_the_differen-IYze [Accessed 4th November 2017].

Smart Parking Systems. (2017) *Shape the future of tomorrow's cities.* Available from: http://www.smartparkingsystems.com/, [Accessed 19th December 2016].

Thanh Nam Pham, Ming-Fong Tsai, Duc Binh Nguyen, Chyi-Ren Dow, and Der-Jiunn Deng. "A *Cloud*-based Smart-parking System based on Internet-of-Things technologies." digital object identifier 10.1109/access.2015.2477299 (2015): 1581-1591.

Vxlabs. (2018) *Which jumper to set on the ITEAD XBee shield v1.1 for use with a 3.3V Arduino.* Available from: https://vxlabs.com/2018/03/23/which-jumper-to-set-on-the-itead-XBee-shield-v1-1-for-use-with-a-3-3v-arduino/ [Accessed 25th October 2017].

Washburn, D., Sindhu, U., Balaouras, S., Dines, R. A., Hayes, N. M., & Nelson, L. E. (2010). Helping CIOs Understand "*Smart City*" Initiatives: Defining the *Smart City*, Its Drivers, and the Role of the CIO. Cambridge, MA: Forrester Research, Inc. Available from http://public.dhe.ibm.com/partnerworld/pub/smb/smarterplanet/forr_help_cios_und_smart_city_initiatives.pdf.

DATA ORIENTED ALGORITHM FOR REAL-TIME ESTIMATION OF FLOW RATES AND FLOW DIRECTIONS IN A WATER DISTRIBUTION NETWORK

Christophe Dumora[1,2,3], David Auber[1], Jérémie Bigot[2], Vincent Couallier[2] and Cyril Leclerc[3]
[1]*Laboratoire Bordelais de Recherche en Informatique, Université de Bordeaux, Talence, France*
[2]*Institut de Mathématiques de Bordeaux, Université de Bordeaux, Talence, France*
[3]*LyRE, Centre de R&D SUEZ, Talence, France*

ABSTRACT

The aim of this paper is to present how data collected from a water distribution network (WDN) can be used to reconstruct flow rate and flow direction all over the network to enhance knowledge and detection of unforeseen events. The methodological approach consists in modeling the WDN and all available sensor data related to the management of such a network in the form of a flow network graph $G = (V, E, s, t, c)$, with V a set of nodes, E a set of edges whose elements are ordered pairs of distinct nodes, s a source node, t a sink node and c a capacity function on edges. Our objective is to reconstruct a real valued function $f(u, v): V \times V \Rightarrow \mathbb{R}$ on all the edges $E \in V \times V$ from partial observations on a small number of nodes $V = \{1, \dots, N_V\}$. This reconstruction method consists in a data-driven Ford-Fulkerson maximum-flow problem in a multi-source, multi-sink context using a constrained bidirectional breadth-first search based on Edmonds-Karp method. The innovative approach is its application in the context of smart cities to operate from sensor data, structural data from geographical information system (GIS) and consumption estimates.

KEYWORDS

Graph Theory, Maximum Flow Problem, Data Driven, Sensors, Internet of Things, Water Distribution Network

1. INTRODUCTION

As reported by the World Health Organization, the urbanization rate (UR) in 2014 accounted 54% of the global population, up from 34% in 1960, and continues to grow. This UR is expected to be slightly above 60% in 2030 (United Nations, 2007). The planet today counts 3.3 billion city dweller, which is four and a half times more than in 1950. By 2030, the urban population is expected to reach 5 billion; there would be as many city dwellers in the world as inhabitants on Earth in 1987 (Veron, 2007). In this context, the concept of smart city has recently been introduced to emphasize the importance of information and communication technologies (ICT). As cities become more attractive and welcoming, it is necessary to be able to understand and master the complex interactions between technological and service delivery systems (Caragliu et al., 2011). The analysis of data collected from sensors and their connectivity offer the possibility to tackle these novel issues. Distributing water that complies with sanitary requirements while providing an irreproachable taste is one of the fundamental services offered by a city to his citizens.

A smart water distribution network (WDN) must ensure the supply of safe drinking water from its extraction to different raw water sources, to the taps of consumers, while controlling the impact on both hydraulic and energetic resources. This task is based on the good management of hydraulic parameters (such as flow rate or operating pressure), on the control of water quality through treatment by purification (such as chlorination), but also by controlling water demand. For these reasons, WDN are instrumented with sensors. Positioning sensors on the production plants, on specific point of the WDN, or closer to the consumer make it possible to monitor and to control key parameters related to water quality (e.g. chlorine, pH, temperature) or the water demand (e.g. consumption). However, just as cities are expanding, WDN are also growing. WDN are increasingly meshed to ensure better security of supply. This looped pipe configuration greatly complicates the hydraulic and increase the risk of stagnation which represent a critic situation that must be avoid prevent water pollution (Obrodovic et al., 1998; Manual of Water Supply Practices, 2005).

The information provided by the sensors therefore leaves shadow areas in which it is difficult to control all the phenomenon taking place on a small spatial and temporal mesh.

One of the main challenges for the control and management of WDN is to be able to estimate the key parameters at any point in the network to remove these shadows areas.

The contribution lies in the methodological approach that consists in modeling a WDN and all available sensor data related to the management of such a network in the form of a network graph $G = (V, E)$. The graph structure use a set nodes E, edges V and properties to represent and store data. This design allows simple and fast retrieval of complex hierarchical structures that are habitually difficult to model when data are heterogeneous. Our objective is to reconstruct a vector of numerical characteristics on all edges $E \in V \times V$ from partial observations on a small number of nodes $V = \{1, \ldots, N_V\}$. This reconstruction method consists in a data-driven maximum-flow algorithm in a multi-source, multi-sinks context. We experimented the method to infer sensors data throughout the Bordeaux Metropolis's WDN in France. With more than 3000 km of pipes this network delivers an average of 170 000 m^3 of water per day for more than 700 000 consumers. The paper is organized as follows. First, we describe challenges related to the management of WDN in the context of smart cities. Second, we present the data generated by the operation of a WDN required to build a flow network. We then describe a constrained Ford-Fulkerson method to estimate flow direction and flow rate inside a WDN. We conclude by a discussion about the future work that will be done to enhance the methodology and results.

2. SMART WATER CHALLENGES

Most of the time the small number of sensors do not allow to obtain sufficient information at every point of the network. Hydraulic models are therefore used to provide complete information on the hydraulic operation of the network (travel times, flow rates, etc.). Nevertheless, these models, although accurate, become more and more complex to solve. They require the use of average consumption profiles and typical configurations (peak days, winter, summer, etc.). This makes them become less adapted to determine, in real time, the state of the network. Estimating the hydraulic condition of the WDN on every point and time meets many challenges. The United Nations Organization estimated that, by 2025, two-thirds of the world's population could live in water stress conditions. The increasing world's population, climate changes, growth in agricultural production and access to drinking water play a significant role in the increased demand. Furthermore, even if in the last few years, the consumer tendency declines, the water demand continues to increase. Future water shortages will require increased efficiency in the treatment and transmission of water. For example, real time flow direction knowledge, would allow us to visualize the water origins at any specific point and time in a WDN. In this way, we could precisely know the path traveled by the water and track all events or interventions that could have an impact on its quality.

This information obtained in real time, could play a key role in improving the management of the WDN, including:

- water shortage risk identification
- water extraction optimization
- pollution impact estimation
- real time water quality monitoring
- enhanced leaks identification
- risk areas prediction (such as red water)
- anomaly detection
- etc.

Thus, the WDN environment must be considered as a whole to get a smarter water management but also more resilience in continuity and quality supply. The interactions between ICTS (Information and Communication Technologies) and WDN structural data need to be further considered jointly. The way we chose to consider this interconnectivity and interdependence associated to the WDN is as a graph network.

3. GRAPH STRUCTURE

Many data initially disconnected from each other can be regrouped and linked together on the WDN. As shown on Figure 1 these data are initially regrouped by theme. This can range from water quality data (e.g. punctual or automatic measure of quality parameters, quality consumer complaint), to field intervention data (e.g. renewal, leak repair, valve actuation), through hydraulics information (e.g. volume delivered to the network, hydraulic simulations, consumed volumes). This set of heterogeneous data, because of their formats, uses and locations, can nevertheless be interconnected to each other at all levels thanks to the graph network. It is important to consider all these data, their interconnectedness and their interdependences to be able to understand the phenomenon that can disrupt the functioning of the network. We propose a more general data structure which is the network graph model. This structure well studied in the field of graph theory, is adapted to intensive calculation and data visualization.

In this part we will focus on two types of information attached to the nodes and edges of the graph, to build a flow network on which we want to apply a flow reconstruction method. 3.1) the structural data which represent the skeleton of the WDN and provide the nodes, edges objects, 3.2) the sensors data which concern the monitoring of all measures related to the flow. We present in section 3.3 how we build a flow network according to the data collected to perform the maximum flow problem.

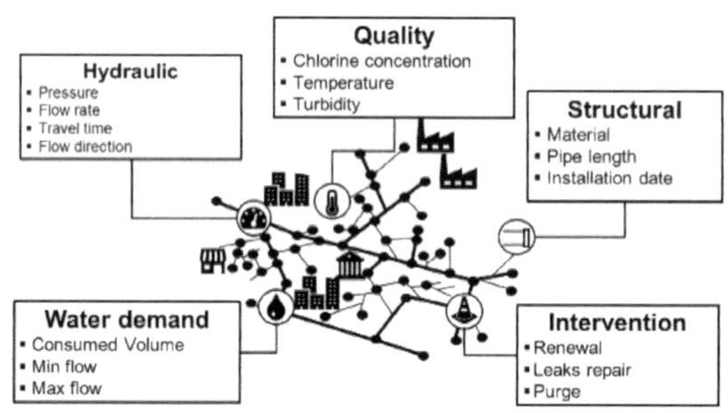

Figure 1. Schematic data representation related to the management of water distribution network

3.1 Structural Data

They represent each of the structural objects of the WDN (e.g. water production plant, pipes, connectors, valves, sensors). All these objects are geo-referenced and described by characteristics such as pipe length, pipes diameter, state of valves etc. These data represent the skeleton of the network. Beyond representing the set of structural data, they have the central role of providing a structure on which all data related to the WDN can be linked.

We now consider the WDN as a graph network $G = (V, E)$, where $V = \{1, \dots, N_V\}$ is the set of nodes and $E \in V \times V$ the set of edges. Each node represents a structural object of the WDN. Each edge depicts physical link between the nodes in our case edges represent pipes. If the nodes u and v are linked by a pipe we create and edge $E_{u,v}$, of length $l_{u,v}$ and internal diameter $d_{u,v}$.

The structural properties of pipes allow us to determine a theoretical maximum possible flow for each pipe depending on their diameters and a maximum flow speed fixed. We define $Cmax_{(u,v)}$ as the capacity of the pipe $E_{u,v}$ representing the maximum possible flow in m^3/h for the edge $E_{u,v}$.

$$Cmax_{(u,v)} = s_{(u,v)} \times V_{max} \tag{1}$$

With $s_{u,v} = \pi \times \left(\frac{d_{u,v}}{2}\right)^2$ the surface and $V_{\max}$ the maximum flow speed of the pipe $E_{u,v}$.

3.2 Sensors

In order to monitor the key parameters related to the management of the WDN, sensors are installed at different strategic points. These sensors provide local information about water that cross through the network on small time step. In the context of building a flow network the sensors in which we will focused are counting devices providing flow direction and flow rate. These flows information are not fixed. They can vary a lot inside the same pipe. Flow direction is not necessary obvious to determine and can reverse depending on the period and the total volume consumed.

These sensors are crucial to obtain real information of the flow rates and flow directions. They measure the amount of water passing through a specific point of the network in m^3/h , with a time-frequency around 1 measure per 15 minutes. We consider in this paper two types of sensors nodes:

- Type a: Those providing inflow or outflow information. Divided into two categories, sources nodes $V_s \; \forall \; s \in V_s = \{1, \dots, n\}$ and sinks nodes $V_t \; \forall \; t \in V_t = \{1, \dots, m\}$, depending if it measures inflow or outflow.
  The sources nodes are mainly located on reservoirs or at the water production plants outputs. They measure the amount of water delivered on the network. The sinks ones can be located on interconnections with other townships networks to provide water in case of shortage or on water tanks when they are filled by water production plant, but especially at consumers level, thanks to Automatic Meter Reading (AMR), counting on an infra-day period the quantities of water consumed. Inflow and outflow information are crucial to be able to reconstruct flow inside a network. It provides quantity and position information of water entering or leaving the network.
  But not all water meters are equipped with AMR. We need to estimate the unknown consumption of the non-AMR to be able to apply the maximum flow problem. These non-AMR consumptions could be estimated in many ways, from smoothing an equal proportion of the missing outflow at all the unknown sinks, to an individual consumption estimate (Ghul & Brémond, 2000). In this paper we used a methodology presented in Claudio et al. (2014) which was the one currently used by Suez who deals with the case study contract. This methodology consists in an annual consumption level group division of the population based on a Horvitz-Thompson estimator. The non-AMR consumption is then estimated according to the average AMR consumption of the group in which they belong.

- Type b: Those providing observations within the network. These sensors measure the quantity of water passing through the node giving local information about the flow rate and flow direction. According to sensors nodes we can constrain the capacity $Cmax_{(u,v)}$, introduced earlier in section 3.1, with x_{obs} the value measured by the sensor. So, for all edges connected to a sensor node in $V_{obs} = \{1, \dots, n_{obs}\}$, the maximum possible flow become an observed flow $Cmax_{(u,v)} = x_{obs}(u) \; \forall \; u \in V_{obs}$. Moreover, the read direction of sensors is known, giving us the flow direction of the flow rate measured. We can then set the direction of the adjacent edges of any sensors.

3.3 Flow Network Construction

In this section we present how we build a flow network according to the data presented earlier to apply a data driven maximum flow problem in our case of a WDN.

First things first, as define in graph-theoretic field (Hieneman et al., 2008; Ahuja et al. 1993) a flow network $G = (V, E)$ must be a directed graph in which each edge $(u, v) \in E$ has a nonnegative capacity $c(u, v) \geq 0$. The nonnegative capacity was set through structural information for non-measured edges and by the sensors observations for the measured ones (section 3.1 and 3.2). But our network is initially semi-directed because all the edges are not observed, and the flow directions are not known.

Because flow could potentially come from any side of the pipe, we duplicate all the edges to create bidirectional edges in the network. For each edge $(u, v) \in E$ we add an extra edge to obtain two antiparallel edges (u, v) and (v, u) and we set the capacity of both edges to the original one $Cmax_{(u,v)} = Cmax_{(v,u)}$. Like in a real-world, flow inside pipe can only go in one direction at a time, so the flow is not allowed to be in both antiparallel edges in the same time. For the measured edges the flow direction is known so the extra edge created will not be used. We will constrain the algorithm to not take a path that could contradict an observed edge.

We need to distinguish two vertices type in flow networks: the sources s and the sinks t. To determine a maximum flow each vertex must lies on some path from the source to the sink. Our flow network has several sources $|V_s| = 60$ and sinks $|V_t| = 34K$ rather than just one. As described in Cormen et al. (2009), we can reduce the problem of determining a maximum flow with multiple sources and multiple sinks to an ordinary problem (Figure 2).

To do so we add a *supersource* node s and directed edges E_{s,s_i} for each of the source nodes. The capacity $Cmax_{(s,s_i)}$ is set to be the measured inflow of the sensor source node s_i.

We also create a new *supersink* node t and add directed edges $E_{(t_i,t)}$ for each of the t_i sink nodes. The capacity $Cmax_{(t_i,t)}$ is set to be the measured outflow of the node t_i.

Intuitively, any flow in the multi-sources, multi-sinks network remains the same. The single source s provides as much as flow as desired by the multiple sources s_i and the single sink t likewise consumes as much as flow as desired for the multiple sinks t_i.

We now have a flow network as a directed graph $G = (V, E, s, t, Cmax)$, where V and E are node set and edge set, respectively; s and t are the *supersource*, and the *supersink*, respectively; and $Cmax$ is a nonnegative capacity on the edges. Let $f(u, v)$ be a real-valued function $f: V \times V \Rightarrow \mathbb{R}$. The nonnegative quantity $f(u, v)$ is the flow from the vertex u to vertex v. We want to reconstruct the flow $f(u, v)\ \forall u, v \in V$ in G that satisfies these constraints:

- Maximum flow: $f(u, v) \leq Cmax_{(u,v)}\ \forall u, v \in V$
- Conservation : $\sum_{v \in V} f(u, v) = 0\ \forall u \in V - \{s, t\}$
- Antiparallel coherence: $f(u, v) > 0 \Rightarrow f(v, u) = 0, \forall u, v \in V$

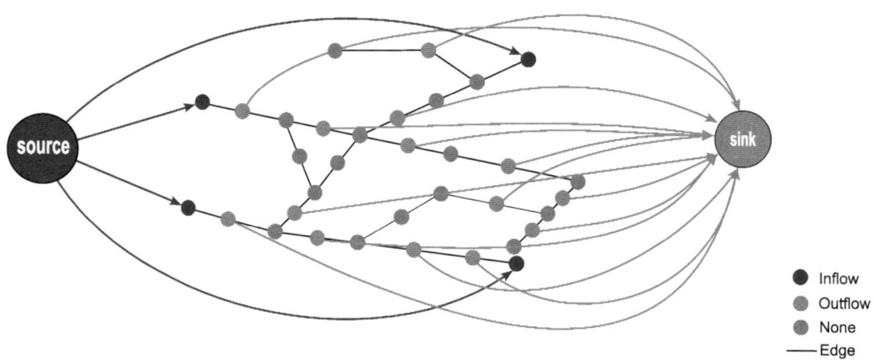

Figure 2. Converting a multiple-source, multiple-sink problem into a problem with a single source and a single sink

4. FLOW RECONSTRUCTION

We choose an implementation in C++ of the Ford-Fulkerson method (Ford & Fulkerson, 1962) to compute the min-cut max-flow problem. Like in Edmonds-Karp method (Edmonds & Karp, 1972) we use a breadth-first search (BFS) algorithm to find the augmenting path. We want to constrain the algorithm to find path first by observed edges to saturate the flow in these edges. To do so we consider, *preferred* = $E_{(u,v)} \forall u, v \in V_{obs} \times V_{obs}$ as a vector containing all the observed edges for which the flow rates and flow direction are known. These edges are considered as *preferred* edges. Because they represent real observation in the network, we must first saturate them while solving the maximum flow problem. These *preferred* edges must be traveled in the observed flow direction. The flow inside them can only increase resulting in a constrained maximum solution but not the maximum flow solution of the Ford-Fulkerson method as described in the figure bellow.

Figure 3. (a) A flow network $G = (V, E)$ with one source s and one sink t. Each edge is labeled with its flow and capacity (flow/capacity). (b) A flow f_1 in G with value $|f_1| = 23$ with no preferred edges. (c) A flow f_2 in G with value $|f_2| = 20$ respecting the observed flow direction and capacity of the edges (v_2, v_1) and (v_3, v_2).

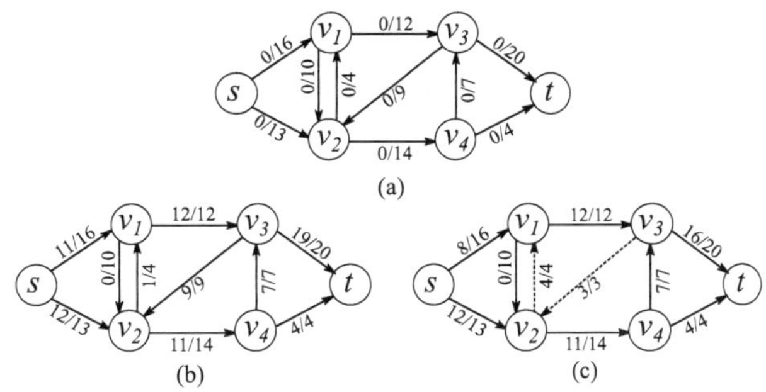

Figure 3

A bidirectional BFS is used to force path to go from the *supersource* s to the *supersink* t passing by all the *preferred* edges. As described in Figure 4, it starts at source node s and explore the neighbors nodes before moving to the next level neighbors. While a path exists and for each nodes of the same level we repeat the same process until the sensor node is reach. The operation is repeated to find a second path starting to the sensor node to the nearest sink passing by edges still unvisited by the first path to avoid loop in the network. If the two paths are not empty, we found a valid path from s to t through the sensor node $s \rightsquigarrow$ *preferred* $\rightsquigarrow t$.

We can add a flow $f_p = min\{c_f(u, v) \; \forall (u, v) \in p\}$ through the path representing the smallest remaining maximum capacity of all edges in the path.

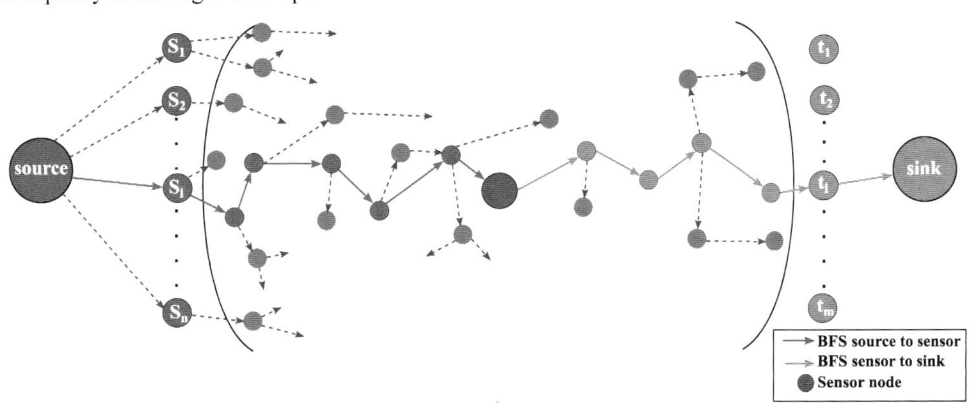

Figure 4. Bidirectional breadth-first search from source node s to sensor node v and from v to sink node t

This process is repeated for all the *preferred* edges until there is no more path available going through them from s to t or if the flow of the *preferred* edges has reach the observed flow $(f(u, v) = Cmax(u, v) \forall u, v \in V_{obs})$. If the sensors capacities are reached or if there is no more augmenting path available for the sensors edges, we try to add all the remaining flow in the network as a classical maximum flow problem by looking at augmenting path from s to t. Decreasing the maximum flow or going through reverse direction on observed edges is still forbidden during this process. For all the non-observed edges both antiparallel edges are available.

But as described in section 3.3 theses antiparallel edges represent the same physical pipe and water can't be at the same time in both. When a new flow goes through an edge in the same direction we simply add it (see line 12 Algorithm 1). When a new flow goes through an antiparallel edge while the edge was already visited in the other direction, the flow must be updated to respect the antiparallel coherence constraint and to determine in which edges the remaining flow is.

Algorithm 1. Pseudo code of the constrained Ford-Fulkerson method

FORD-FULKERSON CONSTRAINED(G, s, t, *preferred*)

while there exists a path
    if all the observed edges are not visited or saturated
        $p_1 \leftarrow$ path from s to *preferred*
        $p_2 \leftarrow$ path from *preferred* to t
        $p \leftarrow p_1 \cup p_2$ path from s to t by *preferred*
    else $p \leftarrow$ path from s to t
    $c_f(p) = \min\{c_f(u,v), \forall(u,v) \in p\}$
    for each edge $(u,v) \in p$
        $e_0 \leftarrow$ first edge of (u,v)
        $e_1 \leftarrow$ second edge of (u,v)
        if edge in path same direction than in graph
            $flow(u,v) \leftarrow flow(u,v) + c_f(p)$
        else
            $flow(v,u) \leftarrow flow(v,u) + \max(0, c_f + flow(u,v))$
            $flow(u,v) \leftarrow \max(0, flow(u,v) - c_f(p))$

The constrained Ford-Fulkerson algorithm presented in the pseudo code Algorithm 1 returns for all edges a flow rate. For all the non-observed edges the flow direction is known according to the nonnegative edges. For all the observed edges we have the flow rate regarding to the expected flow. This information will help us determine if the maximum flow solution is close to observed state of the network. The Figure 5 present an output of the Algorithm 1.

Figure 5. Output of the Algorithm 1 on the Bordeaux Metropolis (France) WDN composed by $N_V = 60K$ nodes and $N_E = 66K$ edges. In light green sink nodes that have been saturated, in light red non-saturated sinks. Squares represent sources nodes. Saturated ones are in blue and those with remaining flow are in yellow. The green dot represents sensor nodes saturated during the bidirectional BFS, and the red ones are those where the flow didn't reach the measured flow.

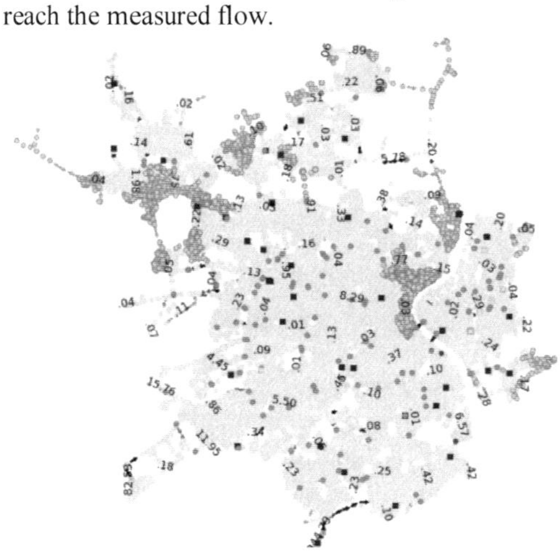

Figure 5

5. CONCLUSION AND DISCUSSION

We presented a methodology to create a flow network to estimate flow directions and flow rates inside a real WDN from sensors and GIS data. These results allow us to determine the age and origin of water in any point and time of the network which is an important result to answer to most of the future WDN operation challenges. We introduced a constrained Ford-Fulkerson algorithm to take advantage of all the sensors information and force the solution to respect the observed value. The result obtained on the case study of the Bordeaux Metropolis WDN are satisfying. They helped us to detect inaccurate information in both structural and sensors data. We could for example check the validity of the flow direction given by a sensor, if no flow was able to go through it during the algorithm and if by reverting it we were able to saturate the edge. The information was then confirmed by a real observation and updated into the database.

The fact that the outflow information isn't completely known on the case study do not allow to saturate all the sensors nodes. Indeed, more than 50% of the outflow is estimated. Since this estimate is based on annual consumption profile, there is area of the network where consumption is overestimated and conversely underestimated. Moreover, to apply the maximum flow problem a proportion of the missing outflow (due to underestimate or leak) is smoothed through all the estimated nodes to obtain inflow equal to outflow. We could detect through connected sub-graph of the network (in which flow entering and leaving the area was measured) that even if sensors were saturated we still have sink node requiring outflow describing the fact that consumption was overestimated in this area. Conversely, we detected that consumption was underestimated in some area because sensors were not saturated, but all sink node were satisfied. We can therefore improve the results provided by the algorithm by spatially refining the consumption estimates by looking at connectivity of the graph.

Future work will be to enhance the methodology with more data related to management of WDN that could constrain the number of solution of the maximum flow problem with for example intervention (e.g. valve operation, pipe break) or leak detection information.

REFERENCES

Ahuja, Ravindra K., Magnanti, Thomas L., Orlin, James B. (1993). *Network Flows: Theory, Algorithms and Applications*, Prentice Hall.

American Water Works Association. (2005). *Manual of Water Supply Practices*. PE-Design and Installation, Denver.

Auber, D. (2004). *Tulip – A huge graph visualisation framework*, Graph drawing software, Springer, Berlin, Heidelberg, pp. 105-126.

Caragliu, A., Del Bo, C., Nijkamp, P. (2011). *Smart Cities in Europe*, in Journalof Urban Technology, pp. 65--82.

Claudio,K., Couallier, V., Le Gat, Y., Saracco, J. (2014). *Water consumption estimation of an hydraulic district from a sample of users equipped with automatic meter reading*, Journal de la Société Française de Statistique, Société Française de Statistique et Société Mathématique de France, 155 (4), pp. 160-177.

Cormen, T.H., Leiserson, C.E., Rivest, R.L., Stein, C. (2009). *Introduction to Algorithms*, third edn. MIT Press, Cambridge.

Edmonds J. and Karp Richard M.,(1972) *Theoretical improvements in algorithmic efficiency for network flow problems*, Journal of the ACM, Association for Computing Machinery (ACM), vol. 19, no 2, p. 248–264

Ford, L. and Fulkerson, D. (1962). *Flows in Networks*. Princeton Univ. Press.

Goldberg, A.V., Tardos, É., and Tarjan, R.E. (1989). *Network flow algorithms*, Tech. Report STAN-CS-89-1252, Stanford University CS Dept.

Guhl, F. and Brémond, B. (2000) Optimisation du fonctionnement des réseaux d'eau potable. Prise en compte de l'aspect stochastique de la demande [Optimization of the operation of drinking water networks. Considering the stochastic aspect of demand]. Engineering - E A T, IRSTEA 2000 edition, p. 15 - p. 23.

Heineman G.T., Pollice G., Selkow S. (2008), *Chapter 8: Network Flow Algorithms. Algorithms in a Nutshell*, Oreilly Media, pp. 226-250

Obradovic, D. And Lonsdale, P. (1998). *Public Water Supply. Models, Data and Operational Management*, E&FN SPON, Routledge, London.

Perrot A., Auber D., (2015), *FATuM –Fast Animated Transitions using Multi-Buffers*. 19th international Conference "information Visualisation 2015", Jul 2015, Barcelone, Spain.

United Nations, Department of Economic and Social Affairs. (2007). *Population Division, World Population Prospects: The 2006 Revision*, Highlights, Working Paper No. ESA/P/WP.202.

Veron, J. (2007). *Population & Sociétés - La moitié de la population mondiale vit en ville* [Population & Societies - Half of the world's population lives in cities], Institut National d'Etudes Démographiques, 435.

EMPOWERING CITIZENS INTO CO-CREATORS OF DEMAND-DRIVEN PUBLIC SERVICES

Diego López-de-Ipiña[1], Pauli Misikangas[2], Mikel Emaldi[1], Unai Aguilera[1], Dejan Drajic[3] and Sara Sillaurren[4]

[1]*DeustoTech-Deusto Foundation, University of Deusto, Av. Universidades 24, 48007 Bilbao, Spain*
[2]*Cloud'N'Sci Ltd, Helsinki, Finland*
[3]*DunavNET, Antona Čehova 1/2, Novi Sad 403774, Serbia*
[4]*TECNALIA, eServices, Spain*

ABSTRACT

Open Government aims to enhance the transparency, participation and collaboration of city stakeholders in order to give place to Smarter Cities. This paper describes the WeLive co-creation fostering methodology together with its associated co-creation tools and a wide range of resulting co-created artefacts. This combination of co-creation methodology, platform and assets have been used to foster higher and better public-private partnerships for addressing citizen needs through new user demand-driven public services in four pilots across Europe. The lessons learned from this piloting on the value of co-creation to enhance participation and collaboration among distinct Smart Cities stakeholders are described.

KEYWORDS

Open Government, CO-CREATION, Open Data, Open Services, Smart City

1. INTRODUCTION

A smart city (Komninos, 2015) is an innovative and sustainable place that uses information and communication technologies, and other means, to improve quality of life, efficiency of urban operation and services, and competitiveness, while ensuring that it meets the needs of present and future generations with respect to economic, social and environmental aspects.

ICT-enabled Open and Collaborative Government is the recipe to deliver "more from less" by promoting higher transparency, more participation and better cross-stakeholder collaboration mechanisms. According to OECD, *Open Government* (Oecd.org, 2018) can be defined as the opening up of government processes, proceedings, documents and data for public scrutiny and involvement - is now considered a fundamental element of a democratic society. Hence, governments should not be any longer the single providers of public services. Empowerment of stakeholders is necessary by incentivizing them to take a more active role. Indeed, this paper argues that it is not enough with the traditional resource efficiency approach of Smart City initiatives. In fact, the "city appeal and dynamicity" will be key to attract and retain citizens, companies and tourists. A way to achieve this is by encouraging a user-driven and centric innovation, i.e. by making citizen and companies in a city more participatory and collaborative – turning them into *prosumers* rather than simple *consumers* of services.

The WeLive project aims at transforming the current e-government approach followed by most public administrations into we-government where all the stakeholders of public administration, namely citizens, local businesses and companies, are treated as peers (collaborators) and prosumers (providers) instead of the usual customer role associated to them. Furthermore, this project also ambitions to turn e-government into t-Government (Transformational Government) by providing the public with the technology tools that enable them to create public value themselves. Additionally, WeLive fully adopts m-Government, i.e. an extension or evolution of e-government through utilisation of mobile technologies for public service delivery.

This paper describes the WeLive co-creation methodology and its platform with a set of tools where open data publishers, citizens and developers can meet and co-create sustainable public services addressing user demand-driven needs. It pursues helping public administrations to move from all controlling and all providing organizations to those that act as facilitators, enablers and orchestrators of public services.

The structure of the paper is as follows. Section 2 offers a related work description. Section 3 describes the proposed WeLive co-creation methodology and its associated infrastructure. Section 4 explains with an example the potential of WeLive co-creation methodology. Section 5 explains how the project contributions were validated in a pilot across 4 European cities. Finally, section 6 concludes the paper and outlines some future work.

2. RELATED WORK

WeLive deals with the following topics: 1) Open Data, 2) Open Services and 3) Open Innovation and Co-creation. To enable a user-centric collaborative public service ecosystem, new types of infrastructure are needed where public value is created by the ability to share, interact and collaborate between actors. Novel processes and approaches are required with a decentralised, cross-government and multi-actor architecture, coupled with the integration of Big Data and the role of social tools (GOV.UK, 2018). Potential problems related to security, privacy and data protection issues have also to be tackled. An open governance framework, as intended by WeLive, also requires interoperability (both at the organisational and technological level), open standards, adoption of Linked Data principles and Cloud Computing. In terms of web evolution, a solution like WeLive has to embrace 3.0 (Vossen, Lytras and Koudas, 2007) development, i.e. machine integration of data. Research demonstrates the potential of mobile apps to transform governments and to provide access to public information; m-Government is therefore emerging as the next big wave for ICT use in public sector (Oecd-ilibrary.org, 2018).

Open Innovation (Baldwin and von Hippel, 2010) provides a framework for involving actual customers in the service and product innovation process. It is a co-creational process that facilitates stakeholder engagement, where companies and governments should use external ideas to develop their services in a collaborative Public Private Partnership setting. With the increased focus on sustainability and development of Smart Cities, a more inclusive public administration is enabled, i.e. one that incorporates citizens into the planning of development activities through different channels enabling their engagement on various matters. This has resulted in Living Labs (Almirall and Wareham, 2011), e.g. cities used as places where new services can be deployed and tested in a real environment, capturing the feedback and contributions crowdsourced by the citizens.

Since the first public administrations started sharing their data as Open Data, the idea of Open Government has been disseminated around the world rapidly. As described by the Open Data Barometer (Opendatabarometer.org, 2018), Europe leads the region ranking, with widely known initiatives like data.gov.uk (UK) or opengov.se (Sweden). However, most of countries which have started adopting Open Government policies have serious lacks on exploiting the potential of Open Data. Many of them are focused only on implementing open data portals, placing little efforts on bringing open data closer to entrepreneurs and citizens through APIs, consumable by application developers, which is aimed by WeLive.

Several European projects have also aimed to realize Open Government in the last few years. CitizenLab (Citizenlab.co, 2018) proposes a ready-to-use civic engagement platform to reach more citizens, manage your participation projects, and drive better decisions. It allows to consult your citizens from bottom-up or within defined council-wide projects. Empatia (Empatia Project, 2018) is a platform for decision-making and implementation cycle of Participatory Budgeting. OpenGovIntelligence (Opengovintelligence.eu, 2018) puts forward a lean and agile process for data-driven co-creation, and defines the core elements of this new service ecosystem. Taking as reference Voorberg et.al. co-creation approach (Voorberg et al., 2017), they adopt a co-creation methodology for data-driven public services consisting of the following stages co-initiation, co-design, co-implementation and co-evaluation. CITADEL (Citadel-h2020.eu, 2018) aims to explore, monitor and analyse the drivers, enablers, impact, risks and barriers of open, innovative and collaborative government across a diverse terrain of PAs through an open and scalable platform based on innovative ICTs to understand, transform and improve by proposing recommendations to enhance the PAs policies and processes with a view to deliver effective, inclusive and high quality public services across Europe. However, overall, when compared with WeLive, the mentioned solutions do not encompass as a whole the co-creation process as we argue WeLive does in the rest of this paper.

3. WELIVE PROJECT

WeLive was created to address the current low take-up of public services (Europa.eu, 2018), traditionally led by public administration. The vision of WeLive is that Public Administrations should not only restrict to supply data and decide on citizens behalf. In fact, they should supply the tools and its associated ecosystem to seek the real collaboration of different stakeholders, i.e. citizens, SMEs and public administration, in the CO-CREATION of truly demand-driven public services. Current public services are built following an administration-centric approach which results into a low usage of those services. PAs are facing key socioeconomic challenges such as demographic change, employment, mobility, environment plus the squeeze on public finances. Citizens' expectations in terms of burden reduction, efficiency and personalisation are growing. Cities and territories should be transformed into hubs of welfare, innovation and economic growth giving place to Smarter Cities or territories.

WeLive pursues to go beyond Open Government Data Portals by turning them into Open Government Public Service co-creation portals. This is, new public services should result from the collaboration and joint investment (and exploitation) of distinct stakeholders. For that, WeLive contributes with a Public Service Product Line (see Figure 1) where collaboratively specified ideas, once refined, are assembled into final public service apps, as result of combining the operation of distinct building blocks, aka. Microservices or constructions bricks, designed to be reusable and composable to ease the construction of new public service apps. Those apps are published into the Service Catalogue or Marketplace component where they can be found, searched, selected and used by final users.

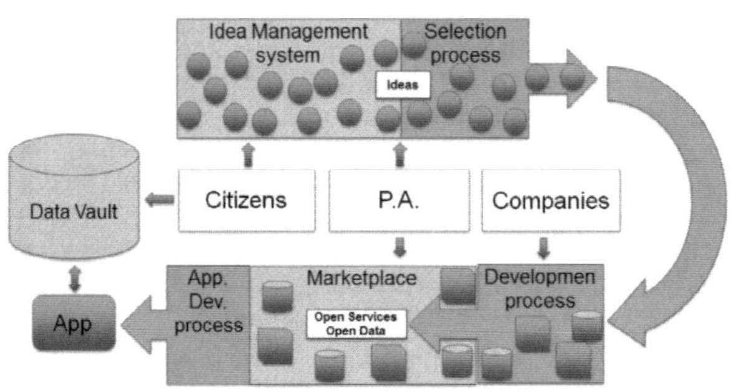

Figure 1. WeLive public service co-creation assembly line

3.1 WeLive Co-creation Methodology

WeLive contributes with a multi-stakeholder (citizens, companies and public administration) CO-CREATION methodology together with a set of web-based supporting tools that streamline and democratize the whole CO-CREATION process, enabling participating stakeholders transit from user-driven *needs* to collaboratively refined *ideas* which then are turned into actual *artefacts* or resources which are finally assembled together to give place to fully-fledge *public service apps*. In this methodology, the CO-CREATION process is divided into CO-DESIGN and CO-EXPLOITATION phases. The *CO-DESIGN phase* further divided into the two following stages: a) *CO-IDEATION stage* which consists on innovating new service ideas together and b) *CO-IMPLEMENTATION stage* which is about designing and implementing ideas into a service. On the other hand, the *CO-EXPLOITATION phase* is further divided into the two following stages: a) *CO-MAINTENANCE stage* which handles keeping the service running and users satisfied and b) *CO-BUSINESS stage* which is about tackling marketing, selling and earning together.

In WeLive, CO-DESIGN implies that stakeholders jointly CO-IDEATE and CO-IMPLEMENT, i.e. they collaborate in the specification of an idea which is turned/implemented as an app or any other type of open government asset. At any stage the collaboration process may be stopped, i.e. the CO-EXIT stage is executed.

CO-DESIGN is followed by CO-EXPLOITATION phase where those involved in the ideation and then implementation collaborate on devising an exploitation strategy for the derived asset. Such exploitation consists at least of two stages, namely CO-MAINTENANCE where the produced asset is deployed, maintained and sustained and CO-BUSINESS where different monetization approaches might be adopted to ensure the asset keeps providing service. Figure 2 depicts graphically the WeLive CO-CREATION process and how those stages are supported by the WeLive platform and associated hosting environments – where business logic of artefacts, i.e. building blocks and apps, is run, described in the next section.

In WeLive, different stakeholders contribute and benefit from the CO-CREATION process. Innovators suggest, refine and give feedback about ideas. App developers develop apps and expect some retribution from it. Similarly, BB developers produce reusable services which can be included in different apps. Hosting providers facilitate computing and storage resources for the execution of co-created assets and expect economic compensation for it. Platform Managers operate and maintain the WeLive platform and the assets developed with it. Data publishers make available information for transparency purposes, e.g. public administration, or in exchange of economic compensation to allow third parties to exploit their company generated or added value aggregated information.

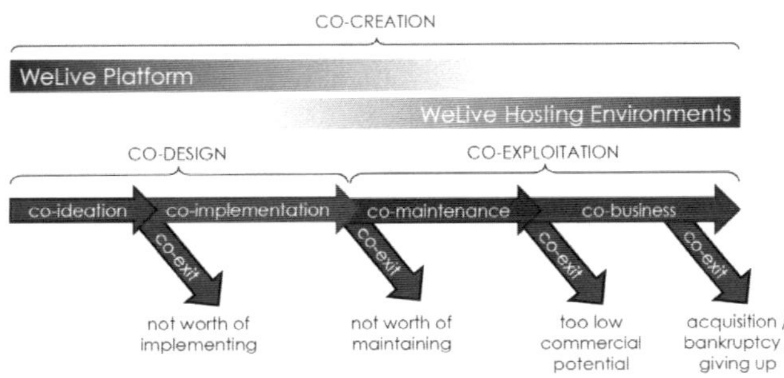

Figure 2. CO-CREATION methodology in WeLive

3.2 WeLive Platform for Co-Creation

The WeLive platform supports all phases of co-creation process, shown in Figure 2, enabling collaborative generation of new public services by all interested city stakeholders. It provides a set of suitable web interfaces, see Figure 6's right hand side, allowing all stakeholders not only to provide ideas for the new services, but also to take an active part in the design and implementation of those ideas to assemble actual services based on their personal needs. It also supports deployment and business development by the Service Catalogue and Hosting Environment made available.

Indeed, the WeLive CO-CREATION methodology is backed by the WeLive platform, consisting of four logical layers, each with a range of components contained within, as shown in Figure 3:

- *Open Data Layer* is responsible for managing Open, Social and even Private Data through the Open Data Stack (ODS) component and to manage personal data through the Citizen Data Vault (CDV) component. It enables data to be created, updated or queried.
- *Open Innovation Layer* embodies the Ideation Board, a component that handles the transformation of needs, into challenges that give place to refined ideas.
- *Open Services Layer* is responsible for hosting and publishing all the generated artefacts in the co-creation process into the Service Catalogue. Besides, it includes the Service Composer component which enables non-programmers to compose new public service apps by mixing and matching the inputs and outputs of various building blocks. Finally, it is associated to the Hosting Environments, where the business logic of artefacts is run.
- *Intelligence Layer*, is responsible for recommending assets related to other assets or assets relevant to different user profiles through the Decision Engine. In addition, the Charts Dashboard shows the evolution in time of certain platform indicators, e.g. usage of generates apps, ideas managed by Ideation Board and so on.

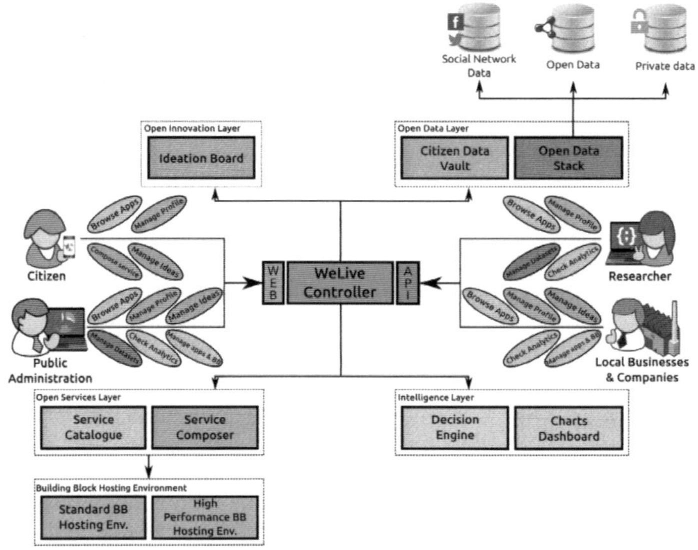

Figure 3. WeLive CO-CREATION architecture

3.3 From Open Data to Open Building Blocks

Remarkably, within the Open Services Layer (see Figure 3), the Service Composer component enables stakeholders to create new services starting from services/datasets already available through a visual paradigm. This component is devised to enable non- ICT-proficient users to design the mock-ups of the apps interfaces (see right hand side of Figure 5), whereas developers and advanced users will be able to use all the operators, functionalities and UI elements to develop complex mashup services and applications (see left hand side of Figure 5). A wizard based template has been implemented to create, in an easy way, a simple web application based on the available mashup projects.

Closely linked to the Service Composer is the concept of *building block* in WeLive. This is indeed a core contribution of WeLive, since it advocates on making available a wide range of building blocks which are readily available easy to use pieces of digital capability of a Smart City.

Even though the increasing availability of datasets in public Open Data portals is a reality, many Open Data portals do not put in place procedures to guarantee the quality and long-term sustainability of their datasets. Fortunately, WeLive helps in this regard through its Building Block (BB) contribution. WeLive allows the creation of BBs as microservices which act as wrappers around datasets. Those BBs include extra functionality to verify the quality and apply corrections measures if we needed. For instance, this was the case of the Bilbao Agenda dataset which was omitting the public event dates that were, anyhow, available in another public web page associated to the event. Thanks to a BB, a corrected dataset of events including the appropriate dates could be provided, mixing the contents of the original dataset with the information (dates) about each event correctly published as HTML in the Bilbao council's website.

Building blocks are made available to developers through REST APIs. Mash-ups developed with the Service Composer can also be exported as building blocks since they offer a REST API well documented through Swagger. In general, BBs either both give access to one or more datasets and apply some business logic around them, e.g. filtering, aggregation, and augmentation/correction of an existing dataset, or they encapsulate business logic which can be easily composed.

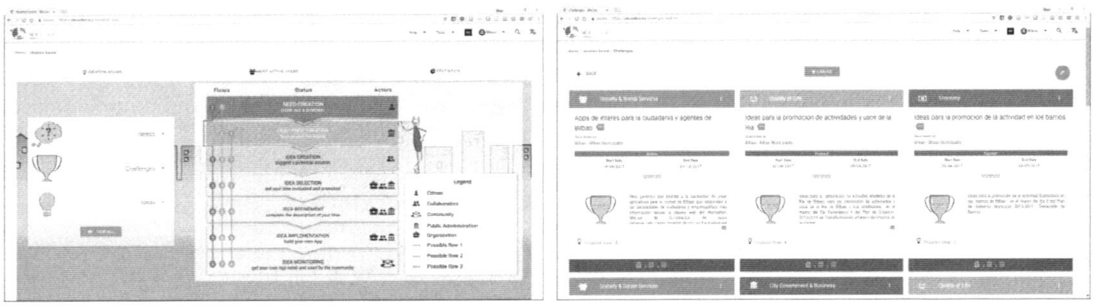

Figure 4. WeLive Ideation board

4. DESIGN, PRODUCTION AND DELIVERY OF CO-CREATED PUBLIC SERVICES

This section illustrates how the WeLive CO-CREATION methodology is applied in practice. The first stage in WeLive CO-CREATION methodology is CO-IDEATION, where stakeholders' needs and comments together with council issued challenges are turned into refined ideas which are selected for progressing towards the CO-IMPLEMENTATION stage. This stage is fully backed by the Ideation Board (see Figure 4), a collaborative tool that enables several users to jointly map needs into challenges given place to ideas. Importantly, the CO-IDEATION stage cannot only be supported by technology, it must be part of a participatory process where face-to-face meetings and workshops take place. Participation techniques such as Game Designs, questionnaires or focus groups are used in this process, as described in section 4.1.

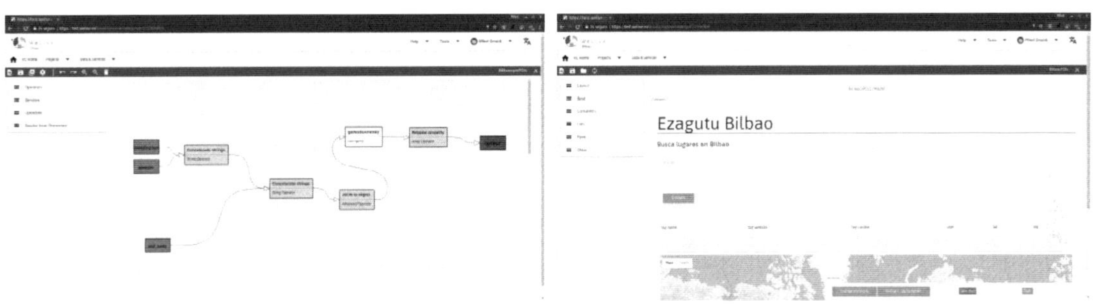

Figure 5. Service Composer: a) mash-up tool (left hand side) and b) mock-up tool (right hand side)

The second stage in WeLive CO-CREATION methodology is CO-IMPLEMENTATION, where selected ideas as result of CO-IDEATION stage, specified in the Ideation Board, area analysed in order to identify artefacts already available in the Service Catalogue (see Figure 6 left hand side), e.g. datasets of building blocks, useful to materialize them. In addition, the Service Composer tool and the WeLive RESTful API (see Figure 6 right hand side) are used by non-programmers and programmers, respectively, to create new building blocks that together with the existing ones can make an idea reality as a new public service app. The newly developed artefacts (new building blocks and app) are published in the Service Catalogue, so that they can be found, consumed and reused by users. Notably, the Service Composer, as shown in Figure 5 left hand side, is a tool that enables users to apply the Drag and Drop paradigm to assemble complex data flows (mash-ups) that are then visualized as mock-ups (see Figure 5 right hand side), without having to write a single line of code. Importantly, once again, the CO-IMPLEMENTATATION stage requires not only technology but also good documentation, direct support or even incentivation events (hackathons).

The third stage in WeLive CO-CREATION methodology is CO-EXPLOITATION, which is sub-divided into CO-MAINTENANCE and CO-BUSINESS steps. The created artefacts published in the Service Catalogue must be maintained to ensure their continuous operation. Besides, their acceptance and usage has to be monitored through the Charts Dashboard (see Figure 7 left hand side). These two aspects are essential to allow for the take-up and usage retention of the produced assets (CO-MAINTENANCE). Besides, co-creators have to pursue the sustainability of the produced assets by developing a business model (see Figure 7 right hand side) which returns their investment and ensures the long term sustainability of the developed public service apps (CO-BUSINESS).

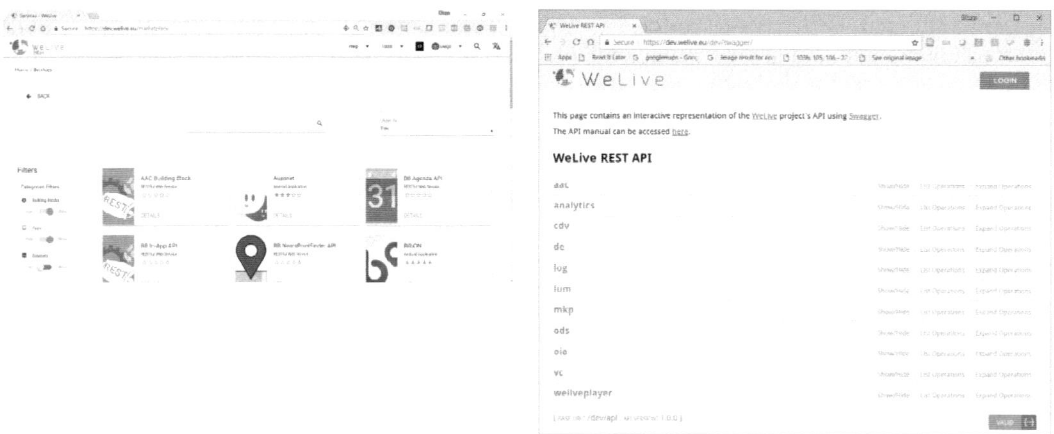

Figure 6. Service catalogue (left hand side) and WeLive RESTful API (right hand side).

Figure 7. Charts Dashboard (left hand side) and Business Agreement (right hand side)

4.1 Participatory Methodologies and Tools

An important conclusion of WeLive is that technological support is not sufficient for successful CO-CREATION of new public service apps. It is very important to organize face-to-face sessions with stakeholders to promote their active participation and collaboration. Two good examples are Game Design Sessions and Gamified sessions.

Game Design sessions are very useful in the CO-IDEATION stage. They are sessions where a set of basic elements and characters are presented, then, based on them, new services and apps concepts are identified, voted and selected. Usage of Game Design methods to inspire and involve different stakeholders (citizens, companies, and the representatives of public and third sectors) to ideate open data based digital services has been proven to be a success. Applying such dynamics, multidisciplinary groups of stakeholders aimed to identify the design problem, or opportunity and the solution space are grouped.

In WeLive, Game Design sessions have been arranged to generate new public service ideas. Cards for challenges, data resources, utilities (Building Blocks) and characters were created, together with a Game Board, see Figure 8, where cards where placed to give place to new ideas addressing a given challenge and making use of already existing or new to be created datasets and BBs (wildcard cards). The board came was filled in following a set of rules or procedure consisting of: a) challenge selection (and its associated card), b) selection of users, idea generation, idea selection, mapping of ideas to artefacts and presentation. Gamers completed the game by publicly presenting the set of challenge-driven new public service apps they devised and depicted on the Game Board.

On the other hand, *Gamified sessions* are useful in the CO-IMPLEMENTATION stage, where new co-created services and apps are publicly presented and stakeholders discover, comment and provide feedback to enhance them as result of using them whilst having fun, e.g. a session with event organizers in Bilbao was organized to publish and discover upcoming events in the city by following a use case. Those teams completing the use case first were given as prize a free entry to a sports event.

Gamified sessions have proven to be a very fruitful type of engagement activity to understand the acceptance of the produced artefacts and, thus, receive direct feedback from actual users to enhance them with over sought features. These engagement events, apart from being related to the dissemination of new public services with the actual citizen and business collectives, aimed also to gather feedback from them and refine these new public services created. They are a natural way of involving third parties into co-maintenance stage.

Finally, the celebration of Ideas and Hackathon contests has enabled non-consortium partners to also take an active part in the co-creation process proposed by WeLive. Still, education and evidence on the value of co-creation needs to keep been promoted and fuelled by the public administration, unless the co-creation process fully embraces the co-business stage proposed in WeLive.

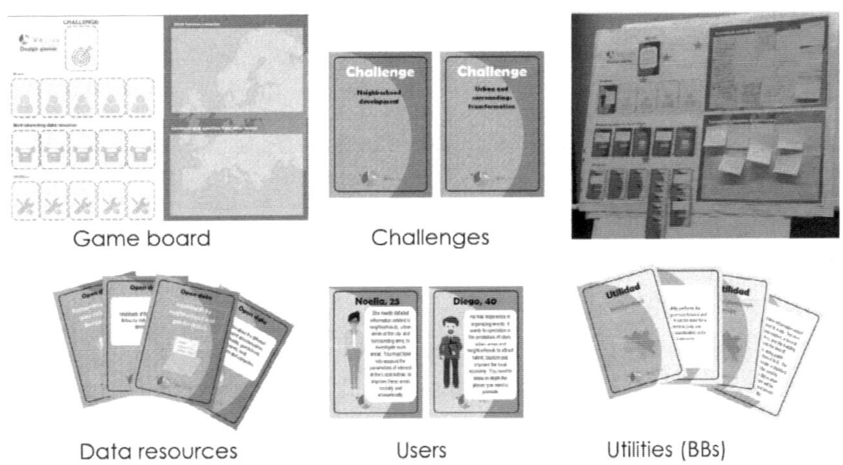

Figure 8. Game Design board, cards and results of execution of Game Design session

4.2 Applying the WeLive CO-CREATION Process

Big Klub is a very good example of the value of the Welive CO-CREATION process. This app allows users to register for entrepreneurship events organized in Bilbao. It is possible to register for events, to get access to documentation after the event has celebrated and even provide feedback about the quality of the event. Besides, the app allows you to contact with other entrepreneurs attending the same event as you or also attending to entrepreneurship events in Bilbao. Finally, the app allows you to retrieve entrepreneurship related news in Bilbao. Next the co-creation process followed to give place to this app is outlined.

First of all, a challenge was published by Bilbao city council looking for ideas to promote entrepreneurship in the city. An Idea Contest event was, then, scheduled in order to get these ideas and as a result 9 ideas were received. 7 of them were accepted and a jury composed by different stakeholders decided which ones were the best 3 which received a prize. One of them, was selected as the most feasible one to be implemented as a service and after an agreement with the idea creators the development of the service started. The economy promotion agency in the council of Bilbao, Bilbao Ekintza, took an important role as a dynamizer between developers (two partners in WeLive consortium) and entrepreneurs and final users of the service. Several meetings took place and the app was constantly refined, e.g. by celebrating two gamified sessions, until the final version of the app was published. Now this app is used as a very useful channel for Bilbao Ekintza and helps in the management of organizing events, being freely available in Google Play as shown in Figure 9.

5. VALIDATION

As result of the public consultation of different stakeholders in 4 pilots across Europe (Bilbao, Novi Sad Helsinki-Uusima and Trento), several new concepts of public services have been developed. At different pilot sites, distinct forms of engagement dynamics were carried out. In phase I of pilots, the focus was on celebrating *in situ* sessions with potential stakeholders to give place to the specification of highly demanded stakeholder-driven public services driven. On the other hand, in phase II, those dynamics were addressed to achieving the actual participation and collaboration of diverse stakeholders in the co-ideation and co-implementation of fully featured public services. In other words, in phase I of experimentation the co-ideation part of the WeLive proposed co-creation methodology was exercised whilst in phase II the whole process, including co-implementation, was tackled. Surveys, focus groups, brainstorming workshops, meetings with public representatives or ideas contests were used to choose novel ideas for public services during phase I. A total of 12 new public service apps were published in Google Play, where the implementation part, in the first phase, was assumed by the consortium.

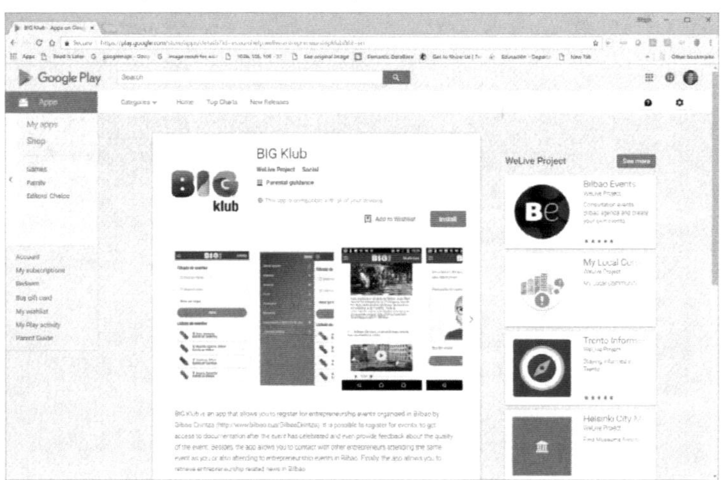

Figure 9. BIG KLUB app published in Google Play

On the other hand, the focus in phase II has been to also involve stakeholders in other parts of the co-creation process, i.e. also in the co-implementation and even co-exploitation of public services. Interestingly, the public service development approach in WeLive does not encourage producing monolithic apps, but rather apps that are assembled as result of combining distinct reusable components, namely building blocks equivalent to the current microservice software architecture conceptual trend. As a result, WeLive artefacts, namely public service apps, building blocks and datasets, are made available through the Service Catalogue component which enables final users and third-party developers, to encounter readily available apps and apps' building blocks which might be reused to give place to other novel public services. The WeLive consortium has given place to 20 apps as result of the co-creation process encouraged through diverse engagement events (Ideas Contests, Design Thinking workshops and Hackathons) at each pilot site. Besides, a wide-range of third party generated artefacts (apps and BBs) has been produced in pilot phase II, i.e. another 20 apps. This implies that the WeLive public service ecosystem has been doubled through the direct contributions of external to the project co-creators in pilots phase II.

In summary, WeLive has delivered more than 110 assets in the form of building blocks and apps, both as web and mobile apps. 21 of such assets are final Android mobile apps that have been published in Google Play[1]. Therefore, together with the development of a CO-CREATION methodology and its supporting platform, the WeLive ecosystem has been populated with a good range of datasets, building blocks and apps which may assist and inspire third parties to continue the CO-CREATION process in their municipalities.

5.1 Validation Process Conclusions

In the piloting of WeLive, a rich volume of evidence during the 1st and 2nd phase of the WeLive project has been collected. Different data sources have been used during the project, e.g. platform and application logging (users participating and artefacts generated among others), questionnaires, engagement events organized and objectives of the pilots, among other things. Some examples of the evidence collection procedure applied are:

- *Alpha testing*: During the early test state of the platform and the services, a simple questionnaire was created in order to gather initial responses about their acceptance, detect technical problems and allow participants to make suggestions.
- *Data logging and KPI monitoring*: All the actions that the users perform on each of the components of the WeLive platform produce log entries that are stored and, therefore, can be later processed to extract the KPIs values which are viewable though the Charts Dashboard (see Figure 10).
- *Questionnaires*: Questionnaires allow gathering the qualitative perception that the participants of the pilot had about the different components of the platform and the developed services during the Pilot Execution. Particularly, there are two types of questionnaires that have been used: a) *demographic questionnaires*, which are oriented to the gathering of information about the characteristics of the attendants to the events; and b) *questionnaires about specific information* about the platform and its perception from the different stakeholders that took part in the events: citizen, companies and public sectors
- *In-app questionnaires*: The in-app questionnaire was oriented to extract information about the user perception and usage of each service developed by each city task force for the Pilot Execution. This questionnaire was shown to the users during the interaction with the mobile applications and it contained 5 rating based questions and one free text question allowing users to provide further feedback about the application.

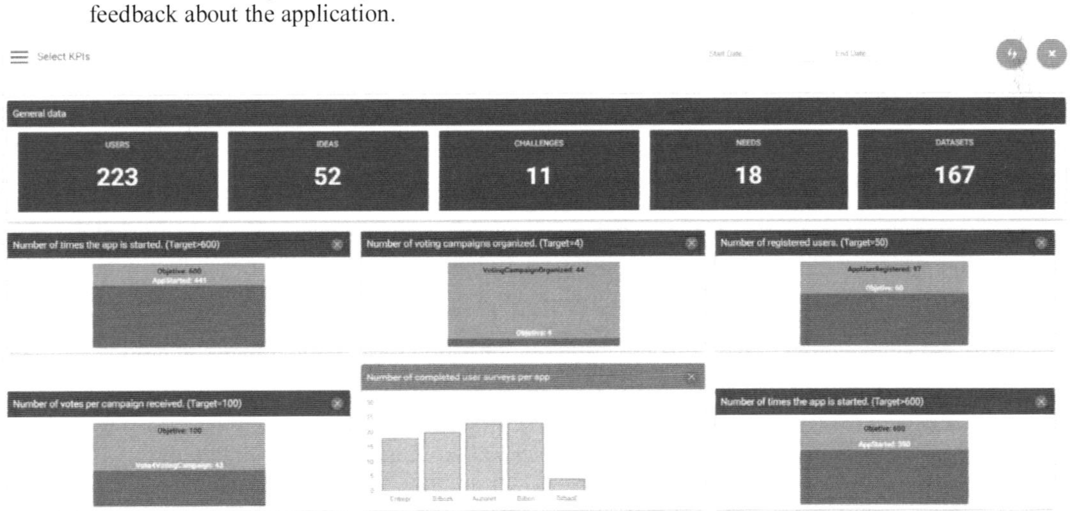

Figure 10. Analytical Dashboard showing KPI information from the platform and the applications

[1] https://play.google.com/store/search?q=welive_project

Based on the analysis of the qualitative questionnaires employed, all participant stakeholders have understood the co-creation process offered by WeLive which maps IDEAS into APP which can be built as the result of mashing-up Building Blocks (BB) and published in the Service Catalogue. But also more than 80% found easy to use and useful the Ideation Board (Ideas management) area to support the CO-IDEATION step of CO-CREATION. They mainly liked from Ideation Board: 1) the easiness to use it, 2) to find all the ideas in one single place and 3) every user can see all the ideas and comment on them (useful to find inspiration for new purposes). In the feedback related to Service Composer, 74% of stakeholders thought that it is useful as a tool to support CO-IMPLEMENTATION (mainly appreciating the quick prototyping of BB and the great potential of the own tool).

Besides, from the analysis of the qualitative data collection referred, stakeholders think that: 1) 85% WeLive platform is easy to use, 2) 75% think that different functions of WeLive platform are well integrated, 3) 74% WeLive platform fulfils ethic requirements, 4) 75% WeLive platform helps to improve transparency in the Pubic Administration and 5) 87% WeLive public services (APPs) respond to the necessities of an Open and Collaborative Government.

However, stakeholders consulted saw some obstacles that may prevent adoption of WeLive co-creation approach among urban app developer community. Some of them are, for example: 1) marketing and money consumption for hosting of artefacts, 2) learning curve (although they think is a valid approach, it needs to be learnt and used, and this takes time and efforts), 3) the lack of private data and 4) the fact of being a little too technical.

As mentioned, in pilot phase II, the focus was put both in developers and companies (to inform them about and to promote the use of Service Composer to come up with new public services), but also in closing the lifecycle of co-creation (passing from CO-IDEATION to CO-IMPLEMENTATION). Besides, in phase II, the initiative of co-implementing apps was assumed not only by the consortium but by third parties, often as result of their participation of hackathons, but also as their involvement in the refinement process of the new services based on the winning ideas gathered from Idea Contests. This fact has led to the point where the stakeholders themselves will be maintaining the new services generated after WeLive project.

6. CONCLUSION

WeLive is Open Government enabling solution which transforms urban stakeholders into co-creators, supported by a Platform and a Methodology. The pillars of Open Government are addressed by WeLive. *Transparency* is tackled since WeLive allows to go beyond Open Data portals also coping with user-generated data which complements public open data and fostering well-document easy to consumed micro-services (building blocks) rather than only raw datasets. *Accountability* is tackled since WeLive allows tracing the journey from needs to ideas into apps composed of datasets and building blocks. An associated Charts Dashboard enables to understand the impact of platform and apps and its integration with a commercial marketplace, namely CNS marketplace, enables to develop artefacts business model (see Figure 7's right hand side). *Participation* is encouraged since WeLive allows to go beyond CO-IDEATION enabling also participation in whole CO-CREATION. For that, inclusive accessible multilingual interfaces in the form of wizards to post new ideas or drag and drop interface to enable non-programmers to assemble simple apps are provided. Besides, these technical tools are coupled with novel collaboration techniques to foster CO-CREATION: Game Design and Gamified User Evaluations. *Collaboration* is also promoted since WeLive has given place to a marketplace to foster public/private partnerships and the CDV component enables to reuse personal data across apps. User and programming interfaces for different stakeholders have also been provided to encourage its adoption, i.e. civil servants, citizens, SMEs, entrepreneurs/developers collaboration.

Open Data and User-generated data, and their combination under the Broad Data (Domo.com, 2018) concept proposed by WeLive, are only the raw material which is not directly usable neither by citizens nor companies. Citizens and companies need to distil added value information which helps them in their daily decisions. There is the need for public administrations to provide easily consumable and actionable information. WeLive has addressed this issue by pushing the Building Block concept, which enables to aggregate, correlate and perform analysis about heterogeneous datasets giving place to views which are directly accessible through simple web methods. Associated tools like the Service Composer can also help democratizing the assembly of new public service apps by others than exclusively developers.

Entrepreneurs, research centres and companies are not yet in the key of reusing public data and even less of participating in co-creation processes where exploitation uncertainty might be the case. New policies are needed to promote reuse to capture the value of the data and the actual benefits of actively participating in co-creation experiences. Therefore, until society fully comprehends the value of co-creation, there is the need to keep organizing activities that continuously fuel the reuse of data and to take part in co-creation processes to boost the economic activity of the city and its area of influence. Further education and evidence on the value of co-creation needs to be showcased and fuelled by the public administration, unless the co-creation process fully embraces the co-business stage proposed in WeLive.

Stronger political leadership on open data and co-creation is needed for WeLive or any similar initiative to realize its potential, thus it is necessary for governments to have their commitments (re)-affirmed to open data as raw material for innovation, and sought to put in place policies that help government, businesses and people realize its benefits. Actions are impending to seek effective collaboration between public and private entities, through the establishment of a relationship framework that contributes to making more dynamic the reuse of data. Actions are also needed to raise the level of training and capacity of society to reduce the digital divide in the definition and management of Public Services.

ACKNOWLEDGEMENT

This work has been carried out within WeLive project H2020-INSO-2014, 645845.

REFERENCES

Komninos, N. (2015). The age of intelligent cities. London u.a.: Taylor et Francis.

GOV.UK. (2018). Public Service Mutuals. [online] Available at: https://www.gov.uk/government/collections/public-service-mutuals [Accessed 18 Jun. 2018].

Oecd-ilibrary.org. (2018). OECD iLibrary | M-Government. [online] Available at: https://www.oecd-ilibrary.org/governance/m-government-mobile-technologies-for-responsive-governments-and-connected-societies_9789264118706-en [Accessed 18 Jun. 2018].

Vossen, G., Lytras, M. and Koudas, N. (2007). Editorial: Revisiting the (Machine) Semantic Web: The Missing Layers for the Human Semantic Web. IEEE Transactions on Knowledge and Data Engineering, 19(2), pp.145-148.

Oecd.org. (2018). *Open Government - OECD.* [online] Available at: http://www.oecd.org/gov/open-government.htm [Accessed 18 Jun. 2018].

Almirall, E. and Wareham, J. (2011). *Living Labs: arbiters of mid- and ground-level innovation.* Technology Analysis & Strategic Management, 23(1), pp.87-102.

Opendatabarometer.org. (2018). *Open Data Barometer.* [online] Available at: https://opendatabarometer.org/ [Accessed 18 Jun. 2018].

Domo.com. (2018). *Introducing Broad Data* | Domo. [online] Available at: http://www.domo.com/blog/2013/03/introducing-broad-data [Accessed 18 Jun. 2018].

Baldwin, C. and von Hippel, E. (2010). *Modeling a Paradigm Shift: From Producer Innovation to User and Open Collaborative Innovation.* SSRN Electronic Journal.

Citizenlab.co. (2018). CitizenLab: online civic engagement made really easy. [online] Available at: https://www.citizenlab.co/ [Accessed 18 Jun. 2018].

Empatia Project. (2018). Home. [online] Available at: https://www.empatia-project.eu/ [Accessed 18 Jun. 2018].

Opengovintelligence.eu. (2018). OpenGovIntelligence. [online] Available at: http://www.opengovintelligence.eu [Accessed 18 Jun. 2018].

Voorberg, W., Bekkers, V., Timeus, K., Tonurist, P. and Tummers, L. (2017). Changing public service delivery: learning in co-creation. Policy and Society, 36(2), pp.178-194.

Citadel-h2020.eu. (2018). Home | CITADEL. [online] Available at: https://www.citadel-h2020.eu/ [Accessed 18 Jun. 2018].

Europa.eu. (2018). European Commission - PRESS RELEASES - Press release - Digital Economy and Society Index (DESI) 2018. [online] Available at: http://europa.eu/rapid/press-release_MEMO-18-3737_en.htm [Accessed 4 Jul. 2018].

IDENTIFIYING PROBLEMS FOR THE PLANNING AND DECISION MAKING OF A SMART CITY IN CHINA: PREPARATION FOR THE 13TH FIVE YEAR PLAN

Ning Zhang[2], Miguel Baptista Nunes[1,2] and Lijun Wang[3]

[2]School of Information Management, Sun Yat-sen University, No.132, Waihuan Dong Road, Guangzhou,510006, China

[3]National Industry Information Security Development Research Center , No. 35 Lugu Road, Shijingshan District, Beijing,10040, China

ABSTRACT

Despite its tremendous success, the Chinese Economy is still controlled by a recurring process of 5 year planning. This comprehensive National planning program occurs at all levels of the Chinese government, educational systems and state owned companies. This paper reports on a study that was made in preparation for the 13th 5 year for the Smart City component of the upcoming city of Tianjin. The objective of this study was to identify problems in informatization, automation and centralization of command and control, so that these could be solved as part of the 5 year plan. The study followed a mixed-method approach in three stages. First, questionnaires were used to assess to sate of development of the smart city features in the different departments of the city government. Second, the study organized thematic joint development groups consisting of expert representatives from different city's departments and units. Third, results of questionnaires and thematic joint development were discussed in departmental focus groups to clarify and specify the problems and assess proposed solutions and viability of those solutions. This paper offers a classification of the identified problems, an integrative conceptual representation of these and a discussion of the importance of this identification in the overall planning process.

KEYWORDS

Smart Cities, Smart City Planning, Planned Economy, Thematic Analysis, Mixed-Methods

1. INTRODUCTION

Smart city as a concept has Information and Communication Technologies (ICT) as the core strategy to record, analyze and integrate key information of captured by core sensors and systems in all of cities' activities. Therefore, smart cities are essentially built by utilizing a set of advanced (ICT), including smart hardware devices (e.g. wireless sensors, smart meters, smart vehicles, and smart phones), mobile networks (e.g. Wi-Fi, 3G/4G/5G network), data storage technologies (e.g. data warehouse, cloud platform), and software applications (e.g. back-office control systems, mobile apps, big data analytical tools) (Peng et al., 2016).

From a conceptual perspective, Hall (2000) defined a smart city as a city that monitors and integrates conditions of all of its critical infrastructures, including roads, bridges, tunnels, rails, subways, airports, seaports, communications, water, power, even major buildings, can better optimize its resources, plan its preventive maintenance activities, and monitor security aspects while maximizing services to its citizens. In China, this is concept of smart city is seen as the product of the Digital City combined with the both Internet of Things and the *Internet+* (Su et al., 2011). Smart city and digital city still lack distinctive definitions and these two topics are often overlapped or confused (Dameri, 2014). A digital city is an open, complex and adaptive system based on computer network and urban information resources, which forms a virtual digital space for a city (Li and Lin, 2001). Couclelis, H. (2004), further elaborated on this concept by defining digital city as a comprehensive, networked representation, or reproduction, of several aspects or functions of a specific real city, open to non-experts. The digital city has several dimensions: social, cultural, political,

[1] Corresponding author.

ideological and also theoretical. These dimensions make planning of smart cities very complex as the understanding and integration of these different aspects is complex, difficult and subjective. In China, planning is made every 5 years since the inception of the People's Republic. This planned economy tradition adopted from the Soviet Union tradition has since then evolved and become dynamic and one of the reasons the Chinese economy has become so stable and progressive. The Chinese government updates its targets and directions for the nation's economic development based on a Five-year planning cycle (Zheng *et al.*, 2012). The last twenty years thus cover that cover the ninth, tenth, eleventh, twelfth and thirteenth Five-year plan periods.

In terms of smart city, planning is seen as the development of a roadmap to provide a first comprehensive and unified view of current and future solutions for the development of the smart city based on explicit National, Regional and City policies and the identification of specific aims, requirements and problems. As proposed by Lee et al., (2013), each city develops their own services based on current technologies using coherent strategic planning following National and Provincial level guidelines as a coordinating view. Ultimately, a smart city plan should offer a developed and customized roadmap that serves as a guiding strategic resource and communication tool to support smart city R&D initiatives and take opportunity of emerging technological trajectories. Therefore, the first requirement in drawing up such a roadmap is the crafting of an identification process of the various problems that need to be resolved and services that should be implemented (Rinne, 2004) according to the cities characteristics, vison and aims.

The study reported in this paper aimed to produce this the first requirement in drawing up such roadmap for smart city development for the city of Tianjin and is the fourth largest in China, after Shanghai, Beijing, and Guangzhou. Tianjin is directly under jurisdiction of the Central Government and is located in the Northeast of China. It is the closest seaport to Beijing and one of the biggest industrial and port cities in China. Tianjin covers an area of 11,000 square kilometers and has a population in excess of 10 million people. Specifically, the study aimed to craft a method to enable the identification of problems that can be resolved by smart city development as well as those that may become barriers to its implementation.

2. RESEARCH QUESTIONS METHDOLOGY

This study was conducted within a much larger project entitled "13th Five-year Plan of Tianjin Smart City Development" that was led by the Tianjin Municipal Commission of Industry and Information Technology (TMCIIT) (http://gyxxh.tj.gov.cn/). This project was conducted in partnership with the National Industry Information Security Development Research Center (NIISDRC) (http://www.etiri.com.cn/index.html) and Tianjin Smart City Research Institute (TSCRI) (http://www.tscri.org/Default.aspx?MenuCurrentID=1). The general aim of this larger project was informed by a city vision of the "Smart Tianjin". The explicit and specific objective of this project group targeted in making the 13th Five-year Smart City Plan of Tianjin. The point of departure to the project was the achievement in informatization, automation and urban development of the previous 12th Five-year plan. Although expected to provide continuity to the previous plan, the 13th Five-year Plan faced more developed and demanding national and city guiding principles, more tight basic rules and more technological driven city operation and missions. The study addressed by this paper occurred at the first part of the planning process and aimed at identification of technological, infrastructure, resource, contextual and geographically localized problems in Smart Tianjin.

2.1 Research Questions

The general aims of this research aimed not only to identify problems in the development of smart cities but also to devise a process that would enable the identification of these problems in the context of an extremely large and complex city like Tianjin. Therefore, two main research questions were set as follows:

R1 – How to identify problems to the development of a very large and complex smart city?
R2 – What are the problems that can be resolve by efficient smart city planning?
- R2.1 – How can these problems be categorized and classified?
- R2.2 – Which of these problems are Chinese in nature and which ones are general to smart cities?

2.2 Methodology

The study followed a mixed-method research design composed of five sequential stages as shown in Figure 1:

1. The first stage consisted of a review of both academic and gray literature. This included National, provincial and city reports and policies as well as a number of Chinese smart cities reports. These cities were chosen according to their similar circumstances with Tianjin, i.e. because they are port cities, large cities or are specialized in the same industry and business sectors. Tianjin is the cradle of China's modern mechanic industry and textile industry, but has recently witnessed a rapid development of the services sectors. Therefore, cities selected had at least one of these characteristics, such Beijing which is a services city, Ningbo a port city and Nanjing a city characterized by well-designed and effective industry parks.
2. This literature review enabled a preliminary identification of problems encountered by other cities. This preliminary identification was used as the base for the design of the questionnaire survey that constituted the second stage of the study. The aims of the questionnaire survey were twofold. First, to assess the comparative state of development of the Smart Tianjin in relation to other cities. Second, to compare problems identified in other cities with those encountered by Smart Tianjin. The questionnaire was sent to all the relevant committees, units and departments of the city municipal government. The questionnaire used mostly open questions to allow rich expressions of problems and situational descriptions. Questionnaires were designed according to the following thematic topic division: Infrastructure; Information security; e-government; urban management; information economy; citizen services; key districts and counties; and key zone. Questionnaires were sent to 53 units as shown in Table 1 and, since this research was done under the auspices of the city government, got a response rate of 100%. No response was not an option.

Table 1. Participating units and departments in thematic joint development group discussions

Thematic Topic	Participating Units	Participating Departments
Infrastructure and Information Security	Municipal Communications Administration, Public Security Bureau, Network Information Office, Maritime Administration, Unicom, Mobile, Telecom, Radio And Television, National Supercomputing Tianjin center, Tianjin Unicom Huayuan Data Port (10 units)	Planning Office, Research Office, Information Infrastructure Management Office, Information Security Office
E-government and Urban Management	Market Supervision Committee, City Appearance and Garden Committee, Construction Committee, Transportation Committee, Planning Bureau, Guotufangguan Bureau, Water Affairs Bureau, Environmental Protection Bureau, Public Security Traffic Management Bureau, Safety Supervision Bureau and Emergency Office (11 units)	Planning Department, Research Department, Information Promotion Department, e-Government Center
Information Economy	Municipal Science And Technology Commission Business Committee, SASAC, Port Office, Oceanic Administration, SME Bureau, Financial Bureau, Tianjin Customs, Tianjin Branch of the People's Bank of China, Banking Regulatory Bureau, Tianjin port (10 units)	Planning Department, Research Department, Integration Department, Electronic Information Industry Department, Software And Information Service Department
Citizen Services	Municipal Development And Reform Commission, Health and Family Planning Commission, Agricultural Commission, Education Commission, People's Social Council, Civil Affairs Bureau, Cultural Radio, Film and Television Bureau, Tourism Bureau, Post Office, Electric Power Company, Municipal Tap Water Group And Municipal Public Transportation Group (12 units)	Planning Office, Research Office and Integration Office
Key Districts and Counties, Key zone	Binhai New District, Heping District, Hexi District, Nankai District, Wuqing District, Jinnan District, Sino-Singapore Ecological City, Development Zone, Bonded District, High-Tech Park (10 units)	Planning Office, Research Office and Integration Office

3. The questionnaire analysis enabled the creation of thematic areas of problems and lists of specific problems as well as the identification of areas where Smart Tianjin seemed to be behind in relation to other cities. However, these were very generic and anecdotal in nature. In order to specify these problems in detail and acquire in depth understandings, the researchers organized a series of thematic joint development groups consisting of expert representatives from different city

departments and units. These group discussions were organized in conjunction with and supervised by the Tianjin city government. The basic method used was a process cognitive walkthrough as proposed by Aleixo et al., (2012) and Wharton et al. (1992). The different experts were asked to elaborate on particular problems, their causes and consequences. Often intense discussion ensued between related departmental experts and problems across departmental borders. The walkthrough process enabled clarification of processes and connections between governmental units as well negotiated agreement over contested issues. The sessions were recorded both by stenographic transcription and audio recording.

4. Nevertheless, the thematic joint development groups occurred with strong time limitations and only attended by selected group of experts from each unit. Therefore, although informative and extremely useful, these discussions often lacked in detail and information that was with other experts not in the room. Therefore, in order to further specify the problems and acquire a full and fine detail understanding of the problems being analyzed, the researchers undertook a series of focus groups with a carefully selected group of governmental units.
5. Focus group interviews are employed to generate data and as a source of data for analysis (McPherson and Nunes, 2006). Group forces or dynamics become an integral part of the procedure with participants engaged in discussion with each other rather than directing their comments solely to the moderator (Catterall and Maclaran, 1997). Thus, a focus group is, in essence, a semi-structured interview in which a moderator keeps the direction of discussions under control by utilizing a list of questions set by one or more researcher or facilitator (McPherson and Nunes, 2006). In this case, closely related groups of experts were asked questions on problems associated with their daily working processes. The research group visited the following specific units were lack in detail or absence of data prevented full understanding of the situation: Tianjin Administration of Work Safety, Cityscape and Landscape Management Committee of the Tianjin Municipality, Tianjin Garrison Command, Tianjin Market and Quality Supervision Administration, Tianjin Planning Bureau, Heping District and Jingnan District. Government staff in these focus groups, illustrated their problems and difficulties in their specific socio-technical infrastructure. The sessions were also recorded both by stenographic transcription and by audio recording.

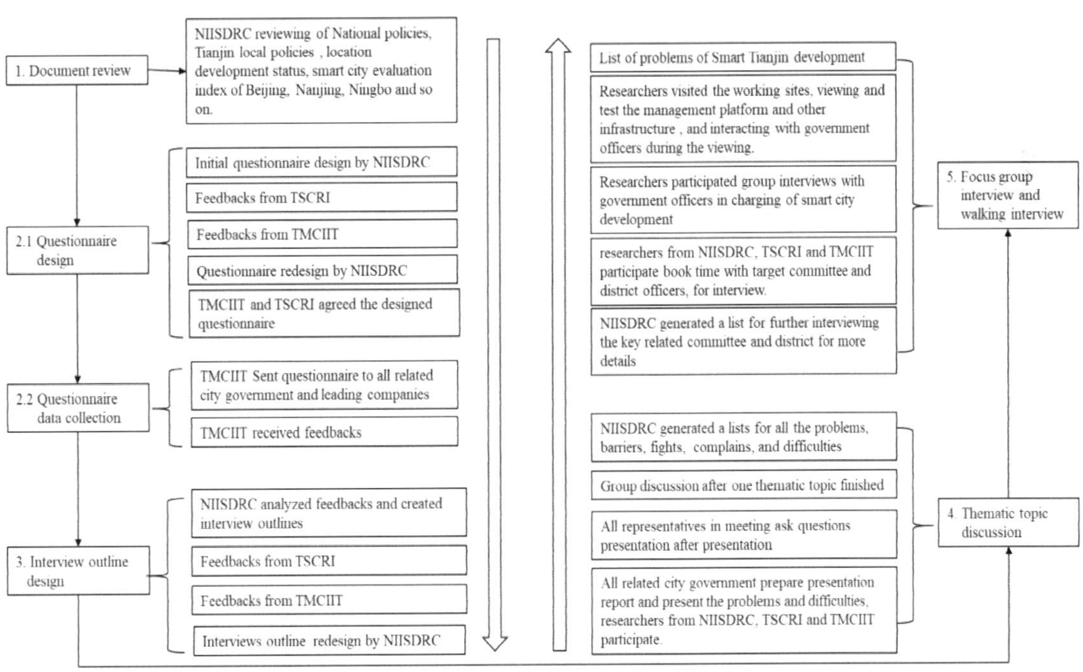

Figure 1. A framework to identify development problems of a very large and complex smart city (FIdDP)

The method of data analysis used was an integrative and evolutionary thematic analysis, that started with the analysis of the open questions in the questionnaire and was then continued, fine-tuned and expanded throughout the following two phases. The research findings presented in the next section are the final result of this evolutionary analysis. Finally, the framework to identify development problems (FIdDP) of a very large and complex smart city presented in Figure 1 aims to be a first contribution as an integrative and evolutionary thematic analysis framework to identify problems to the development of a very large and complex smart city. FIdDP was developed to respond to the research question R1 set for this project.

3. FINDINGS

In this study data collection and data analysis were not separate and sequential processes. After each of the components of the mixed-design framework explained above, data was analyzed and the results operationalized for the next phase. This process enabled a gradual understanding, definition classification of problems to the development of a very large and complex smart city such as Tianjin. The resulting ontology of problems is illustrated in Figure 2.

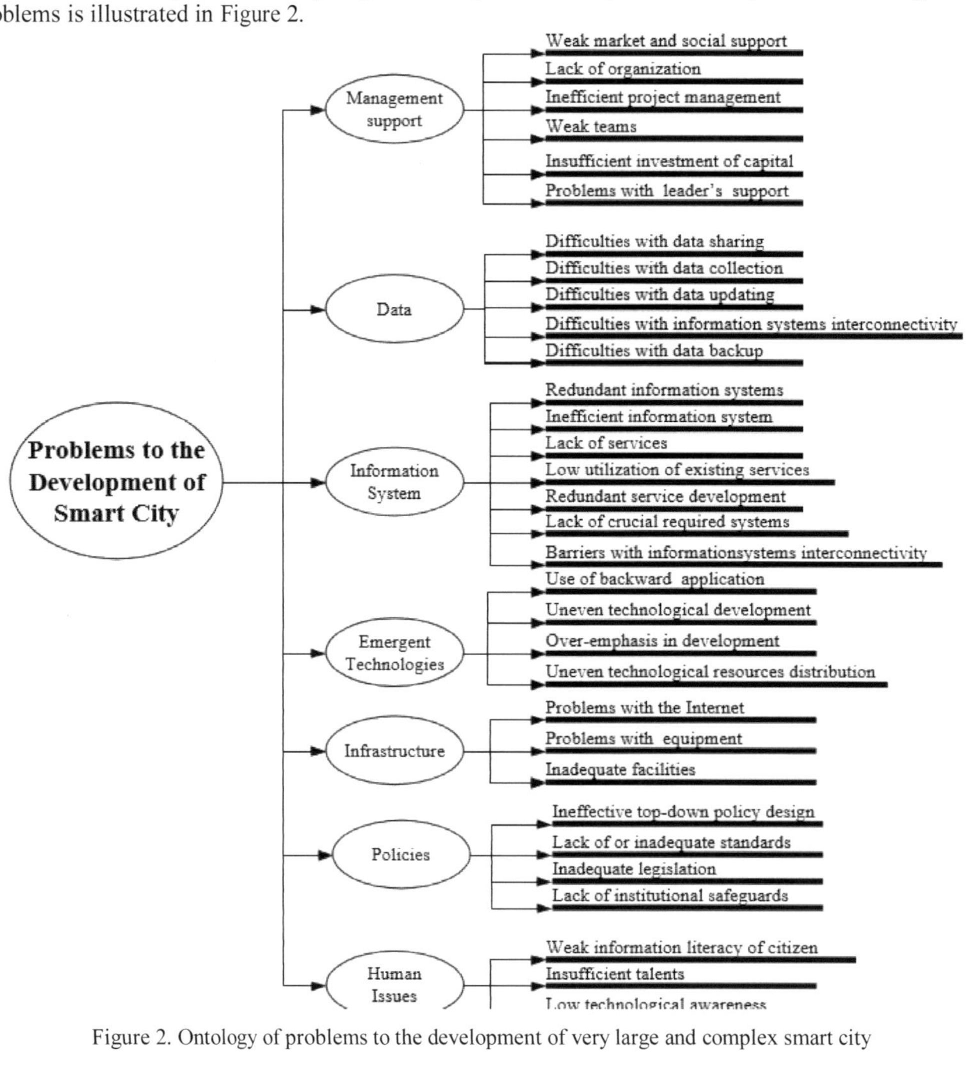

Figure 2. Ontology of problems to the development of very large and complex smart city

The ontology presented resulted from a thematic analysis as explained above and identified 7 main categories of problems and a total of 32 specific problems. All these problems are of high level and strategic nature. Many of them are very specific to the nature of the municipality of Nanjing that includes both urban and rural districts. Other are generic. Another aspect that emerged rather surprisingly is that the perceived problems for the development of Smart Tianjin were not necessarily linked with technological issues, but with resource, human, management and general infrastructure aspects. This is probably due to a more mature understanding of smart city planning by the participants who had to undergo a similar effort of planning 5 years before. The enthusiastic belief in and emphasis on technological solutions has been moderated by the reality of practice and the realization that technology by itself cannot resolve all the problems of an urban space.

One of the most often referred to problems was related to "Management Support". This included lack of interest, engagement and support of management for the implementation of smart city projects that then resulted in obstacles with financial and resource investment. This category also includes problems with project management and support to projects that as a consequence resulted in failure. Finally, lack of management support resulted in weak project and development teams, often under-resourced, poor in influence and unable to take critical decisions. Finally, in China in particular, the lack of senior public manager's involvement often creates both social and market disengagement, leading proposed solutions and applications to be underutilized by citizens and undersubscribed by the business and industrial sectors.

Problems with data and information systems were also often referred to as critical. Participants in the study were particularly worried with difficulties of data sharing across governmental departments as well with the urban environment. Problems of data collection from companies and citizens, consistency of data collected across the different departments on the same entity and data integrity across the different units were mentioned as a critical issue. These critical problems can be made worst with independent upgrading and updating of data collection and data processing systems. A good example of this type of issue happened when in 2016 the city's Public Security Bureau's Monitoring equipment was upgraded to high definition standards, but the digital city management system could not process these. This made it impossible to share the public security bureau's data. Such updates, often decided autonomously by semi-independent city government units create sever problems of interconnectivity and data sharing. Finally, many units mentioned a problem of data backup and storing. Due to the massive quantity of data collected across the city by automatic sensors, many units were only keeping data for short periods of time before deleting it to make space. This may be surprising on our day and age, but the fact is that some of the operating HW is relatively old, partly due to strict National and Provincial regulations regarding the replacing of equipment (some HW can only be replaced after 5 years, some 8 years) , partly due to the disengagement of managers.

Information systems planning and development has also been highly problematic due to the lack integrated and systematic strategic planning and development. Information's systems across the different municipal units and departments are developed autonomously with no guarantee of interoperability and interconnectivity. This results in redundancy for information procession, lack of integrity of data and information across the different government units, lack of consistency in reporting to and informing the citizen and ultimately lack of credible information to the citizen. Sometimes it is difficult outside of China to understand the dimension and responsibilities of municipal government. Tianjin is a city of 15.6 million legal inhabitants (approximately three times the population of Denmark) with a government structure that oversees what amounts to a small country population. The size and responsibility of such a structure is therefore considerable as is the autonomy of different units that compose it. In terms of information systems design and development, this creates real and very significant problems. There is a large problem with redundant services, that causes some to be severely underused and others to be overloaded by users.

On the other hand, there is a general realization that some of the information systems in use are either outdated, obsolete or do not exist yet. Numerous cases were mentioned across disparate units ranging from the lack of an integrated regional health information platform to the need to create a GIS platform that can integrate video and other applications into one platform. Finally, there is also a great demand for public services that enhance the capability of e-government.

Closely related with information systems is another often mentioned category of problems: emergent technologies. There was an overwhelming opinion among participants that there an over-emphasis on technological development in detriment of socio-technical thinking. Emergent technologies and fashionable terminology seem to have influenced both strategic planning and development initiatives sometimes without clear understanding of user requirements or citizen needs. Developing applications for big data analysis, data visualization, cloud computing, Internet of Things, etc., seems to have become an end it is own without clear understanding of their actual role in the smart city systems. Moreover, since these technologies are relentlessly and continuously changing, the technological adoption and development across the different government units becomes unbalanced and uneven, depending on the timing for the development of the different information systems. This then results in uneven development, uneven capabilities, lack of consistency of services and applications and uneven technological resource distribution. Finally, a number of the more technologically sophisticated units point out the in the previous planning there was excessive focusing on technological solutions development and construction and too little thinking on application use and maintenance as well as insufficient integration between business processes and technology.

Additionally, participants stressed the importance of adequately installed infrastructures. The Rural Committee of Tianjin complained bitterly that the network infrastructure in their area was very poor. This idea was confirmed by the Health and Family Planning Commission that claimed that the network foundation was weak and that the network layout lacks in global planning and therefore affects the use and development of their smart city e-health applications. Furthermore, some of the already installed infrastructures resulted in very poor results. For instance the Heping District, is building a Wi-Fi wireless network with very poor effect. This network is a part of the iTianjin initiative that aims at providing free Wi-Fi internet for the whole of Tianjin. This initiative was built for the benefit of the people, but because its poor quality and slow connectivity the district is worried that it was all a waste of resources and has resulted lack of credibility and trust in smart city solutions. Participants also referred to problems with existing hardware and network infrastructures as well as with existing facilities. For instance, the Baodi District participants were rather focused with the construction of new facilities and their integration with older ones that are in urgent need of renovation. Their problem was on how to "form a working complementarity between new facilities and old facilities [... which has become] 'old difficulty' in informatization construction".

The last two categories, in the ontology in Figure 2 are related to policies and human issues. The major concern expressed by participants is directly connected to the absence of detailed top-down policies by the top strategic thinkers on smart cities. Units receive holistic, aspirational and often vague guidelines that are difficult to put into practice. As very clearly put by the Tianjin Planning Bureau: "there are many perfect theories about smart city research, but few of them are implemented in smart city operation. We need detailed and practical policies and regulations". This ineffective top-down policy design is compounded by lack of clear standards and institutional safeguards that can guarantee good quality outputs, adequate monitoring of development initiatives and proper evaluation of implemented applications, services and solutions. Policy inadequacies may some times be justified by weak awareness of the complexity of smart city technological needs and solutions. This lack of awareness is often caused by low information literacy levels and low ICT understanding, that often results in reductionist and limited solutions. Tianjin, despite its status as one of the most developed urban centers in China shares some problems associated with staff teams not being stable due to government salaries not being competitive in relation to the private sector. This led units such as the Public Transportation Group to claim that they have a lack of talent to support intelligent information systems construction for smart traffic management. The Finance Bureau reinforced this statement by complaining that their number of technical teams is low and the comprehensive ability of technical personnel is often not enough to fulfill their role.

4. CONCLUSIONS

This paper resulted from a research project made in preparation for the elaboration for the 13th Five-year Plan for the Smart Tianjin. The paper offers two distinct and useful contributions to knowledge. The first contribution is an integrative and evolutionary thematic analysis framework to identify problems to the development of a very large and complex smart city: the FIdDP framework. FIdDP is based on a transferable and general mixed-method research design composed of four sequential stages. This framework represents a first proposal for a research design that can be used by other researchers if they undertake similar studies and should be tested and improved by other research projects in this area. The second contribution is an ontology of problems to the development of the very large and complex Smart Tianjin. This is an inductively generated ontology grounded on the context of the city of Tianjin. However, the ontology provides practice informed guidance to the main areas that should be considered in a smart city plan, namely: Policy

Implementation and Planning; Management and Project Management Support; Information Systems Design, Development and Maintenance; Emergent Technologies Adoption Strategies; Data Integrity, Consistency and Continuity Safeguards; and Human Resource Issues. The researchers hope, that the paper will also be both timely and useful at a moment in time that China is preparing for a new round of Five-year planning in 2020 and many of the issues discussed in the paper will soon be revisited.

ACKNOWLEDGEMENT

The authors want to acknowledge and thank the Tianjin Municipal Commission of Industry and Information Technology (TMCIIT) (http://gyxxh.tj.gov.cn/) as well as all the members of the operational research team that was at the core of this research, namely: from the Electronic Technology Information Research Center of the Ministry of Industry and Information Technology (MIIT), now entitled the National Industry Information Security Development Research Center (NIISDRC) (http://www.etiri.com.cn/index.html) and the Tianjin Smart City Research Institute (TSCRI) (http://www.tscri.org/Default.aspx?MenuCurrentID=1).

REFERENCES

Catterall, M. and Maclaran, P. (2004). "Focus group data and qualitative analysis programs: coding the moving picture as well as the snapshots", Sociological Research Online, 2(1), available at: www.socresonline.org.uk/socresonline/2/1/6.html (accessed 10 January 2004).

Couclelis, H. (2004). "The construction of the digital city". *Planning and Design,* 31(1), 5–19.

Dameri, R.P., (2014). "Comparing Smart and Digital City: initiatives and strategies in Amsterdam and Genoa. Are they Digital and/or Smart?" In: Dameri, R., Rosenthal-Sabroux, C. (eds) *Smart City*, pp. 45-88. Springer, Cham.

Hall, P. (2000). Creative cities and economic development. *Urban Studies,* 37(4), 633–649.

Peng, G. C., Nunes, M. B. and Zheng, L. (2017). "Impacts of low citizen awareness and usage in smart city services: the case of London's smart parking system." *Information Systems and e-Business Management* 15(4), pp. 845-876.

Lee, J.H., Phaal, R. and Lee, S.H. (2013). "An integrated service-device-technology roadmap for smart city development". *Technological Forecasting and Social Change*, *80*(2), pp. 286-306.

Li Q. and Lin S. (2001). Research on digital city framework architecture. *IEEE International Conferences on Info-Tech and Info-Net*, vol. 1, (pp. 30–36). Proceedings ICII.

McPherson, M. and Nunes, M. B. (2006). Organisational issues for e-learning: Critical success factors as identified by HE practitioners. *International Journal of Educational Management*, *20*(7), pp.542-558.

Rinne, M. (2004). Technology roadmaps: infrastructure for innovation, Technol. Forecast. Soc. Chang. pp. 71 67–80

Su, K., Li, J., & Fu, H. (2011). Smart city and the applications. *IEEE International Conference on Electronics, Communications and Control (ICECC)*, pp. 1028–1031(IEEE Xplore).

Zheng, J., Mehndiratta, S. and Guo, J. Y, (2012). "Strategic policies and demonstration program of electric vehicles in China", *Transport Policy*, 19(1), pp. 17-25.

Wharton, C., J. Rieman, C. Lewis, & P. Polson. (1994)."The Cognitive Walkthrough Method: A practitioner's guide". In Nielsen, J. and Mack, R. L. (eds.) *Usability inspections methods*, (pp. 105–140). New York: John Wiley.

Short Papers

UNDERSTANDING CURRENT RESEARCH ON THE USE AND IMPACT OF BIG DATA ANALYTICS: A SYSTEMATIC LITERATURE REVIEW

Yanqing Duan, Ram Ramanathan, Guangming Cao and Nasrallah Khilji
University of Bedfordshire, Park Square, Luton, UK

ABSTRACT

With the increasing applications of Big Data Analytics, it is imperative for researchers to keep abreast with the rapid development and emerging research challenges in this field. Therefore, the research reported in this work in progress paper aims to update our knowledge and understanding of the state of the art research on the applications of Big Data Analytics by conducting a comprehensive and systematic review of the recent publications. The literature review is mainly focusing on the emerging new concepts and definitions, theories, research models, research methodologies, critical success factors, and impact on business performance. It is expected that the insights gained through this comprehensive review will contribute to our knowledge on the current status of Big Data Analytics research and associated emerging research challenges and opportunities. Due to the increased interests in Big Data Analytics, the critical analysis of emerging literature will identify the research gaps that provides valuable direction for future studies.

KEYWORDS

Big Data, Analytics, Big Data Impact, Big Data Technologies, Systematic Literature Review, Adoption of Big Data Analytics

1. INTRODUCTION

We are living the era of Big Data. The amount of data that we collect and produce daily has dramatically exploded over the last five years (Sena, Demirbag, Bhaumik, & Sengupta, 2017). To make sense of Big Data gathered from emerging digital technologies and IoT smart sensors, Big Data Analytics tools must be implemented. Big Data Analytics can fundamentally change how businesses compete and operate. Therefore, many organizations are increasing their investment in Big Data and are eager to use analytics to benefit from their investment. As the result of the increasing investment in Big Data and Analytics by organisations, research publications on Big Data and Analytics have also been dramatically increased in recent years. It is argued that the information systems' discipline can better serve the needs of business decision makers in light of the emerging Big Data and Analytics (Chen, Chiang, & Storey, 2012). However, information systems' researchers are facing many emerging research challenges as well as opportunities in order to understand how and to what extent Big Data and Analytics is impacting on business operations and performance and to know how to maximise the value of analytics investments.

This research aims to gain a comprehensive knowledge of the current research on the applications and impact of Big Data Analytics. More specifically, the project intents to understand the state of the art development on Big Data Analytics and identify emerging research challenges and opportunities in the following (but may not limited to) areas:

- Emerging concepts, definitions and taxonomy
- Theories
- research models
- Research Methodologies
- The application of specific and novel analytical techniques
- Application areas and economic, environmental and societal impact
- Critical success factors

2. RESEARCH METHODS

To achieve the research aim, the project is conducting a systematic literature review. There are many definitions on what a systematic review is. The operative definition for this project is adapted from Fink (2013) that defining a systematic review as a systematic, explicit, comprehensive, and reproducible method for identifying, evaluating, and synthesizing the existing body of completed and recorded work produced by researchers, scholars, and practitioners. Systematic reviews are characterized by being objective, systematic, transparent and replicable. They involve a systematic search process to locate studies which address a particular research question, as well as a systematic presentation and synthesis of the characteristics and findings of the results of the search (Siddaway, 2014). The systematic review exercise enables us to address the research aims by identifying, critically evaluating and integrating the findings of all relevant, high-quality individual studies. The process of a systematic review can be varied, but it mainly covers the following five steps (Denyer & Tranfield, 2009):

1. Formulate the review questions/objectives
2. Locate and generate a comprehensive list of potentially relevant studies
3. Select and evaluate relevant studies based the predetermined inclusion and exclusion criteria.
4. Analyse and synthesise the relevant studies
5. Report the results

Based on the above suggested steps in conducting a systematic literature review, the project will be completed following three phases:

2.1 Phase 1 – Searching and collecting all Relevant Publications (Completed)

This research mainly focusses on the articles published in information systems (IS) and operation management (OM) journals because IS and OM are the most relevant disciplines for Big Data Analytics research and have been the main research focus of our research center. This phase involves defining the key words and phrases, deciding the period of the search, identifying the main databases to be used, initial screening of the papers, downloading and filing the relevant studies. At the end of this phase, a repository of about 110 relevant papers are established. Nvivo software, which is a qualitative data analysis computer software, is used to store the relevant papers at this stage. Nvivo is a very effective software for content analysis, so it is also used for analyzing and categorizing the key findings in the next phase of this research.

2.2 Phase 2 – Analyzing and synthesizing Selected Papers (Ongoing)

This is the most important phase of this research. A set of analytical themes are agreed and applied in analyzing and coding the articles using Nvivo content analysis tools. The main themes include: the key concepts used in each paper; theoretical underpinnings; research models; research methodologies (qualitative, quantitative, mixed methods, etc.); development and applications of specific and novel analytical techniques; Big Data Analytics application areas; critical success factors; the tangible and intangible business, societal and environmental impact; and suggestions for future research. New themes may also be emerged and coded. Findings are systematically synthesized from different perspectives. Some quantitative and visualization analysis (e.g. heatmap matrix, parallel coordinates plot, and scatterplot) may be used to illustrate the key findings.

2.3 Phase 3 – Mapping and Presenting the Key Findings (Ongoing)

At the end of this research, the findings on the emerging issues of the current research reported in the literature will be mapped out as an overarching framework to systematically integrate the results and guide future research. For example, the technology-organization-environment (TOE) framework (Tornatzky, Fleischer, & Chakrabarti, 1990) may be adapted or elaborated to illustrate the critical success factors. The results will be presented and incorporated in academic publications and presentation.

3. PRELIMINARY FINDINGS ON RESEARCH GAPS

Although this research project is still ongoing, a number of preliminary findings on the research gaps are emerged so far.

Firstly, the term of Data Analytics, Big Data Analytics, Business Analytics, etc. are used widely but there is a no commonly accepted term to define and classify these terms. Therefore, there is an urgent need for clarifications on the concepts and a taxonomy of Analytics in the context of Big Data because Analytics is "not simply a buzz word or hype" (Holsapple, Lee-Post, & Pakath, 2014). For example, what are distinctive differences between traditional data analytics and Big Data Analytics?

Secondly, as Big Data Analytics is an emerging research field, there are no validated measures to benchmark the level and extent of its applications. There are also no effective indicators to measure the various impact of Big Data Analytics.

Thirdly, Many scholars have reflected on big data's possible implications on theory (Abbasi, Sarker, & Chiang, 2016) and call for attention on Big Data theorization. For example, Muller (2005) has showcased how a Big Data Analytics study that is data-driven and predictive in nature can be the basis for theorisation.

Thirdly, the impact of Big Data Analytics is complex and tangled with many other factors, but there is a lack of a suitable theoretical lens to examine and understand the mechanisms of how Big Data Analytics generate business value, and to what extent Big Data Analytics impact on business performance. From an information value chain perspective, some recent Big Data studies and editorials have touched on the role of theory when leveraging Big Data sources for discovering knowledge (Abbasi et al., 2016). A number of theories, such as organisational absorptive capacity, cognitive fit theory, IT affordance theory, contingency theory, resource-based view, dynamic capabilities, etc., are being considered in research on understand the organisations' adoption and diffusion of Big Data Analytics and its impact on organisational performance, but there are challenges when applying them for examining the mechanisms, relationships and factors associated with the use and impact of analytics. Theorizing the impact of Big Data and Analytics has also been identified as a gap by Sena et al. (2017).

Fourthly, achieving a competitive advantage with analytics requires organisational commitment that touches many aspects of organizational behaviour, from revamping information management to adapting cultural norms (Ransbotham, Kiron, & Prentice, 2016). These contextual factors, such as data driven culture, leadership, openness to change, etc. will affect the applications and impact of analytics, but what roles they play in facilitating or inhabiting the implementation and impact are still not sufficiently investigated. From a social-technical perspective, Günther, Rezazade Mehrizi, Huysman, and Feldberg (2017) conduct literature on realizing value from Big Data and argue that we still have limited understanding of how organizations translate the Big Data potential into actual social and economic value. They identify that portability and interconnectivity are two socio-technical features of big data that influence value realization. More studies should be carried out to understand how, why to what extent the organizational and human factors affect the applications success and effective impact of Big Data Analytics. Moreover, there appears very limited research have been reported on identifying counter-productive factors for Big Data success and negative social and behavioral impact. For example, among the very limited studies on negative impact of analytics, Rubel and Jones (2016) question whether learning analytics advances the aims of higher education or runs counter to those goals.

Finally, many small and media enterprises (SMEs) felt that they are left behind large companies in terms of harvesting the value of Big Data and Analytics. However, research on developing suitable Big Data Analytics tools and services for SMEs is still very limited. It appears that none of 110 papers reviewed in this study focuses on the development and applications of Big Data Analytics in SMEs. Comparing with large companies, SMEs has limited financial and human resources, Big Data technology developers and service providers should offer suitable low costs Big Data Analytics tools and services to help SMEs' utilize Big Data Analytics. This is clearly a research gap as well as an opportunity for future research.

4. CONCLUSION

While it is clear that Big Data Analytics can make big impact and offer valuable benefits to organizations across all sectors, preliminary findings from our literature review confirm the argument by Sena et al. (2017) that our understanding of the mechanisms through which Big Data can enhance business growth is still very limited. This research aims to help address this gap by identifying the state of the art research on the applications of Big Data Analytics and their impact on organizational performance. It is expected that this research will provide a comprehensive overview on the applications of Big Dara Analytics, emerging technology-organization-environment issues, research challenges and opportunities that can help advance the field. Final outcomes and key findings of the systematic literature review will be presented in the conference presentation.

REFERENCES

Abbasi, A., Sarker, S., & Chiang, R. 2016. Big data research in information systems: Toward an inclusive research agenda. *Journal of the Association for Information Systems,* Vol 17, No. 2, pp i-xxxii.

Chen, H., Chiang, R. H. L., & Storey, V. C. 2012. Business intelligence and analytics: from big data to big impact. *MIS Quarterly,* Vol 36, No. 4, pp 1165-1188.

Denyer, D., & Tranfield, D. (2009). Producing a systematic review. In D. A. Buchanan & A. Bryman (Eds.), *The SAGE handbook of organizational research methods* (pp. 671– 689). London: SAGE Publications Ltd.

Fink, A. (2013). *Conducting research literature reviews: From the Internet to paper*: Sage Publications.

Holsapple, C., Lee-Post, A., & Pakath, R. 2014. A unified foundation for business analytics. *Decision Support Systems,* Vol 64, No. August, pp 130-141. doi:http://dx.doi.org/10.1016/j.dss.2014.05.013

Muller, D., Yzerbyt, V., and Judd, C. . 2005. When moderation is mediated and mediation is moderated. *Journal of personality and social psychology,* Vol 89, No. 6, pp pp 852-863.

Ransbotham, S., Kiron, D., & Prentice, P. K. 2016. Beyond the Hype: The Hard Work Behind Analytics Success. *MIT Sloan Management Review,* Vol 57, No. 3.

Rubel, A., & Jones, K. M. 2016. Student privacy in learning analytics: An information ethics perspective. *The Information Society,* Vol 32, No. 2, pp 143-159.

Sena, V., Demirbag, M., Bhaumik, S., & Sengupta, A. 2017. Call for papers on Big Data and Performance. *British Jounral of Management,* Vol 28, No. 3, pp 551-553

Siddaway, A. (2014). *What is a Systematic Literature Review and how do I do one.* University of Stirling. Retrieved from https://www.stir.ac.uk/media/schools/management/documents/centregradresearch/How%20to%20do%20a%20systematic%20literature%20review%20and%20meta-analysis.pdf

Tornatzky, L. G., Fleischer, M., & Chakrabarti, A. K. (1990). *The processes of technological innovation.* Lexington, Mass.: Lexington Books.

DYNAMIC DATA ASSIGNING CLUSTERING FOR SCHOOL GROUPING

Olga Georgieva
Sofia University "St. Kl. Ohridski", Faculty of Mathematics and Informatics, Sofia, Bulgaria

ABSTRACT

Following the current trends in data driven solutions, this paper aims to explore a value-creation mechanism for open data of education sector. Dynamic data assigning algorithm for cluster identification is investigated for the ability to group schools based on the students' scores. The primary purpose of the solution is to drive decisions about the education system and policies for reducing the risk of premature leaving the system accounting for the current state of the presented learning deficits.

KEYWORDS

Data Clustering, Data Driven Modeling, Decision Support, Education

1. INTRODUCTION

At the present time the volume of the available data is growing tremendously. Often, the data are from variety of sources, time dependent and have different format and structure. These characteristics are unified in the resent concept of Big Data. The challenge of the contemporary task is their analysis. The data are not only a source of information but resource for new understandings and insights for description of new models and policies of the society. The expectations are to obtain a value added by applying data driven analysis which in case of Big Data is generalized as Big Data Value Chain [Fan].

A common task in this search is identification of groups and structures appeared in the investigated data. These give us information about dependences and could reveal unknown relations. Usually the task is solved according to a clustering procedure. The general question is which clustering technique to use for the considered data. Different clustering paradigms have been invented to solve this common task as hierarchical clustering, also density and distribution based clustering. Among these methods centroid based clustering algorithms are widely applied. They define a prototype as most representative point of each cluster in the data space. Widely applied are K-means and its fuzzy version - FCM algorithm because of their good convergence results. Both they rely on iterative optimization procedure [Bezdek]. Density based algorithms as Subtractive clustering, are another good solution that identifies clusters one by [Chiu]. In comparison to the objective function algorithms the procedure is not iterative, possesses auto-generation capability to detect clusters and needs low computational costs. However, in many data mining problems especially in Big Data Analytics there is no need for a partition of the whole data space. It is often sufficient to find a few interesting substructures that cover only a small proportion of the data set. In seeking this noise clustering have been introduced [Dave] as a way to find only clusters considered as important. Taking the advantage of the centroid and density based algorithms a prototype-based clustering algorithm named Dynamic Data Assigning Assessment (DDAA) explores the idea of noise clustering technique [Georgieva, 2006]. The algorithm keeps the ability to find data structure straight forward finding good clusters and separating the noise data. DDAA presents good separation abilities of real data from different origin as weather data [Georgieva, 2006] and gene expression data [Georgieva, 2008].

The education sector generates a lot of data but it lacks of knowledge about dependences of the different factors for learning deficits and risks of premature leaving the system. This paper aims twofold - to apply the original DDAA algorithm in discovering specific groups of schools and providing this knowledge to facilitate the good education policies. Further purpose is to investigate the incorporation of the algorithm in a common platform for informed and timely decisions.

2. THE CONCEPT OF DDAA ALGORITHM

The concept of DDAA algorithm is based on data separation at the minimization of an objective function J:

$$J = \sum_{i=1}^{c}\sum_{k=1}^{N}(u_{ik})^m d_{ik}^2, \quad (1)$$

where N is the number of data in the data set; u_{ik} denotes the membership degree and d_{ik} - the distance of the k-th data $x_k = [x_{k1}, x_{k2}, ..., x_{kn}]$ to the i-th cluster prototype; n is the number of features in of the data space; c is the number of clusters. Each cluster is represented by its cluster center $v_i = [v_{i1}, v_{i2}, ..., v_{in}]$, i=1,...,$c$. The fuzzifier $m \in [1,\infty)$ is the weighted exponent coefficient which determines how much clusters may overlap. When we choose m=1, we have crisp partition at a minimum of the objective function (1). If the fuzzifier is larger than one, $m \in (1,\infty)$, then fuzzy clustering is explored as a partial membership of data to the clusters is accepted. Widely applicable algorithm in this case is FCM algorithm. In order to avoid a trivial solution of assigning no data to any cluster, the following constraints are imposed:

$$u_{ik} \in [0,1], \qquad 1 \le i \le c, \quad 1 \le k \le N \quad (2.a)$$

$$0 < \sum_{i=1}^{N} u_{ik} < N, \qquad 1 \le i \le c \quad (2.b)$$

Additional constrain is enforced in case of probabilistic clustering:

$$\sum_{i=1}^{c} u_{ik} = 1, \qquad 1 \le k \le N \quad (2.c)$$

The parameters to be optimized are the membership degrees u_{ik} and the cluster centers v_i which determine the distance values d_{ik} as:

$$d_{ik}^2 = \|x_k - v_i\|_{A_i}^2 = (x_k - v_i)A_i(x_k - v_i)^T, \quad (3)$$

where A_i is a positive symmetric matrix. If it is identity matrix then Euclidean distance is applied and spherical clusters are determined

2.1 Noise Clustering

A weakness of the objective function clustering is the grouping of noise data. The arbitrary noise points are allocated with equal membership degree to the significant clusters, which does not reflect the reality. Better is to split the noise data collecting them in a noise cluster, for instance cluster c. A virtual noise prototype with no parameters to be adjusted is introduced. It has always the same distance δ to all points in the data set:

$$d_{ck} = \delta, \text{ for } \forall\, k. \quad (4)$$

The remaining c-1 clusters are assumed to be good clusters. The objective function J_{noise} that considers the noise cluster is defined in the same manner as in the general scheme of functional (1), $J_{\text{noise}}=J$. The distances of each data x_k, are defined by (3) for all good clusters i=1,...,c-1 and for the noise cluster $d_{ck}^2 = \delta^2$. The objective function J_{noise} has a minimum for a fixed distance δ and for two general cases: a) hard noise clustering, $m = 1$, accepts crisp membership degrees of a data to the clusters and b) fuzzy noise clustering, m>1, accepts partial membership degrees of a data to the clusters. The value of the noise distance δ is a matter of consideration. If it is chosen too small then most of the data points will be classified as noise and vice versa. This circumstance is explored in the DDAA algorithm.

2.2 DDAA Algorithm

Let us assume a special case when the data set consists of only one good cluster among noise data being captured in a noise cluster. For a certain δ value the two clusters c=2, could be separated in minimizing the objective function J_{noise}, which gets the simplified form:

$$J_{noise} = \sum_{k=1}^{N}(u_{1k})^m d_k^2 + \delta^2 \sum_{k=1}^{N}(u_{2k})^m, \quad (5)$$

where d_k is the distance between data x_k and the centre v_1 of the single good cluster. Also for the fixed δ:

a) for hard noise clustering, $m = 1$

$u_{1k}=1$ and $u_{2k}=0$ if $d_k \leq \delta$ if data x_k belongs to the good cluster; (6.a)

$u_{1k}=0$ and $u_{2k}=1$ if $d_k > \delta$ if data x_k belongs to the noise cluster. (6.b)

b) for fuzzy noise clustering having, $m>1$:

$$u_{1k} = \frac{1}{1+\left(\frac{d_k}{\delta}\right)^{2/(m-1)}} \qquad u_{2k} = \frac{1}{1+\left(\frac{\delta}{d_k}\right)^{2/(m-1)}} \tag{7}$$

where the centre of the good cluster is determined as weighted mean value:

$$v_1 = \frac{\sum_{k=1}^{N}(u_{1k})^m x_k}{\sum_{k=1}^{N}(u_{1k})^m}. \tag{8}$$

The method introduced by DDAA algorithm separates clusters based on the concept of noise clustering applied via step wise decreasing of the noise distance. The procedure starts by choosing a large noise distance, for instance the diameter of the data set. Then, by decreasing δ with a prescribed decrement step $\Delta\delta$ we can determine the number $N_{in}(j)$ of the data belonging to the good cluster at each level j of the noise distance $\delta=\delta_j$. Obviously, decreasing the distance δ, a process of "loosing" good data and assigning data to the noise cluster will begin. Continuing to decrease the noise distance, we will start to separate points from the real good cluster and add them to the noise cluster, until the good cluster will be entirely emptied. The described dynamics could be visualised by the curve $N_{in}(j)$ via the decremented noise distance and by velocity $\Delta N_{in}(j)$:

$$\Delta N_{in}(j) = N_{in}(j-1) - N_{in}(j). \tag{9}$$

It is clear that if we lose actual noise points that are data from a low density region the curve $N_{in}(j)$ will almost remain in a plateau wise, whereas a strong slope is observed when data from at least one actual cluster are moved to the noise cluster. The peaks obtained from the curve $\Delta N_{in}(j)$ correspond to the slopes of the $N_{in}(j)$ curve. Only significant peaks having area larger than a predefined threshold tol are of real interest:

$$S(s) = \sum_{j:\delta_{\min}(s)\leq\delta_j\leq\delta_{\max}(s)} \Delta N_{in}(j) > tol, \tag{10}$$

where $\delta_{min}(s)$ and $\delta_{max}(s)$ are correspondingly the left and right base of the peak s. The last significant peak occurs when the data points of the good data cluster are moved to the noise cluster. The other significant peaks also correspond to comprehensible cluster. However, data of the insignificant peaks are noisy data. The algorithm could be applied in the context of hard clustering by (6.a,b) or fuzzy clustering (7), where the data are assigned to the good cluster if their membership degree u_{1k} is larger than a predefined value u_{tol}.

The procedure of DDAA cluster identification is summarized as follows:

Step 1 Specify the decrement step $\Delta\delta$ and threshold tol. In case of fuzzy DDAA specify as well u_{tol}.

Step 2 Compute the curves N_{in} and ΔN_{in} over decreasing δ by the prescribed decrement step $\Delta\delta$.

Step 3 Find all peaks of ΔN_{in} curve and select the significant peaks according to (10).

Step 4 Separate one good cluster determined by the last significant peak.

Step 5 Subtract the separated points from the data set and repeat the procedure from Step 2 until no significant peaks could be found.

As in most clustering algorithms due to the scaling effect we normalize the data in advance.

2.3 Comparative Analysis

DDAA algorithm is density based clustering algorithms as the peaks' area $S(s)$ detects the data density. In this sense it could be compared with well-known algorithms of this type as for instance, Subtractive clustering (SC) [Chiu]. SC is also one pass clustering that defines densest cluster at each algorithm pass. A data point with the highest potential is considered as a cluster center. The potential is determined as a function of a distance measure. Unlike the SC algorithm DDAA algorithm does not estimate the cluster centers by any rigorous mathematical computation but as a mean of data that have been heuristically separated at each pass according to equation (10).

However, DDAA takes an advantage of its visibility property as the clustering results could be seen by the curves N_{in} and ΔN_{in} independently of the data dimensionality.

SC clustering needs four parameters that have to be prescribed in advance to define the discovered clusters - cluster radius, squash factor, accept ratio and reject ratio. DDAA is independent of any fine tuning of its initial parameters - decrement step $\Delta\delta$ and threshold *tol*. The choice of the decrement step depends on the density of the data set. However, successful separation can be found for $\Delta\delta$ from 0,01 to 0,001. The threshold *tol* can be determined based on assumption about the minimal amount of data that form a cluster.

3. SCHOOL SCORE DATA PROCESSING AND ANALYSIS

The data set comprises different assessments results collected during one school year of the students of 2363 schools as average score, assessment of two subjects –language and literature (BLL) and Mathematics (Maths) of national external assessments exams, state matriculation exams (SMEs) as well as the average score of the school. The data amount is not related to the Big Data term but the potential of the data to increase during the years and their scalability to other education sectors (universities, other countries) relates the present investigation to the Big Data solutions.

Several procedures as filtering, cleaning and uniform formatting have been applied in order to purify the raw data and to obtain a form appropriate for further analysis and interpretation. The main task regarding data analysis is to achieve significant groups in a space defined by the indicators of school rate results. The exploration of a valuable data space is important in discovering the data structure. BLL is obligatory for all schools and the average score is important indicator for the entire school presentation. Thus, grouping of data space formed by them, $x=[x_1, x_2]$=[BLL, average score] is investigated. The two general groups of schools: a group of poor learning results (934 schools) presenting low BLL and low average score results and second group of schools having good success (1413 schools) are recognized. Dynamics seen from the slopes and peeks of N_{in} curves gives us additional information about the spreading of the groups. First, the smaller and the denser cluster (dots) (Figure 1.a,c) has been separated, whereas the larger one (data are given by cross) was identified at the second algorithm pass (Figure 1.b,c). By reducing ten times the threshold value and the number of data enable to form a valuable cluster we obtain more insights at the larger cluster. This separation gives more detailed view as new five groups that are part of the larger cluster have been revealed (Figure 2). Data given by circles are not assigned to any cluster for each presented partition. These are noise data.

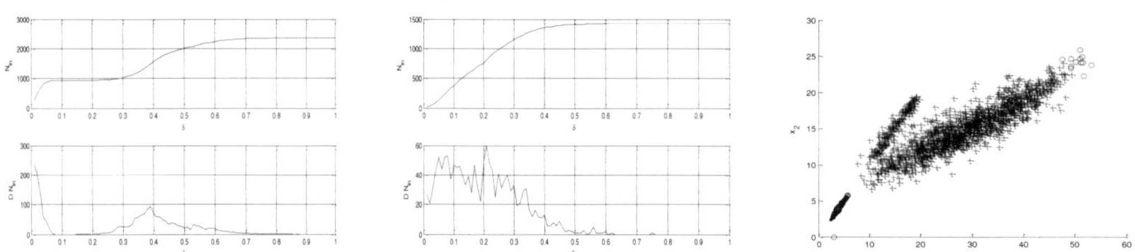

a) b) c)

Figure 1.Two stage clustering dynamics of hard DDAA obtained for δ=0,01 *tol*=500

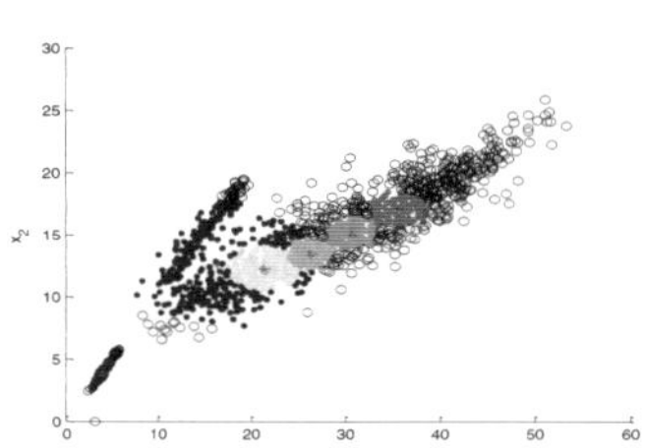

Figure 2. Clustering results hard DDAA obtained for δ=0,001, *tol*=50

Commonly, the sectoral experts need to know the existing school groups depending on more than the two considered features of the data space. In order to answer of this demand DDAA is applied in a three dimensional data space, where besides BLL and average score the Maths scores is taken as a third dimension.

In this case the clustering results are not visible directly, but the dynamics of N_{in} and ΔN_{in} give us information about the obtained 7 groups consisting of 537, 161, 356, 163, 186, 389, 382 schools, respectively (Figure 3). The groups comprise in total 2174 schools and the rest schools are considered as outliers in the context of this partition. The strong slopes (Figure 3,a,b,c) represent separation of very compact school groups, whereas the other five groups comprise more scattered data.

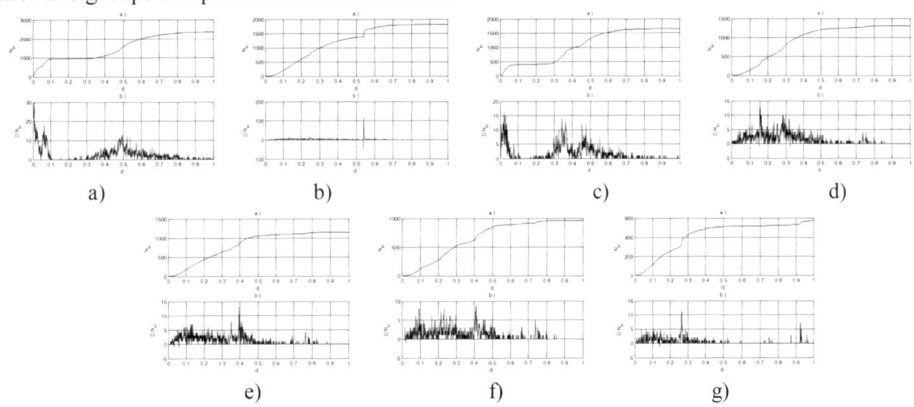

Figure 3. Hard DDAA of schools' grouping, δ=0,001, *tol*=50

4. CONCLUSION

The school groups were easily obtained by DDAA algorithm without rigorous parameter tuning. Furthermore, the algorithm enables to visualize the clustering result independently of the data dimensionality. Despite a heuristic of the algorithm several advantages of the DDAA algorithm could be underlined, which makes it applicable for large open data sets. The algorithm is fulfilled for one pass, determines the number of clusters automatically, and presents the noise data as well. Generally, the algorithm could be easily incorporated in a platform solution where the results could serve for decision support of the sectorial authorities.

ACKNOWLEDGEMENT

The authors acknowledge the financial support by the National Scientific Fund under project grant DN 02/11 and Science Fund of Sofia University "St. Kl. Ohridski" under grand № 80-10-111/2018.

REFERENCES

Bezdek, James C. ,1981, *Pattern Recognition with Fuzzy Objective Function Algorithms*, Plenum Press, New York.

Chiu S.L.1994, Fuzzy model identification based on cluster estimation. *J. of Intelligent and Fuzzy Systems* 2, pp.267-278.

Dave R. 1991, Characterization and detection of noise in clustering, *Pattern Recogn. Lett.* 12, pp.657–664.

Fan W., Bifet A., 2012, Mining Big Data: Current Status, and Forecast to the Future, *ACM SIGKDD Explorations Newsletter*, v. 14, Issue 2, pp. 1-5.

Georgieva O., Klawonn F., 2006, Cluster analysis via dynamic data assigning assessment algorithm, *Information Technologies and Control*, No2, pp.14-21.

Georgieva O., F. Klawonn, 2008, Dynamic data assigning assessment clustering of streaming data, *Applied Soft Computing- Special Issue on Dynamic Data Mining* v. 8, No 4, pp.1305-1313.

IDENTIFYING THE DISTRIBUTION OF THE FLOATING POPULATION IN SEOUL

Jungseok Lee[1], Kyunghyun Min[1], Kiyun Yu[1] and Jiyoung Kim[2]
[1]*Department of Civil and Environmental Engineering, GIS/LBS Laboratory, Seoul National University, Seoul, Republic of Korea*
[2]*Institute of Construction and Environmental Engineering, Seoul National University, Seoul, Republic of Korea*

ABSTRACT

In this study, we analyzed the characteristics of the floating population in three different time zones using the head-tail break method, which is a hierarchical analysis method, to show long-tail distribution using data on the floating population of Seoul, Korea. Results showed that there were areas in which a larger floating population was revealed near the subway station, only during peak commute times. It also showed that there were many factors influencing the floating population, such as large shopping malls and a baseball field. Moreover, there was an increase in the size of the floating population during the workday or at lunch time. Although the movement of pedestrians is largely affected by the location of subway stations, it is also affected by other influencing factors.

KEYWORDS

Long Tail Distribution, Head/Tail Break, Floating Population

1. INTRODUCTION

Recent developments, including portable GPS devices and survey technology, provide navigation services to pedestrians, the disabled, and elderly people in today's modern world. A vehicle navigation system, for example, provides routes by accessing real-time traffic information and the speed of the moving vehicle. Researchers developed studies on navigations for pedestrians considering various moving patterns, the degree of seclusion, and the quality of the scenery. More studies additionally researched indoor spaces, such as museums and exhibition halls, to analyze the movement patterns of visitors using space syntax. Some research was performed on street characteristics and the floating population in an urban environment (Jiang & Claramunt, 2002; Shin & Choi, 2005). Team members recently collected data on moving pedestrians using check-ins from SNS, GPS navigations, and base stations of various cellular service providers. The results were characterized by spatial big data, which are known to follow non-linear properties and long-tail distribution (Pareto distribution) due to spatial autocorrelation(Jiang, 2015; Li et al., 2016). Therefore, to analyze spatial big data, various analyses were performed by applying the head-tail break method instead of conventional statistical methods (Jiang, 2015).

In this paper, we estimate the affecting factors of the floating population data of Seoul in the Republic of Korea (ROK) and carry out basic research on floating population patterns to better determine optimal routes for pedestrians by using the head-tail break method in different time zones.

2. METHODOLOGY

Many studies have shown that spatial data such as city size (Zipf, 1949), street length and connectivity (Jiang, 2009), and population (Brockmann, Hufnagel, & Geisel, 2006; Gonzalez, Hidalgo, & Barabasi, 2008) follow the long-tail (or Pareto) distribution, rather than the Gaussian distribution (Jiang, 2015).

Spatial information is characterized by spatial heterogeneity (Cliff & Ord, 1970) and spatial dependence (Tobler, 1970). Previous research proposed using head-tail breaks to analyze the spatial data instead of using other existing statistics values (e.g., mean, standard deviation, etc.) (Jiang & Yin, 2014).

Head-tail break is a hierarchical classification algorithm for long-tailed distribution, as described in the previous study (Jiang & Yin, 2014). The method is as follows: the data are averaged, divided in half (based on the average), and iterated until the number of the head is not less than the number of the tail (Jiang, 2013). For example, in [Figure 1.a], the graph is divided into Head 1 and Tail 1 by an average of data (μ1). Tail 1 is 60% of the total, while Head 1 is 40%, meaning that the number of heads is less than the number of tails. Thus, Tail 1 becomes Class 1. The remaining (Head 1) is divided into two regions, Head 2 and Tail 2, based on an average of Head 1 (μ2) [Figure 1.b]. Since the ratio of Head 2 (45%) is smaller than that of Tail 2 (55%), Tail 2 becomes Class 2 and Head 2 is divided in half based on an average of Head 2 (μ3) [Figure 1.c]. Since the ratio of Head 3 is the same as Tail 3, the number of heads is not less than the number of tails. Now, terminate the iteration and change Head 2 to Class 3. By utilizing this method, the number of classes and the class intervals are naturally and automatically derived from the inherent hierarchy of data (Jiang & Yin, 2014). These classes, divided by head-tail break, are used to compare different data.

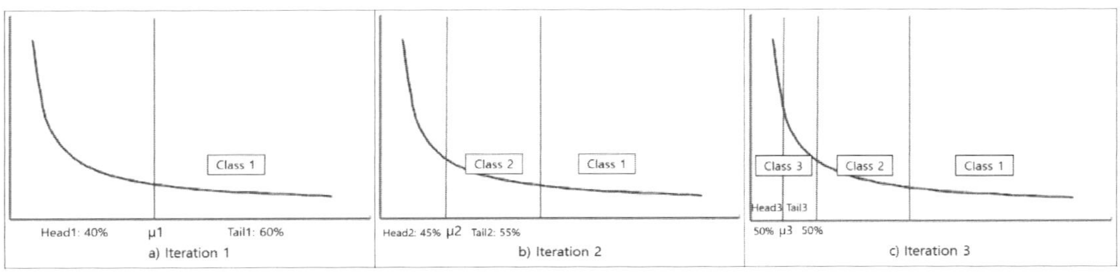

Figure 1. Head-Tail Break

3. TEST AND RESULTS

The floating population data used in this experiment were produced by a company in ROK. The data we used related to the number of communications per hour in a 50m x 50m cell (located in Seoul, ROK) on January 2015. Generally, we expected that the floating population would be high at bus stop and subway station.

In this paper, we divided the time zone into three categories: morning commute time (07:00-09:00), lunch time (11:00-13:00), and evening commute time (17:00-20:00). People use the stations during commuting periods more than at other times. We analyzed the commuting time zones to understand the effect of the stations on the floating population. In other time zones, there may be other influx factors apart from stations. The distribution of the floating population during lunch time is expected to predict the patterns of pedestrians unaffected by bus stops and subway stations. Head-tail break was performed for each of the three time zones.

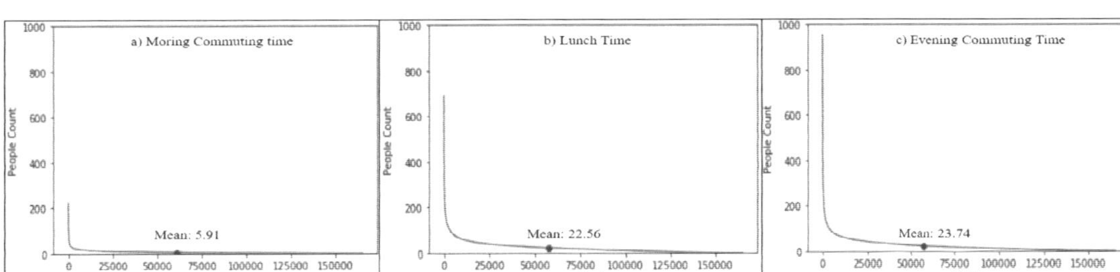

Figure 2. Ranked size plot of floating population by time zone

As shown in [Figure 2], the floating population data by each time zone do not follow normal distributions, making it difficult to derive valuable information. It is also difficult to explain through existing statistical methods (mean, standard deviation, or quantile). [Table 1] provides basic statistical values for each time zone, which, however, could not explain or indicate their data.

Table 1. Statistics value

		Morning Commuting Time (7:00 – 9:00)	Lunch Time (11:00 – 13:00)	Evening Commuting Time (17:00 – 20:00)
Mean		5.91	22.56	23.74
Std		7.09	29.12	32.72
Min		0.00	0.00	0.00
Max		222.63	691.73	955.77
quantile	25%	1.63	5.57	5.52
	50%	4.22	15.03	15.66
	75%	7.97	29.66	31.11

(# of people)

Nevertheless, classes created with head-tail breaks are hierarchically classified so data in different time zones can be compared hierarchically. The number of classes for each time period is 11, 12, 11. As a result of this head-tail break analysis for Seoul city, it was discovered that the highest class (a group with a large floating population) from all time zones was distributed around the station. From among several instances from the experiments, we selected the four most interesting cases. The top four classes (groups with many floating population) are expressed in the following colors: red, orange, yellow, and green.

3.1 Case 1

In Gangnam-gu Office Station, high class distributions were shown only during commuting time [Figure 3]. As time went on, the number of people using the station increased, but the number of classes of floating population did not exceed four during the lunch time zone. This means that the preferred time zone for each station is different and Gangnam-gu Office Station affects the surrounding population only during commuting times. This also implies that people use this station less frequently in the daytime than other stations. When determining floating population patterns or creating pedestrian navigation, the value of cost should be considered differently for each station and time.

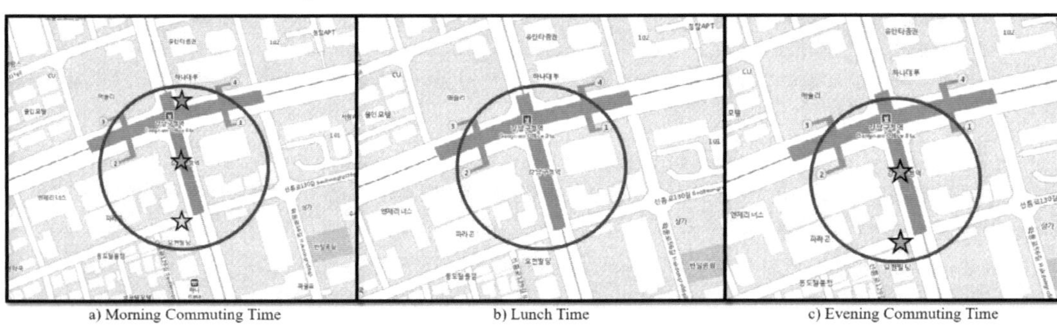

a) Morning Commuting Time b) Lunch Time c) Evening Commuting Time

Figure 3. Gangnam-gu Office Station

3.2 Case 2

When analyzing the Euljiro 1(il)-ga station [Figure 4], we observed high classes in all three time zones. This means that people continue to use this station regardless of the time and that the region causes a continuing influx of individuals that increase its floating population. When analyzing the flow pattern, it is important to study what causes the population flow to continue.

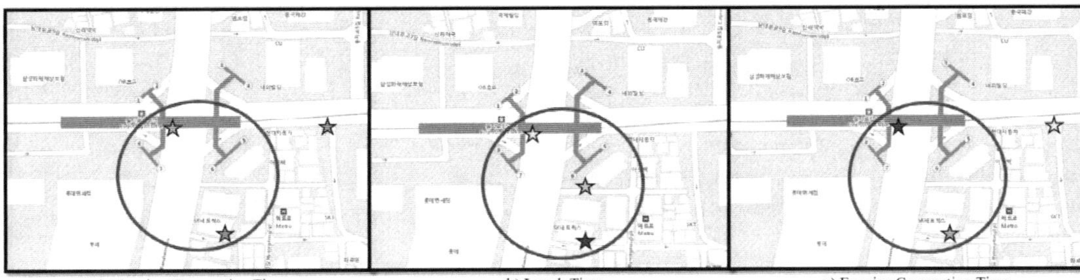

a) Morning Commuting Time | b) Lunch Time | c) Evening Commuting Time

Figure 4. Euljiro 1(il)-ga station

3.3 Case 3

Dongdaemun Station also shows different distribution from other regions. In Dongdaemun Station, the high class is distributed only during lunch time and the low class is distributed during commuting times [Figure 5]. This means that although the subway station affects the floating population, other factors affect it as well. This area, which has a high class distribution, is home to a shopping mall called "Dongdaemun Shopping Town." It is safe to assume that there is a high class distribution during daytime.

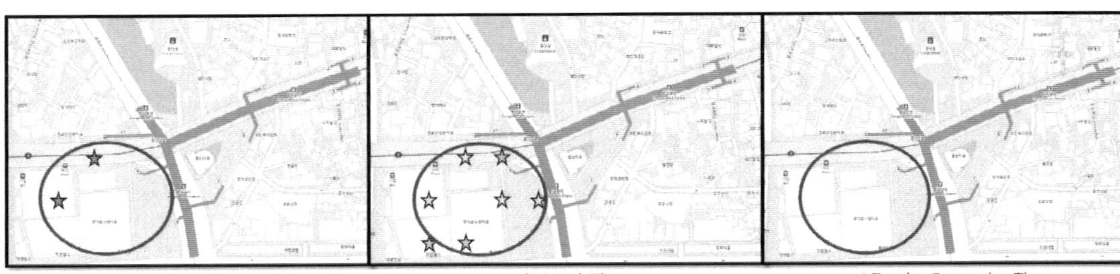

a) Morning Commuting Time | b) Lunch Time | c) Evening Commuting Time

Figure 5. Dongdaemun Station

3.4 Case 4

There is no high class in the morning commuting time near the Omokgyo station, but this is an example where the class is gradually increasing over time [Figure 6]. The highest class (red) appears in the evening. It is interesting that the floating population class is high in this area even though it is located far from the station. There are cultural facilities, such as broadcasting stations (SBS), parks, baseball courts, athletic fields, and shopping malls, near this area. It can be assumed that these various spatial object factors have influenced the floating population. While public transport is an important factor to consider when evaluating the flow pattern, the examination of other factors is necessary as well.

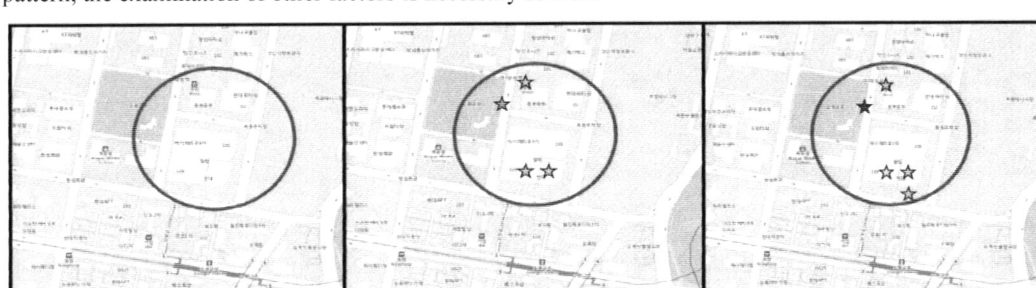

a) Morning Commuting Time | b) Lunch Time | c) Evening Commuting Time

Figure 6. Omokgyo Station

4. CONCLUSION

We have classified the floating population of Seoul, Korea by effectively using the head-tail break method to analyze relative population density and high class distribution (classes with high floating population) in each time zone. When visually analyzed, cases 1, 2, and 4 (large floating populations) revealed high class distributions near their subway stations during commuting times. High class distributions were also observed during lunch or evening commuting times, depending on the influence of other factors, such as large shopping malls and baseball courts. Although the movement of pedestrians is focused around subway stations, we discovered that other influencing factors also affected the movement of pedestrians.

In the future, we will quantitatively analyze the movement of pedestrians using the characteristics of space and street structure by applying space syntax (connectivity, integration, and ERAM), network analysis, and time series analysis. The future study will aim to develop the route search method to meet the various needs of pedestrians.

ACKNOWLEDGEMENT

This research, "Geospatial Big Data Management, Analysis and Service Platform Technology Development," was supported by the MOLIT (The Ministry of Land, Infrastructure and Transport), Korea, under the national spatial information research program supervised by the KAIA (Korea Agency for Infrastructure Technology Advancement) (18NSIP-B081023-05).

REFERENCES

Brockmann, D., Hufnagel, L., & Geisel, T. (2006). The scaling laws of human travel. *nature, 439*(7075), 462.

Cliff, A. D., & Ord, K. (1970). Spatial autocorrelation: a review of existing and new measures with applications. *Economic Geography, 46*(sup1), 269-292.

Gonzalez, M. C., Hidalgo, C. A., & Barabasi, A.-L. (2008). Understanding individual human mobility patterns. *nature, 453*(7196), 779.

Jiang, B. (2009). Street hierarchies: a minority of streets account for a majority of traffic flow. *International Journal of Geographical Information Science, 23*(8), 1033-1048.

Jiang, B. (2013). Head/tail breaks: A new classification scheme for data with a heavy-tailed distribution. *The Professional Geographer, 65*(3), 482-494.

Jiang, B. (2015). Geospatial analysis requires a different way of thinking: The problem of spatial heterogeneity. *GeoJournal, 80*(1), 1-13.

Jiang, B., & Claramunt, C. (2002). Integration of space syntax into GIS: new perspectives for urban morphology. *Transactions in GIS, 6*(3), 295-309.

Jiang, B., & Yin, J. (2014). Ht-index for quantifying the fractal or scaling structure of geographic features. *Annals of the Association of American Geographers, 104*(3), 530-540.

Li, S., Dragicevic, S., Castro, F. A., Sester, M., Winter, S., Coltekin, A., . . . Stein, A. (2016). Geospatial big data handling theory and methods: A review and research challenges. *ISPRS Journal of Photogrammetry and Remote Sensing, 115*, 119-133.

Shin, S., & Choi, J. (2005). A study on the architectural planning of efficient spatial analysis in general hospital.

Tobler, W. R. (1970). A computer movie simulating urban growth in the Detroit region. *Economic Geography, 46*(sup1), 234-240.

Zipf, G. K. (1949). Human behaviour and the principle of least-effort. Cambridge MA edn. *Reading: Addison-Wesley*.

ANALYSIS OF SPATIAL ACCESSIBILITY TO PUBLIC LIBRARIES CONSIDERING DETERMINANT OF USER'S VISIT

Jiwon Lee[1], Kiyun Yu[1] and Jiyoung Kim[2]
[1]*Department of Civil and Environmental Engineering, Seoul National University, Seoul, Republic of Korea*
[2]*Institute of Construction and Environmental Engineering (ICEE) , Seoul National University, Seoul, Republic of Korea*

ABSTRACT

One way to improve the accessibility of public facilities is to increase the facilities' attractiveness to users. This study examined the determinants of public library visits using public opinion poll data and statistically tested the effects of those variables. In addition the accessibility of public libraries in Seoul was calculated by setting determinant of user's visit as supply factors. As a result, accessibility considering library's attractiveness was showed different patterns from accessibility predicted by physical location.

KEYWORDS

Spatial Accessibility, Public Library, LDA, OLS, Gravity Model, 2SFCA

1. INTRODUCTION

Public facilities do not reflect users' willingness to pay for services because they offer free access, so their financial resources tend to be limited. Therefore, public facilities should not be assessed based on industrial or commercial locations under price competition systems, such as markets. They should be analyzed under governmental welfare criteria.

However, the locations of Korea's public facilities often are decided on behalf of the convenience of the provider. In many cases, they are located where land is easy to be obtained. As a result, the characteristics of the surrounding area usually are not considered. Therefore, the results of studies on accessibility of public facilities in Korea can't help concluding only that the ability to access a facility is inconveniently located. Among types of public facilities, it is particularly difficult to establish public libraries because they are related to people's self-actualization, not safety or physiological needs.

This study analyzed the accessibility of public libraries in Korea by focusing on determinants of public library visits. I believe these factors play important role in improving the accessibility to public facilities with fixed locations. In addition, this study assessed the effects of the users' interests. This approach differs from previous studies which concentrated mostly on the provision of the physical facility.

The study area covered the entire public library system of Seoul, Korea. To analyze the libraries' accessibility, visitors' decision-making was employed as a supply factor. To extract the reasons for visiting a library, unstructured data derived from the Public Library Citizen's Forum were analyzed. The Seoul Metropolitan Government held this Forum on November 25, 2017. Altogether, 591 people participated in the roundtable discussions, where they freely gave their opinions on the status and future of Seoul's public libraries.

2. RELATED WORKS

Accessibility has historically been understood as the proximity of one to another specified location(Kwan and Weber, 2003). However, broadly defined, a given location's accessibility is determined by an array of opportunities that exist within a specified distance from that location(O'Kelly and Horner, 2003). Therefore, accessibility might include the ease of transit between a point of origin and a destination or it might include the amounts, qualities, or characteristics of activities available at the destination (Handy and Niemeier, 1997).

So, to determine accessibility, recent studies included demographic and socioeconomic variables as well as physical distance. Joseph and Phillips(1984) defined physical distance as locational accessibility measured by geographical factors and they also defined the social factors as effective accessibility indicated by non-geographical factors.

In the case of public libraries, convenient transportation to the library, its physical distance from a school, and safety near the library have been found to influence the library users' behavior(Palmer, 1981). Examples of the socioeconomic, personal, and geographical factors used in previous studies are population, race, income, wealth, and residential location. However, the influences of these variables tended to be subjectively chosen by the researchers, and there were focused on the physical factors.

3. RESEARCH METHODS

This study's analysis included two parts. The analytical process is illustrated in Figure1. First, the determinants of users' visits were extracted from the unstructured data, and second, the spatial accessibility of the libraries was computed using those extracted determinants.

The first part of the analysis had two steps. The determinants of users' visits were extracted from the roundtable data using Latent Dirichlet Allocation (LDA), a type of topic modeling. This method is widely used because it is easy to interpret the algorithm and it has a high success rate. Then, the variables extracted from the unstructured data were statistically validated. The dependent variable was the number of visitors to the libraries, and the extracted determinants were the independent variables. The effects of the independent variables on the dependent variable were tested in a linear correlation regression analysis.

The second part of the analysis determined the libraries' spatial accessibility as influenced by the variables of the first part of the analysis. The analysis of spatial accessibility has three possible models: 1) travel-cost approach, 2) container-based method, and 3) gravity model. The preferred method was the gravity model because it solved the problems related to the simplicity of the travel-cost approach and the analytical unit problem presented by the container-based method. Many recent studies have applied the gravity model, and the two-step floating catchment area(2SFCA) has been the preferred method when detailed data on facility provision are available.

2SFCA scores are computed in two steps.

$$\text{Step1. } R_j = \frac{S_j}{\sum_{k \in d_{jk} \leq d_0} P_k} \qquad \text{Step2. } A_k = \sum_{k \in d_{jk} \leq d_0} R_j$$

Firstly, the availability of service is determined using a supply-to-demand ratio computed at each service provision point j. Then a cumulative opportunity score is computed by determining the total availability of this weighted service at each population demand centre k. Where R_j is the provider-to-population ratio at service supply location j; S_j the measure of service supply volume at location j; P_k the population count at location k that lies within the service area catchment of j (i.e. $d_{kj} <= d_0$); d_{kj} is the cost in distance between locations k and j, and d_0 is a user-specified maximum threshold cost.

In the second stage, where A_k is the final 2SFCA accessibility score assigned to the population at location k. In this study, the libraries' accessibility related only to population and distance was analyzed using the gravity model, and 2SFCA was used to test the effects of the determinants of visits on accessibility.

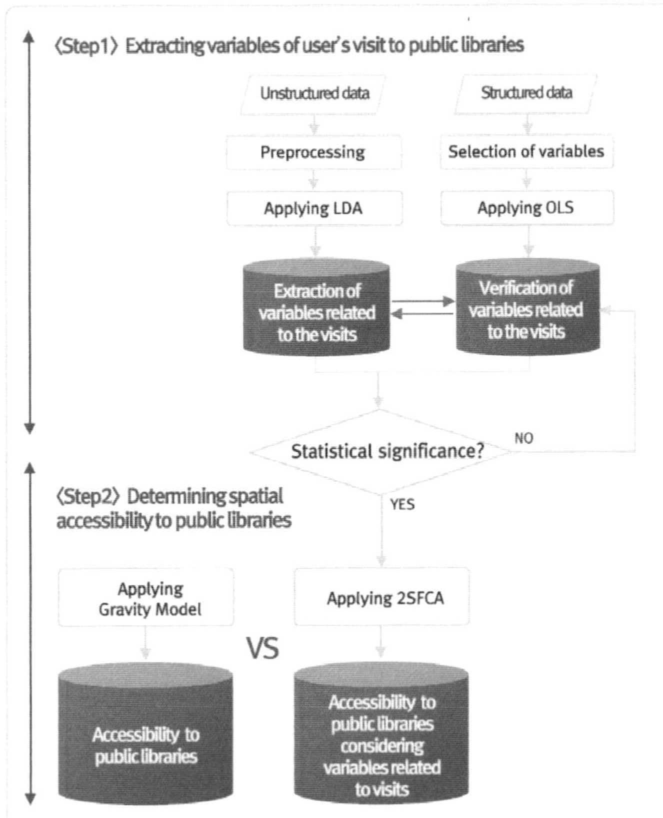

Figure 1. Study Flow Chart

4. EXPERIMENT AND RESULTS

The data used to identify the determinants of public library visits were collected from 3,006 participants' statements provided in roundtable discussions, and LDA was performed after manipulating the data with word segmentation and stop word. The parametric values were adjusted and, after 5,000 iterations with five topics and two words, the following five factors were extracted: program, space, use, book, and librarian.

To verify the factors, data about 147 public libraries in Seoul were collected from the libraries' statistical dataset published on December 31, 2016, by National Library Statistics in Korea. The space per library was measured by the number of seats, including seats for children, elders, and disabled people. The variable measuring library use employed the Google Score ratings for local places. The number of library visitors was regressed on the independent variables, which found that about 68 percent of the variation in the number of visitors was explained ($R_2 = .683$), which was statistically significant. Figure2 provides the detailed results of the analysis.

The accessibility of the public libraries considering variables related to visits was analyzed using the measure of the number of visitors to the library because that variable was statistically found to include all of the visiting factors. The spatial analytical unit was the EupMyeonDong, one of Korea's administrative boundaries, and the distance from the center of the EupMyeonDong to the public library as a straight line was measured. The threshold distance was 2km because 2km indicated that a public library would be accessible within 20 minutes of the sidewalk in its area. The results found that the effects of the visiting factors (program, space, use, book, and librarian) on public library accessibility differed from the effects of population and distance on accessibility.

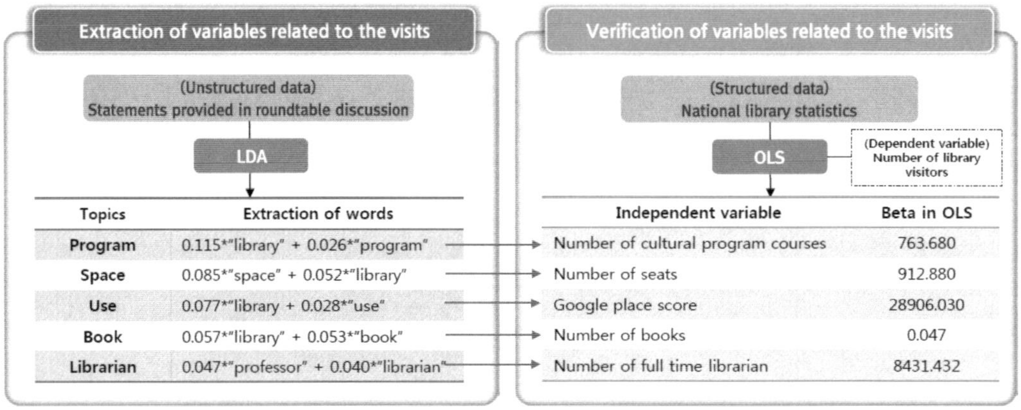

Figure 2. Result of Extracting Variable of User's Visit to Public Libraries

Figure3 illustrates the result of spatial accessibility to public libraries in Seoul between gravity model and 2SFCA model. For index comparisons between different models, the index was standardized by a scoring method among linear transformation methods. In the gravity model, accessibility was mainly determined by the libraries' physical locations. The more libraries there were the better accessibility. However, accessibility predicted from the visiting factors was influenced by number of visitors. To interpret these results, the 147 libraries were categorized by number of visitors and organized into four clusters using the ward method. Visualization using GIS found that accessibility was better for the libraries with good supply factors. In case of Seoul, the libraries with high attractiveness scores were concentrated in the center of Seoul, indicating a regional variation among libraries.

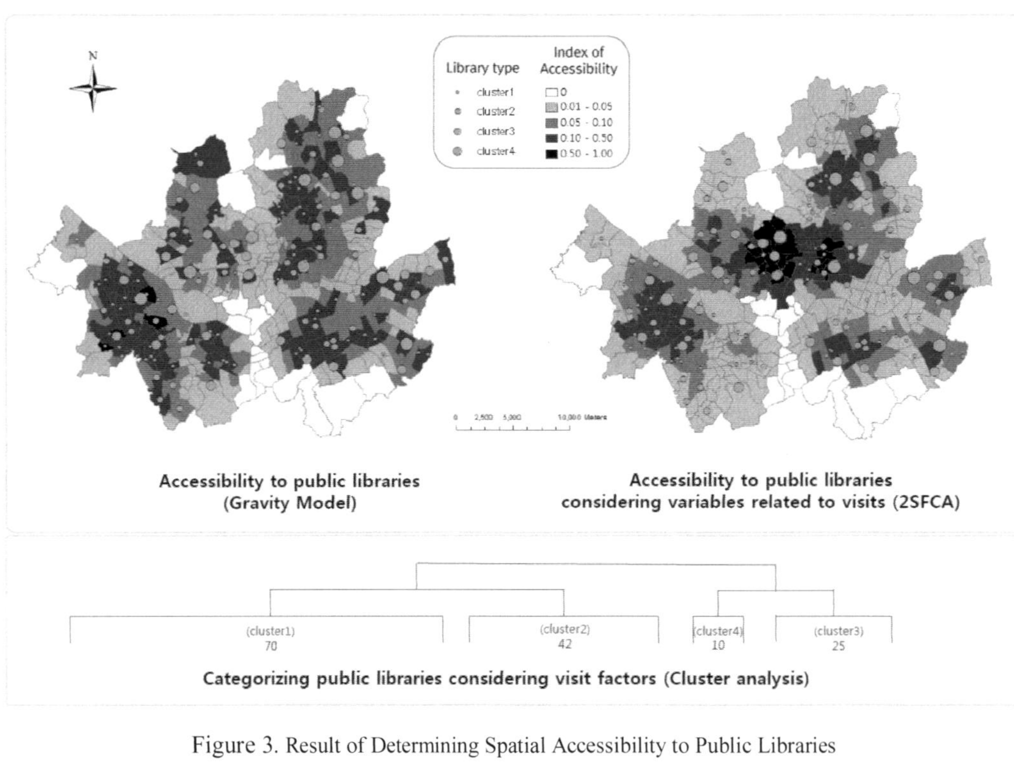

Figure 3. Result of Determining Spatial Accessibility to Public Libraries

5. CONCLUSION

Relocating a public facility is difficult after it has been built and established. Therefore, it is difficult to improve accessibility unless a new facility is built. However, when the attractiveness of a library increases, accessibility improves because of the positive influence of attractiveness on visitors' desires to visit it, even if a location is somewhat inconvenient.

This study extracted the determinants of users' visits to public libraries and analyzed the libraries' spatial accessibility by conceptualizing ability to provide the facility as supply factor. Future research will include aggregated units to improve the precision of the results and use road network data instead of straight-line distance to examine the effects of public transportation.

ACKNOWLEDGEMENT

This study was supported by the research funding of the project on the development of big data management, analysis, and service platform technology for the national land spatial information research project of the Ministry of Land, Infrastructure, and Transport (18NSIP-B081023-05).

REFERENCES

David M Blei, 2012. Probabilistic topic models. *Communications of the ACM*, Vol. 55, No. 4,pp77–84.

Gary Higgs, 2004. A literature review of the use of gis-based measures of access to health care services. *Health Services and Outcomes Research Methodology*, Vol. 5, No.2,pp119–139.

Handy, S.L. et al, 1997, Measuring accessibility: an exploration of issues and alternatives, *Environment and Planning A*, Vol. 29,pp.1175-1194

Joseph, A. et al, 1984, *Accessibility and Utilization: Geographical Perspectives on Health Care Delivery*, Harper and Row, New York, USA.

Kwan, M.P. et al, 2003, Individual accessibility revisited: Implications for geographical analysis in the twenty-first century, *Geographical Analysis*, Vol.35, No. 4,pp 341-353.

Luo, W. et al, 2004, Using a GIS-based floating catchment method to assess areas with shortage of physicians, *Health&Place*, Vol. 10,pp1-11.

O'Kelly, M.E. and Horner, M.W., 2003, Aggregate accessibility to population at the county level: U.S. 1940-2000, *Journal of Geographical Systems*, Vol.5,pp5-23.

Palmer, E.S., 1981, The effect of distance on public library use: A literature survey, *Library Research*, Vol. 3, No.3, pp315-334.

Park, S.J., 2012, Measuring public library accessibility: A case study using GIS, *Library & Information Science Research*, Vol. 34, No. 1,pp13-21.

Susan, L.H. et al, 1997. Measuring accessibility: an exploration of issues and alternatives. *Environment and planning A*, Vol. 29, No. 7,pp1175–1194.

A METHODOLOGY TO IDENTIFY EXTREMIST DISCOURSE ON SOCIAL MEDIA

Frédérique Segond, Sara Monaci, Muntsa Padro and Teodora Dobre
VISEO/INALCO; Politecnico di Torino; Eloquant; MVNIA, Italy

ABSTRACT

Syria may be the first conflict in which a large number of foreign supporters have been documenting their involvement in conflict in real-time and where, in turn, social media represents an essential source of information and inspiration to them. In their minds, social media is no longer just virtual: it has become an essential facet of what happens on the ground. Beyond this function, social media platforms play a substantial role in disseminating terrorist propaganda and then in supporting the process of jihadist radicalization that can have various results, including the recruitment of foreign fighters who leave their country to join ISIS. These recent trends bring our attention in particular to the use of Twitter in spreading extremist messages specifically to reach a European target and on the ways to effectively fight against this phenomenon. This paper mainly aims to present a methodology and an operative tool for understanding terrorist group recruitment discourse strategy in order to put into place a counter propaganda campaign. After determining some criteria and indicators representing strategic keys in terrorist online recruitment, this study develops an IT tool to analyze a large amount of social media data. This IT tool implements the determined criteria based upon the semantic analysis method.

KEYWORDS

Online Extremism, Social Media, Semantic Processing, Foreign Fighters

1. THE ROLE OF SOCIAL MEDIA IN THE FOREIGN FIGHTERS RECRUITMENT PROCESS

Syria may be the first conflict in which a large number of foreign supporters have been documenting their involvement in conflict in real-time and where, in turn, social media represents an essential source of information and inspiration to them. Between 2013 and 2015 social media platforms and especially Twitter played a substantial role in disseminating terrorist propaganda and in supporting the recruitment of foreign fighters who joined ISIS. The presence of foreign fighters coming from Western countries, is a steadily growing element in Middle Eastern conflicts. A study of The Soufan Group (TSG) highlights that in September 2015 the number of foreign fighters in Syria was around 30,000 people from over 100 states. This figure had more than doubled compared to the 12,000 foreign fighters from 81 countries estimated in June 2014 (The Soufan Group 2015, 5). Most of the foreign combatants who join IS and other terrorist groups in Syria and Iraq come from the Middle East and Maghreb. Considering specifically the numbers of European foreign combatants, The Soufan Group analysis showed that France is the leading country from which they leave (1,700), followed by Germany and the UK (760), Belgium (470), Sweden and Austria (300), Netherlands (220), Spain (133), Denmark (125) and Italy (87) (The Soufan Group 2015, 7-10).

Several studies have shown that numerous online platforms and social media apps (e.g. Twitter, Facebook, Tumblr, Ask.fm, WhatsApp, PalTalk) are used by terrorist groups to create a persistent presence for jihadist propaganda online. which is aimed at persuading new followers and even attracting aspiring fighters Social media platforms enable individuals to create contents and documents and to interact with other users. Moreover, online platforms provide an opportunity for using multimedia materials to easily reach a wide and expansive target audience (see Prucha and Fisher 2013; Klausen 2015).

With particular reference to Twitter, Berger and Stern (2015) analyzed how IS strategically used this social platform between April and June 2014 with the application "The Dawn of Glad Tidings", which enabled its users to receive up-to-date news about ISIS progress. The application could also take control of a consenting user's account to send out tweets automatically. Though the application was suspended by Twitter in late summer 2014, the number of pro-IS accounts in 2014 and 2015 remained significant, further enriched by thousands of bots, namely computer software pieces that act like actual Twitter users, tweeting and re-tweeting specific contents. The ISIS Twitter Census, funded by Google, carried out a study in partnership with the Center for Middle East Policy (U.S.) on Twitter profiles that supported Islamic State during the period 2014-2015. They analyzed 46,000 pro-IS profiles on Twitter between Syria and Iraq, and focused on 20,000 accounts to create a general demographic snapshot of Twitter's IS population. The researchers observed that much of IS's social media-based success can be attributed to a relatively small group of hyperactive users in the range of 500-2,000 accounts, which tweet in concentrated high volume bursts.

It is worth now questioning the roles and functions held by those who disseminate propaganda contents via the Internet. They may be affiliated to terrorist organizations operating officially within the framework of its communication strategy, or they may be external supporters. With particular reference to the foreign fighter recruitment process, some authors have identified the "so-called 'disseminator' accounts [of Twitter] which are run by sympathetic individuals who sometimes lend moral and political support to those in the conflict" (Neumann at al. 2014, 15). The disseminators are external supporters who spread information, photos of battles in real-time, new videos and official statements. Their importance is due to a number of specific abilities: they are able to translate official messages from Arabic into English, thereby also reaching a Western audience. Secondly, disseminators provide a general and broader view of events that occur in Syria. In fact, compared to foreign fighters, who have a limited view linked to their locality, disseminators can use a wider range of sources concerning what happens in all rebel zones. Finally, disseminators have the actual opportunity to interact with their followers, gaining their confidence, explaining ambiguities or engaging in discussions (Neumann at al. ib., 17-18). In addition to these people, who mainly use Twitter accounts, other individuals act as guides and source of inspiration, using Facebook as the main online platform. These people are 'cheerleaders' who provide encouragement, justification and religious legitimacy for fighting in Syria. In fact, their Facebook pages usually focus on the syrian conflict, showing videos of battle, pictures of the battlefield and motivational statements for fighters. Moreover, there are the "so-called 'facilitators', people with the necessary contacts to open a privileged channel with a specific jihadist group.. Facilitators introduce new followers and aspiring European jihadists to members of small cells scattered throughout Europe and belonging to the informal network named Sharia4.

2. IDENTIFYING TWITTER PROFILES: A METHODOLOGY

In such a context, SAFFRON aims at building an advanced IT tool, SafApp, able to identify and analyze online textual content related to potential online recruitment of European foreign fighters. This article presents the methodology used and the linguistic processing of identified sources to fill the general information model. The SafApp tool performed the selection of the relevant Twitter profiles automatically. However, in order for the tool to derive accurate results, in the preliminary stage, a first set of data was introduced via individual selection performed by the team of researchers involved in the project. The data resulted from a combined conceptual and pragmatic approach. The structural framework was provided via a field literature review, focused on a multidisciplinary understanding of cultural, behavioral and discourse markers that can indicate the emergence of a radicalization process and that can prove relevant in the early detection of radicalization and foreign fighters' recruitment.

All conceptual criteria were subsequently translated into a questionnaire submitted to an Intelligence and Security Experts Working Group (ISEWG) specifically identified to offer support to the SAFFRON project. The ISEWG included practitioners, experts and psychologists working in the field of radicalization and terrorism who constantly guided and offered feedback to the research team. As a result of this process, the specific methodology included (1) a review of scientific literature with regard to radicalization early warning indicators, (2) constant inquiry and consultation with experts and practitioners in counterterrorism and, last but not least, (3) direct observation effected by research team members on site on the daily routine of the experts and practitioners that agreed to offer guidance to the needs and requirements of everyday open source intelligence collection. Finally, the selection was performed with the help of content analysis and following a step by step gradual risk scaling model. To create the risk scaling and detection model researchers used searching sequences relevant for violent radicalization. Results showed a series of alternative accounts out of which, based on the image displayed by the avatar, the account public content and displayed connections, a series of accounts were chosen for further search. The "Following" list was also analyzed for relevant details. Criteria used in the selection include: the meaning and resonance of the online adopted name, the images used as avatar and the presentations of own account holder, as well as suggestions of a radical mind frame established via content and emotion analysis of the public posts (non-cumulative conditions). Furthermore, studying the "Following" list of the mentioned accounts has allowed the identification of other accounts with strong radical content, which were then also fed into the testing process. Content and emotion analysis combined with an analysis of the related social networks created around posts and comments of the above-mentioned accounts indicated the possibility that an information network might exist between a series of account owners with a significant (violent) extremist content. As a result of the findings, the methodology was applied for further testing within the app format.

2.1 Keywords

In order to automate, to a high extent, the merger and evaluation of available information using computation tools so as to provide insight on radicalization trends, a basic requirement for the development of the tool is a collection of basic keywords, interconnected clusters of words and a set of relationships established among them. The semantic grounding enforces a logical structure and provides an ontology for foreign fighter's recruitment roles and types of interactions. To generate an ontology, the primary objective of this particular task was to construct a core distinct semantic architecture based on recurrent vocabulary used by terrorist propaganda sources and consumers in creating the terrorist master-narrative. This architecture provides an adequate, relevant and sufficient knowledge for the description and analysis of online recruitment and radicalization, from early stage propaganda, alienation, conversion to online violent content and manifestation of availability to join terrorist groups. In identifying the most relevant keywords used by terrorist organizations to disseminate radical content, we used both a quantitative and qualitative approach and grouped the keywords into clusters, based on the associated message they conveyed.

For the quantitative analysis, the database used to identify the communicational patterns of the terrorist networks consisted in data collected from static sources such as "Dabiq" and "Inspire". Based on a frequency analysis, we extracted from the compiled database the most used keywords and semantic constructions and grouped them based on the magazine issue that they originated from. The list was filtered, as it contained (1) connection words and nouns with no relevant connection to radical and (2) words that could have been used in a variety of contexts non-related to radical propaganda and that could have resulted into false-positive results. The qualitative approach consisted in organizing the above-mentioned ISEWG, thus creating the framework for discussion and consultation with representatives that have direct responsibilities in the field of preventing and countering terrorist threats. The researchers developed a questionnaire focused on identifying the requirements of the practitioners, as well as identifying a model of their activity log, in order (1) to harmonize the operational needs of the practitioners with the capabilities of the SafApp, as well as (2) to increase the efficiency of the tool in what regards the workflow. The questionnaire was applied to practitioners whose professional tasks include monitoring online activities in connection to terrorism and radicalization. In order to avoid any institutional or cultural biases, the questionnaire was send to other security and intelligence organizations of the EU member states. Under anonymity protection, four services agreed to contribute and provided the research team with answers to the questionnaire above-mentioned. The results were analyzed, filtered and integrated, limiting the list to a set of specific words, which are defined more precise. They were further correlated with the quantitative results obtained in the first stage, which confirmed that the results obtained match both their professional routine and need for support.

The OSINT experts provided insight into the type of contexts the keywords may appear, as they made a clear distinction of the two main stages of the online radicalization process: (1) promoting an idealistic image of the Muslim faith, seeking to attract Muslims or determine to convert non-Muslims, through messages posted on public profiles and open/public online communities, (2) promoting a violent discourse towards the "enemies of Islam", usually within closed online communities or dedicated groups and profiles. The keywords identified were grouped on 22 thematic clusters (e.g. Greatness of Islam, Conversion, Migration, etc.). The clusters, as they were defined by the research team, sought to be mutually exclusive and contain as few words as possible that can generate false positive results. To facilitate the calibration of the searching process, online sources promoting radical content (e.g. archives and collections of non-attributed radical messages like archive.org, justpaste.it) were manually checked and filtered to identify relevant contexts for each cluster of words.

2.2 Indicators

The list of clusters represents a preliminary model of knowledge structure that can be useful for practitioners in the field of counterterrorism. However, it lacks any analytical insight and increases the efficiency of the practitioner only quantitatively, in the sense of a faster retrieval of information and can generate false positive results if are not correlated with other information regarding that user (e.g. locations and/or names pertained to terrorism are also used as regular hashtags by journalists and non-radical media outlets). Therefore, the research team developed a framework of concepts and relationships established among them, to enable efficiency in identification of means and patterns of online recruitment and radical content online. The team developed a list of indicators corresponding to the radicalization process, varying from interest manifested towards terrorism activities to posting hate speeches and inciting to violence. For a better understanding, each indicator was structured as a partonomy that provided the basis for correlating the clusters of words using logical operators. As the indicators and associated subclasses and clusters do not occur in mutual exclusive situations and there are cases in which one cluster is consistent with several indicators, it was necessary to formulate a structure of relationships established between clusters of words and indicators in a matrix-based form. To generate added-value to the analysis, the Saffron tool was then technically structured to trigger alerts, to be then further validated by the practitioners, based on their own individual assessment.

3. SAFAPP TOOL

The SafApp tool (Derbas et al. 2017) is based on semantic and machine learning technologies and allows to semantically analyze a large number of social media textual data and to detect automatically the criteria and indicators, previously defined, representing online recruitment. SafApp comprises four principal steps: (1) Data acquisition from identified sources, (2) Filtering the input data to remove irrelevant and noisy data, (3) Linguistic analysis to identify indicators representing strategy keys in terrorist online recruitment information, (4) Visualization allowing users to explore, discover and visualize the enriched and analyzed data. For data collection, two crawlers have been developed to collect information from target social media sources, which might contain relevant information: one for Twitter and one for web sites based on WordPress. Each crawler extracts textual content (posted messages) and the available associated metadata (e.g. publication time, author, localization). Since the crawling step extracts a huge amount of information, a filtering step needs to be implemented to retain only the potentially interesting text. We addressed this task as a classification problem (related or nor related to radicalization) using the Radom Forest algorithm.

Once relevant content has been filtered, it serves as input to the semantic module, which implements several types of linguistic analysis in order to extract as much information as possible from different sources:

Named Entity Recognition: consists in detecting in sentences groups of words referring to an entity and to determine the type of the entity (person name, organization, location, time expression, etc.)

Terminology detection: detects in sentences words or groups of words that belong to the clusters presented in section 2.1 and associates the semantic cluster to them.

Topic Categorization: consists in assigning to each text one or more pre-defined categories which represent its topic. This categorization will help us to perform a domain-based information extraction. The categories have been defined to match the indicators established by the sociologists and the intelligence searchers but also considering the set of topics extracted automatically from the crawled data via topic modeling (Blei et al, 2003).

3.1 Graphical User Interface

SafApp offers several ways of manipulating and exploring the semantically enriched data to support their understanding and evolution in time. Users can see details of each message, user who posted them, filter them based on different criteria, etc. Those are the main functionalities:

Interactions: SafApp provides a view of the interactions (shares, replies or just "simple" messages). Users can click on an interaction to see the message thread details with the corresponding semantic labels. The linguistic features which helped to detect semantic labels are highlighted. An extensive search tool is also available to allow users to filter interactions. The list of interactions can be sorted based on the number of likes or retweets, shares or on the creation date.

Social users and social users interactions: fine-grained view on the net of social users is provided. Summary information is presented about each user, for instance the number of messages they have posted. Sorting and searching is available on this page, in a similar manner to the messages page. The tool also provides an analysis of the set of social users and their interactions using different aggregating visualization methods.

Word cloud of semantic labels: This visualization provides an aggregated view of the output of the "terminology detection" step (shares, simple messages, likes). The more a label occurs in the text the bigger the font is. The user can click on any of the displayed semantic label to access the detailed list of interactions carrying this label through the linguistic analysis performed by the system.

Analytical interactions network: This view draws a graphical representation of the social user's network based on the different way of interaction. For each user with whom the current social user interacts by replying, liking or sharing a message, a bubble is shown with the user's name. The bigger the bubble, the more interactions there are with this user.

4. CONCLUSIONS

Providing an analysis of the latest tendencies in the online radicalization, taking into account the large scale use of social media resources used by terrorist organization in promoting violent messages has been the main aim of our work. We described how the Saffron project contributes to the development of automatic semantic analysis instruments that aim to detect and understand online textual content related to potential recruitment of foreign fighters by terrorist groups. The added value of the IT tool, SafApp, stands in its ability to identify in a timely fashion both internet activities of direct and indirect recruitment of foreign combatants and the signals (weak and strong) that we can find online and that can point at radicalized individuals. Furthermore, in addition to supporting the automatic analysis of social networks, SafApp is technically structured to contribute, in a concrete and timely manner, to increasing the understanding of radical groups, cells and patterns of online behavior. It also provides practitioners with an easy to use tool that automatically triggers alerts and therefore makes their work significantly more efficient. Alerts are then validated by the practitioners, based on their own individual assessment. Secondly, SAFFRON proposes a semantic analysis software that focuses on the content disseminated publicly on social media platforms such as Twitter and blogs. Having as end-user/beneficiaries national and international institutions responsible with ensuring security, the software aims to firstly, efficiently identify the content related to potential recruitment of foreign fighters and secondly, generate alerts to practitioners concerning their potential to act violently.

REFERENCES

Blei D.M., A. Y. Ng, and Jordan M. I., 2003. Latent dirichlet allocation. J. Mach. Learn. Res., 3: 993-1022.

Derbas, N., Segond, F., Padró, M., Dusserre, E., Dobre, T., Monaci, S., & Mastrobuoni, G., 2017. Semantic analysis supporting de-radicalisation. In Database and Expert Systems Applications (DEXA),. IEEE

Klausen, J. (2015). Tweeting the Jihad: Social media networks of Western foreign fighters in Syria and Iraq. Studies in Conflict & Terrorism, 38(1), 1-22.

Neumann P. et al. 2014. #Greenbirds: Measuring Importance and Influence in Syrian Foreign Fighter Networks. Report by ICSR, King's College. Available from: http://icsr.info/wp-content/uploads/2014/04/ICSR-Report-Greenbirds-Measuring-Importance-and-Influence-in-Syrian-Foreign-Fighter-Networks.pdf

Prucha N. and Fisher A., 2013. Tweeting for the caliphate: Twitter as the new frontier for jihadist propaganda. CTC Sentinel 6, (6): 19-23

Stern J. and Berger J. M. 2015. ISIS: The state of terror. London, UK: HarperCollins.

The Soufan Group. 2015. FOREIGN FIGHTERS. An Updated Assessment of the Flow of Foreign Fighters Into Syria and Iraq. Available from: http://soufangroup.com/wp-content/uploads/2015/12/TSG_ForeignFightersUpdate3.pdf..

EXTRACTION OF CLASSIFICATION MODELS USING A BEE SWARM APPROACH

Sadjia Benkhider and Mohamed Badache
Computer Sciences Department; University of Sciences and Technology, PoBox 32 EL Alia, Bebe Ezzouar, Algiers 16111

ABSTRACT

This paper provides a metaheuristic-based of classification rules. Indeed, The classification problem is a data mining task which belongs to the NP-Complete problem class. This is a combinatorial problem which may find good solutions using metaheuristics approaches. We are interested in adapting the Bee Swarm Optimisation (BSO) algorithm which is relatively a new metaheuristic. Our aim is to discover a classification model. This BSO approach already gave some interesting solutions for the well-known SAT problem and we will show the efficiency of the method for the Problem of the Extraction of Classification Rules also.

KEYWORDS

Data Mining, Supervised Classification, Rules, Michigan Optimisation, Bee Swarm

1. INTRODUCTION

Currently, possibilities to collect a large amount of data in various fields of science, economy, industry and others are very various and specific. This is made possible and efficient because of the rapid and efficient progress of computerization and digitization techniques. These data can provide a valuable resource for the discovery of new knowledge and decision support.

To understand, analyze and potentially use this huge amount of data, a multidisciplinary approach, called "data mining" has been proposed for this challenge. One area that is gaining much attention in the field of Data mining is the supervised classification task, in which we see two distinguished groups: non rules-based classification methods and those rule-based. The methods of rule-based classification derive from explicit knowledge data directly. This is why users of these classifiers can often assess the accuracy and utility of the discovered knowledge.

Unfortunately the problem of the classification rules extraction belongs to the NP-complete class. The meta heuristics are a set of methods used to solve optimization problems considered difficult.

Many studies using metaheuristic techniques to address this problem have been published. One may cite (Freitas et Al, 1998), (Tan, K. C et al, 2006), (Freitas, A. A. and Holden, N., 2008), (Tan, K.C. et al, 2010), (Benkhider , S. et al, 2013 a), (Benkhider , S. et al , 2013 b).

In this paper, we are interested to solve this problem using an algorithm called "Bee Swarm Optimisation" (BSO) which is based on the life of bees, developed by (Drias, H. et Al , 2005).

Our paper is organized as follows: section 2 describes previous works for the Classification Rules Extraction Problem. The third section presents some details about the BSO approach and is followed by a fourth one which presents details of our adapted BSO approach to the problem of classification rules extraction. Section 5 gives details about our tests and some experimental results obtained. The paper will be concluded in section 6 and will present some future works which we think are promising.

2. PREVIOUS WORKS FOR THE CLASSIFICATION PROBLEM

The classification is one of the most studied tasks in data mining. It consists in identifying a class, to which an object belongs out of its descriptive features (Berry, Linoff, 2004) (Freitas et Al, 1998). It includes several application domains such as human activities, like business particularly banking and risks analysis, diagnosis in medicine, computer security and is mainly appropriate for decision-making problems. The classification task is divided into two groups: non-rule-based and rule-based classification techniques.

Rule-based classifiers are more comprehensible (Tan et al., 2006)] when application domains necessitate comprehensibility. The Rule-based classifiers are divided into two groups: Decision Trees and some heuristic techniques. Among the most popular existing decision trees methods, we find CHAID (G. V. Kass (1980), CART (Breiman et Al, 1984) and C4.5 (J.R. Quinlan, 1993).

Heuristic techniques are commonly used to extract classification rules. Among these techniques, we may cite: Decision Table (R. Kohavy, 1995), OneR (Budhinat and Derry, 1995) which is also a simple greedy classification heuristic. Recently, several works have been developed using hybridizations of metaheuristics to extract classification rules. In this connection the studies of (K.C. Tan , Q Yu et J.H. Ang , 2006) , (A.A. Freitas, N. Holden 2008), (K.C. Tan, J.H. Ang, A.A. Mamun, 2010), (S. Benkhider , A. R. Baba ali, H. Drias 2013), (S. Benkhider , H. Drias, 2013) are worth mentioning.

3. DESCRIPTION OF THE ARTIFICIAL BEES IN THE BSO ALGORITHM

In the literature we find the "Artificial Bee Colony" (ABC) algorithm which is a relatively new swarm intelligent algorithm. ABC was proposed by Karaboga in Erciyes University of Turkey in 2005 (D. Karaboga, 2005).

The metaheuristic BSO was defined and proposed by Drias, Sadeg and Yahi in 2005 (H. Drias et Al, 2005) which is completely different than ABC.

BSO is based on the behavior of a swarm of artificial bees cooperating together to solve a problem in the same manner like natural bees in the process of food seeking. This algorithm finishes when a good solution is found or after a certain number of iterations. The BSO algorithm is illustrated by the following steps.

```
  begin
  Let Sref be the solution found by BeeInit;
  While not condition of stop do
   begin
     insert Sref in taboo list;
     determine SearchArea from Sref;
     affect a solution of SearchArea to
     each bee;
     for each Bee K do
     begin
       search starting with the solution
       affected to it;
       store the result in the tableDance;
     end;
     Choose the new solution of reference
     Sref;
   end;
end.
```

4. ADAPTATION OF THE BSO ALGORITHM TO THE PROBLEM OF CLASSIFICATION RULES EXTRACTION

To adapt the BSO algorithm for the extraction of classification rules, the following steps are to define:

- The Knowledge representation
- The trategy of identifying research areas
- The strategy of calculating the neighborhood.
- The evaluation function of a solution,
- The Sequential coverage algorithm to extract a classification rules set
- The performances of the classification model obtained using a Test Set.

In our works, we adapted the bee swarm algorithm to the classification rules extraction using a Michigan approach (Holland, 1978) which considers that a solution of the problem is a rule and consists in evaluating the rules each one on its own. This is using a whole pass of the algorithm to produce one optimized rule. We have adopted this approach because of its production of an accurate classifier knowing that only one rule is optimized at each time.

4.1 Knowledge Representation

In our works a rule presents the following form:

If A Then C = c

where A is the antecedent part of the rule which includes several premises and we adopted an integer representation of a solution which is a rule. This last is represented using a vector of integer values which contains n attributes that characterize the considered dataset for classification. This representation is well described in (Benkhider, S. et Al, 2013 a)

Example: Let us Consider a training set where the instances are characterized by 7 attributes. Our adopted coding is illustrated by Figure 1.

S1

0=0	1=2	0=0	0=0	1=5	1>6	0=0

S2

1=3	0=0	0=0	1<3	0=0	1=8	0=0

Figure 1. Illustration of the rules coding

The first vector represents the following rule

R1: IF Att(2) = 2 AND Att(5) = 5 AND Att(6) > 6 THEN Class =C

And the second one represents the rule

R2 : IF Att(1) = 3 AND Att(4) < 3 AND Att(6) =8 THEN Class =C

4.2 Search Area Determination

In this section we made 3 strategies for determining regions to fully explore the search space for each bee. These strategies respectively called (modulo, next, continuous), are detailed in (Drias, H. et Al, 2005)

4.3 Neighborhood Determination

- Case of nominal attributes: For each solution S the computation of its neighbors is performed as follows: for each value of a nominal attribute, we add 1 or substract 1 to the active attribute and we take the first value of the attribute when this last is not active.
- Case of the numeric attributes:

We replace the value of the attribute by a random chosen of a value belonging to its domain of values.

To generate a new value of an operator in a premise we choose randomly a code of operator from the four operators =, <,>, ≠.

4.4 Fitness Function

Each new generated solution has to be evaluated. In our case a solution is a classification rule. In previous works, we found several metrics to evaluate performances of classification rules. Among these metrics we are convinced that the Precision Rate and the maximum of coverage and the size of a rule are the metrics that may give good performances for a classification rule. So, our fitness function is expressed as follows:

Fitness(R) = a*(Number of covered instances / total number of instances) * b*(number of instances correctly classified by R/ number of instances covered by the rule R) – c*(size of a rule)

Where a, b and c are three parameters belonging to [0,1] and their sum equals 1.

4.5 Sequential Cover Algorithm

When all these steps have been modeled we have to implement the Sequential Cover Algorithm to extract our model of classification using the approach BeeSwarm BSO. This last may be summarized by the following pseudo code.

```
Begin
    RS = Ø
    For (each value C of the class attribute) do
        TS = {Training Set}
        While (Number of Instances with Class=C != 0) do
               - Perform BSO( ) to generate the best rule
                 BestRule
                - RS = RS U BestRule
                - TS = TS - {the covered training instances  by
                BestRule)
        end do
     end do
    SORT RS by decreasing quality of rules
    Return (RS)
End
```

When the best rules have been found by the BSO Search they constitute the classification model. This last has to be checked using a Test Set which is a set of new instances. The model has to predict the class for each Test instance.

With the aim to show the efficiency of our approach we present in the following section the different results of tests using different UCI benchmarks (C.L. Blake, C.J Merz 1998).

5. TESTS AND RESULTS

Our tests have been conducted on several UCI Benchmarks. Table 1 presents the used datasets in our tests.

Table 1. Used benchmarks of the UCI to tests

Datasets	Number of Instances	Number of attrib	Number of classes
IRIS	5	150	3
Hepatitis	20	155	2
Breast-cancer	10	286	2
Tic-Tac-Toe	10	958	2
Car	7	1728	4
Zoo	18	101	7
Pocker-Hand	11	25010	10

In order to show the efficiency of our approach we made comparisons with 3 classifiers DOEA (K.C. Tan, Q. Yu et J.H. Ang, 2006), PSO/ACO (A.A. Freitas N. Holden 2008) and GA_NRIP (Privanka Sharm, 2014) which consists in a genetic algorithm GA with Non-Random-Initial-Population to extract classification rules. These three metaheuristic-based approaches extract a set of classification rules as well as our approach.

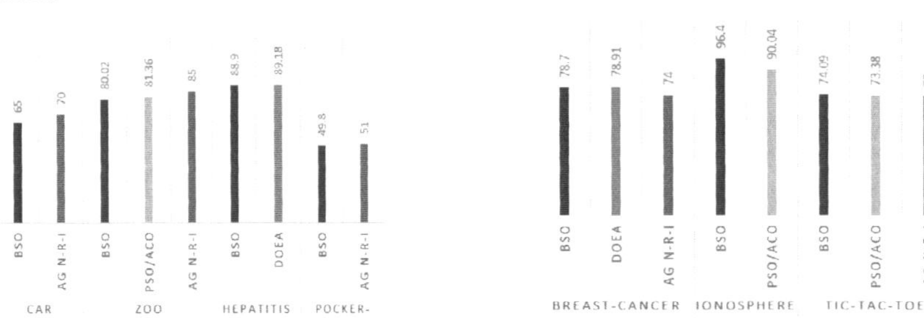

Figure 2. Illustration of the performances of our classifier vs 3 others

When observing (Figure 2) the obtained means by our approach BSO and in comparison with the 3 others approaches one may notice that BSO has the best or the equivalent rate of correctly classified datasets instances. We also notice that the 3 other classifiers are hybrid metaheuristics-based when our approach based on BSO has not been hybrided with an another metaheuristic. The efficiency of the approach is good with no hybridizations.

6. CONCLUSION

This paper deals with the classification rules mining using a relatively new metaheuristic called Bee Swarm Optimistaion (BSO). We studied this approach and its parameters and showed its efficiency when applied to a complex problem like the knowledge discovery. The two important operations (determination search areas with several strategies and neighborhood search) provided by BSO, permit to improve the solution quality. Indeed BSO gave us good and promising rates of correct classification and a small number of rules when applied to several datasets of the UCI. The obtained rates of correct classification are better or equivalent to those obtained by DOEA, PSO/ACO and GA_NRIP which are hybrid metaheuristics while BSO is a simple metaheuristic. The hybridization of BSO to a genetic algorithm as a local search to produce a memetic algorithm may give excellent performances in terms of accuracy and comprehensibility of the obtained classifiers.

REFERENCES

Drias, H. et al, 2005. Cooperative Bee Swarm for solving the Maximum Weighted Satisfiability Problem. Computational Intelligence and Bioinspired Systems, pp. 318-325.

Berry, M. and Linoff, G.,2004. Data Mining: Techniques for Marketing, Sales and Customer Relation Ship Management, *John Willey Publishing*.

Freitas, A.A. et al, 1998. A Survey of Evolutionary Algorithms for Data Mining and Knowledge Discovery, *Internal report of the university*.

Tan, K. C et al, 2006. A Dual-Objective Evolutionary Algorithm for Rules Extraction in Data Mining', Computational Optimization and Applications, Vol. 34, pp. 273-294, Springer: Netherland.

Kass, G.V., 1980. An Exploratory Technique for Investigating Large Quantities of Categorical Data. Applied Statistics, vol. 29, No. 2, pp. 119–127.

Breiman, L. et al, 1984. Classification And Regression Trees, Wadsworth, Belmont CA. 1984.

Quinlan, J. R., 1995. C4.5: Programs for Machine Learning. Morgan Kaufmann, San Mateo, CA.

Kohavy, R., 1995. The power of decision tables, Machine Learning 1995: *8th EuropeanConference on Machine Learning, Greece*, SpringrVerlag.

Budhinat, G. and Derry, D.,1995. A Simple Enhancement to OneR Classification', available at http://goanna.cs.rmit.edu.au/~gjyati l/ Other Links/Documents/Iproved OneR Algorithm.

Freitas, A. A. and Holden, N., 2008. A Hybrid PSO/ACO Algorithm for discovering Classification Rules in Data Mining. *Journal of Artificial Evolution and Applications*, Hindawi Pub. Corporation, Article ID 316145.

Tan, K.C. et al, 2008. A memetic Evolutionary Search Algorithm with variable length chromosome for rule extraction. *Proceeding of the IEEE International Conference on Systems*, Man and Cybernetics SMC 2008.

Tan, K.C. et al, 2010. An evolutionary memetic algorithm for rule extraction, *Journal of Expert Systems with Applications*, Elsevier, pp 1302-1315.

Benkhider, S. et al, 2013 a. Evolutionary Approaches for the Extraction of Classification Rules. *International Journal of Applied Metaheuristics,* IGIGlobal.

Benkhider, S. et al, 2013 b. A New Memetic Approach for the Classification Rules Extraction Problem. *International Journal of Data Mining, Modeling and Management,* Special Issue on Evolutionary Computation and Related Metaheuristics, Inder Sciences Pub, Accepted on April 2011, published December 2013.

Karaboga, D., 2005. An idea based on honey bee swarm for Numerical Optimization. Technical Report-TR06.

Sharm, P., 2014. Discovery of Classification Rules using Genetic Algorithm with non-random Population initialization. *International Journal of Artificial Intelligence and Knowledge Discovery IJAIKD*, Vol. 4, No. 3.

Blake, C.L and Merz, C.J., 1998. Available at www.uci.edu/~mlearn/MLRepository.html., Irvine, CA University of California, Department of Information and Computer Science.

Holland. J.H. and Reitman, J.S., 1978, *Cognition Systems Based on Adaptive Algorithms*, in Pattern-Directed Inference Systems, D.A. Waterman and F. Hayes-Roth, Eds., Academic Press, New York, 1978.

VISUAL ANALYTICS IN THE PUBLIC SECTOR: AN ANALYSIS ON DIVERSITIES AND SIMILARITIES OF LONDON'S WARDS

Daqing Chen[1], Beatriz Martin Sanz[2] and Erlong Zhao[3]
[1]*School of Engineering, London South Bank University, London SE1 0AA, UK*
[2]*News UK, London SE1 9GF, UK*
[3]*School of Information Science and Technology, Northwest University, Xian 710127, China*

ABSTRACT

In this paper, an analysis is presented on the diverse and common characteristics in different geographical areas across London's wards with respect to certain social, economic, and welfare measures. 18 data sets from different sources are used in the study. The principal component analysis and the *k*-means cluster analysis have been applied by using SAS Enterprise Guide and Miner. Visual analytics has been implemented with Tableau to identify patterns and correlations among various measures. It has been found that a geographical distance or proximity does not necessarily indicate a significant difference or similarity between different areas on a given social and economic measure. The work suggests that collaborative management across all the London's council boroughs is meaningful.

KEYWORDS

Visual Analytics, Data Mining, Principal Component Analysis, *K*-Means Clustering Analysis, Inequality

1. INTRODUCTION

For more than two decades, a large amount of data from the public sector has been collected and accumulated to a massive scale. The data is rich involving various social and economic measures. Exploring and analyzing such as a data asset has been evidently crucial for the central and local governments to make tangible informed decisions in their strategic management processes (Syvajarvi and Stenvall, 2010).

As one of the most unique, multiple-cultural cities in the world and the global business and finance hub, London has posed a great challenge to the local authorities in terms of how to make London's social and business environment stabilized, healthy, and sustainable. Inequality and poverty in London, for instance, is a long-established problem since the capital has been recognized as the most unequal city in the UK (Trust for London, 2015). This research presents a case study of identifying and analyzing the diverse characteristics in Greater London, aiming to provide some insight to help the central and local governments better understand the capital from multiple perspectives.

Geographically, London is currently divided into 33 Borough Councils. Each council constitutes several smaller areas known as wards, representing different electoral districts. There are 629 wards in total in London. These wards share some common features; however, each ward may its own characteristics as well. As such, completely different and diverse wards might be found within a borough. Understanding the diversity of London's wards and the major causes for the diversity will help the local authorities adopt appropriate strategies and policies to tackle problems.

18 data sets from different sources are used in the study. All the data is publicly accessible, and the data can be categorized into several groups by measure including demographics, economics, quality of life, crime, and accidents and emergencies. The principal component analysis (PCA) and the *k*-means clustering analysis have been employed in this study. Detailed analysis on different ward groups is provided along with a visualized presentation on a polygon map.

The reminder of this paper is organized as follows. Section 2 provides a brief literature review on the relevant works and findings. Section 3 gives a detailed account about the data collection and pre-processing, and how the PCA and the *k*-means cluster analysis have been conducted. The diverse characteristics and the common features of the wards are identified. Further in Section 4, a correlation analysis is presented to explore possible causes for the diversities and similarities. Finally, in Section 5, the main findings of this research are discussed with recommendations for future work.

2. BACKGROUND AND RELEVANT WORKS

Due to its political, social and economic importance, nationally and globally alike, London has always been a great research focus. Many case studies are available in the literature with regard to what impact that various social, economic, and welfare characteristics can have on the quality of living in London, such as, inequality, poverty, and housing affordability, to name just a few.

Boyne and Cole (1998) analysed the structure of London's local government and its evolution in the history for over a period of 150 years. Based on the Survey of Londoner's Living Standards in 1987, Harloe (1992) examined the association of certain social characteristics with housing inequalities in London. The research established that economic position, household structure, gender, and ethnic identity of the Londoners have shown having the strongest association with different housing circumstances, and the housing affordability concerned a wide range of people, not only the poorest classes.

Aldridge *et. al.* (2015) examined the characteristics of London's poverty in their report for Trust for London. They measured the role of different indicators relating to inequality, housing, employment, and education in all London's boroughs. On the other hand, some studies have concentrated on a particular London borough. Watt (2003) studied the impact caused by the labour market restructuring in the late 1990's on the employment circumstances of the local tenants in Camden. Arbaci and Rae (2012) conducted an analysis on mixed-tenure neighbourhoods in order to understand if the social and tenure-mixing policies have helped with alleviating deprivation effectively or had no positive effect at all. Using quantitative and qualitative longitudinal analyses, they concluded that diversification of housing tenure had positive effect on mitigating deprivation in London. Kirkbride *et. al.* (2014) studied whether the social deprivation and inequalities in East London were associated with the emergence of non-affective psychotic disorders. Hamnett and Butler (2011) have also placed their research emphasis on East London, studying how the distance from school has caused educational inequalities in the area. They argued that increasingly geography has been becoming the basis for rationing access to some forms of welfare including allocating secondary school places. The study on the NEET issues in London boroughs by Chen *et. al.* (2016) suggested that the median property price could be considered a simple and seemingly accurate indicator of areas likely to suffer from NEET.

Interestingly, Green (2012) applied a different approach to investigate the inequalities around London by choosing the London underground map to depict the distinct deprivation scores and provide a picture of a divided city, with areas wealthier than others.

In summary, much of the relevant research shown in the literature has been conducted at a borough level using multiple measures and exploratory data analysis techniques.

3. DATA COLLECTION, PRE-PROCESSING AND ANALYSIS

In this research we place our emphasis on identifying diversities and similarities across London's wards based on multiple measures to provide a detailed analysis at an appropriate granular level. SAS Enterprise Guide, SAS Enterprise Miner and Tableau have been used as the main tools in this study.

A group of data sets of year 2014 has been collected from different data repositories as shown in Table 1. Each of the data sets involves a single measure only and therefore represents a variable in the analysis.

A target data set has been created by integrating the original data sets, in which, there are 629 rows, each corresponding to a particular ward.

Table 1. Data sets and sources (Note: All measures are numerical data type)

Measure	Description	Measure	Description
Theme I: Demographics		Theme IV: Crime	
Population	London population	Crime	Number of total crimes
Births	Number of births	Deliberate Fires	Number of all deliberate fire incidents recorded by the London Fire & Emergency Planning Authority
Deaths	Number of deaths	Assault Incidents	Number of assaults attended by the London Ambulance Service.
Theme II: Economics		Weapon Injuries	Number of weapon injuries attended by the London Ambulance Service
Incapacity Benefit	Number of claimants	Drugs	Number of drug crimes in the Metropolitan Police Area.
Income Support	Number of claimants	Theme V: Accidents and emergencies	
Employment & Support Allowance	Number of claimants	Ambulance Attendance	Number of all incidents attended by the London Ambulance Service
Jobseekers Allowance	Number of claimants	Road Casualties	Number of road causalities
Houses Sold	Number of houses sold	Binge Drinking	Numbers of incidents where someone suffering from an alcohol related illness
House Price	Average house price in sterling		
Theme III: Quality of life			
Public Transport Accessibility (PTA)	A score represents an accurate accessibility, where 8 is the highest level of accessibility.		
Data sources: In general: http://data.london.gov.uk. Theme I: https://data.london.gov.uk/dataset/birth-and-death-rates-ward. Theme II: https://data.london.gov.uk/dataset/average-house-prices. Theme III: https://data.gov.uk/dataset/17136b47-d5b4-4df7-9e88-b9653b34a060/crime-rates-in-the-metropolitan-policearea-by-ward. Theme IV: https://data.london.gov.uk/dataset/crime-rates-metropolitan-police-area-ward. Theme V: https://data.london.gov.uk/dataset/ward-profiles-and-atlas.			

The analysis started with the PCA for dimensionality reduction of the target data set. The first three principal components have been recognized significant and the cumulative value of the eigenvalues of these components was 75%. Accordingly, each ward instance in the data set has been transformed and represented in the 3-dimensional principal component space. This transformation is essential, especially when the data set under consideration contains many variables and/or many of the variables are categorial data type with many distinct values.

Using the transformed data set, the *k*-means cluster analysis has been further performed with 5 centroids and range normalization for variable normalization. Note that outliers in the data set, if any, wouldn't be removed due to the context of the analysis that each instance is related to a specific ward. As such, a very small-sized cluster would be expected from the cluster analysis.

The statistics summary of the resultant clusters is given in Table 2. Each ward has been assigned to one of the 5 clusters uniquely. The clusters are also visualized on a polygon map as illustrated in Figure 1, where, as an example, the corresponding wards contained in Cluster 5 are highlighted.

For comparison purposes, the following discussions are based on the relative frequencies of the values in Table 1, i.e., the ratio of a given measure value to the total population in a cluster.

Table 2. Statistics summary of clusters (Note: OBS stands for number of observations)

Variable	Cluster 1 (OBS: 2)				Cluster 2 (OBS: 222)			
	Mean	Std Dev	Min	Max	Mean	Std Dev	Min	Max
Population	11460	511	11099	11821	15116	1992	11024	22100
Births	87	1	86	87	247	63	97	465
Deaths	48	11	40	55	72	19	38	133
Incapacity Benefit	103	11	95	110	131	28	75	235
Income Support	115	14	105	125	310	83	135	575

Employment Support	440	120	355	525	596	127	320	975
Jobseekers Allowance	203	88	140	265	369	103	175	805
House Price	1986482	537463	1606439	2366526	401366	194921	191601	1601476
House Sold	231	106	156	306	166	66	37	431
PTA	8	0	8	8	4	1	2	8
Crime	12419	1315	11489	13348	1427	570	699	4233
Deliberate Fires	6	1	5	6	9	8	0	67
Assault Incidents	403	92	338	468	64	28	15	197
Weapon Injuries	13	1	12	13	7	3	0	17
Drugs	575	112	495	654	99	79	21	754
Ambulance Attendance	7845	1291	6932	8758	2009	504	958	4030
Road Casualties	340	86	279	401	59	29	4	174
Binge Drinking	1144	187	1012	1276	63	51	6	348

Variable	Cluster 3 (OBS: 33)				Cluster 4 (OBS: 177)			
	Mean	Std Dev	Min	Max	Mean	Std Dev	Min	Max
Population	17477	3213	11667	24567	11056	1710	5283	15423
Births	260	65	109	367	155	48	54	324
Deaths	120	38	45	219	55	16	16	91
Incapacity Benefit	96	33	35	170	69	30	5	160
Income Support	216	102	45	440	134	71	0	335
Employment Support	420	163	110	815	307	132	20	671
Jobseekers Allowance	223	101	75	470	156	75	10	395
House Price	404228	150746	219095	862243	763924	663197	184410	5257978
House Sold	334	144	97	897	151	48	53	303
PTA	3	1	2	6	4	2	1	8
Crime	1728	1097	562	5371	796	440	231	3627
Deliberate Fires	9	8	2	46	3	3	0	20
Assault Incidents	60	46	10	200	24	14	4	91
Weapon Injuries	5	4	0	17	3	2	0	11
Drugs	96	99	21	464	42	34	6	286
Ambulance Attendance	2602	1433	1508	9465	1181	333	617	3155
Road Casualties	74	37	24	169	37	23	7	159
Binge Drinking	84	80	16	315	32	24	4	209

Variable	Cluster 5 (OBS: 195)			
	Mean	Std Dev	Min	Max
Population	13423	2153	7702	18066
Births	186	56	82	379
Deaths	90	26	21	166
Incapacity Benefit	74	31	15	185
Income Support	146	75	30	485
Employment Support	296	116	100	705
Jobseekers Allowance	158	74	40	370
House Price	431669	186606	192270	1330065
House Sold	217	69	71	486
PTA	3	1	1	8
Crime	804	327	281	2167
Deliberate Fires	5	5	0	28
Assault Incidents	25	14	2	77
Weapon Injuries	2	2	0	11
Drugs	38	26	6	154
Ambulance Attendance	1490	355	719	2687
Road Casualties	39	20	6	128
Binge Drinking	29	20	3	115

As shown in Figure 1, wards located in different boroughs can have some common characteristics although they are quite far one from the other geographically. For instance, the wards in Cluster 5 have the lowest crime rate (5.88%) across all the 5 clusters and this is coincided with the lowest rates of assault incidents, drugs relevant problems, and road causalities (0.19%, 0.28%, and 0.28%, respectively). On the other hand, a borough can have quite diverse wards although geographically those wards are close to each other. For example, Southwark Borough has wards belonging to Clusters 2, 4, and 5 as shown in Figure 2, where Cluster 2 has a much higher crime rate (9.44%) and higher rates of assault incidents, drugs relevant problems, and road causalities (0.44%, 0.62%, and 0.45%, respectively).

4. AREA OF ATTENTION

In this Section we examine the patterns of correlations among certain variables to provide indications for possible causes of diversities and similarities. It is worth noting that correlation not necessarily indicates a causation.

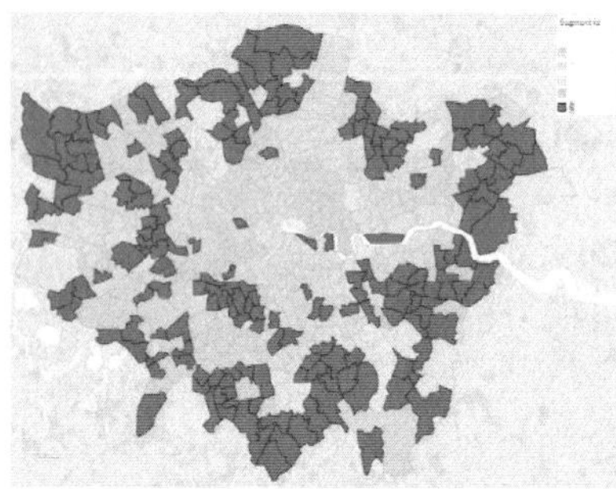

Figure 1. Examples of wards geographically located in different boroughs are grouped in a cluster

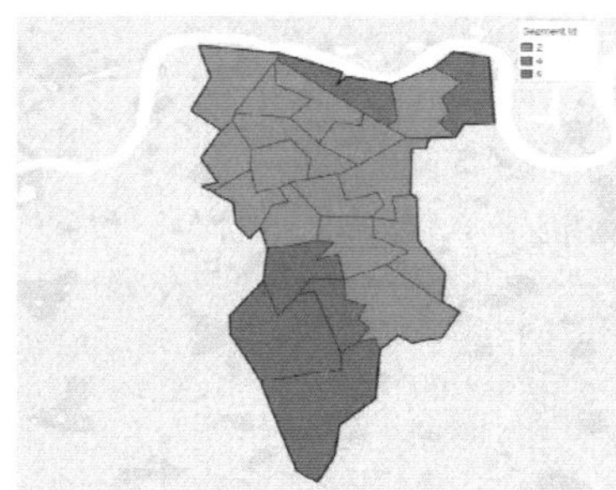

Figure 2. Example of a borough can have diverse wards that belong to different clusters

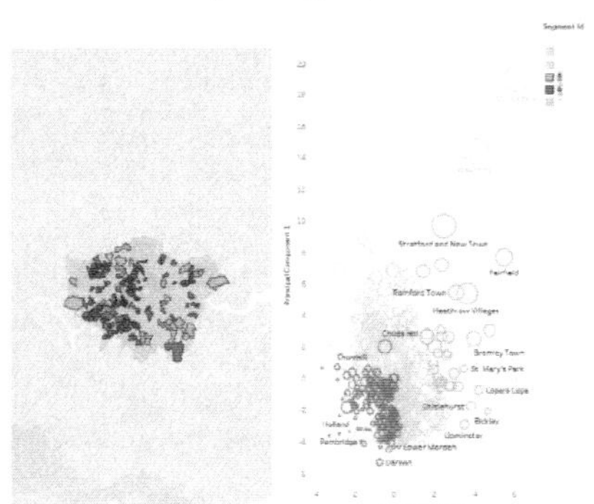

Figure 3. Variation in different clusters

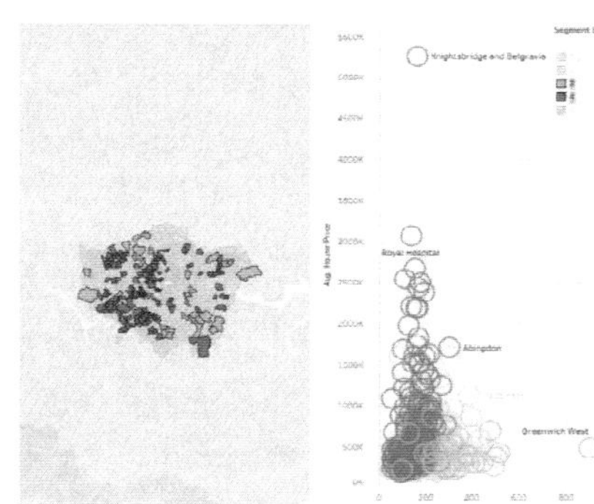

Figure 4. Variation of average home price vs. average number of homes sold

Unemployment related issues such as crime is always a major concern for the central and local governments and authorities. Checking with the clusters established, it can be seen that a higher employment support is usually coincided with a higher crime. However, there are some specific areas where a much higher ratio of crime to employment support can be evidenced. In general, all the groups have a relatively concentrated value in terms of the ratios of crime to employment support, drugs related problems, and assault incidents except for Cluster 3. This cluster only contains 33 wards and has the highest variation with all these ratios. The wards particularly concerned attributing to the variation are Stratford and New Town, Heathrow Villages, and Fairfield as shown in Figure 3. These wards have a much higher variation against the trend line compared with the other wards. In comparison, Cluster 3 has a very low variation with the ratios as indicated in Figure 3, where a bigger circle indicates a higher crime rate.

House price and the number of houses sold are always an important economic indicator reflecting collectively the popularity of an area, quality of life, social development and inequality, etc. In the clusters created, Cluster 4 has many wards that have a high ratio of average house price value to the average number of houses sold. On the other hand, Cluster 3 has many wards that have a comparably low ratio value for average house prices vs. houses sold, as displayed in Figure 4. Considering the patterns identified in Figures 3 and 4, it becomes evident that there is a clear and strong correlation among employment support, crime, house price and houses sold. Similarly, a correlation analysis can be performed with other measures and concerns.

For areas that have some common characteristics as reflected by certain measure values, it is advisable that probably similar strategies and policies could be adopted in practice for the local governments in their management processes. Therefore, an effective mechanism for collaborations and communications across all the boughs should be established to support regular and collective reviews on the wards.

5. CONCLUSION AND FUTURE WORK

In this paper, the diverse characteristics and common features across London's wards with respect to certain measures have been analyzed. It has been shown that a geographical distance or proximity does not necessarily indicate a significant difference or similarity between different areas with regards to a given social and economic measure. A council borough usually constitutes many diverse wards as reflected by certain measures. On the other hand, wards from different boroughs can have very similar social and economic features. This suggests that collaborative management across all the London's council boroughs is meaningful. The local authorities need to consider how to apply similar strategies to the wards that share some common features. A strong correlation among the measures has been established which may suggest implicitly causes for the diversities and similarities.

Future research includes analysis at a further refined granular level, the LSOA level (known as Lower Layer Super Output Areas). In addition, in order to examine how diversities and similarities have evolved over time, data from different years should be collected and analysed.

REFERENCES

Aldridge, H., Born, T.B., Tinson, A., and MacInnes, T., 2015. London's Poverty Profile. *https://www.npi.org.uk/files/5714/4533/2889/LPP_2015_report.pdf*

Arbaci, S. and Rae, I., 2012. Mixed-tenure Neighbourhoods in London: Policy myth or effective device to alleviate deprivation? *International Journal of Urban and Regional Research*, Vol. 37, No. 2, pp. 451–479.

Boyne, G.A., Cole, M., 1998. Revolution, Evolution and Local Government Structure: An Empirical Analysis of London. *Urban Studies*, Volume: 35, Issue: 4, pp.751-768.

Chen, D., Asaolu, B., and Qin, C., 2016. Big Data Analytics in the Public Sector: A Case Study of NEET Analysis for the London Boroughs, Proceeding of International Conference on Big Data Analytics. *Proceedings of Data Mining and Computational Intelligence*. Funchal, Madeira, Portugal, pp.171-178.

Green, M.A., 2012. Mapping Inequality in London: A different approach. *The Cartographic Journal*, Vol. 49, No. 3, pp. 247–255.

Hamnett, C. and Butler, T., 2011. 'Geography matters': the role distance plays in reproducing educational inequality in East London, *Institute of British Geographers Transactions*, Vol. 36, No. 4, pp. 479-500.

Harloe, M., 1992. Housing inequality and social structure in London. *Housing Studies*, Vol. 7, No. 3, pp. 189–204.

Kirkbride, J.B., Jones, P.B., Ullrich, S., and Coid, J.W., 2014. Social deprivation, inequality, and the neighborhood-level incidence of psychotic syndromes in East London. *Schizophrenia Bulletin*, Vol. 40, No. 1, pp.169–180.

Syvajarvi, A. and Stenvall, J., 2010. *Data Mining in Public and Private Sectors: Organizational and Government Applications*, IGI Global, Hershay, USA.

Trust for London, 2015. London's Poverty Profile, Inequality Indicators. *http://www.londonspovertyprofile.org.uk/indicators/topics/inequality/.*

Watt, P., 2013. Urban marginality and labour market restructuring: Local authority tenants and employment in an inner London borough. *Urban Studies*, Vol. 40, No. 9, pp. 1769–1789.

BRING YOUR OWN SECURITY RISKS WITH BYOD

Fenio Annansingh
York College, City University of New York, 94-20 Guy R Brewer Blvd, Jamaica, NY 11451, USA

ABSTRACT

One of the most significant challenges facing organizations today is the fact that corporate data is being delivered to mobile devices that are not managed by the IT department. This practice brings presents many new opportunities which businesses can exploit but present associated security risks. With these unmanaged devices, companies have less control and visibility, and fewer mitigation options when protecting against the risks of cyber-attacks. This research adopted a survey approach, which employs the use of questionnaires as the main data collection tool. From the questionnaire, descriptive data analysis is employed to synthesize, analyze and interpret the data. The results indicate the need for layered security protection between the organization and personal data, which focuses on balancing the thin line between empowering employees while enabling greater business agility.

KEYWORDS

Bring your own Device Policy, Mobile Devices, Risk Management, Security

1. INTRODUCTION

Bring Your Device or BYOD was first proposed by Intel's chief security and privacy officer Malcolm Harkins in 2009. After observing employees at Intel bringing their own mobile storage devices, Harkins proposed embracing this trend as a means of cutting cost and improving productivity (Zakaria, 2014). BYOD allows employees to use their technological devices to connect and access data or information from the employing organization. Companies with BYOD policies allow users to access systems network and services via their tablets, smartphones, and other devices.

Employees are highly dependent upon using any of portable devices such as laptops, iPad, smart-phone or even a USB stick for both work and personal purposes. The proliferation of these available devices and the growth of the Internet of things provides further motivation for companies to consider, including loss of standardization benefits, lack of control over hardware. To be competitive organizations are facilitating technological advancement by allowing employees to access corporate e-mails, documents, applications, and networks with technologies not corporately owned. These same devices are also used to conduct personal transactions such as internet banking, texting and engaging on social media. However such practices have been recognized as compromising the security of corporate information and end-user privacy as organizational critical and sensitive data can be downloaded onto the personal devices. Once this information leaves the organization, it is no longer under its control. Company-owned devices consist of security policies which are enforced and require the use of passwords and encryption of sensitive data. They, however, cannot implement these policies on machines the company does not own.

The threat of unauthorized access and knowledge leakage increases with the introduction of each unmanaged devices. Identifying the devices within the BYOD policy and thereby ensuring that potential areas of knowledge leakage are blocked and implementing measures which will ensure that unknown machines have limited access. Some of the other potential issues with allowing BYOD usage are:
Consequently, the research questions guiding this study are as follows:

- How do you secure data on a mobile device which the organization does not own?
- What security measures can and should the enterprise require for employee-owned devices used for business purposes?

2. LITERATURE REVIEW

The concept of BYOD was driven by several factors firstly, by the enhancement of mobile technology capability; secondly, the rise of the cloud computing for personal use and finally, the changing expectations of employees who are demanding high IT performance. As part of this consumerization, BYOD allows employees to access corporate email or view text documents on any device they choose thereby increasing productivity and reducing costs (Disterer and Kleiner, 2013). Since the practice of BYOD is not just about mere permission to employees to use their devices or technologies to access sensitive enterprise resources, companies often find it difficult to provide a proper and secure IT infrastructure to incorporate efficient working and communication among various types of devices and technologies. Allowing employees to use company-owned devices for personal use without any restrictions, would have security and compliance risks, as well as higher costs. Companies are hardly able to provide sufficient equipment that can meet the high, divergent, and quickly changing demands of users experienced with consumer devices (Disterer, and Kleiner, 2013; O'Leary et al., 2017). The main security concerns identified as a result are confidentiality, integrity, and authenticity of company data. Confidentiality is breached when an unauthorized person gains access to sensitive private or confidential information by manipulating devices or through the interception data transmissions. Manipulation takes place when company data on personal devices is insufficiently secured. Likewise, authenticity is threatened when BYODs are used to trigger business transactions that cannot be traced clear without ambiguity. Mobile devices that are insufficiently secure can lead to unauthorized use and modification of data due to intentional or negligent actions. When personal devices are used, it must be assumed that the careless or the naïf behavior of users could pose security risks (Disterer, and Kleiner, 2013). Personal devices left without security software, or protocols are vulnerable to various cybersecurity threats. This includes drive-by-downloads where an application is downloaded to the device without the person's knowledge (Tode, 2013), downloads can consist of viruses, spyware, and malware which as stated earlier can not only be transferred onto the corporate network but also exploit the data already existing on the device. Other security risks include phishing where hackers acquire user's passwords, credit card details, and additional sensitive information by pretending to be a trustworthy source. Quite often these devices are operating with outdated software. This is a critical for businesses as data retrieved via the attack could be the company intellectual property or confidential information. With the number of professionals using free Wi-Fi hotspots, these security risks are increasing. Each endpoint should have its associated vulnerabilities. Indeed, an effective policy should identify and mitigate each risk individually. The threat of unauthorized access and knowledge loss increases with the introduction of unmanaged devices. Identifying the devices within the BYOD policy and thereby ensuring that potential areas of knowledge leakage are blocked and implementing measures which will ensure that unknown devices have limited access. In addition, to protecting corporate data, employees' private data must be secured against a company's access. This need for a dual type of security that is, for the protection of company and personal data, adds to the complexity and cost of the system as BYOD requires the development, use, and management of various new and sophisticated devices with different applications. Even with corporate BYOD policies, the IT department is faced with the task of ensuring company software applications work with multiple operating systems on a range of device models as employees will inevitably choose a device they are familiar with but not necessarily what the company's IT department selection(Qing, 2013). Hence, the organization's technical infrastructure must be robust enough to support this diversity. When connected to organization's ecosystem, BYODs have access to all corporate data. Nonetheless, an attacker can easily compromise personal devices than corporate-issued devices, which are protected using more sophisticated security measures. This amalgamation of sensitive corporate applications and data on unmanaged personal devices open up security risks (Jain and Shanbhag, 2012). As the nature and types of cyber-attacks rapidly evolve mobile devices have become a critical part of corporate cyber-security strategy. Even though these solutions can be useful in safeguarding corporate network and data, these are inadequate to provide complete protection. Consequently, forward-thinking companies need to recognize that to protect sensitive corporate data and increase productivity, innovation, and employee satisfaction they must create and maintain an effective and well thought out BYOD policy regarding personal devices.

3. METHODOLOGY

This research adopted a survey method which sought individual perception by testing different concepts which reflects the attitude of people on a specific topic. Survey method can be used in both, quantitative and qualitative studies. For this study, a quantitative technique was chosen, namely two cross-sectional questionnaires. The benefits of using surveys over other methods are:

- They can be conducted faster and cheaper compared to other methods of data collection;
- They are relatively easy to analyze.
- Their ability to use smaller groups of people to make inferences about larger groups (Barlett et al.,2001)

In this study, a cross-sectional survey was used to drive this study. Cross-sectional surveys involve the collection of data at a single point in time from a specific population. They are most often used to document the frequency of particular characteristics in a population. Cross-sectional surveys do offer the opportunity to assess relations between variables and differences between subgroups in a population. Survey research method can make use of different data collection tools, in this case a questionnaire was employed as the primary data collection tool (Bryman, 2015, Fowler, 2013).

3.1 Cross-sectional Survey

The research employed a questionnaire survey by querying company's involved BYOD practices. When it was determined that the questionnaires meet the required standards, via a series of pilot test, they were distributed. The questionnaires were sent out to 70 companies within the city of New York. Questionnaires (A) were sent to the IT department a total of 41 valid surveys were returned. Questionnaire (B) was sent to general employees/ users, of which a total of 60 valid questionnaires were returned. This was a based on simple random sampling technique, which assures that each element in the population had the same chance of being selected (Saunders et al., 2009 and Lewis-Beck et al., 2004). Participants included cybersecurity engineers, software developers, IT Security Specialists, IT Business Analysts, System Support Analysts, Senior Software Engineers, Security Engineers, Information Security Analyst, Chief Information Security Officers, amongst others. These IT personnel have considerable knowledge of BYOD and its security implications. Unstructured, open-ended questions were used to encourage participants to construct their meaning of the phenomena – meanings that have been forged through dialogue and interactions with their colleagues. Data analysis for the survey was done using univariate and bivariate descriptive data analysis, both techniques involve the use of a number of tools which includes: frequency counts and distributions, summary values for frequencies and/or comparison between categories, pictorial representations of distributions and contingency tables/correlations (Saunders et al., 2009).

4. PRESENTATION AND DISCUSSION OF FINDINGS

From the questionnaire with the IT personnel, the majority of participants (62.5%) were between the ages of 18-33 which reflect a young task force who are in line with the younger and more technological savvy employers/trendsetters who are distorting the lines between work and personal time, space and data. As typical of the IT industry, 70.7% of participants were male, with the over 61% being employed by large corporations employing more than 250 people. 73.2% of the participating companies have a BYOD policy which allows employees to bring their smartphones, tablets, and laptop. Employees engaging in BYOD scheme used it primarily for email purposes (82.9%) and (77.1%) for communicating with the organization and their colleagues.

How do you secure data on a mobile device which the organization does not own?

Managing data on a mobile device can be quite daunting even for the most thorough IT company. In addition to malware, there are a number of other security risks which could impact the company. These include lack of authentication, unsecured Wi-Fi networks, outdated operating systems, and accidental knowledge loss resulting from sharing the mobile device with friends, family, or coworkers. With over 75% of employees sidestepping or disabling the security features on mobile devices it is essential for organizations to develop and implement appropriate mobile security policies which would control or mitigate the associated risks (Ponemon Institute, 2012). From the questionnaire survey, 74% of IT departments claimed they have a BYOD policy. The remaining 16% allowed employees to bring their device but did not have a formal system to govern and monitor usage. These devices include smartphone 43%, tablets 30% and laptops 28%. Owing to their size and portability these devices are typical of the technology used for BYOD purposes. The prospect of using one's own devices in the workplace has been a driving force behind the innovation of BYOD practices, especially for business and operations purposes.

However, not all employees felt that their data is secured and protected under the BYOD policy. The results from the findings show that 83.3% of employees were satisfied with the level of security implemented but the remaining 16% of participants were cynical that their organization can prevent a mobile cyber-attack or breach from occurring thus leaving employees' personal information vulnerable to theft. There are several factors which could contribute to this belief. One possible reason is the IT departments had not communicated the security controls mechanisms that were implemented to secure the corporate ecosystem as well as employee's personal devices. With employees being unaware of the security measures they may believe they not be held accountable if they leak or lose corporate data. Hence, company training for employees should focus on security awareness to help users understand the risks their actions or lack thereof poses to the company. Nonetheless, the IT department needs to proactively communicate the benefits of BYOD program and continue communicating these inside the business as improvements are made.

Mobile devices are designed to make it easy to find, acquire, install, and use third-party applications. This poses obvious security risks, especially for mobile device platforms that do not place security restrictions or other limitations on third-party application publishing. From the questionnaires, employees were asked to identify who was responsible for deciding which applications are implemented on mobile devices. The results show that 33% of IT departments were responsible for vetting or selecting the types of applications which are downloaded to the device, a further 39% claimed the applications were decided by the organization, and they had to choose from the options give and 25% allowed employees to select their application

Hence, companies should plan their security directives for a mobile device based on the assumption that unknown third-party mobile device applications downloadable by users should not be trusted. There are several risks which are inherent to these practices consequently the installation of third-party applications should be strictly prohibited, and mobile devices should be checked for all unapproved applications. Every third-party application should be thoroughly vetted to ensure it does not pose any security risks. It is important to note that even if these mitigation strategies are implemented for third-party applications, employees can still access dubious applications through commercial web browsers.

What security measures can and should the enterprise require for employee-owned devices used for business purposes?

Companies allowing BYOD privileges should examine both the macro and microenvironment and develop, design or acquire the solution/s considered most suitable. Based on risk management principles access to software and wireless network interfaces should be restricted. Corporate network should be managed and automatically monitored, to detect and report any policy violations or security breach. Also, encrypting data communications and data storage, wiping data from the device once employees leave, and remotely wiping the device once it is lost or stolen are all factors which should be included in the BYOD security policy to prevent unauthorized users access to sensitive data. Security deliberations should then be given to data which may have been copied to another location, such as cloud storage, local backup files or forwarded email ((Wong, 2012 and Agudelo et al., 2016). Companies, participating in BYOD and allowing cloud storage need to be aware of the intangibility of cloud storage and the fact that information in the cloud may not be readily accessible and forensically viable in the case of a breach. Consequently, employees should be encouraged to use time and cost-effective cloud-based tools, but only under careful supervision and according to agreed rules and guidelines of the existing policy.

Quite often employees are also operating with outdated software and patches. Therefore the IT department should install and update applications. From the results, it was seen that software updates were done when new updates are issued (45%) and weekly by 10%. However, 25% never updated the software on their mobile device and they are operating either with outdated software which poses several security risks, or the devices are being updated by the IT department who access to the system. Therefore, technical staff should ensure that participating devices do not unexpectedly return to default settings. From the questionnaire, employees/users were asked to identify the types of data protection employed by their organization, from which the majority 30% claimed using a combination of user authentication, anti-virus software, and encryption. All companies participating in the study had a method of protecting the network and applications. Any BYOD policy should consider the following security factors: confidentiality, connectivity, data integrity, protection, authentication, application functionality, and performance. For any policy to be successful employees, buy-in, and adherence to the rules is imperative. Hence for the BYOD policy to be effective, employees must be educated to understand not only the strategies in place but the controls and consequences of ignoring or overriding these mechanisms. Control and mitigation strategies are not valid unless employees/users appreciate and understand the importance of restrictions and the effects of ignoring or disregarding the controls. The training program should include the ability of employees/users to recognize an attack and notify IT personnel immediately when they suspect that a mobile device has been infected or compromised.

5. CONCLUSIONS

Synonymous with the creation of any BYOD policy is the identification of business and technical threats resulting from the use of mobile devices. Companies are now recognizing that seemingly benign devices can be dangerous especially when employees are oblivious or careless in their approach to security and protection of sensitive corporate information. Consequently, many organizations are struggling with how to adequately define the impact on their security posture and establish acceptable procedures and support models that balance both their employees' needs and their security concerns. On the other hand, the implementation of a BYOD policy can be intrusive to users are it interfere with their personal life. The cost of mitigating those risks and developing a layered security approach can be significant. Consequently, organizations are wrestling with the balance between empowering employees and enable greater business agility against security risks and spiraling costs of control

As with any data protection policy, the key is creating a framework that reduces the risk of knowledge leakage while limiting the impact on user's freedom. Hence developing a proactive and integrated risk management approach with the BYOD policy would help the IT department being ahead of the risks of knowledge leakage.

REFERENCES

Agudelo, C. A., Bosua, R., Ahmad, A., & Maynard, S. B. (2016). Understanding Knowledge Leakage & BYOD (Bring Your Own Device): A Mobile Worker Perspective.

Barlett, J. E., Kotrlik, J. W., & Higgins, C. C. (2001). Organizational research: Determining appropriate sample size in survey research. *Information technology, learning, and performance journal*, *19*(1), 43.

Bryman, A. (2015). *Social research methods*. Oxford University press.

Fowler Jr, F. J., (2013), *Survey research methods*. Sage publications.

Disterer, G. and Kleiner, C., (2013). BYOD bring your own device. Procedia Technology, 9, pp.43-53

Jain, A. K., and Shanbhag D., (2012) Addressing Security and Privacy Risks in Mobile Applications, IEEE Computer Society: Mobile & Wireless Technologies.

O'Leary, D., Zimmermann, R., Grahn, A., Poarch, D., Cook, M., Pirchard J., (2017) Mobile Device Security in the Workplace: Key Risks and a Surprising Challenge. Available at: https://www.google.com/search?q=Mobile+Device+Security+in+the+Workplace%3A+5+Key+Risks+and+a+...&oq=Mobile+Device+Security+in+the+Workplace%3A+5+Key+Risks+and+a+...&aqs=chrome..69i57.7144315j1j7&sourceid=chrome&ie=UTF

Ponemon Institute, (2012), Global Study on Mobility Risks, Survey of IT & IT Security Practitioners, Ponemon Institute Research Report, Websense, Inc

Poarch, D., Zimmermann, R., Grahn, A., Cook, M., (2016). Mobile Device Security in the Workplace: 5 Key Risks and a Surprising Challenge. IT Area Security. Available from: http://focus.forsythe.com/articles/55/Mobile-Device-Security-in-the-Workplace-5-Key-Risks-and-a-Surprising-Challenge.

THE METHOD FOR DETECTING THE DEPENDENCIES BETWEEN TECHNICAL FUNCTIONS AND PHYSICAL EFFECTS

Dmitriy M. Korobkin, Sergey S. Fomenkov and Sergey G. Kolesnikov
Volgograd State Technical University, Russia, Volgograd, Lenin av., 28

ABSTRACT

Authors use the physical effects (PhE) for the synthesis of the physical operation principle of a technical system. PhEs realize the technical functions that compose the selected functional structure of the designed technical system. Authors developed the method for extraction the physical effects descriptions from the patents of USPTO and RosPatent databases, and the method for extracting of technical functions from Natural Language documents including patent texts. The method of automated construction of a matrix of physical functions performed by physical effects is based on the detection of latent dependencies in the consolidated matrix "Physical Effects – Technical Functions". Developed software has been tested for tasks of extraction of the physical effects and technical functions from patent documents.

KEYWORDS

Patent, NLP, Fact Extraction, Data Mining, Physical Effect, Technical Function, SAO

1. INTRODUCTION

Analysis of the computer-aided innovation systems (CAI) (Orloff, 2006) such as Goldfire Innovator, TechOptimizer, Innovation Workbench, Idea Generator, Pro / Innovator, etc., shows these CAI systems do not solve the fundamental problem of updating the information component of the new technical systems generation. Using the world patent database (more than 20 million patents) and open databases of scientific and technical information as a global knowledge base most correctly. The engineer/inventor realizes the required functions of the designed technical system on the basis of heuristic morphological synthesis or the physical operation principle (POP) (Vayngolts, 2016), which is a sequence (network) of physical effects (PhE) (Korobkin, 2016). Therefore, it is required to extract the following data from the global information space: physical and technical effects, morphological features and their alternatives (elements of functional structure, technical realizations of objects), i.e. information necessary to solve the problems of information support for the synthesis of new technical solutions.

The task of determining the most effective physical operation principle of a technical system with a selected functional structure that synthesized on the basis of a morphological matrix is solved by 2 methods: 1) the method for automating the procedures for synthesizing the physical operation principle based on the database of technical functions performed by physical effects, and 2) the developed method for verification the practical realizability (Korobkin, 2015) of the synthesized POP on based on the criteria parameters of the physical effects that are part of a POP structure.

2. THE METHOD FOR EXTRACTION THE PHYSICAL EFFECTS DESCRIPTIONS FROM PATENT OF USPTO AND ROSPATENT

For the task of extraction of the physical effects descriptions from patent texts are used the previously developed procedures (Fomenkova, 2017) for segmentation of complex sentences of patent texts, morphological and semantic analysis with the construction of dependency trees, and building the deep-syntactic structures based on the Meaning-Text Theory (Mel'čuk, 1988) for reduced Stanford dependencies.

Example of deep-syntactic structures from the sentence of patent US20130307109A1 "(1)When (2)light (3)enters (4)the (5)semiconductor (6)junction (7)of (8)such (9)an (10)element (11), (12)the (13)incident (14)light (15)causes (16)photoelectric (17)conversion (18), (19)generating (20)charges:

I(enters-3, light-2)
OPER(ROOT-0, enters-3)
II(enters-3, junction-6)
ATTR(juction-6, semiconductor-5)

ATTR(light-14, incident-13)
I(causes-15, light-14)
OPER(ROOT-0, causes-15)
II(causes-15, conversion-17)
ATTR(conversion -17, photoelectric-16)
COORD(causes-15, generating -19)
II(generating -19, charges -20)

According to the PhE model (Korobkin, 2014) developed at the CAD Department of Volgograd State Technical University, input cause-action produces an output effect-action on the environment or object. For extraction of physical effect from text it is necessary to find the predicates (verbs) such as "change", "increase", "decrease", "dependence", "change", "generate", "act", "cause", etc. that show some "action" with arguments. For these predicates, authors correlated the arguments: actant relations "I" (something that acts), "II" (something that has an effect, where an action is realized) with elements of PhE description: input cause-action (A), output effect-action (C) and object (B).

Authors developed the new PhE model on basis of developed ontology "Physical Effect" (Korobkin, 2017):

$$M_{PhE}=<C, D, B, R_C, R_B>, (1)$$

where C – set of predicates (verbs), $c_i \in C$; D - set of actant relations of arguments $\{I, II\}$, $D_i \in D$ – set of actant relations of predicate c_i, $d_j \in D_i$; B – set of elements of the PhE description (A, B, C), $B_k \in B$; $\forall c_i \in C$ $\exists d_j \in D_i$ $d_j \xrightarrow{def} B_k$, R_C – relation $C \times D$, $(c_i, d_j) \in R_C$ determines an element(s) of the PhE description with actant relation d_j of predicate c_i; R_B – relation $R_C \times B$, $((c_i, d_j), B_k) \in R_B$ determines a set of ontology concepts that correlated with an element of PhE description b_k , $b_k \in B_k$. The authors have developed a set of patterns for extraction of the PhE descriptions from NL patent text (104 patterns in Russian, 36 patterns in English) on the base of model MPhE,

Authors also improved the method of building a semantic network of PhE description that extracted from the NL text: a) node $V_i = (T_i, B_i)$, where T_i – argument (Natural Language terms) of predicate c_j, $T_i \in R_B$; B_i – PhE element(s) which is represented as T_i in the NL text, $B_i \in R_C$; b) arc C_j – the predicate that extracted from NL text. The Table 1 shows the example of the semantic network from the sentence: «When light enters the semiconductor junction of such an element, the incident light causes photoelectric conversion, generating charges».

Table 1. Example of Semantic Network

Node	Parent node	Predicate	Object	Type of actant relation
O_1			T_1= {light}, B_1= {Input}	I actant relation
O_2	O_1	C_1= enter	T_2= {semiconductor junction}, B_2= {Object}	II actant relation
O_3			T_3= {incident light}, B_3= {Input}	I actant relation
O_4	O_3	C_2= cause	T_4= { photoelectric conversion }, B_4= {Output}	II actant relation
O_5	O_3	C_3= generate	T_5= {charges}, B_5= {Output}	II actant relation

Authors developed the algorithm of PhE extraction from NL patent texts on the basis of model M_{PhE} and method of building the semantic networks that consist of the next steps: a) The semantic analysis of patent text with procedures of segmentation of complex sentences, morphological analysis, construction of the dependency trees, building the deep-syntactic structures based on the Meaning-Text Theory for reduced Stanford dependencies; b) Search in the NL patent text the predicates (verbs) from a thesaurus of database "Physical Effects"; c) Detecting from received deep-syntactic structures the important arguments (with actant relations I, II) of found predicates. Arguments (NL terms) must be found in ontology thesaurus "Physical Effect Input", "Physical Effect Output", "Physical Effect Objects"; d) Building a semantic network; e) Construction of PhE description with using the procedures: a) concept joining, and b) exception of the concepts that not found in their corresponding concept classes "Physical Effect Input", "Physical Effect Output", "Physical Effect Objects". For this example (Table 1) the authors obtained a description of PhE "Photoelectric effect" which have "light" as input cause-action, "charge" as the object and "semiconductor" as output effect-action.

3. THE METHOD FOR EXTRACTING OF TECHNICAL FUNCTIONS FROM PATENT TEXTS

Currently, the problem of the patent databases analysis for the extraction of technical functions in the SAO form (Subject-Action-Object) is actively studied by scientists H. Park (Park, 2012), D.U. Yufeng (Yufeng, 2016), S.Choi, K.Kim, JYLee, J.Hu, J.Yoon, J.Guo, S.Fang, and others. For extraction the technical functions in SAO form from NL patent texts are also used the previously developed procedures (Korobkin, 2017) for building the deep-syntactic structures (Meaning-Text Theory). The root node of the deep-syntactic structure is a verb (Figure 1) ("Action"), its child nodes are extracted with actant relations I ("Subject") and II ("Object"), and for each node "Subject", "Object" and "Action" the child nodes are extracted with attributive relation.

The description of the PhE "Photoelectric effect" was found in the patent US20130307109A1. Then in this patent, it is necessary to search for descriptions of technical functions. Example of SAO extracting from sentence "(1)Most (2)solid (3)image (4)sensors (5)are (6)used (7)to (8)detect (9)visible (10)or (11)infrared (12)light" shown in Table 2.

Table 2. Results of Analysis the Patent US20130307109A1

Deep-syntactic structures	Example of extracted technical function
ATTR(sensors-4, solid-2) ATTR(sensors-4, image-3) I(detect-8, sensors-4) OPER(ROOT-0, detect-8) ATTR(ligth-12, visible-9) ATTR(ligth-12, infrared-11) II(detect-8, ligth-12)	Action: "detect" (root node - "detect"); Subject: "solid image sensors" (I actant relation - "sensors", attributive relation – "solid", "image"); Object: "visible or infrared light" (II actant relation - "light", attributive relation – "visible", "infrared").

The result of SAO extracting from the sentence of patent US20130307109A1: "The element isolation may achieve by impurity diffusion using a PD junction": a) Action: "perform" (root node - "achieve"); b) Subject: "impurity diffusion" (I actant relation - "diffusion", attributive relation – "impurity"); c) Object: "element isolation" (II actant relation - "isolation", attributive relation – "element").

Structuring of the set of SAO components values was made on the basis of a set of terms most often encountered in the technical function descriptions (for example, in the International Patent Classification and in the field "Practical application" of the PhE database (1200 descriptions). Using this information structure the class of verb "achieve" are defined as a "perform". The obtained components of the technical function representation according to the SAO model recognized in the patent sentences are listed in Table 3.

Table 3. Technical Functions from Patent US20130307109A1

No	Action	Subject	Object	Action class
1	detect	solid image sensors	visible or infrared light	DETECT
2	perform	impurity diffusion	element isolation	PERFORM

The algorithm of grouping (comparison) SAOs (Korobkin, 2017) is used to combine several "Subject-Action-Object" structures into one common structure.

4. CONCLUSION

The experiments are performed using a multiprocessor computer system (cluster) of the Volgograd State Technical University. The cluster entered the 22nd edition of the Top-50 rating of the Russian supercomputers. The 990,000 USPTO and RosPatent patents are stored in the HDFS file system.

Authors developed the method for extraction the physical effects descriptions from the patents of USPTO and RosPatent databases, and the method for extracting of technical functions from Natural Language documents including patent texts.

The method of automated construction of a matrix of physical functions performed by physical effects is based on the detection of latent dependencies in the consolidated matrix "Physical Effects – Technical Functions". The consolidated matrix is formed from two term-document matrices: a) the first matrix describes the frequency of occurrence (TF/IDF) of each term (technical functions in SAO form) in all patent documents, b) the second matrix describes the frequency of occurrence of physical effects in all patens.

Table 4. The Evaluation Criterions of Technical Functions Extraction

No exp	R_{rel}	NR_{rel}	R_{nrel}	Recall	Precision
1	82	23	14	0.78	0.85
2	133	42	31	0.76	0.81
3	301	86	96	0.78	0.76

Table 5. The Evaluation Criterions of Physical Effects Extraction

No exp	R_{rel}	NR_{rel}	R_{nrel}	Recall	Precision
1	12	6	8	0.67	0.6
2	18	17	20	0.51	0.47
3	25	14	23	0.64	0.52

where R_{rel} – the number of retrieved relevant PhE / TechFun (technical functions); NR_{rel} – the number of not retrieved relevant PhE / TechFun; R_{nrel} – the number of retrieved irrelevant PhE / TechFun.

ACKNOWLEDGEMENT

The reported study was funded by the Russian Foundation for Basic Research (research project No. 18-07-01086 A, research project No. 16-07-00534 A).

REFERENCES

Fomenkova, M. A., Korobkin, D. M., Fomenkov, S. A., 2017. Extraction of Physical Effects Based on the Semantic Analysis of the Patent Texts. *CIT&DS 2017 ed A Kravets, M Shcherbakov, et al* , Russia, pp. 73-87.

Korobkin, D. M., Fomenkov, S. A., Kamaev, V. A., Fomenkova, M. A., 2016. Multi-agent model of ontology-based extraction of physical effects descriptions from natural language text. *In Journal of Physics*, pp. 498-501.

Korobkin, D. M., Fomenkov, S. A., Kravets, A. G., 2017. Extraction of physical effects practical applications from patent database. *Proceedings of IISA 2017, DOI: 10.1109/IISA.2017.8316402*

Korobkin, D. M., Fomenkov, S. A., Kravets, A. G., Kolesnikov, S. G., 2017. Prior art candidate search on base of statistical and semantic patent analysis. *Multi Conference on Computer Science and Information Systems 2017 ed Y Xiao, A P Abraham*, pp. 231-238

Korobkin, D. M., Kolesnikov, S. G., Fomenkov, S. A., Golovanchikov, A. B., 2015. Evaluating an operation principle practicability of new technical system. *Proceedings of IISA 2015, DOI: 10.1109/IISA.2015.7388068.*

Korobkin, D.M., Fomenkov, S.A., Golovanchikov, A.B., 2018. Method of identification of patent trends based on descriptions of technical functions. *Journal of Physics: Conference Series,* DOI :10.1088/1742-6596/1015/3/032065

Korobkin, D.M., Fomenkov, S.A., Kolesnikov, S.G., 2014. Ontology-based extraction of physical effect description from Russian text. *Proceedings of the MCCSIS 2014,* pp. 321-330

Mel'čuk, I. A., 1988. *Dependency Syntax: Theory and Practice*. SUNY Publ., NY.

Orloff, M. A., 2006. *Inventive Thinking through TRIZ: A Practical Guide.* Springer Science & Business Media, Germany.

Park, H, Yoon, Y., Kim, K., 2012. Identifying patent infringement using SAO based semantic technological similarities. *In Scientometrics)* 90: 515, DOI:10.1007/s11192-011-0522-7.

Vayngolts, I. I., Korobkin, D. M., Fomenkov, S. A., Golovanchikov, A. B., 2017. Synthesis of the Physical Operation Principles of Technical System. *Proceedings of CIT&DS 2017 ed A Kravets, M Shcherbakov*, Russia, pp. 575-588/

Yufeng, D. U. et al., 2016. Patent Similarity Measure Based on SAO Structure. *Chinese Sentence and Clause for Text Information Processing*, 30(1), pp. 30-36.

CITIES INFORMATION AND COMMUNICATION TECHNOLOGIES (ICT) BRIDGE TOWARD VILLAGES FOR WOMEN EMPOWERMENT

Muhammad Yasir Faheem[1], Syed Anees Haider[1], Shunan Zhong[1] and Muhammad Basit Azeem[2]
[1]*Beijing Institute of Technology, 5 South Zhongguancun Street, Haidian District, Beijing, China Postcode: 100081*
[2]*University of Engineering and Technology Lahore , UET Lahore, Faisalabad Campus Faisalabad, Pakistan Postcode: 38000*

ABSTRACT

This paper presents a new approach to empower rural women at/near their door steps. Under this approach, government ICT departments will establish ICT centers in some of the easy accessible places. Universities of that area will provide its academic and technical assistance to these centers for example, training provision in the centers. The centers will train the women with the help of universities for enhancing their I.T knowledge, online banking skills, employment opportunities etc. Once the training is completed, mobile applications will be introduced to implement the ICT Training thus, these ICT centers will be converted into SMART Centers. Further, ICT centers will be relocated to some other area so that maximum women can get technical training from such centers. We believe that such ICT trainings will perk up not only the life of rural women but also whole rural communities. This idea will be very fruitful in achieving smart cities goals.

KEYWORDS

Smart ICT Centers, Women Empowerment, Smart Cites, Skill Conversion

1. INTRODUCTION

To build powerful economies through sustainable development, Women empowerment is essential in all sectors. Women participation in economic activities leads the countries towards higher economic development. For example, if women are empowered, there will be increase in opportunities, total output and trade of the country will be higher, more finance will be available, and quality of life will improve. A big technology gap exists between cities and villages, according to some international surveys the women users living in villages of smart technology and communication in developing countries are around (5% to 10%) only. On the other hand women population is almost more than 50% of the total. Village women can contribute in sustainable development of any nation with the use of smart technologies. In developing countries, there are many barriers like poverty, lack of resources, language barriers, and unavailability of modern technology. Such barriers create a digital divide in the developing countries. But education through modern technology can rapidly change the conditions of poor countries. ICT infrastructure can play a backbone role in economic development. In some countries, where female population is featured as sheltered, tough to access and conservative up to some extent. There has been a global research interest for international and sustainable development. Therefore, it is imperative to study the emerging issues related with female sector. International development organizations like United Nations Development Program (UNDP), Organization for Economic Cooperation and Development (OECD), United Nations Development Fund for Women (UNDFEM) consider ICT as an essential tool for economic development. Abbasi (2001) argued that ICT possess unique social infrastructure based on knowledge and skill. It can be of great importance for women marginalization. Ningo, (1999) stated that development through ICT is only possible if gender issues are properly considered. ICT can best serve in increasing women access to knowledge and information because there are fewer opportunities for women in developing countries (Sharma, 2001). The proposed idea is to give the awareness and job opportunities by implementing the Smart ICT Centers in rural areas. This idea is possible through government and university linkage. Universities will be resource organization in terms of technical and training assistance. Students of final year will be required to train uneducated women in these ICT centers and such trainings will be considered as a degree course hour. Practical implementation of students' knowledge will give them confidence. Women can contribute by making small applications, collecting and uploading data, making record of official data and many more. This should be public private partnership which include transparent audit by random third parties quarterly in year. The funds and salaries should be transferred directly in the bank account of the working women. This will make a strong relationship with the undeveloped areas of the countries; it will give an abrupt push to the train of development, because a huge amount can be circulate with some fruitful contribution of women. Unwin,T (2009) stated in his book "Information and Communication Technology for Development" (ICT4D) described the major ingredients of ICT related projects. He argued that we must first assess the needs for designing suitable hi-tech solutions that are sustainable. For economic development, we need vision and commitment to provide infrastructure through effective partnerships. Then monitoring and evaluation of such ICT projects is very important for sustainable development.

2. PROBLEM STATEMNET AND LIMITAIONS

2.1 Problem Statement and Limitation

The rural women usually have ample spare time after the completion of their daily routine works. Utilizing their potential is very important for sustainable development. The country where women are not supposed to work in industry freely, ICT can play a vital role so that such women may contribute in the development by sitting in their homes. To encourage and empower such women segment, skill oriented ICT centers convertible to Smart ICT centers are much needed. Limitations of Women over the Ages are Family and social pressures, Gender imbalance, Caste differences and social issues, scarce access to useful resources, Poverty, inadequate advancement opportunities and Less Power.

In developing and some developed countries the villagers have a limited life style as it is well known that the populations of the villages have a significant value in any country. Men and women both are the equal rights to participate in the development but in villages the women are limited with their house liabilities. Arif, Eman Muhammad (2007) stressed on I.T training for women empowerment to perform better in the knowledge economy and worldwide competition. ICT centers can make a strong bridge between cities and villages. The aim of these centers is to educate and deliver skills to the village women, because they have enough time to learn and adopt new skills. These centers will be mainly controlled by government. Government will provide all the facilities including initial funding, where the universities should provide services by arranging training programs and workshops with the help of students and teachers. ICT centers can give a better life style to the villagers; on the other hand, it will open the job opportunities for the needy persons. ICT centers can be converted in to smart ICT center after some successful years of ICT centers parties.

3. PROPOSED SOLUTION

This paper proposes an innovative concept of temporary mobile ICT centers convertible to smart and portable ICT centers are proposed. After the successful completion of trainings; smart phones will work as a mobile ICT centers with the ICT applications and every latest technology should have no boundaries. In Figure 1 we can see the complete flow of working including two way directions, where AD represents the Audit Department in Figure 1.

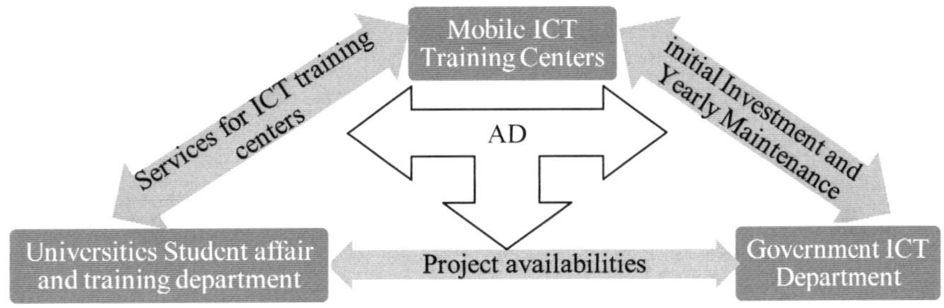

Figure 1. Block Diagram of Proposed Solution

First of all temporary and Mobile ICT centers should be installed in those villages which are very near to the city, after the training and conversion of skills and Smart technology using smart phone those mobile centers reinstall to the next nearest villages and so on. The responsibilities and duties of each part of this project are defined as below one by one.

3.1 Universities Student Affair and Training Department

This department is a back bone of proposed solution. University should be responsible for the fruitful training and make sure that the duration and material should be up to the mark, for this university will recruit the professional trainer. After training and conversion of skills a practical implementation test should be conducted for the villagers to confirm the required output. There will be an internship program for university student which will provide the initial training to the ICT women students and after that trained professional faculty should deliver the final and effective training. In figure 2 the complete working hierarchy of ICT training is shown given by Universities.

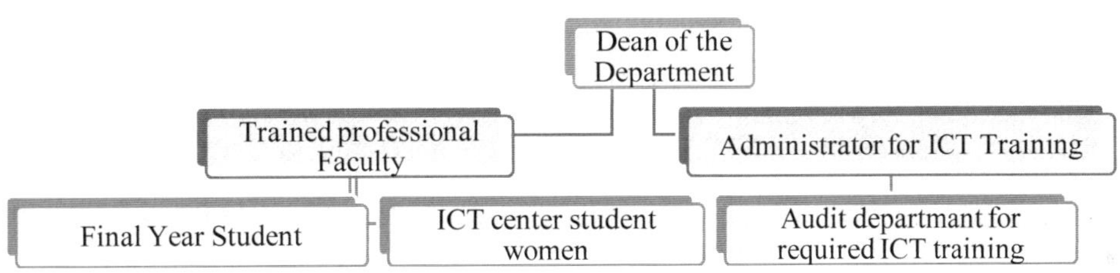

Figure 2. Working hierarchy of ICT training

3.2 Government ICT Department for Sustainable Development

This department should invest the initial cost of the mobile ICT centers which can be easily installed and uninstalled from one place to other place, for this Govt. not need to spend so much money because these centers can be uses many times. When the training and skill about the ICT will complete properly then this department makes sure the availability of the projects and access of business men by introducing and advertising the smart phone applications developed by universities training and student affair department. So each woman in the village can easily run an online shop or can do online business. The steps of the working of Government ICT department are as follows.

- Step 1. Installation of mobile ICT centers in the nearest village
- Step 2. Make sure all the requirement are fulfilled properly
- Step 3. Coordinate with the university training department and the women from the villages with the help of female faculties
- Step 4. Handing and taking process with proper documentation
- Step 5. After the completion of project uninstall and reinstall Mobile ICT centers in the next nearest Village

3.3 Mobile ICT Training Centers

These centers should have all the latest technology and equipment regarding ICT including laptops, smart phones, latest computers, broadband, 4G/5G and digital library. These mobile ICT centers can be installed at any place provided by the villagers which is safe and convenient for the women. Final year students will teach and train initial or basic knowledge to the ICT center students. Every student will give training at least once in a month and submit his/her report in university concern department for next training session to the same mobile ICT center. When this basic training will comes to its final stage then professional trainers will start their training with practical and will implement some user friendly tools for women to empower them. There are two types of training the first one is basic training from final year students of the university and the second one is from the professional training from the professional trainer and faculty after that we found skilled and independent women which will surly contribute for the sustainable development.

3.4 Audit Department for Proposed Solution

This department should have three persons from three departments which includes Government, Concern University and Technologist for auditing of services and founds. The business and projects which will provide government and university should be transparent. There will be only one Audit program for funds and services where in funds audit program the audit includes funded projects, salaries/wages for project completion, bank transactions, completion/duration of projects, women access to their bank accounts and standard of projects. On the other hand services audit program includes goal of training, course of training, and duration of training and implementation of ICT trainings for the transparency of the project.

4. EXPECTED RESULTS

ICT training is important from women's perspective also because most of them have desire to get fundamental ICT skills to improve their knowledge and information or for job purposes. There are many immediate and long term benefits of ICT training through Smart centers to women. Keeping in view Sustainable Development Goals (SDGs) described by United Nations, we in this paper, talk about only five major SDGs. Developing countries can effectively cultivate the benefits of ICT in following five major areas:

1. Digital financial services through ICT can help the rural women connect with digital economy. There is evidence that financial inclusion is helpful in reducing the poverty. With the help of digital finance, more and more people can have access to financial services. ICT centers can provide digital training and facilities to people for accurate and timely financial services.

2. From earning and trading point of view, ICT provides update information like weather forecasts, training courses, and freelancer job opportunities. Thus, by sitting at homes, women can earn handsome amount in their spare time.

3. ICT centers can be used to provide medical training to rural women and these centers can become a bridge between health organizations, hospitals, medical practitioners and patients. There can be a direct contact between patients and healthcare facilities. With the help of ICT centers, there can be quick diagnostics and treatment possible.

4. E-learning methods are very helpful in educating the learners with the help of ICT system. Smart systems are capable to evaluate the learning patterns of learners which can be used to devise future plans for maximum output. Thus, these ICT centers will be very supportive in delivering quality education to rural women at their door steps.

5. ICT helps the women to realize their dynamic and reproductive roles at the local, national and even at global levels. Sustainable development is not possible without the contribution of women in a society. We believe that these ICT centers will bring a reform in competition, education and telecommunication sectors of developing countries. Gender inequality will be diminishing in years to come. ICT has vast potential for women empowerment including entrepreneurship, advocacy, service provision, community development activities, I.T based projects, free-lancer assignments etc. So, women potential can be captured in all sects of economy and their socio-economic and political roles are imperative for the economic development.

Presently, annual GDP growth rate of developing countries is approximatly1.95% shown in figure 3. We expect 1-3% increase in GDP growth rate if we implement this idea and train at least 10% of rural population every year. But it all depends on government policies and university contribution to social communities.

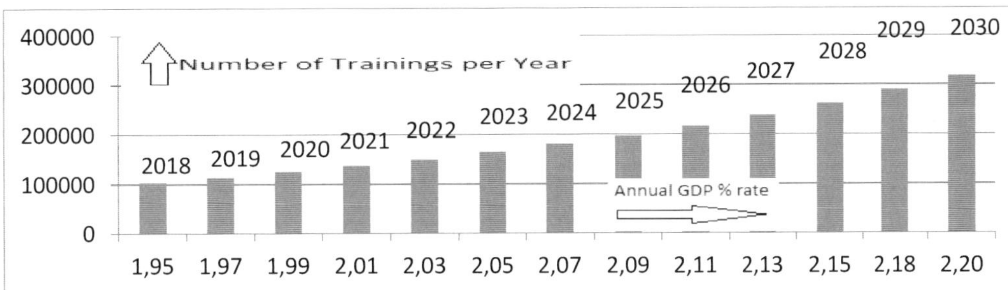

Figure 3. ICT trainees and GDP growth

5. CONCLUSION

The proposed idea will not only empower the women living in village but also all the men living there. The proposed solution is low cost and easy to implement; not a big investment is needed for services and trainings. Under this approach, government ICT departments will establish ICT centers in some of the easy accessible places. Universities of that area will provide its academic and technical assistance to these centers for example, training provision in the centers. The centers will train the women with the help of universities for enhancing their I.T knowledge, online banking skills, employment opportunities etc. Once the training is completed, mobile applications will be introduced to implement the ICT Training thus, these ICT centers will be converted into SMART Centers. Further, ICT centers will be relocated to some other area so that maximum women can get technical training from such centers. We believe that ICT trainings will improve overall living standard of rural women. This approach will be very productive in achieving sustainable development goals about smart cities. After the completion of proposed ICT project all the villages will participate equally to the cities of the country for the sustainable development. Women will get awareness about the modern banking system including modern trends of business. The women are no more dependent; as all the new terms of business and access at their door steps. Smart ICT centers are safe and low cost solution for the villagers.

REFERENCES

Abbasi, Z. F. (2001). Pro-Poor and Gender Sensitive Information Technology: Policy and Practice. Electronic Publication, http://www.comminit.com/st2002/sld 6845.html [accessed Jan 28 2018].

Arif, Eman Muhammad (2007).Training in information technology and the empowerment of women in the light of the educational requirements to work in the knowledge society. Studies in Higher Education-Egypt, AR-15, (2007), pp.252-310.

Khali S. Rabaya'h (2009). Economic and Social Empowerment of Women through Information and Communication Technology: A Case Study. *The Journal of Community Informatics, 5(3-4),* 2009.

Ningo, N. (1999). ICT and Sustainable Good Governance in Sub-Saharan Africa: Countering the Hegemonic Drive for Power. Washington DC: World Bank,http://www.worldbank.org/ [accessed Jan 28 2018].

Sharma, C. (2001) Using ICTs to Create Opportunities for Marginalized Women and Men: The Private Sector and Community Working Together. Washington, DC: World Bank 2001. http://www.worldbank.org/poverty/voices/globcoal/cspres.htm [accessed Jan 28 2018].

United Nations: Women's Empowerment Principles: Equality Means Business. Available online at http://www.unwomen.org/en/digital-library/publications/2011/10/women-s-empowerment-principles-equality-means-business#view accessed date [Jan 28, 2018

Unwin T. (2008). Information and Communication in development practices. ICT4D: Information and Communication Technology for Development, Cambridge University Press, 2009, chapter 3, 39-69.

Reflection Papers

TOWARDS A BIG DATA PLATFORM TO ENHANCE ROAD SAFETY IN THE MENA REGION

Driss Kettani
Al-Akhawayn University in Ifrane, Morocco

ABSTRACT

This paper describes a Big Data Platform that we developed in order to fulfill the needs of an international development project we recently were involved in. The focus is on the potential of this new technology on enabling the data revolution in developing countries and obstacles that might drastically restrict its usage/benefits.

KEYWORDS

Big Data, Transport sector, Black Spots, MENA Region

1. GENERAL CONTEXT

I recently was involved in an interesting Project titled 'Harnessing the Economic Power of Data in the Middle East and North Africa', funded by the International Development Research Centre of Canada (www.idrc.ca). This project aimed at exploring the potential of Big Data Driven Innovations to improve data collection, management, and usability, particularly in the areas of Entrepreneurship and youth employment in the Middle East and North Africa (MENA) region1.

The specific objectives of this 2-year Project were to:

- Inform policies and regulations to effectively produce, manage, and use data, particularly for entrepreneurship and youth employment,
- Study, develop, and test innovative approaches to produce, manage, and use data,
- Build capacities in data production, management, and use among policymakers, statistical agencies, NGOs, and youth,
- Disseminate knowledge and lessons learned from the project ,
- Engage key stakeholders, including NGOs, entrepreneurs, journalists, researchers, and the public.

As a partner in this project, along with colleagues from the American University in Cairo and Birzeit University in Palestine, I was tasked to develop and deploy a testbed to experiment and enable the new usage/exploitation models and semaphores proposed by the research team, and to elaborate an innovative data model, which takes into account the limitations and challenges of the MENA Region. This paper describes the application that we have developed to fulfill the needs of the global project, states its potential in enabling the data revolution in developing countries, and indicates some obstacles that drastically restrict its usage/benefits but, yet, open the doors to further research investigations that we intend to undertake in a near future.

2. IDENTIFYING AN EXPERIMENTAL PLATFORM

One fundamental issue the research team needed to address very early was to identify several fields of common interest/benefit in all MENA Region countries. Our main idea here was to ensure that the testbed that we will develop can benefit to all countries of the region and their population, and would allow us, as Researchers, to draw some observations and lessons learnt to feed our Data Model.

[1] https://www.idrc.ca/en/project/harnessing-economic-power-datamiddle-east-and-north-africa

Three fields were initially shortlisted (Sustainable Energy, Education and Transport) and, after several discussions, we retained the Transport sector for our experimental application.

The transport sector is central to the development targets of MENA countries and crucial in the acceleration of their economic growth. It is also key to regional integration and vital to improving the quality of life and reducing poverty (Yamouri 2010). However, most countries in the MENA region are suffering serious problems related to road accidents leading to more than 75,000 causalities every year. In terms of fatalities per 10,000 registered motor vehicles, the MENA region's average rate 189 of road crash fatalities is currently one of the highest in the world. And, worst of all, in several countries of this region, an average of one person is killed in road crashes every hour (Habibzadeh 2012).

Despite governmental attempts to bring about infrastructural developments that would lead to positive repercussions, the transport sector and the prospect of mobility in the MENA countries still face major challenges.

For example, in Morocco, the Ministry of Transport and Logistics estimates that the social cost related to road accidents and fatalities is 2.5% of the country's annual GDP. With a death rate-per-100,000 of 19.89 %, more than 4,000 people die in traffic accidents every year, which is by far the first death cause in the country.

In Egypt (in the top 10 countries, worldwide, for the number of fatal road accidents), the annual death toll from road accidents in is more than 25,000, as well as more than 70,000 serious injuries, with financial losses that amount to between LE30 billion and LE35 billion annually[2].

It is noticeable that in Morocco, in Egypt and in most MENA Region countries, accidents often happen in the same location and for the same reasons (bad infrastructures, road conditions, heavy traffic, Speed, signalization, etc.), leading to black spots that continuously trap new victims although they are known to local/central officials (Naji and Djebarni 2000). This is a "Pattern" that has been highlighted and documented in many countries, along with many other patterns one could find in the specialized literature (Naji and Djebarni 2000).

Hence the need of an application/system whose exclusive goal is to manage the Accidents Black Spots (ABS), through an innovative technology platform, in a way that could significantly reduce their impact on safety and security of people in the MENA Region.

3. BIG DATA OR NOT?

As the broader research project we are involved in deals with Big Data technologies, we needed first to make sure ABS is a good testbed of Big Data application for development. The term "Big Data" is used here and there to convey different kind of concepts (and associated expectations), including: huge quantities of data, social media analytics, next generation data management capabilities, real-time data, and much more (Kettani) 2016. One of its most accepted/cited definitions is included in (Beyer and Laney 2012), which proposes a threefold definition encompassing the volume, velocity and variability of Data, marking upon the increasing size of data, the increasing rate at which it is produced and the increasing range of formats and representations employed. No particular quantification of big data has been indicated. This definition has been extended afterword to include two other important Data aspects (Beyer and Laney 2012) & (IBM 2013) veracity to take into account the truth value of data, and variety to stress on the huge diversity of data sources.

We can safely confirm that ABS fulfills most of these features considering that the potential number of its users and the number/nature of documents that are included in the data repository in order to serve as evidence of blackspots, will result in a very high volume of data (Petabyte range) in different formats (GIS, audio, video, text, narration, etc.). Also, the combination of the high numbers of accidents / users / blackspots necessarily leads to a high data velocity (or database access/update rate). Finally ABS accepts multiple sources of data to build/consolidate its database, ranging from mobile phones and handheld devices to direct access through voice recorders, cameras and any other USB input devices.

[2] http://www.egyptindependent.com/egypt-top-10-road-traffic-deaths-officials-still-seeking-solutions/

4. ABS SPECIFICATIONS AND DESIGN

ABS is a Big Data platform that we developed to manage black spots and provide real time information on key events related and associate to them, to drivers so that they can anticipate road conditions and adapt/adjust their driving behavior accordingly. Hence, as a driver gets close to a black sport area, a warning is delivered to his mobile phone using various modalities (particular rings, various volumes, vibrations, vocal indications, video illustrations, etc.) depending on the seriousness of the situation. The information that is provided includes the total number of fatalities in the particular black spot, the frequency of accidents per year, the black spot graveness level and supporting multimedia contents to increase the awareness of the driver and "bring" him to pay attention to the area he is crossing. The ABS is designed to fit the needs of drivers who plan their journey ahead of time and of those who use it, sporadically, when they are driving. In the later situation, it is strongly recommended that the mobile phone that reeves the warnings be held/used by a co-driver.

ABS visualizes traffic black spots with all "common" mapping functionalities, including zooming, moving, displaying available information on a particular black sport, etc., and allows users/drivers to add new black spots and include all supporting documentation/ information (testimonies, photos, statistics, etc.), which will be validated by the System administrator before posting them.

Data related to traffic black spots is gathered both from the field (testimonies, user feeds, etc.) and from the national archives (official organizations that govern the transport sector in any particular country). It (Data) is collected at the back office level and geo-referenced including established itineraries, time-stamped positions along the itineraries, the events published, and the notifications received, etc. These data serve the purpose of applying some analytics that we developed. Some of these are descriptive (including what happened in a particular black-spot, the number and facts, the images and testimonies, etc.), and the others are prescriptive (including recommendations on the best course of events for drivers to follow, speed limitation, change of itinerary, etc.).

In terms of Design, and as shown in the following figure, the system comprises 5 modules:

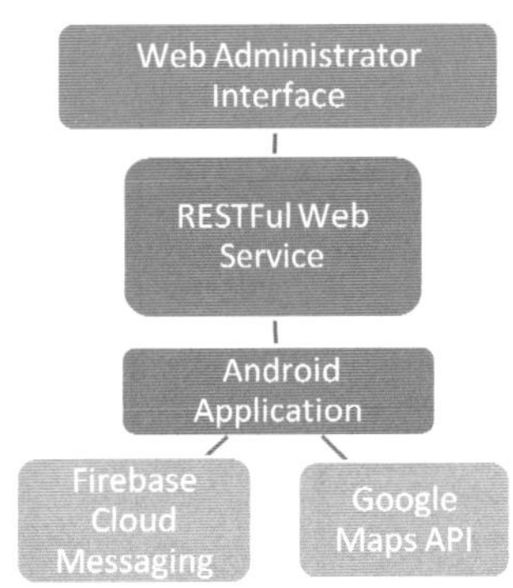

Figure 1. System Architecture

- **RESTful Web Service**: an Object-Oriented PHP built API that reads/writes from a MySQL database, both hosted on a shared Linux web server running Apache.
- **Web Admin Interface**: a web interface built using HTML/CSS/jQuery/PHP that consumes the RESTful API by allowing administrators to manage users, events and their categories.
- **Mobile Application**: an Android application that consumes the RESTful API, as well by allowing users to view and publish events.
- **Google Maps Android API**: this API is consumed by the mobile application to display maps to the users. These maps are customized using a custom JSON Map Style and custom markers.
- **Firebase Cloud Messaging**: the system relies on this messaging platform to monitor the application, manage analytics and deliver real-time notifications to the users.

5. DISCUSSION AND CONCLUSION

As the ABS platform has been developed in the framework of a broader research project related to Big Data for Development, several underpinning hypothesis needed to be investigated by our research team before and after the development of the ABS platform, including:

- **Transport Sector Governance**: How do e-Transport Services improve the safety and Security of Road Users? How does this impact on development in general? Does increased information and services lead to greater drivers' security and safety? Does this facilitate the formation of new groups, associations and more generally, the development of civil society in relation to the transport sector?
- **Users and Usage of e-Transport services**: what segments of Society are more likely to benefit or to be excluded from such technologies? What are the gender differences? How are users using the services? How are they benefiting? What behavioral changes came about? Is this a form of empowerment? What are the obstacles and challenges to their using it?
- **Access to services and technological appropriateness:** what kinds of political, social and economic strategies can be thought of and utilized so as to integrate a greater number of people into these services and "democratize" access to them. What tools are most apt to ensure the use of these is widespread? What factors can ensure this type of project's sustainability and usefulness in the long-term?
- **Data Collection and Analytics:** One important feature of ABS is to collect and put together Data related to black spots. So far, aside a sample that we are using to demonstrated the purpose and usefulness of our platform, the whole aspect of data gathering related to accidents records (old and of new) is still being investigated. For example, as ABS will be used and disseminated on a larger scale, its Data will be directly enriched and consolidated by the end-users. However, we don't know yet if countries of the MENA region would accept such a new model of creating and sharing data? Also, as ABS platform is mainly based on Data directly coming from end users, (testimonies, comments, pictures, etc.), the issue of truth/veracity of Data is crucial to address. Who is going to record the events and how? Would simple users/drivers be officially allowed to create new records? How to validate these records?
- **Ownership and Dissemination:** Although the ABS platform seems interesting given the road safety records in the MEA Region, its actual usage has been low since we made it available for the public (about 6 months ago now). This is not surprising since we have not advertised for it, aside within our academic environment, which is indeed very limited and limiting. We are still exploring ways to efficiently (and cost effectively) disseminate this app and how to make people know about it and about its importance. In fact, the whole issue related to the appropriate model (B2B Model vs. Social Model) to be used in order to maintain and to sustain our platform is still being investigated.

ACKNOWLEDGEMENT

This is to express my appreciation and gratitude to the International Development Research Centre (IDRC) of Canada for funding this Project. Without such assistance this Research could not have been achieved.

REFERENCES

Beyer M.A and Laney D., 2012. *The Importance of Big Data: A Definition*, Gartner, Stamford, USA.

Habibzadeh F., 2012. *Traffic Collisions in the Middle East*, The Lancet, Vol. 380, Elsevier, NYC, USA.

International Business Machines, 2013. *What is Big Data? - Bringing Big Data to the Enterprise*, http://www01.ibm.com/software/data/bigdata/, Sillicon Valley, USA.

Kettani D., 2016. *Towards a Framework for Executives and Decision Makers to Discriminate Big Data Projects for International Development*, Volume-2, Issue 5, International Journal of Engineeering Research, India.

Naji J.A. and Djebarni R., 2000. *Shortcomings in Road Accident Data in Developing Countries*, the International Association of Traffic and Safety Sciences (IATSS) , Vol. 24, No. 2, Elsevier, NYC, USA.

Yamouri N., 2010. *Transport in the MENA Region*, http://web.worldbank.org/archive/website01418/WEB/IMAGES/TRANSPOR.PDF, The World Bank, Washington DC, USA.

A MACHINE LEARNING APPROACH TO FORECAST THE USAGE OF ANALYTICAL SERVICES

Laura Gerlach[1], Dragan Milosevic[1] and Vera G. Meister[2]
[1]*AWIN AG, Germany*
[2]*Brandenburg University of Applied Sciences, Germany*

ABSTRACT

The need to store and analyze ever-increasing amounts of data has motivated us to design high performing analytical services. To overcome the challenge and need for enormous hardware resources, we used machine learning methods to forecast the need for future analytical services based on historical usage. This forecast will enable us to execute queries and cache results before they are actually submitted allowing us to prepare the analytical services for the upcoming user queries. Initial experiments show that both, a 77% accuracy in predicting future queries and a response time of 1 second, can be achieved.

KEYWORDS

Data Mining, Clustering, Machine Learning, Prediction, Analytical Services

1. INTRODUCTION

Data has an important role in our daily life and its amount grows at an impressive rate (Danova, 2014). In 1992 the global data usage on the internet was around 100 GB per day, in 2016 it was already 26 TB per second. One reason for the increase is the number of internet-connected devices (Gartner, 2017). The first challenge to be solved is storing the data. Companies that need to handle huge amounts of data have already come up with different solutions. On one side, Netflix (Netflix, 2011) uses simple-DB, Hadoop/HBase and Cassandra. On the other side, Facebook (Fong, 2014) built a system with HBase to store their huge amount of data. More importantly, the interest in analyzing the huge amount of data stored is growing because we want to learn and benefit from the experience of the past. One way to achieve this is through analytical services that enable us to first analyze a specific situation in the past, and afterwards make an optimization for the future in order to produce a better result.

In this paper we present a novel approach to optimize the analysis services used by Awin AG, Europe's largest affiliate marketing network. It uses three different systems to support analytical services. The first system is built with Hadoop (HadoopR, 2014) (White, 2015) and Lucene (McCandless, 2012), where several Hadoop-jobs are used to process the data and to create Lucene indexes. The second system is based on a multidimensional data Cube built up with Microsoft SQL Servers and the full text-searching tool Elasticsearch (Gheorghe, 2010). The third system is based on a relational database system built with MySQL. The fact that three complex systems are needed in order to support analytical services was the motivation for us to see how machine learning can help cope with the increased amount of data in a completely different way (Devulapalli, 2015) (Ganapathi, 2009) (Mitchell, 1997).

This paper is structured as follows. In the problem description section, we will briefly describe the most important challenges of using existing data and machine learning methods to create performance optimizations. The machine learning techniques used will then be introduced in related work section. In the approach section we will focus on the analytical services that provide individual user relevant reports. These reports are customized by using specific filter settings that capture user interests and can be used for prediction. The evaluation section explains how we have compared different techniques and how we have decided which one to use.

2. PROBLEM DESCRIPTION

The biggest challenge is ensuring a fast response time in the case of a massively increased amount of data. Although every system that Awin AG uses scales horizontally, due to the massive increase in volume of data that needs to be processed and analyzed, we have decided to try to predict future usage and execute requests in advance before they are actually submitted. The high-level overview of the system is presented in Figure 1. As soon as a user logs in, we will retrieve their profile and compute how many requests we can afford to execute for them beforehand. There are many factors that need to be examined when computing the number of requests to execute in advance. The most important ones are the current load of the system, the number of reports that given user typically requests and the importance of a given user for Awin AG.

After computing the number of requests to execute in advance, we will use machine learning to predict which requests to execute in advance. The biggest challenge here is handling the huge amount of data while being able to generate predictions relatively quickly. Generating predictions quickly is necessary because the user has already logged in and at any moment real queries can be expected.

At the end of the user's session, we are able to update their profile because it is clear which queries are really executed and how accurate our predictions were. In the optimal case the updated profile should be used when the user logs in the next time, so that the user can experience better performance as a result of the machine learning. As we will show this fast learning is a real challenge for many machine learning approaches, which whilst being able to generate very accurate predictions are not able to integrate gained knowledge quickly enough.

3. RELATED WORK

There are many different methods for forecasting (Sridharan, 1999) the request that the user will send to the analytical services. They can be divided into two groups, being incremental and model-based ones (Wu, 2008). The incremental methods immediately use all available data while generating predictions. This is their biggest advantage as every request can be immediately used when generating future predictions. Model-based methods often need a long time for training. This further means that we have to wait up to several hours before being able to benefit from the most recent user interactions with the system.

The simplest incremental methods are the ones based on different clustering techniques. The k-Means clustering (Bentley, 1978) is an explicit and distance-based algorithm. It is explicit because it assigns each data point to one cluster. The other version is fuzzy c-means (Lu, 2013), where each data point is assigned to more than one cluster. Yet another method to create clusters are density-based algorithms (Ester, 1996) (Sander, 1999), which build clusters by analyzing the neighboring data points. By using created clusters, a simple K nearest neighbor (kNN) (Muja, 2009) (Yong, 2009) technique can be implemented. Another incremental technique is Naïve Bayes (Bayes, 1764) (Joyce, 2010) that calculates probabilities for each outcome based on historical observations.

There are many model-based methods, most frequently used for forecasting are the ones based on logistic regression, decision trees, neural networks and support vector machines. Common to all of them is a training phase that integrates observations into the model that is afterwards used for forecasting. As the ability to quickly react to new trends is fundamental for us, we will evaluate only the simplest logistic regression (Mitchell, 1997) (Witten, 2011).

4. APPROACH

We show the main steps of the process we planned to apply in Figure 1. The initial user profile is based on historical usage of the analytical service and contains all queries that a given user has ever submitted. It is updated after the next login of the user and as soon as new queries were received. Those queries will be added to the profile, so that when the user logs in, we will be able to forecast more accurately.

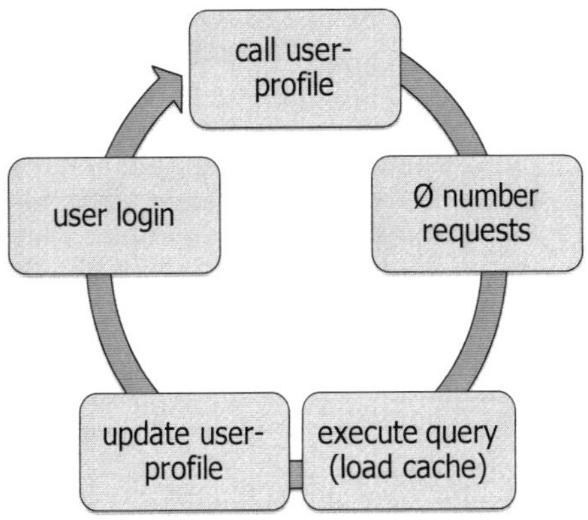

Figure 1. User-Profile Cycle

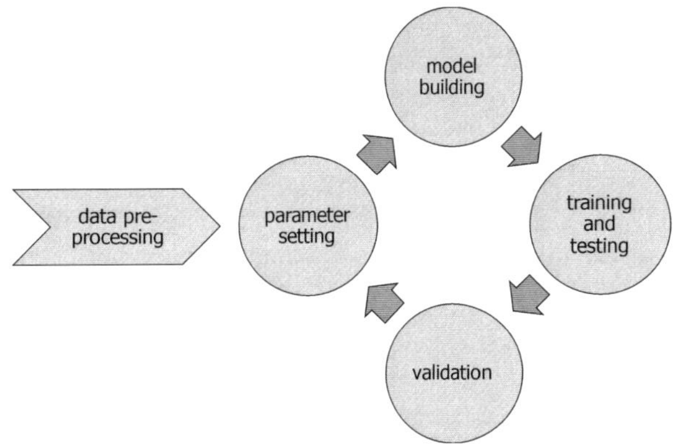

Figure 2. Model Processing

It is always possible to log how the services are used and if running a successful business, huge amounts of useful data is produced. The general idea on how to gain knowledge from the collected data is illustrated in Figure 2. The first step is "data pre-processing". As already mentioned, Awin AG uses three different systems for supporting the analytical services. Consequently, the logged historical user requests, are in different formats. We have SQL statements from MySQL databases, JSON format from logged Hadoop requests and MDX queries form MSSQL data cube. For the forecasting purposes, they all need to be cleaned and converted into one dataset. To reduce the amount of data, we will delete irrelevant information and keep only attributes that might be useful for the particular machine learning technique. Furthermore, as most of the algorithms work better with numeric attributes, we will transform the non-numeric values to numeric ones. If an attribute has labels, they get an index and get replaced with the corresponding index key. Additionally, one attribute of the data set has to be the one which will be predicted. In our case, we will forecast which query will be submitted by the user in the future to which system. In the "parameter setting" step on Figure 2, every machine learning technique has to be correctly configured. For example, in the case of kNN technique, distance function and number of neighbors should be determined. The next step is "model building" where the most useful attributes should be selected. We have found out that the best results are obtained if using user-id, timeframe-filter and the weekday on which a query was submitted. For "training and testing" and "validation" phases, the dataset needs to be split in to two parts. One is to train the algorithm and fit the parameters. The second one is for the validation of the training. Depending on the test dataset the predicted outcome of the training will be checked. In Figure 3 we show that three weeks of data has been used for the initial experiment. As training dataset we used the first two weeks and for testing the third week.

As each algorithm has different parameter settings which can change the outcome, it makes sense to start with fewer attributes and add after each run another one and validate the result. These steps should be repeated as long as the accuracy of the prediction increases. Additionally, different attribute combinations have to be tested and validated. As in the pre-processing step we have selected only the most important attributes, we used Grid Search (Mitchell, 1997) for parameter selection, i.e. we have checked all possible combinations. In the case where more attributes have to be checked, heuristic techniques like evolution programing should be used for parameter optimization. After tweaking the algorithm settings, a cross-validation is carried out. This is done to check if by partitioning the dataset in different ways the percentage of correct prediction still holds.

5. EVALUATION

The evaluation is not only necessary to find the best method to make the predictions, but also to find the best attribute combination for the selected method. Because we used Grid Search to exhaustively check each attribute combination, we had to limit attributes being checked to user-id, timeframe-filter, filter-type, aggregation-level and weekday of query submission. The best results were obtained with user-id, timeframe-filter and weekday, and those results will be further discussed in this section. In the future, we use a plan to increase the number of candidate attributes, use heuristic to select the best ones, and apply layered evaluation (Paramythis, 2010). A dataset of 1.4 million historical queries was used to train and test our system. These queries were collected over a 3-week period and their distribution by system and day is presented in Figure 3. The evaluation is performed on a standard notebook with an Intel i5 processor and 16 GB internal memory. We want to check two hypotheses. The first one is that the accuracy of the prediction increases by increasing the number of queries that are available to generate predictions. The second hypothesis is that the incremental methods are significantly faster than the model-based ones. Additionally, to find the best working attribute combination we manually tested other combinations.

To evaluate the first hypothesis, three different methods are asked to generate predictions in the case where the different number of training queries are available. The obtained results are given in Figure 4. It shows the achieved accuracies for three methods kNN, Naïve Bayes and Logistic Regression. While Naïve-Bayes achieved the best results for runs with 95 and 110 queries, kNN managed to continuously increase the accuracy as the number of training queries grown. As at the same time the achieved accuracy for kNN is superior compared to Naïve Bayes, we are able to conclude that hypothesis 1 holds for the best performing incremental approach. Unfortunately, due to the complexity we were only able to execute Logistic Regression for the first iteration and consequently we were not able to check if hypothesis 1 also holds for model-based methods.

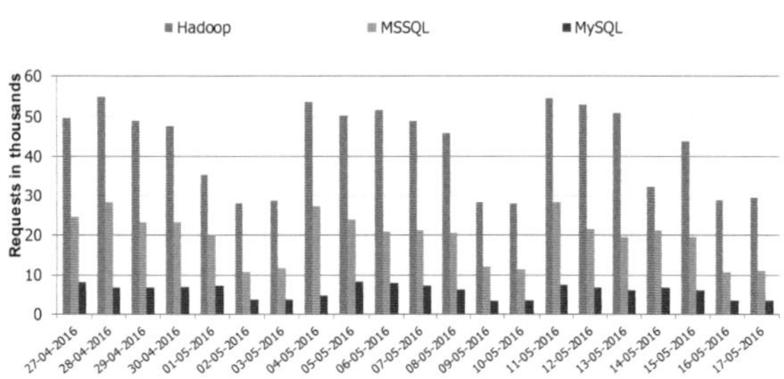

Figure 3. Query Distribution

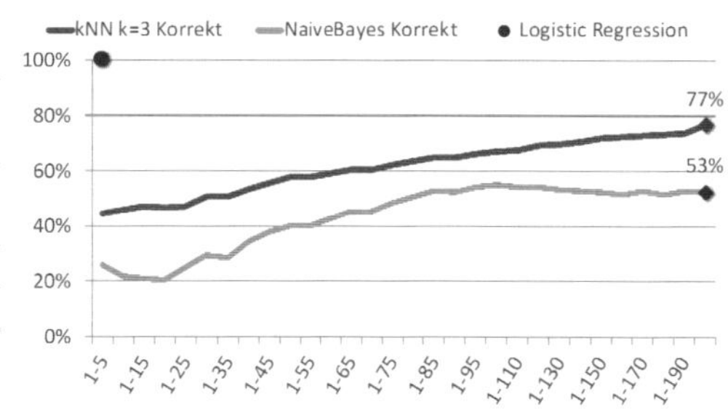

Figure 4. Experimental Results

The best execution times we achieved were 1 second for kNN, 4 seconds for Naïve Bayes and 15 hours for Logistic Regression with the smallest dataset. Those durations are either response time to generate prediction, in the case of incremental methods, or time that is needed to train models. While both kNN and Naïve Bayes responds within a few seconds, Logistic Regression needs several hours to train its model. Consequently, we proved hypothesis 2 and made clear that we have to use an incremental method in order to achieve the requested reaction time.

6. CONCLUSION

While Logistic Regression demonstrates the superior prediction accuracy, it has an unacceptably slow training phase, most likely due to the huge amount of data that needs to be processed. Therefore, we decided to use incremental methods that are able to generate predictions within a few seconds. The next stage of investigation will focus on using distributed machine learning frameworks, such as Mahout, in order to speed training phase and check if they can be applied.

ACKNOWLEGEMENT

Authors gratefully acknowledge the financial support from Awin AG that also granted access to a real dataset which made it possible to evaluate different machine learning techniques. The indebted gratitude deserves the anonymous reviewers for their insightful comments, which greatly helped to strengthen the paper. Special thanks also go to Ben Poole, Chris Loonan and Simon Edwards, whose suggestions and proofreading helped make the presented matter easier to understand.

REFERENCES

Bayes, T. (1764). *An Essay Toward Solving a Problem in the Doctrine of Chances. the original essay with an introduction by his friend Richard Price* http://www.stat.ucla.edu/history/essay. pdf. Philosophical Transactions of the Royal Society of London 53, 370-418.

Bentley, J., Friedman, J., and Center, S. L. A. (1978). *A Survey of Algorithms and Data Structures. Stanford Linear Accelerator Center*. S.L.A.C. pub [Series],2189. Stanford Linear Accelerator Center.

Netflix Tech-Blog, N. T. (2011). *Nosql at netflix*. Website. https://medium.com/netflix-techblog/ nosql-at-netflix-e937b660b4c.

Danova, T. (2014). *The internet of everything: 2014*. Website. http://www.businessinsider. com;BI Intelligence.

Devulapalli, S. K. (2015). *Machine learning use cases in telecom - cogni- tive computing meetup*. Website. http://www.slideshare.net/SaiDevulapalli/ machine-learning-use-cases-in-telecom;.

Ester, M., Kriegel, H.-P., Sander, J., and Xu, X. (1996). *In A Density-Based Algorithm for Discovering Clusters in Large Spatial Databases with Noise, Institute for ComputerScience*, University of Munich Oettingenstr. 67, D-80538 München, Germany.

Fong, Z. and Shroff, R. (2014). *Hydrabase – the evolution of hbase@facebook*. Website. https://code.facebook.com/posts/321111638043166/ hydrabase-the-evolution-of-hbase-facebook/.

Ganapathi, A. S. (2009). *Predicting and Optimizing System Utilization and Performance via Statistical Machine Learning*. PhD thesis, EECS Department, University of California, Berkeley.

Gartner - world's leading information technology research, G. I. and advisory company (07-2017). *Gartner Says 8.4 Billion Connected "Things" Will Be in Use in 2017, Up 31 Percent From 2016.* https://www.gartner.com/newsroom/id/3598917

Gheorghe, R., Hinman, M., and Russo, R. (2015). *Elasticsearch in Action*. Manning Publications.

HadoopR , A. (2014). *What is Apache Hadoop?* Website. https://hadoop.apache.org/ #What+Is+Apache+Hadoop%3F; The Apache Software Foundation.

Joyce, J. (2003-06-28). *Bayes' theorem. Stanford Encycl. of Philosophy*. http://plato.stanford.edu/entries/bayes-theorem/;.

Lu, Y., Ma, T., Yin, C., Xie, X., WeiTian, and Zhongl, S. (2013). *Implementation of the fuzzy c-means clustering algorithm in meteorological data.* Technical report, Nanjing University of Information Science and Technology, Nanjing.

McCandless, M., Hatcher, E., and Gospodnetic´, O. (07-2012). *Lucene in Action, Second Edition*. B&W.

Mitchell, T. M. (1997-03-01). *Machine Learning. McGraw-Hill* Science/Engineering/Math.

Muja, M. and Lowe, D. G. (2009). *Fast approximate nearest neighbors with automatic algorithm configuration. In VISAPP International Conference on Computer Vision Theory and Applications*, pages 331–340.

Paramythis A., Weibelzahl S., Masthoff Judith. (2010) *Layered Evaluation of Interactive Adaptive Systems: Framework and Formative Methods*

Sander, J. (München 1999). *Generalized Density Based Clustering for Spatial Data Mining*. Herbert Utz Verlag.

Sridharan, M. (07-2015). *Machine learning algorithms mindmap.* Website. https://jixta. wordpress.com/2015/07/17/machine-learning-algorithms-mindmap/;.

White, T. (03-2015). *Hadoop: The Definitive Guide, 4th Edition, Storage and Analysis at Internet Scale*. O'Reilly Media.

Ian H. Witten, Eibe Frank, and Mark A. Hall. (2011) *Data Mining: Practical Ma- chine Learning Tools and Techniques.* Morgan Kaufmann Publishers Inc., San Francisco, CA, USA, 3rd edition, 2011.

Wu, X., Kumar, V., Ross Quinlan, J., Ghosh, J., Yang, Q., Motoda, H., McLachlan, G. J., Ng, A., Liu, B., Yu, P. S., Zhou, Z.-H., Steinbach, M., Hand, D. J., and Steinberg, D. (2008). *Top 10 algorithms in data mining. Knowledge and Information Systems*

Yong, Z., Youwen, L., and Shixiong, X. (2009). *An Improved KNN Text Classification Algorithm Based on Clustering. Technical report, School of Computer Science and Technology, China University of Mining and Technology.*

Posters

EXTENDED NODES OF ARTIFICIAL NEURAL NETWORK FOR GESTURE RECOGNITION

Hye Yeon Cho and TaeYong Kim
GSAIM, Chung-Ang University, Seoul, Republic of Korea

ABSTRACT

Hand gestures can easily express ideas to others and these hand gestures can be applied to various fields such as art, game, and smart home. In this study, we propose a method to improve recognition rate for various kinds of 3-dimensional hand gestures. We extract the features from the gesture data distribution by Mahalanobis distance and construct the feature nodes, and feature nodes are added to the input layer of a neural network. Experimental results show that the proposed method has better performance than the conventional artificial neural network.

KEYWORDS

Artificial Neural Network, HCI, Accelerometer, Gesture Recognition, Pattern Recognition

1. INTRODUCTION

As a smart environment is built recently, the interface technology between humans and computers is studied for more natural interaction. To communicate between humans and computers, in the past, interfaces such as a keyboard, mouse, touchpad, etc. were used, but these existing interfaces were cumbersome. Thus, natural interface technology has been developed, and among them, a hand gesture is a means of expressing ideas conveniently and abundantly. Since the technology recognizing a hand gesture can be used in a variety of areas including smart home, games, medicine, arts, etc., studies on recognition of hand gestures for natural interface are conducted actively [Watson]. As a typical technology for hand gesture recognition, camera-based motion recognition technologies are frequently studied, but they are vulnerable to environmental changes or their spaces for motions are limited [Rautaray]. Therefore, wearable devices such as a smart watch and smart band may be used to obtain the hand gesture information at low cost without spatial limits. The hand gesture information collected by sensors can be processed and classified in a variety of methods, but the classification of general patterns should analyze different statistical distributions. If these sets of data are various or their sizes get bigger, the distributions of the data sets may be overlapped. Since various types of hand gestures are used in real life, the overlap of data distributions makes classification difficult [Parate]. Therefore, a more accurate method to classify diverse hand gestures used in actual life is required.

2. EXTENDED NODES OF ARTIFIICAL NEURAL NETWORK

In this study, the method of improving the hand gesture recognition based on ANN which adds the extended node is composed of pre-processing, extended node constitution, training ANN, and test process. The pre-processing normalizes the database consisting of trajectories, removes noises, and conducts linear interpolation. After the pre-processing, the features that can express the characteristics of a distribution in the database are extracted, and features are processed to constitute extended nodes. Then, the extended node would be added to the back of the database consisting of the existing trajectory information. Finally, the trajectory data and the extended nodes are added to the input of ANN, and the process of training and testing would be provided. Fig. 1 describes the overall system structure to improve the recognition of hand gestures.

We constitute the feature nodes using the similarity information inferred by Mahalanobis distance and the number of the extreme values in the hand gesture trajectory to find out which data set the hand gesture to be classified belongs to. The extended node generated in this way is added to the database, and they will be input additionally in the input layer when training and testing take place through the ANN.

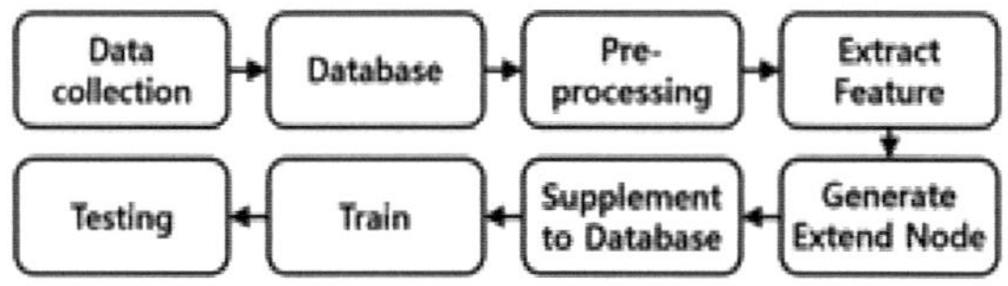

Figure 1. System structure of the proposed method

To constitute the feature nodes, the similarity information calculated in the features of data distribution is used. Regarding certain database which is classified as type of k, start point, end point, or mean point of the hand gesture trajectory should be selected as features that may express the characteristics of each hand gesture to find the data set closest to an arbitrary single data stream. The distance between all k hand gestures' feature information with feature information of a single hand gesture is calculated, and the sets meeting the shortest distance are found to be closest to the arbitrary single hand gesture feature vector. Generally, the linear distance between the two points in n-dimensional vector space is expressed in Euclidean distance. In this study, to express not a simple linear distance but the distance in the probability distribution, Mahalanobis distance is used to calculate the difference. If Mahalanobis distance is used, the distance between the single hand gesture and arbitrary hand gesture sets can be expressed in a way that how many times the distance is greater than the standard deviation of the arbitrary sets. When the selected feature information is a and the gesture feature information sets of k consisting of a, the feature information is $A=[A_1, A_2, ..., A_k]$, the arbitrary ath hand gesture feature information set can be expressed as $A_c=[a_1^c, a_2^c, ..., a_i^c]$. To calculate Mahalanobis distance, $\overline{A}_c$, the mean vector of A_c, the arbitrary ath hand gesture feature information set, and S_c, the covariance matrix, should be calculated together. If the single hand gesture feature vector is $\boldsymbol{B}$, Mahalanobis distance between $\boldsymbol{B}$ and $\overline{A}_c$, the mean vector of a certain feature information set, can be calculated as Equation (1).

$$MD(\overline{A_c}, B) = \sqrt{(\overline{A_c} - B)^T S_c^{-1} (\overline{A_c} - B)} \tag{1}$$

Where S_c^{-1} is the inverse matrix of covariance matrix of A_c. With Equation (1), the sets of k and all Mahalanobis distances are calculated to find out the ath hand gesture feature information which meets the shortest distance. As the distribution of a certain data set and an arbitrary single vector are closer, Mahalanobis distance will be shortened. Therefore, the index number of the ath hand gesture feature information which satisfies the shortest distance should be constituted as one feature node.

3. EXPERIMENTAL RESULTS

In the experiment data are obtained by wearing a Smart Watch in the right wrist of a user. The data are collected at sample speed of 10Hz, and 8 different users conducted 20 different hand gestures with 20 times repeatedly. The data consists of acceleration data of 3,200 hand gestures (8 users conducted 20 hand gestures 20 times each). To divide the data, whenever the user starts and finishes one hand gesture, the Smart Watch is directly tapped to distinguish the start and end of the hand gesture manually. For hand gesture consisting of 3,200 types of acceleration information of 3-axis, because the length of sequence of every hand gesture is different, it should be processed to form a column vector of constant length. After the 3-axis hand gesture data are normalized and noise is removed for each axis, 15 data are processed with constant length by the linear interpolation. Then, a total of 15*3 (45) pieces of information can be obtained. To input the pre-processed data to the input layer of ANN, each set of hand gesture data composes the database in the form of column vector with 45 vectors, and the database is converted with 3,500*45 matrices with constant length. For training and verifying the ANN, 2880*45 training database and 320*45 testing database are divided and experimented.

Table. 1 shows that, even with only one addition of extended node, the recognition rate is higher than the composition of the trajectory data for the input layer. However, if the combination of extended nodes is appropriately constituted according to the feature of the database, better recognition rate is shown. Particularly, the recognition rate is the highest when the similarity information inferred by the end position of hand gesture and the information of the extreme values are constituted as the extended nodes.

Table 1. Hand gesture classification results according to the combination of extended nodes for input layer

Feature Nodes	**Accuracy (%)**
None	95.9
Start position	96.6
End position	96.9
Extreme value	96.6
Start, End	96.4
Start, Extreme	96.9
End, Extreme	**98.1**
Start, End, Extreme	97.8

4. CONCLUSION

In this study we propose a method of improving the recognition rate of hand gestures by adding feature nodes when the hand gesture data collected from the acceleration sensor is made to be learned and classified by ANN. The accuracy of gesture recognition is improved by extracting features by a simple calculation and constituting them as extended nodes without increasing the complexity of the implementation. It is found that if the extended node is added to the input layer consisting of trajectory information of existing hand gestures, the recognition rate would gain positive influence. Various sensors such as a gyroscope sensor or electromyogram sensor will be used to conduct the recognition of hand gestures.

ACKNOWLEDGEMENT

This research was supported by the Basic Science Research Program through the National Research Foundation of Korea (NRF), funded by the Ministry of Education, Science and Technology (NRF-2015R1D1A1A01058394) and by Brain Korea 21 PLUS Project in 2018.

REFERENCES

G. H. Watson and K. Gilholm, 1998, Signal and image feature extraction from local maxima of generalised correlation, Pattern Recognition, vol. 31, no. 11, pp. 1733-1745.

S. S. Rautaray and A. Agrawal, 2015, Vision based hand gesture recognition for human computer interaction: a survey, Artif Intell Rev, vol. 43, no. 1, pp. 1-54.

A. Parate, M. Chiu and C. Chadowitz, 2014, Risq: Recognizing smoking gestures with inertial sensors on a wristband, Proceedings of the 12th annual international conference on Mobile systems, applications, and services,149-161.

ANALYSIS AND VISUALIZATION METHODS FOR TOPICAL BUSINESS NETWORKS

Donghun Lee and Kwanho Kim[1]
Dept. of Industrial and Management Engineering, Incheon National University
Dept. of Industrial and Management Engineering, 423-ho, A-dong, Building No.8, Incheon National University, 119, Academy-ro, Yeonsu-gu, Incheon, South Korea, 22012
[1]Associate Professor

ABSTRACT

The importance of convergence activities among business is increasing due to the necessity of designing and developing new products to satisfy various customers' needs. In particular business representatives with top decision-making are required to maintain network connections to obtain suitable convergence partners. It is important for business not only to make a large number of contacts, but also to understand the networking relationship with business with similar topic information. However, there is a difficult limit in collecting the topic information that can show the lack of current status of business and the technology and characteristics of business in industry sector. In this paper, we solve these problems through the topic extraction technique and analyze the business network in three aspects. Specifically, there are C,S,T-Layer models, and each model analyzes amount of business relationship, network centrality, and topic similarity. As a result of experiments using real data, it is necessary to activate network of strengthening network with highly centrally located companies when the corporate relationship is low. In addition, we confirmed through experiments that there is a need to activate the topic-based network if the topic similarity is low.

KEYWORDS

Topical Extraction, Text Mining, Social Network Analysis, Visualization

1. INTRODUCTION

Due to the necessity of designing and developing new products to meet the needs of various customers in the fourth industrial revolution era, the importance of human convergence activities of small business are increasing and it is essential to manage the network of small business. Small business are experiencing stagnation of industry due to factors such as rapid diffusion of technological innovation due to the development of information technology. In addition, it has difficulties in developing new technologies for entering new business fields, such as lack of expertise and lack of workers. Most small business have difficulty finding suitable business partners to solve them, so it is important to pre-form the connections between small business.

On the other hand, it is important for small business to form a network with entrepreneurs who have technology or similar topic information that entrepreneurs possess when forming a network. For example, company A is a manufacturer of semiconductor equipment and precision processing; company B is a manufacturer of office supplies and painting supplies; company C is a display and monitor manufacturer; both companies A and B have their own technology Because the characteristics are different, there is a limit to the fusion of the unit technology and the creation of the new technology and value. On the other hand, both companies A and C have similar characteristics of technology, so they can form new management strategies based on convergence activities and can help to advance into new industries and fields or to create new characteristic technologies.

However, due to the lack of information on the status of small business, there is a difficulty in convergence activities among small business. According to (Cho, Y., and Kim, E), the number of commercial enterprises in Korea is 5,377,000, of which 5,373,000 (99.9%) are small business. Although most companies are small business, they can only know information such as the number of workers by sector and the number of employees by region, and since there is no update, only the topic information of three years ago can be confirmed. Therefore, it is difficult to gather the topic information that can represent the skills and characteristics possessed by each small business, so there is a limit to forming a network with small business with similar topic information and conducting convergence activities.

In order to solve these problems, many researches are being conducted to analyze the importance and activation of convergence activities. (Borés *et al.*) have studied industrial convergence analysis for specific technology development and technology management centered on IT industry technology (Hacklin *et al.*) Analyzed technology fusion patterns using Nutraceuticals and Functional Foods (NFF) technology and IPC co-classification information in patent information.

However, in the existing studies, there is no research using the characteristics of the company, and the focus is on the analysis of the convergence pattern and the convergence of technology using the patent information and the existing network analysis technique. Therefore, this study solves the problem that the information that can represent the characteristics of the small business is extracted automatically from the topic information on the web site where the small business operates, and does not reflect the characteristics of the small business. We propose a network analysis and visualization technique based on topic information.

2. THE PROPOSED METHODS

2.1 Network Analysis based on $C - Layer$

The c-layer model analyzes quantitative aspects of corporate connection based on corporate connection information of small business. To analyze the network, we construct corporate connection information of small business $u_{j,k}, j = 1, \dots, m, k = 1, \dots, K$ corresponding to corporate connection for any small business $u_i, i = 1, \dots, n$. Equation (1) shows the equation for calculating the amount of connection for small business u_i.

$$\sigma_C(u_i) = \frac{\sum_{j-1}^{m}\sum_{k=1}^{K} count(u_i, u_{j,k})}{max_{j'}\left(\sum_{j-1}^{m}\sum_{k=1}^{K} count(u_i, u_{j,k})\right)} \quad (1),$$

Where k is represents the information of hop, and $\sum_{j=1}^{m}\sum_{k=1}^{K} count(u_i, u_{j,k})$ represents the total number of corporate connections up to k for u_i. $max_{j'}(\sum_{j-1}^{m}\sum_{k=1}^{K} count(u_i, u_{j,k}))$ represents the number of corporate connections among small business, which have the largest number of corporate connections among all small business.

2.2 Network Analysis based on $S - Layer$

S-Layer (Social Influence Layer) is model or analyzing influencers that can serve as hubs for networking as well as social networks. We use the closeness centrality method of social network technique and measure the degree of concentration by calculating the total distance (hops) based on the *C-layer* model. If the degree of concentration is large, it can act as a corporate human hub as an influencer or key player in the network (Kim *et al.*). Equation (2) represents the centrality measure calculation of the model for the small business. In the case of a network with a direction, we use a reciprocal instead of a reciprocal of the sum of the distances (Rochat, Y). Specifically $\sum_{j=1}^{m}\sum_{k=1}^{K}\frac{1}{hop(u_i, u_{j.k})}$ represents the sum of the reciprocal of the shortest distance of u_i and u_j, and $max_{j'}\left(\sum_{j=1}^{m}\sum_{k=1}^{K}\frac{1}{hop(u_i, u_{j.k})}\right)$ represents the greatest value of the total of the reciprocals of the distance in the small business.

$$\sigma_S(u_i) = \frac{\sum_{j=1}^{m}\sum_{k=1}^{K}\frac{1}{hop(u_i, u_{j.k})}}{max_{j'}\left(\sum_{j=1}^{m}\sum_{k=1}^{K}\frac{1}{hop(u_i, u_{j.k})}\right)} \quad (2)$$

2.3 Network Analysis based on $T - Layer$

T-Layer (Topic Relevance Layer) is a model for analyzing networks through visualization based on corporate topic analysis as well as influencers. In order to visualize topic information of small business and analyze network, topic information is expressed in RGB color based on color embedding model. The color embedding model uses the skip-gram model. The skip-gram model is learned by setting the parameters Iteration, Windows size, and Dimension as *a*, *w*, and *v*, respectively, using noun text data (Mikolov *et al.*).

The topic information of small business is defined as $u_{i,t}$ $t = 1, \ldots, N$, the topic vector is defined as $\vec{u}_{i,t}$, and topic color vector is defined as $\sigma_r(u_{i,t})$. Equation (3) represents the calculation of the topic color vector for the topic information of the small business u_i.

$$\vec{\sigma}_T(u_i) = round\left(\frac{255 \cdot (\sum_{t=1}^{N} \sigma_r(u_{i,t}) + 1)}{2}\right) \quad (3),$$

Where $round$ represents rounding. The range of $\sum_{t=1}^{N} \sigma_r(u_{i,t})$ vector value is a value between -1 and 1.

3. CONCLUSION

First, we will analyze the cumulative distribution of companies' scores based on the proposed model. We will analysis a network analysis of all companies. We also analyze each company's model according to each proposed model and evaluate the network of the company with differences for each model.

ACKNOWLEDGEMENT

This research was supported by Research Program through the Korea Industrial Complex Corporation (Analyze business announcement of small business based on deep learning and develop convergent partner matching system) funded by the develop customized technology on site (No. RIC17019) and this work (Grants No. C0531925) was supported by Business for Cooperative R&D between Industry, Academy, and Research Institute funded Korea Small and Medium Business Administration in 20.

REFERENCES

Cho, Y., and Kim, E., "A Corporate Strategy on Technological Convergence Through Analyzing Patent Networks and Strategic Indicators", The Journal of Intellectual Property, Vol. 9, No. 4, pp. 191-221, 2014.

Borés, C., Saurina, C., and Torres, R., “Technological convergence: a strategic perspective”, Technovation, Vol. 23, pp. 1-13, 2003.

Hacklin, F., Raurich, V., and Marxt, C., “How Incremental Innovation becomes Disruptive : The Case of Technology Convergence”, Proceedings of the IEEE International Engineering Management Conference, vol. 1, pp. 32-36, 2004.

Wirtz, B. W., “Reconfiguration of Value Chains in Converging Media and Communications Markets”, Long Range Planning, Vol. 34, pp .489-506, 2001

Lee, H., and Kang, P., "Topic modeling and technology management research trend analysis", Proceedings of the Korean Institute of Industrial Engineers Autumn Conference, pp. 5208-5229, 2016.

Kim, H., Park, H., Lim, J., Chul C., and Kim, K., “Function-Property based Causality Network of Patents for Technology Convergence”, Proceedings of the Korean Institute of Industrial Engineers, pp. 1205-1219, 2012.

Mikolov, T., Sutskever, I., Chen, K., Corrado, G. S., and Dean, J., "Distributed Representations of Words and Phrases and Their Compositionality", Advances in Neural Information Processing Systems, pp. 3111-3119, 2013.

Lee, D., and Kim, K., “WebSite Keyword Selection Method by Considering Semantic Similarity Based on Word2Vec”, Proceedings of the Korean Institute of Industrial Engineers, pp. 923-938, 2017.

Rochat, Y., “Closeness Centrality Extended to Unconnected Graphs: The Harmonic Centrality Index”, In ASNA 2009.

AUTHOR INDEX

International Association for Development of the Information Society (IADIS)
Rua Sao Sebastiao Da Pedreira
No. 100, 30, 1050-209
Lisbon, Portugal

ISBN 978-1-5108-7012-3